LESLIE MARMON SILKO

LESLIE

MARMON

SILKO

A Collection of Critical Essays

EDITED BY
Louise K. Barnett
& James L. Thorson

University of
New Mexico Press
Albuquerque

FIRST EDITION

Library of Congress Cataloging-in-Publication Data
Leslie Marmon Silko : a collection of critical essays /
edited by Louise K. Barnett and James L. Thorson.
— 1st ed.
  p.   cm.
Includes bibliographical references (p.   ) and
index.
1. Silko, Leslie, 1948 — Criticism and interpretation.
2. Women and literature — West (U.S.) — History —
20th century.   3. Western stories — History and
criticism.   4. Indians of North America in
literature.   5. Laguna Indians in literature.
6. West (U.S.) — In literature.   7. Silko, Leslie,
1948–   .   I. Barnett, Louise F.   II. Thorson,
James L.
ISBN 0-8263-2033-3 (cloth)
PS3569.I44   Z77   1999
813'54 — dc21   98-58058
                                                          CIP

CONTENTS

PREFACE

Silko's Power of Story

Robert Franklin Gish

T here are certain key books in every writer's life that once read change everything. These books — and in various associations both real and imagined, their authors — become inspirational "spots of time," literary interludes and mentors, interlocutors and companions of considerable moment and memory.

Such an effect in certain more or less random writers goes much beyond any reputed anxiety of influence, in the sense that the writer become reader or reader waiting to become writer worries little about matching or surpassing the creative process and result that the book re-created through the transformations of reading. The effect in question, however, is transcendent.

Reader response, like literary taste is, as every reader or critic knows, a fascinating process filled with all kinds of causality and, in certain cases, casualty. Authors who are never or seldom read become the worst of trage- dies — more regrettable even than books never written. There are, we know, much beyond clichés of commonality and solidarity in the writers' craft, major and minor authors. Major authors perhaps know this best of all (assuming their books are read, are engaged) as they sit back and marvel at the various meanings, interpretations, and significance bestowed on them and their worded "creations" that suddenly become popular or canonized.

Leslie Silko is a decidedly major author whose books have come to mean much to many readers, and especially critical readers, as these assembled analytical essays demonstrate. Certainly among contemporary authors Silko enjoys much esteem — whether labeled as an American author, an American Indian author, an American Indian woman author, or a regional author. Silko's place is secure in the "tradition" of modern American Indian literature. Just why this is so in the more technical critical sense is perhaps best left to the critics assembled here.

My own critical assessments of Silko have for the most part sought to see and understand her in the tradition of an august group of nature or environmental writers — writers of what might be called "ethnicity and the land." Here, however, by way of preface to these collected critical assessments that demonstrate, each in its own way, Silko's special significance as an artist, I offer a more personal testimonial to Silko's power of story.

I first read Silko some years ago when she was in Alaska and I was in Iowa. And that happy convergence in many ways changed my life. The first stories I read by her were in Kenneth Rosen's seminal book *The Man to Send Rain Clouds: Contemporary Stories by American Indians* (1974), which took its title from Silko's story of the same name. Rosen positioned it as the first story in his volume, a story Silko first published in 1969. There were five other stories by Silko in Rosen's book, almost making it a Silko anthology, and making her someone of note even at that early time.

They were wonderful stories, each leading me back to my home in New Mexico, a place that at that time called to me with all the lure and nostalgia that exile in the frozen flatlands of Iowa could evoke. Like Silko, I too came from New Mexico, had attended the University of New Mexico, and was now, as a young instructor of composition, freezing to death — physically and spiritually — in what to me was a most alien place where the sun would disappear for days on end.

The contributors' notes to Rosen's book indicated that Silko too had been born in Albuquerque and that her present home was Ketchikan, Alaska. She said in her entry, "This place I am from is everything I am as a writer and human being."

And so I felt a kinship with Silko and through those five stories struck up a friendship with her. I liked them all immensely! I liked "Tony's Story," and "Uncle Tony's Goat," and "*from* Humaweepi, the Warrior Priest." I especially liked "Bravura," though I didn't know why. I remembered hearing about the Nash Garcia case, the New Mexico state patrolman Silko tells about (as does Simon J. Ortiz in a companion story Rosen reprinted.) I had been to the settings of most of Silko's stories. I knew those places. I felt the spirit of that place. I was a New Mexico reader! And soon, out of the augmented influences of teaching repeated sections of composition, I started to write some stories myself.

I had argued back and forth with Geary Hobson about James and Howells in graduate seminars at UNM but much respected his critical judgment and liked him. We were fellow Cherokees in ways that went beyond fadishness. When his prototypic anthology of "contemporary Native American literature," *The Remembered Earth* (1979), came my way and I read Silko's "Storyteller" and the four poems Hobson included, especially "Story from Bear Country," my feelings were confirmed that Silko's words held more than ordinary literary power for me. They registered deep inside me.

What was happening to me was not unlike walking in bear country in that I was changing. I knew. I knew "By the silence / flowing swiftly between the juniper trees / by the sundown colors of sandrock / all around. . . . " I was there. There was a metamorphosis underway and I was in my own strange way like the walker in bear country "dark shaggy and thick." I was on a path back to my most primordial intuitions, a path from which I could only return through writing.

By the time *Ceremony* was published in 1977 I had proposed and was teaching a new course in Native American literature. Certain colleagues teased and typified me as a professor of "buffalo chip lit" and needled me for corrupting the "Great Tradition." But I knew truth and beauty when I saw them. I too had seen a shadow of the magnitude.

Momaday had influenced me. Welch, especially *Riding the Earthboy 40* and *Winter in the Blood*, was tremendous. But Silko's *Ceremony* was everything that a book could be, everything that literature was supposed to be, the realization of all the adages and quips, all the epigrams and sayings that I had heard and had quoted to students. Indeed, I did feel like Keats when first reading Chapman's Homer. I had found what Dickinson and Frost and Sandburg and company had said "poetry" was supposed to do. I "understood" Silko's novel in so many ways that I had a hard time expressing them — to myself or to others.

When I became deeply involved in the intrigues of the shifting boundaries between biography and autobiography and the relationship of those forms to fiction — telling lives and telling lies — I came across *Storyteller*. There, in the same way Momaday opened my eyes to the role of family in *The Way to Rainy Mountain*, Silko's mixed forms about her family helped me through the writing of a literary biography of novelist Harvey Fergusson (i.e., *Frontier's End*) by pointing me back along the pathways of my own genealogy through a work that turned out to be a memoir called (with the borrowed blessing of Harold

Littlebird's title) *Songs of My Hunter Heart: A Western Kinship*. Family scripts, myths, and stories do augment our own special family photo albums, in spirit and in memory.

I understood the power of story, the efficacy of words, through them and simultaneously beyond them. In reading Silko and thinking about her artistry I was somehow back home in New Mexico and the sacred mountains, there with Grandma A'mooh and Aunt Susie, with Tayo and T'seh and the Hunter. I knew, of course, that I didn't really understand all there was to know about Silko's special power of story, about *Storyteller* or *Ceremony*, didn't know what a Laguna or other Pueblo Indian would know about such published stories, for example. But Silko helped redefine New Mexico for me, the place and the people I had known all my life. I too could say with Silko and her human and godly characters, "This place I am from is everything I am as a writer and human being."

By the time *Almanac of the Dead* appeared I had moved to California. As political "text," it seemed a case study of the skirmishes and battles in the central California theater of the "culture wars" I was experiencing in establishing a new ethnic studies program and department. Students and faculty of color were protesting, requesting, predicting a new era, a new "majority." Old wrongs were meeting new rights. The result of such accumulating social and political injustices would bring about an apocalypse (or was it an apotheosis?) not unlike the promises of the Ghost Dance.

And the anger I heard Silko, among others, express about ethnic fraud and cultural appropriation in the arts and in society at large, at the first Returning the Gift gathering in Oklahoma echoed the turmoil and change I felt everywhere in California. Ghosts of the dead were abroad bringing new life to new coalitions of race and gender and class. My understanding of the strands and fragments of *Almanac* were as troubled (but true) as my dismay at attempting to comprehend California.

Silko's most recent book to date, *Yellow Woman and a Beauty of the Spirit* (1996), offers a somewhat more patient but still passionate insight into the intersections of the personal and the political forces not just in Silko's or in "Native American Life Today," as the subtitle states it, but in all of contemporary society — from immigration to U.S. Indian policy over three centuries, to discourses and confessionals on art, on nonfiction, and on the writing of *Almanac of the Dead* and just what those long years of compulsion if not obsession to write meant to Silko as a person, an artist, a friend, a mother, and as a family member. Her essays on the interrelationships between ethnicity and the land, internal and external landscapes, surface again — something quite special and significant, something profound.

It is, then, with considerable gratitude, and appreciation of the most heart-felt kind, that I say — along with the critics assembled here — that Silko's legacy is her own beauty of spirit and the myth of her life as Thought-Woman, a heroine of her own occasion who brings her personal power and inspiration, the power of story, into all our lives. She is naming things, still, and as she names them they appear. . . .

INTRODUCTION

The publication of her widely praised first novel *Ceremony* in 1977 established Leslie Marmon Silko as a notable new talent in contemporary American literature. Modifying the traditional novel to reflect her Native American culture, Silko revealed a willingness to experiment with form that would continue to characterize her writing. The long-awaited *Almanac of the Dead* (1991) exhibited new facets of her extraordinary talent: this second novel is more complex, more shocking, and more apocalyptic than *Ceremony* — in fact, than any other novel of the latter part of the century. Poised between these two texts, the collection of short fiction, photographs, and autobiography entitled *Storyteller* (1981) confirmed Silko's determination to alter traditional Euro-American literary forms to accommodate her own heritage.

A collection of essays devoted to Silko's writing is overdue, to some extent the consequence of our culture's unfortunate tendency to categorize and marginalize writers on the basis of ethnicity and gender. Silko is indeed significant as a Native American woman writer; she is also a significant American writer, a dazzlingly original voice who should be confined to no special classification or restricted field. Although she speaks passionately for her Pueblo culture, she also speaks from the borderland where cultures and languages meet and from a modernist literary praxis.

While the purpose of this collection is to present a group of new essays on Silko, covering her career down to the present moment, no effort was made to give precisely equal attention to Silko's three major texts. There are no essays completely devoted to *Ceremony*, for example, because this early novel has been overwhelmed with critical attention while the more recent *Almanac* has instead been neglected, perhaps because its powerful vision of cultural decadence, racial conflict, and fearful retribution has been so unpalatable to many readers that it obscured the novel's achievement. This volume accordingly gives a generous amount of space to essays that demonstrate the artistry and meaning of this complicated, original, and wide-ranging text.

Robert Nelson's "Laguna Woman" is an overview of Silko's career that emphasizes her relationship to the land where she grew up, the Laguna Pueblo and the surrounding territory. While the basic outline of Silko's career is available elsewhere — recognition came early and one prestigious fellowship followed another in rapid succession — the strength of Nelson's presentation of Silko's life is in its constant evocation of the dramatic landscape that Silko has repeatedly acknowledged as a formative influence. He carefully sites the village on its "domed, white gypsum mesa that looks over the river and the highway beyond it" and deploys the surrounding geography: red rocks and lava flats to the east, pueblos to the west, sandhills to the south, looming Mount Taylor to the northwest. The Marmon family, with its mixed heritage, has a long history in the pueblo, one replete with official roles within its polity and a tradition of storytelling that Silko experienced early on.

Although Silko left New Mexico to spend two years in Alaska, during which time she wrote *Ceremony,* Nelson quotes from a letter written to the poet James Wright to establish that she had been devastated by being away from her home terrain: "the writing was my way of re-making that place, the Laguna country, for myself." Silko has mostly lived in the vicinity of Tucson, Arizona, since 1977; nevertheless, Nelson shows that Laguna has continued to nurture her art. At the same time that *Almanac* was taking shape centered in Tucson, Silko pursued filmmaking in Laguna, founding the Laguna Film Project and filming one of her own stories there. And in spite of its huge canvas and dozens of characters, *Almanac* ultimately ends with Sterling, a native of Laguna, returning to the village moved to tears by the word "home."

In both novels Nelson discerns the same pattern, a movement away from Laguna to encounter "non-Laguna forces" and an eventual return with the "acquired knowledge of how to live with those forces." Whether Silko herself ever follows the trajectory she has inscribed in her fiction, she remains, as Nelson demonstrates, a Laguna woman.

Paul Taylor's contribution to this volume stands at the beginning of the critical essays because of its ambitiously comprehensive approach—one that encompasses a number of perspectives. Taylor builds on the work of contemporary literary and cultural critics such as Louis Owens, Geary Hobson, Jana Sequoia, Vine Deloria, and Arnold Krupat; he also alludes to other American Indian writers such as N. Scott Momaday, D'Arcy McNickle, James Welch, Ray Young Bear, Jim Barnes, and Linda Hogan as well as the contemporary Chicano writer Rudolfo Anaya. Other texts he uses to develop his rich argument range from Icelandic and Anglo-Saxon through Greek, English, and American classic literature.

Taylor's argument focuses on the secret meanings of American Indian writing, particularly Silko's, and their ultimate relevance to her representation of the cultural malaise of Anglo society. He maintains that American Indians, whose cultural vitality has been sapped by their encounters with the dominant American culture, are now in the process of reclaiming what has been lost. Their literature "has moved well along in its strategic process of reappropriating from the mainstream American literary economy something of its own . . . story tradition, which the white has taken and transformed." Taylor applies this idea of appropriation and reappropriation to *Ceremony* and *Almanac* and some of Silko's short stories.

According to Taylor, Tayo recovers the ability to read the natural world in *Ceremony,* while the Euro-Americans of *Almanac* are notably impervious to signs. He sees the turning of story into English as "effectively reappropriat[ing] the Anglo's wasted word while correcting the Indian's wasted sight," a process that culminates in Sterling's successful reappropriation of his ability "to read and fuse differences."

In "Native Designs: Silko's *Storyteller* and the Reader's Initiation," Linda Krumholz addresses the issue of reading a cross-cultural text correctly, that is, *without* appropriating it as a Native American artifact and assimilating it into an American "Master Narrative." Specifically, in *Storyteller* Krumholz finds that the text instructs the reader in a Native American way of reading. She identifies *Storyteller* in Barthesian terms as a "readerly" text, one that requires the reader to actively connect its disparate parts and in doing so to learn how the Laguna Pueblo culture creates meaning. Building on Arnold Krupat's application of dialogics to *Storyteller* (and that of James Ruppert's to *Ceremony*), Krumholz finds that Silko's multivocality is more complex than the dichotomy of dominant versus minority discourse that characterizes a similar work, Gloria Anzaldúa's *Borderlands:* in *Storyteller* contemporary American discourse is "an *already* multicultural, multilingual, 'mixed' discourse." Rather than positing a monolithic dominant discourse that must be destroyed—as Anzaldúa does—Silko sees this discourse as already fragmented. During the course of the book it becomes increasingly marginalized, opening a space for other voices and destabilizing the reader's "normative discursive foothold."

Through a "ritual of initiation" the reader replaces this normative reading practice with a new approach, communal and accretive: "In this way, Silko initiates the reader into a Laguna interpretive practice." The breakdown of generic boundaries is another destabilization that makes room for a nontraditional reading experience.

Krumholz illustrates this method by reading one short section of the book, the Spirits section (187–211), as an intertextual exploration of death, loss, and renewal in Pueblo culture — expressed in photographs, family stories, poems, and conventional fiction. Through a detailed examination, Krumholz exposes the connections between the cycles of nature and culture, the individual and the community. As she concludes, "whether one experiences pain or pleasure, the cycles are beautiful because they weave our acts and our lives into the deep mesh of interrelationships that sustain the world." Juxtaposed with this spiritual understanding is the archaeologists' investigation of Enchanted Mesa, an expedition that collects and removes artifacts without regard for the power and mystery of the site.

Emphasizing the centrality of spiritual transformation in *Storyteller*, Krumholz ends her discussion of the text with a consideration of two versions of a story about a boy's adoption by bears and his return, through the efforts of a singer, to his human family. As Krumholz reads these stories, Silko is the singer whose mediation between two cultures guides the reading experience, one whose profoundly transformative qualities are moral and political as well as aesthetic.

Helen Jaskoski's "To Tell a Good Story" treats Silko as a mediating figure between two cultures. What unifies the diverse individual consciousnesses of *Storyteller* for Jaskoski is language, "the origin and guardian of the self." Language creates story, but it can also lie: the opposition Jaskoski finds in *Storyteller* is between lying and story, not lying and truth. In the title story the protagonist, surrounded by the lies of others, fiercely insists on her own language, "the only way she has of maintaining her sense of self in this disintegrating world."

In Jaskoski's reading, each story addresses issues of sexuality, identity, language, and violence. In "Lullaby," for example, a family tragedy ensues when a Navajo woman is taught to sign her name in English: rather than empowering her, as conventional wisdom would have it, the accomplishment makes it possible for her to unwittingly sign away her children. The alien language has also been the instrument of a disastrous change in the woman's world, one that is killing her own culture and replacing it with a cold and spiritually empty efficiency. In "Yellow Woman," the protagonist enjoys a guilt-free romantic idyll ended by the intrusion of the dominant culture in the person of a white rancher. The confrontation that ends in violence begins with a failure of communication between two languages that contrasts with the protection and certitude available within the woman's native language community.

More violence and more failure of communication in the contact zone ensue in "Tony's Story," where a non-Indian policeman and two young Indians, Leon and Tony, clash within a colonial context reminiscent of the power relations of "Storyteller." However, Jaskoski traces a subtle shift in power in the last four stories of *Storyteller:* the non-Indian world recedes ("Uncle Tony's Goat" and "Coyote Holds a Full House in His Hand") or shows a new flexibility, one that indicates the possibility of symbiosis if not cooperation or mutuality. Jaskoski analyzes the richly textured "Geronimo Story" as both a revisiting of the themes treated elsewhere and a departure. Here, bitterness is replaced by comedy, and the persistent association of language and identity leads to accommodation rather than tragedy. Considering the range of accomplishment in this volume, Jaskoski concludes that Silko's short fiction belongs with the very best of modern literature in its rendering of a particular community.

Elizabeth McHenry's "Spinning Fiction of Culture: Leslie Marmon Silko's *Storyteller*" also examines the mixed genre work first published in 1981. Whereas Krumholz approaches the text from the perspective of how it is to be read, McHenry examines how it exists and how it was created. Though the volume "follows the traditional conventions of bookmaking," including Silko's name's appearing as the book's author, "everything about the text and the presentation of *Storyteller* suggests Silko's denial of conventional authorship." Using the work of cultural anthropologists who attack the division between ethnology and literature, McHenry sees this unconventional book as both, and most important, as an exploration by Silko of the dynamics of storytelling in an era of print: "Silko's assessment of the difficulty of conveying what was traditionally oral cultural material and stories is expressed again and again in the text."

One unusual feature of *Storyteller* is its use of snapshots from Silko's family, which in McHenry's view helps Silko answer some difficult questions. McHenry asserts that "the process of restoring pictures to their narrative contexts provoked questions never before asked or answered about Silko's sense of self, family, immediate community, and the larger myths and legends of her region."

McHenry uses a number of Silko's own words in her examination of *Storyteller,* many of them from letters exchanged with the poet James Wright during the process of creating the book, but also vocabulary drawn from the work itself and other interviews and presentations. Though Silko says the volume is not a "big piece," McHenry sees her as "walking a fine line . . . blurring the boundaries between art and social science, she is able to introduce her readers to the fullness and fragmentation of her own private life and the life of Laguna culture." Through these innovations, *Storyteller* reveals the potential of storytelling.

In their "Shifting Patterns, Changing Stories: Leslie Marmon Silko's Yellow Women" Elizabeth Hoffman Nelson and Malcolm A. Nelson examine the Yellow Woman figure of Keresan myth adapted by Silko in *Storyteller* and *Ceremony*. While Ts'eh in the latter text is usually identified as Yellow Woman, the Nelsons argue that Tayo also plays this role. Both texts modify the traditional Yellow Woman stories to make them part of a modern context.

In the story "Yellow Woman," which antedates *Ceremony,* the young Pueblo wife who meets a stranger at the river and is instantly attracted to him grasps the similarity of her adventure to the traditional Yellow Woman stories. With *Storyteller*'s typical destabilization of identity, the nameless protagonist at first resists her inscription into the story as an impossibility; later, the narrative itself supports her acceptance of the attractive stranger: "This is the way it happens in the stories, I was thinking" (56).

The Nelsons explore the protagonist's alternation between her old and new identity, and the effect of story itself in shaping her responses. Her ultimate decision to return to her old life as both Yellow Woman and storyteller makes her "part of a new (and renewing) set of stories." She is, the Nelsons suggest, a strong new version of Yellow Woman, more accessible than the traditional Keresan figure because she speaks a first-person narrative set in a contemporary milieu.

Ceremony presents a more complex case because aspects of Yellow Woman can be found in both Ts'eh and Tayo. While a number of details identify Ts'eh with Yellow Woman, she has a "freedom and power that most traditional Yellow Women lack." Instead, she plays the role of a benevolent ka'tsina whose instruction saves and rehabilitates Tayo. The Nelsons adumbrate a number of similarities between the unnamed protagonist of *Storyteller*'s "Yellow Woman" and Tayo, who are drawn to their ka'tsina lovers by passion and who develop new identities as a result of their encounters with these powerful and mysterious others. Both Tayo and the unnamed woman return to their pueblos, but both hope to see their lovers again. Most important, they share an "understanding of the significance, the power, of the newly created stories." Through their combination of continuity and change, the Nelsons conclude, the Yellow Woman stories of *Storyteller* and *Ceremony* affirm Betonie's authoritative pronouncement that "only this growth keeps the ceremonies strong" (126).

In "Antidote to Desecration: Leslie Marmon Silko's Nonfiction," Daniel White focuses on a body of writing that is little known or commented on but that nevertheless deserves serious attention, especially now that the essays have recently been collected in *Yellow Woman and a Beauty of the Spirit: Essays on Native American Life Today* (1996). Although the subjects of the individual essays are disparate, White finds a common theme of opposing the destructive tendencies of modern culture with a Pueblo-based philosophy. He divides this large topic into two areas, "how people should relate to each other and . . . how they should relate to the earth." Addressing the first concern, Silko's essay "Yellow Woman and a Beauty of the Spirit" contrasts racism, which she identifies with the Puritans, with the Pueblo assessment of people according to their treatment of others, including animals and the earth itself. She also contrasts sexism in the dominant culture with the egalitarian and communitarian spirit of Pueblo society, which values individuals in terms of their contributions, not their gender. Pueblo religion, moreover, "reinforces the people's ties to each other and to the land" rather than emphasizing a heavenly afterlife.

In White's reading of Silko, the motivating force of Euro-American behavior is greed, a desire to own and exclude that has usurped Indian land and created the border patrol to keep others out. On this timely subject Silko asserts that "borders haven't worked, and they won't work. . . . The great human migration within the Americas cannot be stopped" (122–23).

Concerning nature, the other major focus of the essays, Silko is equally committed to a Pueblo wisdom that opposes the dominant culture's waste and desecration. As White points out, most of the tenets of Euro-American nature writing are a part of Native American culture. Living in an arid and unforgiving land, the Pueblo people learned to respect nature in order to survive. Here the motif of communal action introduced above is invoked in an extreme form: "greed, even on the part of only one being, had the effect of threatening the survival of all life on earth" (29–30).

Comparing the original and revised versions of the essay "Interior and Exterior Landscapes," White notices Silko's "deepening anxiety" at the ravages of the land and the breakdown of traditional culture. In her limited edition publication *Sacred Water* (1993), Silko describes her own struggle to resist these forces, encapsulated in the saga of her backyard pond. Contaminated in various ways, the pond was slowly brought back to purity by Silko's efforts, but this success is fragile: the desecrators of nature are a powerful and omnipresent multitude. White describes the conclusion of *Sacred Water,* which focuses on the increasing pollution of water in the Southwest, as only slightly less bleak than the conclusion of "Landscapes." Yet, while we may poison ourselves to death, Silko believes, the earth will survive.

David L. Moore's "Silko's Blood Sacrifice: The Circulating Witness in *Almanac of the Dead*" focuses sharply on that powerful novel, but brings in a number of comparisons to the earlier *Ceremony* and *Storyteller* as well. His discussion, informed by postmodern literary theory, identifies two themes in *Almanac* that reprise elements of *Ceremony* and *Storyteller:* "the witness of death, through the trope of the Tayo/Arrowboy myth, and the narrative of circulation of life and death, through the trope of blood itself."

In *Almanac* the radical patience of the elders will ultimately cause the defeat of the liars who are so often the representatives of Euro-American society in the Northern Hemisphere. Silko, Moore asserts, "subverts the ideology of colonialism, founded on the historical opposition between the European as Self and the Native as Other" by equating "witchery with oppositional thinking." In Moore's treatment of *Almanac,* the force of time, land, and dreams works slowly but surely against the colonial thrust of manifest destiny. As Silko asserts in *Ceremony,* to witness the attempted activities of witches is to interfere with the effectiveness of their witchery. Silko is that witness in the first instance, but in Moore's view, she also implicates the reader: "Thus witnessing is a double power circulating in the silent power of sight, a necessary event that precedes the power of telling." Moore contrasts the positive force of witness with voyeurism, which plays a prominent role in *Almanac.* In its double role of witness and voyeur, "the reading eye watches torture as a perverse exercise of colonial pressure on the human psyche . . . [and] this watching becomes a strategy of undoing." Moore brings Native American myths into his analysis as well as the work of Bakhtin and Lacan.

Blood, the second significant trope Moore finds in *Almanac,* is a marker for both life and death and a sign of the circular relationship between life and death. In Moore's view, "the novel's ontology of blood and the circulation of 'energies' of life and death shapes both its circulating narrative structure and its historical theme of the ultimate transcendence by the land and the land's people over colonialism."

Similarly concerned with circulation and diverse perspectives, Ami Regier, in her "Material Meeting Points of Self and Other: Fetish Discourses and Leslie Marmon Silko's Evolving Conception of Cross-cultural Narrative," focuses on ways of looking at objects in *Ceremony* and *Almanac*—both sacred and secular. Her purpose is to explore how the narrative takes on both an aesthetic and a political meaning: "In the world of *[Almanac],* characters are often placed according to their attitudes toward sacred texts and objects, and the politics of the transmission of those objects would seem to extend beyond individual lives. Silko's expansive narrative might thus be said to follow materialist histories through the complicated politics of the histories of artifacts rather than following a logic of the narratives emerging from character development." Regier analyzes the evolution of this narrative practice from the earlier novel, which had a centered subject, to the later one, which features multiple persons and, importantly, multiple objects.

Noting that fetishism was part of anthropological discourse from the beginning, Regier traces its development from Frank Hamilton Cushing in 1882 through contemporary anthropologists Emily Apter and James Clifford. Evoking the work of Jean Baudrillard, sometimes pointing out how that work has evolved and sometimes showing how Silko's work contradicts it, Regier produces a powerful argument that "logic of the fetish animates this vision of revolution, spreading from objects contextualized in tribal belief systems to the technological objects of postindustrial capitalism."

Regier also compares Karl Marx's concept of commodity fetishism with tribal fetishism, asserting that "Silko links the oracular fetish to the commodity fetish in order to problematize Marx's comparison of capital's operations to tribal fetishisms" by presenting them comparatively. Relying on a close analysis of some discussions in *Almanac,* she compares this result with the earlier presentation of the same questions in *Ceremony,* and shows how Silko's practice has evolved here, too.

In the final section of her essay Regier argues that "fetishism becomes a mode of articulating a substantive tribal identity in a technological, contemporary society." Here she points out that Silko's novel incorporates a coalition of the dispossessed that includes Africans as well as Native Americans. The fetishes of these minority cultures embody the clash of their belief systems with the dominant culture. "By deploying a comparative object discourse that includes a revisionist fetishism," Regier concludes, "Silko links tribal histories, reformulations of identity, and cultural change."

Janet St. Clair's "Cannibal Queers: The Problematics of Metaphor in *Almanac of the Dead*" tackles one of the most uncomfortable aspects of the novel, its harshly negative presentation of homosexuals. As St. Clair says, "the novel is admittedly full of savage white homosexual men who prey on weak and unsuspecting victims to feed their insatiable lusts for sex, money, and power." She argues that this portrayal is a "metaphor of the insane solipsism and androcentric avarice that characterize the dominant culture." Further, "homosexuality as metaphor is amplified through the emblem of cannibalism, which figures the insatiable greed that inevitably attends undisciplined individualism and amoral objectification."

St. Clair's examination of the homosexual males reveals that the only positively presented gay male is ultimately destroyed by the others — Beaufrey, Serlo, and Trigg — who are the most negative examples among "literally countless male homosexuals" in the novel. In each of these examples, St. Clair illustrates how Silko's "focus on the characters' psychotic self-absorption rather than on their sexual gratifications reiterates in various specific ways her use of homosexuality as an elaborate figure of speech."

Each of the characters "illuminate[s] a different facet of Silko's complex metaphor for a savage society of 'Vampire Capitalists.'" St. Clair demonstrates how Silko utilizes the established stereotypes of antihomosexual attitudes found in Western culture, including psychoanalytic writings, to create these characters, characters who bear a strong resemblance to the monsters conjured up by unscientific authors such as Charles W. Socarides and Edmund Bergler. Noting the lack of lesbian as well as successful gay male relationships in the novel, St. Clair points out that *Almanac of the Dead* is not about love: it is about the death of love; about the love of death."

Caren Irr's "The Timeliness of *Almanac of the Dead,* or a Postmodern Rewriting of Radical Fiction" views the text as fitting in the tradition of the radical novel. She notes that Silko's predecessors in the 1930s wrote utopian narratives because they were responding, not unreasonably, to contemporary social conditions; in particular, they were resisting the mainstream culture's standardization or Taylorization of time. Silko has a similar concern: the novel's appearance on the eve of the five hundredth anniversary of Columbus's arrival in the Western Hemisphere allows her to use the occasion to contrast the past with the present and assess the toll taken by time. The almanac form that binds the various elements of the novel together and the almanacs that appear in it are both "commemorative and prophetic." They retain the past in present memory and promise a "renewal that will lessen the weight of dead fellow travelers." Examining in detail the role of time in the novel, Irr finds that "Silko contrasts traditional Native American beliefs about the spatial nature of time with the linear concept of time implicit in white people's gradualist mode of aging." Yet another concept of time that Irr analyzes derives from Navajo myth cycles, which include both sacred and historical times. The current epoch of the "Death-Eye Dog" is recognized in the novel by native persons as such, and the coming of Columbus is explained by *Almanac* not as the historical agency of change but merely as a development foreseen by native culture—as will be the demise of white rule in the Americas.

Examining the text in terms of Walter Benjamin's distinction between story and novel, Irr asserts that Silko contradicts Benjamin by incorporating most of the elements of story into her novel, which should be resistant to the nonlinear temporal elements in story. In these terms, Sterling's exile early in the novel and his return "Home" at the end follow a "Lukàcsian development."

Finally, Irr brings in Einsteinian relativism, Henri Bergson's response to it on temporal matters, and Steven Hawking's ruminations on the future of time, in which it is possible that "an ancient sense of the future returns. The pre- and postmodern fuse, and a timely new form of radical novel emerges."

Daria Donnelly's "Old and New Notebooks: *Almanac of the Dead* as Revolutionary Entertainment" also treats the novel as a radical document, but her focus is as specific as Irr's vision is broad. Noting that Silko's use of Pueblo materials has changed since the immensely successful *Ceremony,* Donnelly asserts that Silko is deeply indebted to Western apocalyptic literature and Marxism for her narrative structure, but unlike these models, she delays narrative and dialectical resolution. Postmodernism is also an influence, but Silko departs from postmodernist theory in expecting an ultimate "narrative resolution," albeit one that occurs beyond the concluding pages of the book in history itself.

After glancing at Silko's anticipation of the uprising in Chiapas and the 1992 "Ant March" to Mexico City, Donnelly focuses on the various notebooks and instances of notebook-keeping that are rich sites for considering the relationship between storytelling and historical change, and for understanding the importance of unauthorized, marginal storytellers to Silko's vision of history. She provides detailed though succinct analyses of the notebooks of Clinton, the "notes" of Lecha, the notebooks of Angelita, and most centrally, the ancient notebooks that are the almanacs. To Donnelly, in opposition to a negative reviewer, Sven Birkerts, the almanac "is not meant to be a site of social commentary, but rather of proliferating storytelling." The stewards of the almanac, most notably Yoeme, Lecha's grandmother, add their own stories to the ancient ones. The power of the stories, according to Donnelly, does not depend on their circulation: they will remain vital regardless of whether they are or can be retold, in contradiction to Angelita's view that if the stories had been lost, the people would also be lost.

Donnelly believes that both of Silko's novels are centrally concerned with the reintegration of an Indian protagonist into his community. She concludes that radical change does not depend on mass movements or individual initiatives: "Change is inevitable, charted and promoted by multiple and fragmentary stories told or inscribed in private notebooks, all of which converge upon the prophecies recorded in the ancient notebooks."

In "Mapping the Prophetic Landscape in *Almanac of the Dead,*" Janet M. Powers discovers that "Silko's prophetic narrative bears striking parallels to Dante's great allegory, the *Commedia.*" Powers makes a convincing case, though necessarily pointing out some of the differences: "As a Native American of the late twentieth century, Silko does not present a synchronic Christian cosmology but rather a diachronic one beginning with the arrival of Europeans in the New World at the end of the fifteenth century." She observes that the Five Hundred Year Map that Silko includes in the novel has both linear geographical and moral dimensions, with Tucson serving as its blighted center as Florence did for Dante.

After efficiently summarizing the five levels of interpretation used in the *Commedia,* and consulting the old, but still extremely useful work of Evelyn Underhill on mysticism, Powers proceeds to show how the five levels all enrich a reading of *Almanac.* Quoting an anonymous member of the Laguna Pueblo who stated that "the novel contains truths, but the ugliness of that book is not necessary," Powers remarks that the entire narrative is "disruptive" in the sense that a series of ruptures forces the audience to move from lower to higher levels of understanding. Powers then specifically applies the five levels of interpretation to interpret Silko's vast narrative, beginning with the autobiographical, which in *Almanac* is represented by Sterling: "Sterling's preoccupation with tribal law parallels Dante's focus on government." At the literal level, Silko's southwestern United States and northern Mexico have innumerable details that operate at the spiritual level as well, though many of the malign characters are not sensitive to any spiritual dimension. Even some of the Native Americans in the novel — such as Menardo, Rose, and Calabazas — at first appear to be problematical figures. "Perhaps because the church seems powerless to address the destructive aspects of contemporary life, Silko deals with church affairs (god-centeredness in time) only briefly," though, Powers notes, church officials are as corrupt in *Almanac* as they are in Dante. For Powers, "the anagogical meaning of Silko's novel (god- or spirit-centered out of time) is presumably what justifies the enormous tapestry of moral depravity that she weaves."

Powers sees Yoeme as the transcendent character, just as the almanac within *Almanac* symbolizes the novel, the key "to the lost will to rebel." Arguing that "if we are truly horrified, we will take steps toward change," Powers finds that Silko's intent, like Dante's, is "to put an erring society back on track."

Connie Capers Thorson's bibliographical essay and her bibliography are self-explanatory aids to the student of Silko's work. Both contributions are meant to be selective, not exhaustive: many short reviews and brief articles have been quietly omitted in the belief that they offer little help to the reader of Silko.

Louise K. Barnett and James L. Thorson

Every book has a history, and this one is no exception. Part of its history goes back more than thirty years, when Leslie Marmon enrolled in a freshman reading seminar in the general honors program at the University of New Mexico where I was one of her teachers.

It was obvious to the coteachers of the seminar that we had a wonderful class that was exceptionally diverse and lively. Leslie was a sparkling member of that group, and we believed she would have a remarkable career, whatever she chose to do. Several years later, after graduating with an honors degree in English and spending some time in law school, she returned to graduate study in English, and I was able, as director of graduate studies at the time, to help her a bit in graduate school. There she worked on her writing, though I would hesitate to say that her study had an enormous impact on her very self-directed talent. She later wrote that her best teachers in the program [wisely] didn't try to change what she was doing.

I was her colleague at New Mexico when her first novel, *Ceremony,* came out to rave reviews, though she had already gained recognition as a writer of fiction. She had been awarded some fellowships to advance her writing career, and she obviously utilized them well, in part by creating *Ceremony.*

I continued to read and admire her work when a notice of a planned MLA session on *Almanac of the Dead* as a contemporary *Divine Comedy* came across my desk. The session was being proposed by Professor Louise K. Barnett of Rutgers University, and we struck up a correspondence in mutual admiration of the writings of Leslie Marmon Silko. That session never made it to the program of the MLA, nor did another one that the coeditors planned for the next year, but the quality and enthusiasm of the people who proposed papers for these sessions so impressed us that we suggested this book to the University of New Mexico Press. Its essays testify to the power of Silko's talent and the importance of her contribution to American literature.

Jim Thorson

A LAGUNA WOMAN

Robert M. Nelson

S torytelling comes naturally enough at places like Old Laguna. Each house, and each crumbling adobe shell of a house, has stories attached to it; every mesa, cerro, arroyo, and spring in the surrounding countryside is home to some recountable event, or waiting to become so. As a child, Leslie Marmon grew up attaching herself, in memory and imagination, to the village and then to the land around it; and because this is Laguna land, many of the stories she grew up with were stories from the Keresan oral tradition, the stories of her father's people and their shared history. In her art as in her life, Silko has continued to maintain her identity with the story of the people of *Kawaika,* the People of the Beautiful Lake. The story of Laguna, like the biography of Silko and the fictional lives of her novels' protagonists, has always been a story of contact, departure, and recovery.

Leslie Marmon Silko was born in Albuquerque, New Mexico, on 5 March 1948. Her mother, Virginia, was originally from Montana; her father, Lee Howard Marmon, was at the time just out of the army, beginning his career as a professional photographer and managing the Marmon Trading Post in the village of Old Laguna, about 50 miles west of Albuquerque. Along with her two younger sisters, Wendy and Gigi, Leslie was raised in one of the houses on the southeast edge of Old Laguna village, just a short walk away, even for a child, from the Rio San José that arcs below the village on its south and southeast sides, separating the village from—or, seen differently, connecting the village to—what is now Interstate 40 and before that was U.S.

Route 66. In several of Silko's *Storyteller* pieces, particularly those featuring the Kochinninako/Yellow Woman motif, this part of the river figures as a contact zone,[1] where a female representing Laguna identity "within" meets a male who represents some other cultural or spiritual identity "out there."[2] This place is also the liminal zone in which the spirits of the Katsinas, passing through it from the direction of sunrise into the village in November, take on the corporeal form of the masked dancers, a transformative event recalled in *Ceremony*.[3] In the work of many writers, such places take shape as wastelands, deserts, and lifeless or life-threatening expanses; in Silko's work, as at Laguna, the site of such transformative contact events appears as a place of comfort and regenerative energy, a place characterized by the twin blessings of shade and moving water even throughout the long summer months. Silko's own affinity for this place reflects, perhaps, her own felt "position," occupying as she does a marginal site with respect to both Laguna "within" and the dominant Anglo mainstream "out there" — and as she depicts it, it's not a bad place to be.

This same sense of contact zone becoming meeting ground also characterizes the position of the family household with respect to its Keresan and non-Keresan surroundings. From the perspective of the east-west highway, the Marmon house stands below and in front of the rest of the village; most of the rest of the village's houses are built farther up on the domed, white gypsum mesa that looks over the river and the highway beyond it. On the top of the mesa at the northwest corner of the village is the gleaming whitewashed Mission San José, the setting for her first published short story, "The Man to Send Rain Clouds." Along the south and southeast edge of the mesa are the commercial buildings that during Silko's childhood included the Marmon Store, the U.S. Post Office, and the old railroad depot building that was later to become her father's house. During the 1940s and into the mid-1960s the Marmon family's general store, located a house or two nearer the highway interchange than the house in which Leslie grew up, served not only residents of Laguna and the surrounding Laguna Pueblo villages — Paguate, Mesita, Encinal, Paraje, Seama, and Casablanca — but also cross-country automobilists and truckers.

Born and raised at this cultural intersection, Silko grew up becoming part of both Anglo and Keresan cultural traditions, as had most of her Marmon ancestors at Laguna. The first Marmons to come to Laguna, Ohioans Walter and his brother Robert, came as surveyors just after the Civil War, married Laguna women, and stayed on, Walter as a schoolteacher and Robert as a trader; both eventually were elected to serve as governor of the pueblo. Conversely, Silko's Keresan great-grandmother Marie Anaya Marmon (Robert's second wife), the Grandma A'mooh of *Storyteller*, left Laguna to attend the Carlisle Indian School in Pennsylvania, and Robert and Marie sent their son Henry, Silko's paternal grandfather, to the Sherman Institute in California. Another of the Laguna women among Silko's forebears, her great-aunt Susie (née Susan Reyes, who was married to Henry's brother Walter), attended both the Carlisle Indian School and Dickinson College (also in Carlisle); upon returning to Laguna she served the community as a schoolteacher and also as a Keresan cultural historian—a "storyteller" like Grandma A'mooh, in one of the most important senses of that term. Leslie's father, Lee, served as tribal council treasurer during the time that uranium began to be mined at Laguna. Not surprisingly, given such a heritage, Leslie Marmon Silko grew up in a house full of books and stories, part of an extended family whose members have always been prominent in Laguna's history of contact with Euro-American social, political, economic, and educational forces. The story of the Marmon family at Laguna is a story of outsiders who became insiders and of insiders who became outsiders—a story about the arts of cultural mediation, from both sides of the imaginary borderline.

In *Storyteller* and elsewhere, Silko acknowledges the extended Marmon family of storytellers, including her aunt Susie, her grandma A'mooh, her grandfather Henry, and her father, as a powerful shaping influence on her own creative vision and storytelling repertoire.[4] But as Silko has also pointed out, the extended landscape of her early years was shaping her vision and providing stories as well.[5] Beyond the village and the river to the east lay the red rocks of Mesita, patches of rich wet grazing land, and the Cañoncito Navajo reservation on the other side of some lava flats; to the south were sandhills, red and yellow mesas dotted with springs, cool clear water on the hottest summer days; to the west lay most of the other Laguna settlements, and Cubero and Budville, and the Malpais; to the northwest, looming over it all, high and blue in the distance, rose Mount Taylor, the place for deer hunting, bear country; and due north, up the long hill where bulldozers and Cats would change the landscape forever while creating the Jackpile open-pit uranium mine in the 1950s, was the conservative village of Paguate, where many of the old-timers lived, and beyond that Seboyeta, near the site of the original Laguna sipapu or emerging place in some of the Keresan origin stories. By the time she was a teenager Silko knew something of these places and their stories:

My father had wandered over all the hills and mesas around Laguna when he was a child, because the Indian School and the taunts of the other children did not sit well with him. . . . I started roaming those same mesas and hills when I was nine years old. At eleven I rode away on my horse, and explored places my father and uncle could not have reached on foot. I was never afraid or lonely—though I was high in the hills, many miles from home — because I carried with me the feeling I'd acquired from listening to the old stories, that the land all around me was teeming with creatures that were related to human beings and to me. ("Interior and Exterior Landscapes," 166)

In addition to the informal education she was receiving from the land and the storytellers in her extended family, Leslie attended the BIA school at Laguna through the fifth grade and then parochial schools in Albuquerque during her teenage school years. She spent her undergraduate years at the University of New Mexico, where she was enrolled in the general honors program, and received her B.A. in English (with honors) in 1969, the year the Pulitzer Prize for fiction was awarded to Scott Momaday's *House Made of Dawn*. She then enrolled in the American Indian law program at the University of New Mexico Law School, but later transferred into the creative writing M.A. program there.

Though her interest in writing predated her college years — she was already writing stories in elementary school — that interest blossomed during her years at the University of New Mexico, during which time she took several courses in creative writing and saw her first work published ("The Man to Send Rain Clouds" in *New Mexico Quarterly* [winter-spring 1969]). By 1971 she had chosen writing, rather than the practice of law, as her vocation, and in 1974 (at the end of a two-year teaching stint at Navajo Community College) her career became effectively established with two publications: her collection of poetry *Laguna Woman* (Greenfield Review Press) and Kenneth Rosen's *The Man to Send Rain Clouds,* an anthology of 19 Native American short stories, seven of them (including the title story) by Silko. In that same year, another of Silko's short stories, "Lullabye," was published in *Chicago Review,* and Silko was awarded an NEA writing fellowship. She then moved to Ketchikan, Alaska, for two years; there, supported partially by a Rosewater Foundation grant, she wrote most of what was to become the novel *Ceremony* (1977). The time she spent in Alaska at Ketchikan and the small community of Bethel strongly engaged her imagination — "Storyteller," the title story of her major collection of short works and the only piece not set at or near Laguna, is unmistakably Alaskan in setting and character. But even while living in Alaska, Silko's creative vision remained profoundly rooted in the landscape of her native Laguna: "When I was writing *Ceremony,*" she wrote to poet James Wright in 1978, "I was so terribly devastated by being away from Laguna country that the writing was my way of re-making that place, the Laguna country, for myself" (Wright, 27–28).

Returning to the Southwest from Alaska, Silko continued to write while holding academic appointments first at the University of New Mexico and then at the University of Arizona. In 1981, after her marriage to John Silko had been dissolved,[6] Seaver published her book *Storyteller*, which brought together much of her previously published poetry and short fiction, reembedded in a webwork of family narrative accompanied by photographs of the sources of her storytelling identity — photographs, that is, of the people and the settings to which those stories attach. In that same year, Silko was awarded a five-year, $176,000 MacArthur Foundation Prize Fellowship, allowing her to devote herself full time to her artistic pursuits, including writing the novel that over the course of the next ten years would become *Almanac of the Dead*.

A few years earlier Silko had been the subject of a short film, "Running on the Edge of the Rainbow" (1978), in which she played herself as a Laguna storyteller;[7] during this time Silko began to develop her own interest in the visual arts, in particular filmmaking, an interest encouraged earlier in several graduate courses as well as by her father's career as a professional photographer (arguably, the combination of verbal and photographic texture in *Storyteller* anticipates this phase of Silko's career). During the late 1970s and early 1980s, even while her written work was relocating itself in a much larger sociopolitical context with Tucson rather than Laguna at its center, Silko's filmmaking efforts remained anchored at Laguna. There, she founded the Laguna Film Project and, with some additional support from an NEH grant and with an eye to eventual PBS release, began filming and producing "Arrowboy and the Witches," a 60-minute video version of her story "Estoy-eh-muut and the Kunideeyahs" (*Storyteller*, 140–54).[8] To film it, she returned to the mesa country south and west of Old Laguna, a landscape of cottonwoods and sandstone caves in an area locally known as Dripping Springs, which has been in the care of the Marmon family for several generations. As part of the setting for this film but also partly, perhaps, fulfilling the words she attributes to her father in *Storyteller* — "You could even live / up here in these hills if you wanted" (161) — Silko erected a stone cottage near the base of the Dripping Springs mesa. It burned down shortly thereafter, but its ruins are still there, along with the shell of the dwelling occupied by Spider Grandmother in that film, parts of yet another story attaching to this place.

As *Storyteller* does mainly in print and "Arrowboy and the Witches" does mainly in motion-picture form, much of Silko's nonfiction work of the past decade continues to integrate the conventional domains of visual and verbal art. In 1989, for instance, an essay entitled "The Fourth World" appeared in *Artforum*, a journal of the visual arts, and in 1995 her photo essay "An Essay on Rocks" appeared in a special issue of *Aperture* magazine. In these essays, as in her filmmaking, Silko's creative vision remains grounded in her years growing up at Laguna: in "The Fourth World," Silko speculates about the connections between the high teenage suicide rate around Laguna and the open Jackpile uranium mine, while in "An Essay on Rocks" her story about a boulder in a Tucson arroyo ends with an allusion to the story of a similar rock on Mount Taylor that first appeared in *Storyteller* (77–78).

Leslie Silko lives today on a ranch in the mountains a few miles northwest of Tucson, Arizona, where she has been living since the publication of *Ceremony*. In her most recent novel, *Almanac of the Dead* (1991), Silko portrays Tucson, the novel's apparent center of gravity and the setting for much of the story, as a hopelessly corrupt city, "home to an assortment of speculators, confidence men, embezzlers, lawyers, judges, police and other criminals, as well as addicts and pushers" (frontispiece, *Almanac*), trembling on the edge of apocalyptic redemption thanks to its locus with respect to the Azteca migration motif. But even in *Almanac of the Dead*, Sterling, Silko's on-again-off-again protagonist, is a native of Laguna, and the novel can end only when the "Exile" of the novel's second chapter returns to Laguna in its final chapter, titled "Home": "Sterling hiked over the little sand hills across the little valley to the sandstone cliffs where the family sheep camp was. The windmill was pumping lazily in the afternoon breeze, and Sterling washed his face and hands and drank. The taste of the water told him he was home. Even thinking the word made his eyes fill with tears" (757).

Like Tayo's in *Ceremony*, Sterling's personal history is a story of contact with attractive but dangerous non-Laguna forces, departure from Laguna, and eventual return to Laguna with the acquired knowledge of how to live with those forces — the "Yellow Woman" motif that Silko so strongly associates with the image of the river at Laguna. In *Ceremony*, Tayo completes his return by crossing this river from south to north at sunrise (255); in *Almanac*, the water-spirit of Kawaika is presented in its alternate shape: in the open pit of the Jackpile uranium mine, the giant spirit snake Maahastryu, who formerly inhabited the lake after which the Laguna people were originally named, has reappeared, "looking south, in the direction from which the twin brothers and the people would come" in fulfillment of a prophecy of which the Laguna story is but a small part (763).

Despite her Arizona address, Silko was recently named a Living Cultural Treasure by the New Mexico Humanities Council. In 1994 she also received the Native Writers' Circle of the Americas lifetime achievement award, an honor she now shares with N. Scott Momaday (1992), Simon Ortiz (1993), and Joy Harjo (1995). No doubt there will be more honors forthcoming.

Perhaps Silko, who has never ceased to write out of her experience as a Laguna woman, will, like her fictive protagonists, one day return to Kawaika and receive them there.

NOTES

1. The term is Mary Louise Pratt's; see "Arts of the Contact Zone." See also Gloria Anzaldúa's *Borderlands/La Frontera*.
2. See, for instance, "Yellow Woman" (62), "Storytelling" (94–95), and "The Man to Send Rain Clouds" (182).
3. *Ceremony*, 182; see also Auntie's story about Tayo's mother, Laura, which positions her at this place at sunrise, returning to Laguna (70). This is also the place that Tayo positions himself at the first sunrise following the autumnal equinox (and the Jackpile mine episode) at the end of the novel (255). A videotaped image of this site, marked by a large cottonwood tree, appears in "Running on the Edge of the Rainbow."
4. For a discussion of these sources see Linda Danielson, "The Storytellers in *Storyteller*." For photographs of the family storytellers Silko credits in *Storyteller* see Lee Marmon, "A Laguna Portfolio."
5. See, for instance, "Landscape, History, and the Pueblo Imagination." Silko reiterates her formative connection to the landscape of Laguna Pueblo in one of her most recent essays, "Interior and Exterior Landscapes."
6. This was her second marriage; her first, also short-lived, was to Richard Chapman while she was still a student at the University of New Mexico. She bore two sons (one from each marriage), Robert and Cazimir.
7. "Running on the Edge of the Rainbow: Laguna Stories and Poems" is one of the series of videotapes of oral literary performance entitled *Words and Place,* produced by Larry Evers at the University of Arizona. It is available from Norman Ross Publishing, 330 West 58th Street, New York NY 10019.
8. Silko's project was originally for a trilogy of films, to be collectively entitled *Stolen Rain.* "Arrowboy and the Witches," the only one of the three to be completed (though it has not undergone final editing), is available from Video Tape, 10545 Burbank Boulevard, North Hollywood CA 91601–2280.
   In a 1978 letter to James Wright, Silko had this to say about her intentions for this project:

> I am pushing to finish the first of the scripts which attempt to tell the Laguna stories on film using the storyteller's voice with the actual locations where these stories are supposed to have taken place. In a strange sort of way, the film project is an experiment in translation — bringing the land — the hills, the arroyos, the boulders, the cottonwoods in October — to people unfamiliar with it, because after all, the stories grow out of this land as much as we see ourselves as having emerged from the land there. . . . [I]f you do not know the places which the storyteller calls up in the telling, if you have not waded in the San Jose River below the village, if you have not hidden in the river willows

and sand with your lover, then even as the teller relates a story, you will miss something which people from the Laguna community would not have missed. (Wright, 24)

WORKS CITED

Anzaldúa, Gloria. *Borderlands/La Frontera: The New Mestiza*. San Francisco: Aunt Lute, 1987.

Danielson, Linda. "The Storytellers in Storyteller." *Studies in American Indian Literatures* 1.2 (fall 1989): 21–31.

Marmon, Lee. "A Laguna Portfolio." *Studies in American Indian Literatures* 5.1 (spring 1993): 63–74.

Pratt, Mary Louise. "Arts of the Contact Zone." *Ways of Reading: An Anthology for Writers*. Ed. Donald Bartholomae and Anthony Petrosky. 3d ed. Boston: St. Martin's, 1993. 442–56.

Rosen, Kenneth, ed. *The Man to Send Rain Clouds: Contemporary Stories by American Indians*. New York: Viking, 1974.

"Running on the Edge of Rainbow: Laguna Stories and Poems. With Leslie Marmon Silko." Videotape in the series Words and Place: Native Literature from the American Southwest. Produced by Larry Evers. New York: Clearwater Publishing, 1978.

Silko, Leslie Marmon. *Almanac of the Dead*. New York: Simon and Schuster, 1991.

———. *Ceremony*. New York: Viking, 1977.

———. "An Essay on Rocks." *Aperture* 139 (summer 1995): 60–63.

———. "The Fourth World." *Artforum* 27.10 (summer 1989): 125–26.

———. "Interior and Exterior Landscapes: The Pueblo Migration Stories." *Landscape in America*. Ed. George F. Thompson. Austin: U of Texas P, 1995. 155–70.

———. *Laguna Woman*. Greenfield Center, NY: Greenfield Review, 1974.

———. "Landscape, History, and the Pueblo Imagination." *Antaeus* 51 (1986): 83–94.

———. *Storyteller*. New York: Seaver, 1981.

Wright, Anne, ed. *The Delicacy and Strength of Lace: Letters between Leslie Marmon Silko and James Wright*. Saint Paul, MN: Graywolf, 1986.

SILKO'S REAPPROPRIATION
OF SECRECY

Paul Beekman Taylor

To you it is given to know the mysteries of the kingdom of heaven, but to them it is not given. . . . Seeing they do not see, and hearing they do not know.
MATTHEW 13:11, 13

The act of appropriation [is] essential to the marginalized culture that would wrest authority from the authoritative center.
LOUIS OWENS (1992a)

The critical perspective in the pages that follow is pointedly and purposely Eurocentric because it emanates from my ethnic background and an academic nurture and cultural interest in the history of ideas in medieval Europe and particularly in the literary vestiges of non-Christian culture in the European north. This point of view, however, gives me a distinct if not privileged perspective on the American Indian's cultural convergence with mainstream American civilization and upon his strategies of appropriation and reappropriation of cultural goods. I find the Indian example instructive for the European who senses that his own cultures are in a deeper crisis now than they were five hundred years ago when the competition for conquest and appropriation of the riches of the Western Hemisphere began.[1] The arts, and particularly the literatures of the American Indian, are effective tools for shaking the European's perspective loose from tight ideological shackles to engage him in alternative realities. If I can have myself and my students appreciate, if not acquire, something of the knowledge and power that American Indian arts transmit across cultural boundaries, I can pose with some purpose and profit the urgent questions: What does this literature mean for us? To what use can we put it? These questions are not directions for an engagement in the romantic and nostalgic pageantry of the popular media, or for picking up beads, leather, feathers, shedding a tear, and becoming Indians,[2] but rather for coaxing us to take a halting step toward analyzing and treating our own cultural malaise, for we in Europe have in large part lost touch with the land, our ancestry, and with those primal mythic values that are figured and refigured in American Indian story from its native oral matrix into the Eurocentric compartments of word and graph. To show anything of the manner in which the literature of the American Indian — among other emergent cultures in North America — has turned the homoglossia of the literary hegemony of America toward a fresh and dynamic heteroglossia is of inestimable value for the European who is suffering the fracturing of cultural hegemonies within borders of body and thought he has taken for granted as enduring realities.[3] I have found that overlaying the European and American literary map with contemporary American Indian written lore brings into sharp relief lines of convergence and divergence of cultures and exposes much of its promising power to rejuvenate what many lament as a stale and moribund mainstream American literary koine, and if that, its power can touch world literature. To review what has been taken from his artistic expression is to appreciate what the Indian has retrieved, or reappropriated.

THE POLEMICS OF INDIAN SECRECY

American Indian literature has moved well along in its strategic process of reappropriating from the mainstream American literary economy something of its sacred, or "secret," story tradition, which the white has taken and transformed along with other cultural goods to perpetuate a comforting image of the Indian as an object of study and nostalgic reflection. In his discussion of N. Scott Momaday, Louis Owens says that with *House Made of Dawn* (1968) "the American Indian novel shows its ability to appropriate the discourse of the privileged center and make it bear an other world view" (1992a, 92); that is, to retrieve his own, the Indian must tap the Anglo's stock and reshape it in his own style.

Since appropriating the discourse of the Euro-American entails a confluence of indigenous with imported story — blending a distinctive indigenous spirit with a foreign language — not every Indian is happy with the assimilation of English into tribal cosmologies (Owens 1992a, 103), regretting that while the Indian alters what he himself has appropriated of white literary culture, what is retrieved of his traditional story is inevitably altered by its presence in the Euro-American literary economy. Controversy over Hollywood versions of the stories of Squanto and Pocahontas reveal the extent to which such transformation of story splits Indian opinion into traditionalist and modernist camps. The former see in such film adaptations a "re-inventing and distorting of the tribe's culture for future generations," while the latter assign less importance to accurate reflection of tradition than to the emergence of "a rare positive portrait" for young children (Faiola 1995, 20).

Reshaping popular images of the Indian for white and Indian youth is politically corrective, but the crucial issue for the Indian is not *who* should translate Indian story (the Indian himself, of course), but *what* story may be commodified for scientific research and educational entertainment, if any at all, and *who* is its appropriate audience. Before the Anglo translated Indian lore into English film story for "disposable entertainment," anthropologists and ethnographers were writing Indian "autobiographies" and recording material the Indian often guarded as "sacred." As Leslie Marmon Silko states quite directly: "The . . . implicit racist assumption still abounding is that the prayers, chants, and stories weaseled out by the early white ethnographers which are now collected in ethnological journals, are public property" (1987, 212). Indian story, she adds, is no different in this context from the museum artifact, since shifted location and occasion for performance necessarily distorts its meaning by misrepresenting its matrix in oral story. In short, removing artifact and story from its traditional performative context, like removing the Indian from his ancestral land, breaks the sacred bond between person and thing.

Geary Hobson sees "interested" scholarship depriving the Indian of something of his viable culture: "The assumption seems to be that one's 'interest' in an Indian culture makes it okay for the invader to collect 'data' from Indian people when, in effect, this taking of the essentials of cultural lifeways, even if in the name of Truth or Scholarship or whatever, is as imperialistic as those simpler forms of theft of homeland by treaty" (1993b, 101). Appropriation of artifact and story, whether for museum, library, or film, is a Eurocentric strategy for possessing what cannot be understood if not mastered, and not mastered as long as it is not understood. Appropriated story on the library shelf or in the video cassette, like medicine bundles in museum dust and stale air, lies fossilized and inert, deprived of a natural power of growth, change, and adaptation. Silko's opening to *Ceremony* announces that *loss* is precisely what the white wants, "so they try to destroy the stories / let the stories be confused or forgotten" (2). As Josiah reminds Tayo in the novel, "droughts happen when people forget, when people misbehave"(47).

Many Indians believe hopefully that nothing *essential* is absolutely irretrievable of their lore. Owens says that the Indians "knew they had lost something precious and indispensable and they lived in a world bereft and haunted. But they believed that what they'd lost was still there, somewhere if they could only understand the clues. The solution was just out of reach" (1994, 39). The Azteca del Norte Rudolfo Anaya has argued that although the capacity to retrieve the old sacred secrets has been blocked by the white, it is not lost:

> [There are] secrets that hint at the deeper spiritual and humanistic relationships the pre-Columbian societies had with the Earth and with the deities of their cosmos . . . we no longer understand, in paintings and in ancient writings that puzzle us. . . . We see the truth hidden in these symbols and secrets and stories of the past. This is what the pilgrim seeks a key to turn, a door to enter, a new way to see his role in the universe. (Anaya 1986, viii)

He adds optimistically: "You can be separated for a hundred years, for two hundred, for four hundred, for a thousand years, from what is essentially your mythology, but the separation is a veneer. The myth will always emerge. It has to surge out and be known, because you carry it with you" (Gonzalez-T.1990, 428–29).

It is hidden in the dark recesses of an ancestral memory, illuminated by signs and symbols on the landscape. In *Ceremony*, Ts'eh explains to Tayo the painting of an elk on a cliff: "Nobody has come to paint it since the war. But as long as you remember what you have seen, then nothing is gone" (218). Similarly, in *The Way to Rainy Mountain*, Momaday laments the vanished culture of the Kiowa, while holding out hope for retrieval of secret lore the white man has systematically obliterated. "East of my grandmother's house," he muses near the end of his story, "south of the pecan grove there is buried a woman in a beautiful dress. Mammedaty used to know where she is buried, but now no one knows. . . . She was buried in a cabinet, and she wore a beautiful dress. . . . That dress is still there, under the ground (1969, 82). Like the Navajo Changing Woman, who incarnates time in the cycles of life, the body of the Kiowa woman in her attire incarnates time and story. It is enough, for the moment, that she is remembered so that, wherever she is, she can be regenerated in story. Story functions to reclaim secret lore the Indian has forgotten or the Anglo has metamorphosed.[4]

Retrieval of what has been forgotten is a major concern for those Indians whose sense of cultural vitality has been severely sapped, but the Indian who revitalizes and makes public his people's story in written form runs the risk of being charged with adding to the desecration already caused by the white's appropriation of it. Jana Sequoya says of Silko and Momaday that "although . . . both are concerned with the recuperation of indigenous sources of identity . . . the first novels of both directly incorporate elements of traditional sacred story cycles — a practice constituting, along with an emergent literary form, an ethical question vis-à-vis the particular communities of which these authors write" (456). In brief, they "betray the 'origins' . . . from which they derive their canonical status as representative Native American writers" (464).

A conciliatory view concedes that "Native Americans have had to make a variety of accommodations to the dominant culture's forms, capitulating to them, assimilating them, sometimes dramatically transforming them, but never able to proceed independent of them" (Krupat 1989, 57). Owens notes that "the form of the novel may thus represent a necessary 'desacralization' of traditional materials, a transformation that allows sacred materials — from ritual to myth — to move into the secular world of decontextualized 'art'. . . . This transformation can be problematic" (1992a, 11); and yet, to Allen's warning that "to use the oral tradition is to run afoul of native ethics" (1990, 379), he responds: "The risk is one that many Indian authors appear ready to assume" (24).

Sequoya argues that the risk, nonetheless, has a negative effect on Indian children, because their stories are told "outside the sanctions of their context . . . [and] will be confused in the terms of their communal context and hence forgotten because in the secular domain of the novel they *are* just 'entertainment'" (1993, 460). The implication here is that entertaining *(delectare)* is clearly distinct from instructing *(docere)*. Therefore, "to the extent that authors and critics alike deny the real difference between the cultures in way of having stories, they silence crucial aspects of those tribal traditions they would reclaim" (468). Clan stories aren't just entertainment, she continues, "but have a survival function in sustaining the identity of the community" (467). That is, their power remains intact as long as they remain secret as the private property of the clan. So, she observes, Momaday errs when he incorporates explicitly sacred oral story in *House Made of Dawn* (466). Paula Gunn Allen echoes that charge when she says of Silko's *Ceremony:* "Being raised in greater proximity to Laguna than I, she must have been told what I was, that we do not tell these things outside. . . . The story she lays alongside the novel is a clan story, and it is not to be told outside of the clan" (1986, 95–96). "To use the oral tradition directly," she states elsewhere, "is to run afoul of native ethics" (1990, 379). Because Silko validates her novel's representation of sacred story by taking on Thought Woman's voice, she legitimates the non-Indian reader's access to traditional narrative by blurring the differences between secular and sacred uses of story (Sequoya 1993, 466).

The heart of the matter is understanding precisely the differences between secular and sacred uses of story, for each one of us reads story through the cultural lens our culture has clamped on our vision.[5] The Indian suffers from having his idea of the sacredness of story reduced to mundane entertainment, and the white misses the significance of Indian sacred secrets by reading them at best as exotic lore and at worst as retrograded barbarism. Insofar as the sacred is secret, it is to be guarded from eyes that cannot understand it, so the secret that is made public has its sacred content banalized. For the outsider, it is difficult to either appreciate or measure the extent to which medicine bundles removed from their proper locations have their secret power laid waste, or even effaced, such as the "grandparent" figures in a glass case in the Santa Fe museum, stolen eighty years earlier from the Laguna Pueblo (1991, 31), which are, effectively, violated by the eyes of museum visitors. If power for the good of the pueblo is denied as long as their outward forms are appropriated as fragments of "exotica," how much of their power is irretrievably lost if returned to their sources? So, for Indian lore, how can the outsider, let alone the Indian himself, measure how much sacred power of Indian story is irretrievably lost once it is taken out of oral instructional context and placed in the public literary market? If Franz Boas had collected Laguna stories, including the account of Tayo's ascension of Tse-pi'na, scores of years before Silko wrote her story of Tayo, has she violated its sacred character only because she is an Indian?

The answer is, in a sense, yes, because the boundary between secular and sacred is hermeneutic; that is, it depends upon the way in which texts and contexts converge to shape sense. To the child, the madman, and the enlightened, all texts and contexts — the world and everything in it — are sacred. "All is written for our doctrine" says Saint Paul (Romans 15:4), and there is nothing secret in nature for those who are not aware of the existence of hidden things; but he who has lost his innate sacred view of the world, as Christ explains the parables, can no longer see the sacred meaning behind mundane appearances. The word "secular" itself pertains only to a world fallen from grace. Children are taught *out* of a pristine innocent view of all things as sacred and must be "re-instructed" to read a sacred sense back into common secular forms.

The kiva's exclusive and sacred space, and story told there, are clearly indicated to the Indian, but written story occupies a free area whose sacred limits are often difficult for teller and hearer to discern. In short, the written text is superior to the oral text because written law and holy scripture certify a truth that is not context-bound, while Indian ceremony evokes its power in particular contexts. Allen recognizes the hermeneutic complexity of story when she argues that ceremonial literature "frequently uses language of its own, archaisms, 'meaningless' words, or special words not used in everyday conversation" (1993, 235). For these reasons one might assume that the total secrecy of meaning is never known except to those who make it.[6] To say that "only those who already know the mysteries can discover what the stories really mean" (Kermode 1979, 3), is to trace a hermeneutic circle.

Institutions like the kiva teach the sacred truths residing beneath the secular appearances. Just as the casual tourist is pleased with the language and pageantry of the coronation of an English monarch, despite ignorance of the secret meanings derived from the sacral context of its origins, looking admiringly at the image of Kokopelli on a belt buckle and at Gogyeng Sowuhti on a bolo tie does not give the tourist a privileged peek into the sacred mythic lore to which the images allude. Their familiar outward array may be merely ornamental to him, but even the instructed are often reluctant to attribute to royal pageantry or to mythic images in these contexts a cosmic power. Nonetheless, while American Indian story in translation is enjoyed by many in the mainstream literary circuit as local color, and by anthropologists as a people's myth essential to a sense of being, many if not most Indians are educated to sense a cosmic power in their people's stories, dances, prayers, and fetish artifacts. When critics like Sequoya and Allen argue that public audience and witness to these things violate their secrets, if not waste their power, they are right in the sense that there are unbridgeable gaps between white and Indian cultural perspectives, but wrong insofar as there are, in all cross-cultural contacts, inevitable "fusions of horizons" in interpretation (Kermode 1983, 203).

The hermeneutic challenge to fuse horizons of interpretation is precisely what the Salish D'Arcy McNickle's Indian agent in *Wind from an Enemy Sky* comes to realize; that is, to understand Indian ways, one must learn to read two different realities, if not live in them. It is an epistemological as well as hermeneutic issue, for the Indian's world is both subject and object of his attention. Momaday has said in many different ways that to be "Indian" is to have a certain idea of oneself, and the Anglo who moves into the "other" reality can witness and read its sacred lore, simply because he has realized its pertinence to *his own* life. The Anglo who cannot transfer an understanding of that other reality to his own being, it seems to me, can neither read nor violate its secrets as long as the secret is in the meaning of the artifact rather than in the artifact itself. So it is with Navajo sandpaintings and Hopi Kachina dolls sold on the open market whose transfer of place and occasion masks that secret form and function the Indian would hide from the white.[7] So it is as well with the translation of story from oral to literary performance, for the audience that does not "know" the local and topical uses to which oral story is put cannot understand its performance in terms much else than features of plot.

Since it is difficult for the general reader to recognize a violation of a secrecy of whose existence and substance he is ignorant, it is impossible to judge the violation of the "misread" secret where there is no authoritative exegetical guide. The outcast Sterling of Silko's *Almanac of the Dead* represents the general white reader when he questions why he is exiled for having allowed the filming of a secret idol, when those who filmed it didn't know what they were looking at (31). For his tribal elders it is enough for the white to see a secret for him to want to steal it (92), but theft constitutes violation of secrecy in the limited sense of removing its access to those who can read it. One can only transmit secret lore to one qualified somehow to understand it. Ancestral spirits and the old sages who guard tribal secrets must wait for the right ear to hear their secrets. In the Blackfoot James Welch's *Fools Crow*, the spirit woman So-at-sa-ki reveals only to the well-instructed hero the origins and ends that contain and give meaning to the confusion of the tribe's present conditions (1986, 350–59). The old Stehemish Jim Joseph in Louis Owens's novel *Wolf Song* feels himself caught between revealing and hiding a tribal secret, knowing that it is bad luck to tell the old stories about Wolfspirit that shouldn't be told (1995, 34–35). He dies before he is able to pass on more than a few fragments to his nephew Tom, who needs that lore to retrieve his lost bonds with the land and its people.

Like Jim Joseph, the Indian novelist who writes of traditional culture seems to face a choice of either transmitting secrets from one generation to another, translating one cultural form to another, or — lacking an appropriate audience to hear and understand — letting the secret lie dormant with the hope that someone will rediscover something of it with which to remake fresh story. Sequoya sees the choice as one between respecting traditional sanctions and hiding sacred texts or assimilating them into the "dominant institution" as "fragments of an exotic subculture (1993, 468). She would prefer to respect a border between Anglo and Native American cultures, beyond which Ameri-can Indians could hide their secret lore from the "enemy" alien. Leigh Jenkins says of the Hopi that if "the conflict arises when *non-Indians* want to preserve Hopi culture by publishing their secrets . . . the tribe would prefer to lose its traditions" (qtd. in Sequoya 1993, 457, my emphasis). The choice to have the secret disappear rather than be exposed appears to be self-defeating, but it is made most often in personal terms as an avowal to keep one's *own* story inextricably bound to one's own experience. So, the Mesquakie Ray A. Young Bear writes:

> I remember well
> my people's
> songs.
> I will not reveal to anyone

that i
know these songs.
it was
intended for me
to keep
them
in
secrecy
for they are now
mine to die with me. (Hobson 1993, 353)

The Choctaw poet Jim Barnes adds, as a prefatory warning to the reader:

Let us all carry into death the words we could not,
Lifebound, bear and in whatever other worlds
    Say them unafraid. (1982)

The choice in these lines is between *not* transmitting a frozen idiom of a people's sacred lore to where it would be classed and stored as an ethnographic curiosity and forging an organic bond between the life of story and its maker. The secret "dies" for the white as soon as the Indian writer adapts, alters, and reshapes received story into a new life. This is what Silko's Betonie means in his explanation to Tayo in *Ceremony* that story must change with each experience that recontextualizes it. Anaya puts it another way in his story of the ancient Inca runner who "would read the message of the Quipus, record it in his language, and pass it on. Each new time had its runners, those whose work carried them into new realms of reality" (1995, 260). In like fashion, Momaday and Silko recode sacred lore in new secret forms that renew old sacred power.[8] Recognizing that they have lost something of the vital secrets essential to their ancestors' survival with the dignity of distinctive being, they retrieve sacred lore by entering themselves into new myths (Gonzalez-T. 1990, 426). Citing the Anglo Gary Snyder's assertion that "you must create your own new myths," Silko quips: "That's good advice to follow" (1993b, 215).

Reshaping myth is not only a manner of retrieving and adapting indigenous lore; it is also a strategy of resistance to the white's continuing appropriation and secularization of Indian secrecy. Silko's prologue to Tayo's story insists on the resistant as well as curative powers of story:

You don't have anything
If you don't have the stories.

Their evil is mighty
but it can't stand up to our stories. (1977, 2)

The medicine man Betonie tells his patient Tayo quite simply: "I tell you, we can deal with white people, with their medicines and their beliefs," and the way of dealing is recycling "the leftover things the whites didn't want" (1977, 139, 133).[9] For the Indian, recycling the white's disposable cultural debris in story reclaims a vital culture of sacred lore from the dustbin of the Euro-American's public economy. Furthermore, the Indian's recycling of European language and literary forms enriches the Anglo mainstream with the particular value of Indian experience. Finally, translation of place and language re-effects secrecy by shifting attention away from the original hieratic nature of community story to the distinctive constituents of new forms whose simple demotic cover is all the more resistant to the hermeneutic scrutiny of the uninstructed.

In short, that which retrieves and revitalizes the power of sacred lore is the writer's, singer's, dancer's, or painter's memory of his own experience conjoined with the lore of ancestral or communal experience. Retrieval depends upon re-creating myth that has something to do with life now (Gonzalez-T. 1990, 426). For example, in Momaday's later novel, *The Ancient Child*, the half–Kiowa Locke Setman, under the care of a young medicine woman, recovers his Indian being by actualizing the nominal secret force in his name, Set ("bear") and by entering the traditional Kiowa myth of the bearchild Tsoai. Betonie effects the first stage of Tayo's cure using story as medicine (1977, 135–58). Like the Kiowa arrow that carries the teeth marks of its maker, story has the force to destroy those who do not know the maker's language (Momaday 1969, 46).

In this manner, the Indian writes *over* European story, not only over the romantic mythology that the Euro-American invented to validate his claims to the Indian past but also over the European's dominant lore of secrecy. His intent, finally, is not to reveal secrets, but to re-create, reconceal, and resacralize them. The white has taken Indian story, as he has taken Indian foodstuffs, reformed and commercialized them into bland and unpalatable forms, while the Indian has nurtured the white's language and literary forms, as he had adopted the white's gun and horse, to make new and efficient tools for survival and resistance.

So, in such terms, what does American Indian story mean to the white reader? It is obvious, first of all, that secrecy in fiction and the fiction of secrecy lie at its core. It is clear that in the translation of Indian cultural experience into the English literary idiom two ontologies as well as two cosmologies exist, and that the Indian writer conjoins received images and meanings of English words with his own distinct image and word-making traditions. The English language of the Indian writer ineluctably appropriates the traditional lore of Anglo culture while empowering that idiom with a fresh resonance and reference that unsettles conventional reading expectations. In effect, the Anglo reader finds himself challenged to reshape his own hermeneutic procedures to grasp multiple epistemologies and realities. To appreciate the secret lore in American Indian fiction, then, the European reader must review his conventional topoi of secrecy, just as the Indian reader who would appreciate the cultural distinctions between his own and the white's traditional lore should scan the history and form of secrecy in the European literature the Indian takes to trace over his own landscape.

EUROPEAN SECRECY

Secrets are bound to time more than to space in European lore. In Greek myth, secrets of past, present, and future are embodied in the Fates. In Plato's story, Lachesis sings the things that were; Clotho sings the things that are; and Atropos the things that are to be (*Republic* 10, 671e). This triad is reduplicated in Anaya's *Heart of Aztlán* by the Aztec Crispín who sings all three to merge the historical past of the Mexican with his imaginative present and hoped-for future, a conception that moves man's imaginative possibilities close to Augustine's God who lives in one tense, while man lives in what the grammarians identify as three tenses. Divine Creation is the fundamental secret of the past in almost all mythic traditions, and its hidden end in the indeterminable future is coded in the material signs of nature. The secrets of creation and its process are, then, hermeneutic mysteries encoded in the shapes of the world's landscape. Man's limited means to see "the whole picture" is a universal condition, and it appears from anthropological research that all earth's extant mythologies address themselves to this same triadic relationship between unwitnessed beginnings, hidden ends, and present signs of both. In the pre- or non-Christian story of the Germanic north, trickster figures like Loki of Nordic myth know something of the secrets of creation and destruction that are guarded zealously by the primal giants. They work their trickery to bring about the inevitable destruction of the world for the same sort of purging and renewing that American Indian tricksters work.[10] Tricksters like Saynday and Coyote of Plains Indian story and Quetzalcoatl of Aztec lore are forces of time that span creation and destruction in sacred story, but who populate secular space as instructors in practical wisdom. Like Silko's Gambler, they destabilize the balance of accounts on the landscape in order to provoke the wit and energy necessary to set things right. In these worlds of belief, there is no necessary distinction between science, myth, and story, and all secular activity plays out sacred processes.

If the use of time to earn grace, make one's mark, leave a monument, and a name and fame for story, if not for salvation, is particularly Christian and Eurocentric, the Indian is concerned with space and with his collaboration with the land to live spiritually well, rather than with exploitation of the land in order to live materially better. In European lore, then, secrecy has much to do with what is to come and with what can be done about it, while the Indian is sensitive to what can be read of all time in the present moment. Tayo, on his ride to find the missing Mexican cattle of his past, "knew then why the oldtimers could only speak of yesterday and tomorrow in terms of the present moment" (1977, 201). In short, while the fallen world of the Christian can only be redeemed after life, Indians like Tayo on a path of retrieval can grasp something of the paradisiacal in mortal experience.

In Christian lore, the essential secrecy that mediates between Creation and Doomsday is sin. While the first and last secrets are inviolable public and universal mysteries, sin is a private spiritual shame. In the Judeo-Christian tradition, sin and salvation are linked secrets of hidden causes and public consequences of evil acts. The biblical Tree of Knowledge, which figures man's fall from innocent ignorance to knowledge of sin, has parallels in most Indian myths of emergence. In Blackfoot and Ojibwa myth, Feather Woman digs up the sacred turnip and is released from the sky by her husband Sun to fall treeward (Welch 1986, 350–52). In Kiowa story, emergence is through a hollow log, and in Pueblo story, witches emerge out of the underworld with the people.[11] In *Ceremony,* Silko tells the story of a contest in magic among medicine men during which an outsider, Pa'caya'nyi, identifies himself as a Ck'oyo medicine man and performs tricks that divert the attention of his audience away from tending the altar of Corn Mother. In anger she leaves, taking the rain clouds with her (1977, 48–50).[12] The error in such stories, as in Greek and pre-Christian Germanic story, is a community matter not a private matter between a person and his maker. There is no substantial category of secrecy that has to do with salvation as an individual or eternal spiritual reward in such stories. Cliff House and Sand Hills are neither heavens nor hells.[13]

A crucial difference between Indian and Christian morality is brought into focus in Indian story. Whereas for the Christian, man is responsible for the sin that only God can expiate, the Indian is taught that he has the power in collaboration with his community to redress natural, moral, and social ill. In *Ceremony,* Betonie tells Tayo that the evil of the present situation is the fault of the Indian himself who invented the Anglo (139), and so the Indian, in collaboration with the earth, has the power to cure the Anglo. "Because the powaka [witch] has gone with the Bahanas, they will grow strong," says a traditional creation tale. "They will learn evil as well as good, and they will have secrets that are not known to us" (Courlander 1987, 31). In the same story it is prophesied that a good Bahana will come from the east and rejoin the other Indian clans. In Aztec myth, the good one who will return is Quetzalcóatl. The story of the opposition to him by the evil alliance of Moctezuma's sorcerers with the European is told briefly in *Almanac of the Dead* (57), and in a full form in Anaya's *Lord of the Dawn*.

From its inception, European secret story has progressively secularized the epistemological issues of the creation and destruction of the world and of the pageantry of life between. Plato's *Timaeus* offers a "likely" account of the origin of all things, and his fable of the warrior Er in *The Republic* (10, 614b–620a) illustrates public and secular rather than sacred concerns, similar to Aeneas' and Ulysses' instruction in the underworld. Homer's Er returns from the land of the dead where he is charged by its judges to report back to the living the secrets of life and death. Instruction by the dead is common to both Greek and Indian story and, like Indian mythographers, Plato is concerned less with the secret design of the universe than with man's urgent civic need to distinguish between the good and the bad life (618c). Transmission of essential lore from inhabitants of an "otherworld" is a major feature in the fiction of Momaday, Silko, Welch, and Owens.[14]

Perhaps the most comprehensive story of secrecy in European lore reflected in American Indian story is Ovid's myth of Arachne's weaving contest with Pallas Athena (*Metamorphoses* 6, 1–69). Weaving creation stories, both women reflect spider women creators like the Aztec Coatlicue and the Hopi Gogyeng Sowuhti. On her loom, the goddess weaves images of the supernal power of the twelve gods, while Arachne weaves the stories of Juno contending against Antigone, Bacchus against Saturn, and Jupiter raping Europa in the form of a bull and Leda in the form of a swan. When the judges accord Arachne the laurel, Pallas tears up the web and strikes Arachne, who in shame moves to kill herself. In pity, Athena turns Arachne into a spider with her skill of weaving intact. This story is an archetype of art resisting oppression, but it is also an exemplum of the force of art to maintain life and cultural identity for one whose sense of being has been violated. Another European example of a text as weapon of resistance is Penelope's secret design, woven by day and unraveled at night in Homer's *Odyssey*. Her text retards time and resists the sexual advances of her unwanted suitors. The most telling instance of a woven secret as weapon against oppression in European story is Ovid's tale of Philomena. Raped by her sister's husband Tereus, who cuts her tongue out to prevent her disclosure of the act, she is kept prisoner in a cave for his delight. There she weaves a coded tale of her plight, has it sent to Progne, who deciphers it and rescues her sister. Reunited, they take their revenge on Tereus by killing his sons and serving their flesh to him, before they castrate and kill him.

A complementary story that has signifying force for American Indian story is of Daedalus's flight from the Cretan labyrinth. In Virgil's version, after crossing the Aegean sea, Daedalus dedicates a temple on Mount Chalcidius to Apollo/Helios and on its walls inscribes the story of Minos, Pasiphae, and the Minotaur. Virgil identifies the half-bull, half-man shape of the king himself as the first mixed breed:

> hic crudelis amor tauri, suppostaque furto
> Pasiphaë, mixtumque genus prolesque biformis
> Minotaurus inest, Veneris monumenta nefandae.

> [Here (he depicted) the bull's harsh passion and the secret submission to Pasiphae, and as a warning against evil love their mixed-breed child the double-formed Minotaur.] (*Aeneid* 6, 24–26) [15]

The "double-formed" Minotaur, part man and part animal, imprisoned in a labyrinth to serve his master's design for rule, figures the "breed" Indian, and Daedalus, whose art enables him to escape his insular prison and translate to his homeland the cultural goods of his captor, even if at the price of the life of his son, figures the Indian who profits from the goods of his oppressor at an awful price. On a broader scale, the story of the Minotaur figures the violence and mixed heritage that engenders cultural change. Bloodline carries secrets of origins, and those origins are necessarily mixed in the European, even if the Spanish invaders of Mexico vaunted their *peninsulares'* pure blood, and theorists of the Third Reich evoked a pure Aryan strain. With few exceptions, the founding myths of Europe are of rape and abduction in which male invaders either carry foreign women off or sire new bloodlines after killing rival occupants of the land they conquer. So Zeus rapes Europa, the Romans rape the Sabine women, Paris carries off Helen, and Aeneas kills Turnus and appropriates Lavinia for his own dynastic purposes. On the other side of the Atlantic, Cortés takes Malintzin as his mate in his project to found a dynasty in a new Troy. Yoeme's story in *Almanac* of the bloodline of Lecha and Zeta Cazador from Guzman and Amalia reflects all these stories, but few dramatize the cultural potency of the mestizo better than Anaya in his story of Abrán González in *Alburquerque* and Owens in *Bone Game*.[16]

While prying behind the veil of creation to see something of the secret person of the creator describes the primal sin of disobedience in Christian story, the technological extension of human curiosity to know the "facts" of origins incited the European in the twelfth-century Renaissance to obviate cosmic secrets along with the notion of secrecy itself. The concept of the inviolable secrecy of God's being and his purpose was challenged by a shift of attention back to the pragmatic observation and analysis of physical matter practiced by Greek and Arabic philosophers. In an environment of exploration and experimentation, secrecy became not so much a cover of sacred things as an irrational mystery. Reason was applied to divulging the secrets of the earth, to laying bare the body of God, and to analyzing the process by which he created the world. Nothing was sacred to the explorer of the undiscovered things of land, sea, and air. In brief, the goal of empirical science was to obliterate secrecy, and under scientific scrutiny the Bible was read literally as an almanac of man's providential curve, or vector of grace.

Consequently, the individual's sense of community was abrogated by the church's insistence on individual responsibility for sin. The bond between man and God took precedent over man's bond with the earth and its other denizens, a development that Tayo considers in *Ceremony* when he regrets how Christianity separated the people from themselves, how Christ would save only the individual soul (70), whereas what happened to his mother Laura happened to *all* her people (71). From the church's campaign against rural heresy came a doctrine of sin that demanded revelation of secret thoughts and deeds. Chicano witnesses of the first atomic explosion wondered at the determination of the white man to master all things: "They compete with God, they disturb the seasons, they seek to know more than God Himself. In the end, that knowledge they seek will destroy us all" (Anaya 1972, 183). Tayo's grandmother also tells him the story of the Trinity Site explosion and concludes: "Now I only wonder why, grandson. Why did they make a thing like that?" Now Tayo, experienced in the evil of the whites, does know (257).

The concomitant development of Nominalist conceptions of language and epistemology denies a world of hidden forms behind the substance of words and things. The philosophic insistence on the priority of thing over idea constitutes a phenomenology that reached a culmination in Deistic reasoning that empties nature of its essential magical force. Nature was perhaps irretrievably demystified during the Industrial Revolution when advances in biology, medicine, astronomy, psychology, economics, and sociology mapped deterministic forces that isolated individual and family values from the larger human community, while binding them to political and social structures. In the Western world, national economies, languages, and political ideologies intruded upon man's sacred relationships with the earth. The Euro-American notion of Manifest Destiny and the dialectical materialism of Communism are but two manifestations of this ideology of progress. It is of little wonder that the Euro-American habit of thought secularized the pursuit of happiness. In such an environment, secrecy is either a secular inconvenience, a banal social and psychological game, or a hidden cause behind natural phenomena that must be divulged. Hegel put the prevalent European view well when he said: "America has always shown itself physically and psychically powerless, and still shows itself so. For the aborigines, after the landing of the Europeans in America, gradually vanished at the breath of European activity. In the United States of North America all the citizens are of European descent, with whom the old inhabitants could not amalgamate, but were driven back. . . . A mild and passionless disposition, want of spirit."[17]

If the sacred secrets of American Indian cultures have resisted the European's ideological secularization, it is because they have resisted the commodification of space that has been vital to the European view of the world's sky-, land-, and seascape as inchoate properties to be transformed into material goods. As Vine Deloria reminds us, the Indian has not, like the European, concerned himself with a philosophy of time either in the church's providential sense or in a secular program of "progress" (1973, 111–28). It is easy to understand, then, why the Euro-American, in his appropriation of Indian story, would reduce its secret sacredness to banal riddle and exotic lore that can be converted and commodified for a dominant economy, and hence, why the Indian writer would "remythologize" appropriated story.

In the modern era, the European topos of the secret text has dwindled into psychological and sociological mysteries that promise or threaten to reveal something sinister of one's self in the world. Poe's *Narrative of A. Gordon Pym,* Wilde's *Picture of Dorian Gray,* Stevenson's *Doctor Jekyll and Mr. Hyde,* James's "Jolly Corner," Pynchon's *Crying of Lot 49,* represent the current dominant shift of the idea of secrecy from the mystery of the forms behind creation toward sublimated chemical, social, and psychological forces hidden within man over which he has little or no control. Secrecy is conceived of as a dark and forbidding sexual force and a fearful bleakness of perversity and guilt.[18] The secret sin known to God and the sinner, revealed and hidden in the dark confession to an ear without voice, and the secret thought unveiled to the psychoanalyst who imprisons it in word invite analytic procedures rather than stories as cure. Silko responds to these procedures by castigating the "idea restricted to the white man" of a " 'power' to inhabit any soul, any consciousness" (1993b, 212). It is over the banal secrets of a spiritless society that the Indian writer conscientiously inscribes his story.

SILKO'S FICTION IN THE TRADITION OF AMERICAN INDIAN SECRET STORY

No other writer I know of has so pointedly addressed the issue of contrasting and reappropriated Euro-American secrecy than Silko in *Almanac of the Dead,* but before scanning that text in isolation, I need to review its context in contemporary American Indian fiction. Typical in Indian story is a secret place like the kiva, comparable to the hidden, or invisible, world the Christians call Paradise, because it is a place where one, like Silko's Tayo, can be reintegrated into a harmonious relationship with his people. Furthermore, while the Christian Paradise is more a text than a place, Indians in novels traverse borders between the visible "real" worlds and the hidden worlds in ceremonies as well as in vision and dream. Welch's Fools Crow visits the otherworldly green sanctuary of Feather Woman where the cosmogony of the Pikuni is revealed to him. In *Ceremony* the ranchito of Ts'eh is where Tayo reads vital secrets in a blanket pattern (218), and Black Swan's white-curtained room from which music and cool air float both figures and is a secret bower of woman's magical sexuality (103). The hidden inner bat cave and the Hill Indians' settlement in Hogan's *Mean Spirit* are places hidden from the white where sacred powers are guarded. Aztlán in Aztec and Chicano story is a secret place of origins, like the Keres T'se-pina, or Kawestima.[19]

In American Indian chthonic thought, the secret of origins pertains not only to the generative force of man's being but also to the force resident in all things on the landscape. Everything from stone and tree to eagle, coyote, and man contains story of its generic bond with all other created things. The more story that is lived, the stronger is the collaboration of all things on the landscape in maintaining harmony. The release of story from artifact is a hermeneutic act, perhaps not so different from Michelangelo's idea that the art of sculpture is a release of form from its material matrix. In either case, the act collaborates with matter, rather than seeks mastery over it. The Blackfoot hero of James Welch's *Fools Crow,* for instance, learns the story of the raven, frog, beaver, and wolverine—his "power animal"—to communicate and collaborate in maintaining the health of the land.

The health of the land is often encapsulated in a magical artifact, comparable to the Celtic Cornucopia, the Finnish Samppo, and the Christian Grail. The Kiowa *Tai-me,* or Sundance bundle, in Momaday's *Way to Rainy Mountain,* the Featherboy bundle in D'Arcy McNickle's *Wind from an Enemy Sky,* and the slave-girl's corn pouch in his *Runner in the Sun* are life-giving and sustaining forces. Tacho's opal eye in *The Almanac of the Dead* and Joe Billy's bat pouch in *Mean Spirit* convey messages from ancestor spirits. In Paula

Gunn Allen's *Woman who Owned the Shadows,* the two sacred pouches of Spiderwoman, or Sussistinaku [Thinking Woman], contain Uretsete, or she who matters, and Naotsete, she who remembers. The first is Corn Woman; the second is sacred story.[20] Mose's amulet in Welch's *Winter in the Blood,* and Yellow Calf's in *Indian Lawyer* lie dormant, though they finally draw attention to their latent powers. A destructive counterforce is the rawhide bag of Kaup'a'ta the Gambler in *Ceremony,* who has his victims wager their lives that they can guess what is in it (180).

Secret places and secret things contain story, but only the instructed — those who have achieved "self-actualization" by reconnecting themselves to the earth — can enter into vital story and its making.[21] Though Owens's Uncle Jim says it is bad luck to transmit the story that shouldn't be told about wolf spirit, the secret, like Silko's story of the gambler, *must* be told, even if it risks in its telling the engendering of evil. Jim knows he must do it, but when Tom goes away, the story is left unfinished and its power seems to be lost. The truth in what is not told him, however, is retrieved in Tom's own experience, and the telling of his story connects the teller and his adventure to the original secret power. Story transmitted is the germ of new story for the one receiving it. This point is made hopefully and comprehensively in Momaday's *Ancient Child* in the story of and within the hero's name, *Set* (Kiowa for "bear"), whose meaning emerges as he identifies himself progressively with both the animal and its mythic avatar. His name-sense takes shape in both writing and picture, and is retrieved as a physical object and a mental concept hidden within a magical process in which a girl, Grey, materializes a text floating free and unshaped over the landscape and nurtures it within the core of Set's own being. The hidden text here, like the painted Elk Ts'eh explains to Tayo in *Ceremony,* is the authenticity of an identity retrievable in a personally manifested myth.

Set also moves himself toward his personal myth of being in the process of painting a mysterious self-portrait whose central figure is a vague shape that is both man and bear. Painting looses Set's atavistic imaginative force that shapes the being hidden in his subconscious. The hidden text that mediates between person, people, and the land is a mark of identity alive *within* the individual as well as *about* him. The Yaqui heroine of Alma Luz Villanueva's *Ultraviolet Sky,* paints into actualization her hidden cultural identity as Quetzalpetlatl, the sister of Quetzalcóatl.[22] Painting the world with continents shaped into women's bodies, Rosa remakes a world whose female informing spiritual source is a defense against male violence and his sexual and social domination. Like Momaday's Set, Rosa observes the text of her personal mestizo myth emerge slowly and painfully in the shapes and colors of the sky in a painting more generated than invented. Through their arts and their acts, Set and Rosa discover something essential of their social and natural connections, and both make story of it in which they can read themselves in a process rather than as a product of self-actualization.

What is distinct from mainstream Euro-American fiction in these and other American Indian novels is the extent to which hidden racial difference and cultural mix matters. What is obviously common to both traditions at first sight is the English language and the novel "genre" that the Indian storyteller appropriates; but similarities in cultural perspective cannot be taken for granted. Today's English language and European literary forms have appropriated Native American secret lore for their own story for the past four hundred years since Cabeza de Vaca's *Relación* and Gaspar Pérez de Villagrá's epic *Historia*. In Meso-America, the Spanish conqueror who destroyed indigenous texts rewrote in Spanish what he wished to appropriate from them. The European history of Mexico is but one example of appropriation of local lore with all its secret glyphs and linguistic codes. English versions of that material follow the Spanish versions; and now Indian versions reshape much of that lore whose meanings remain secret to the European, if only in the sense that its codes, like the parables of Silko's *Almanac,* resist traditional Eurocentric hermeneutic procedures, reading, for example, within structured unities of time, space, and character with a Coleridgean "suspension of disbelief."

In all her writing, Silko has developed an ideology of secrecy that serves to distinguish Indian identity in story from lies that have imprisoned the image of the Indian and his sacred lore in Eurocentric secular frames.[23] One of her stylistic strategies is to lay her own story against and over the Anglo's, and she does this pretty much as the Gambler does to dupe others, that is, by challenging them with new secrets about themselves. Her stories expose the sterility and waste of Anglo secrets in contrast with the latent and realized vitality of Indian lore. The short story "Yellow Woman" features a girl who is spoken into myth by the man she sleeps with, and hearing his story, she realizes that her participation in it requires making myth herself. This "promotion" of person into story prefigures Yoeme's account to Lecha in *The Almanac of the Dead* of her own entrance into the almanac's secret text (130). The life of a text consonant with the life of its teller is a conception distinct from a prevalent European view typified by statements like "art is art precisely because it is not reality" (Voltaire) and "never trust the teller; trust the tale" (Lawrence).

Silko's "Storyteller" opposes native and European forms of story in the Eskimo's struggle to maintain a sense of distinct being. The girl who visits the trailer of the red-haired man discovers his secret perversity in the picture of a dog coupled with a woman, which he hangs above his bed to incite his sexual performance. The obscene banality of this Anglo's secret is tantamount to the bland logic of the Anglo police who cannot grasp the girl's secret motives and methods for killing the shopkeeper. The red tin whose alcohol poisoned the girl's parents, and that destroys nature as it lies idly rusting away in the grass, symbolizes the killing power of the white's deceptions. Listening to the old Eskimo's story of the giant polar bear stalking a lone hunter across the Bering Sea ice, the girl understands that story has the *real* power to resist the way of life the white man has forced upon the Eskimo and to defeat the white's machinery of destruction. The last words of his story, uttered as he dies — "and the blue glacier bear turned slowly to face him" — figures the confrontation of Eskimo with white, and figures the hunted's turn to face the hunter. The girl enters this story herself to reenforce it with her own experience.

Engagement in story to maintain its life is undertaken directly at the beginning of *Ceremony* when the narrative voice declares that it is telling the story that Thought-Woman is thinking (1), and then defines ceremony as stories to "fight off illness and death . . . Their evil is mighty / but it can't stand up to our stories" (2). Story, then, is a fetus with the name "ceremony" growing in the womb of Indian life. The entanglement of the white's technological and sexual perversity with the Indian's curative and redemptive secrets is a critical issue in *Ceremony.* Tayo's own birth is wrapped in the social and moral secrecy of the filth and degradation of Gallup prostitution and poverty; his military duty ensnares him in the world of fake identities among Los Angeles whores; and his war-induced sickness and his pueblo's drought are an interlaced ill that he is convinced he brought about by cursing the jungle rain. His cure and the cure of his pueblo depend upon the story which can retrieve its past prosperity and redress "what they did to the earth with their machines, and to the animals with their packs of dogs and their guns" (212–13). There is a telling confrontation in the Dixie Tavern between the war stories of Emo, Harley, and Leroy (41–42, 54, 64–65) and the story Tayo tries but fails to tell in order resist the "history" of the white's world of war and destruction. Black Swan's earlier instruction to Tayo in sex did much to counter the malefic image he had been given of his mother, and the Navajo Betonie retrieves for him later a sense of the "comfort" of the land before the whites made Gallup into a den of spoilage. In his hogan, Betonie points out the calendars and phone books he has collected, dates and lists constituting hidden story: "All these things," he confides, "have stories alive in them" (127). They are kept alive by the hermeneutic perspicacity of their user, who applies story as medicine. Story is the pharmacopeia of all Navajo healing ceremony, and Betonie has rescued story from the white's discarded medicine cabinet.

Betonie's hogan is a secret story in itself for Tayo to read. "I brought back the books with all the names in them. Keeping track of things" (127), he continues, making it quite clear that these discarded "out of date" things can be read as records of the past and prophecy of the future, both attached to one enclosing time (201). They are the American Indian's organic almanac, whose power is actualized by the mind reading it, just as the spirit woman Ts'eh achieves the story in natural things (235). It is no wonder that she, like Thought Woman, knows the secret story in things unfolding for Tayo, those hidden properties of things with which he must relearn to live in harmony. So Tayo finds the missing cattle once he realizes the story they are making (236). Like the Gambler's riddle, such story hides its power from those who can neither find nor read it. If the secret evil of the Gambler can be erased by the story Spider Woman tells Sun Man (182), and if the Anglo is an Indian invention, then the Anglo can be deconstructed and reconstructed by story.

The contrast between the physically and morally shameful secrets of the white man and the secret ceremonies of the indigenous peoples is represented by the opposition between the secret force in the uranium mined out of the hidden entrails of the earth, used for the powers of destruction, and the secret message of the stars, which Betonie reads as a map for Tayo's retrieval of his lost Mexican cattle. His recovery of the cattle and his own health depends upon his erasure of the Euro-American's hermeneutic appropriation of his native environment. For example, the white reads flies as disease and discomfort, while the Indian reads them as collaborators in maintaining and engendering life. It is precisely the hermeneutic designs of nature that Tayo must reread. The death he had read in the jungle rain and green is canceled finally by the story in Ts'eh's storm-pattern blanket that reinforms nature with its proper life-sustaining role.

Not only does Tayo erase the white story overlaid upon his landscape, he overlays his own vulnerary story upon the elements of mass destruction the white has torn out of the ground: "They had taken these beautiful rocks from deep within earth and they had laid them in a monstrous design" (258), but he reforms that design into "the story that was still being told." In effect, Tayo reappropriates the earth's secret force of uranium for his own life-redeeming story: "He had arrived at a convergence of patterns. . . . Accordingly, the story goes on with these stars of the old war shield; they go on, lasting until the fifth world ends, then maybe beyond" (266). Tayo can return now to the pueblo to tell the story and render the white's actualities innocent by his making new story of them to add to the cumulative mythology of his people. His experience in story merges with the sacred story of hummingbird and bee. Reappropriation, conversion, and transformation retrieve *hózhó,* his and his pueblo's sense of natural well-being.

Like *Ceremony, Almanac of the Dead* disengages Indian from white story in order to reconverge them. Its central Indian character, Sterling, sloughs off, as Tayo does, the destructive story of the white world and reads a new story of its impending destruction. The narrative voice of his story carefully and deliberately takes what is useful of white story to recode the Indian's prophecy of the disappearance of the white from Meso- and North America. If story is one thing stolen from the Indian, it is reappropriated cleverly in the front matter and on the title page by the generic identification "novel," a label that conventionally engages the reader in a suspension of disbelief in texts known variously as bildungsroman, picaresque, naturalist, realist, crime, mystery, science fiction, etc.[24] In this respect, however, the generic label converges with the title label, for while the almanac is a distinctive genre itself with a history longer than that of the "novel," the title implies both a subject and a form. In effect, the title holds a secret.

Yoeme's old notebooks appropriate the European word and the object "almanac" for Meso-American myth. One of its early entries has the phrase "Quetzalcoatl gathered the bones of the dead and sprinkled them with his own blood, and humanity was reborn" (136). While there is something here recalling the myth of Christ's self-sacrifice, the reference is to Aztec story in which Quetzalcoatl returns to his people in the year Ce Acatl, "One Reed," the first year in the Aztec calendar 52-year cycle. The next entry, "Sacred time is always in the present" (136), is followed by a cryptic history of the almanac in Europe, in seven items. The first has simply "almanakh: Arabic." The second item cites the form *almanac* in English from the Arabic in A.D. 1267. The date A.D. 1505 locates the word in Spanish in item 3, and items 4–6 list conventional functions of almanacs from calendar tables to good luck glyphs. Item 7 lists "Madrid, Paris, Dresden: Codices."

This brief excerpt alludes to a number of stories. To begin with, the location of sacred time "always" in the present, conventionally dislocating the Christian notion of difference between God's timelessness and man's temporality, has us participate in that continuous present. At the same time, the calendar designation "A.D." appropriates Christian myth and measure for an indigenous text dedicated to deleting it. The cryptic "almanakh," despite its Arabic appearance, hides a mixed form that was unknown in Arabic of the time outside of Spain. The thirteenth-century date in the second item does not locate the word in the English language, but in England where Roger Bacon cites *almanac* in a Latin treatise as a word for astronomical tables. He probably formed the word from earlier Latin *manacus,* which designates the circle in a sun dial containing the zodiacal signs of the months. This intertextual allusion is a link to the next item, the date of Pedro de Alcala's *Castilian-Arabic Vocabulary,* which not only lists *al manach* but also the word *manah* for *relox del sol,* or "sun-dial."[25] The origin of both *manacus* and *manah* may be *manæus* "month," a definition that explains the statement "The Month was created first, before the World" in Yoeme's "Fragments from the Ancient Notebooks" (570). In this overwriting of the Christian's Genesis, the Month measures the footstep of God and then walks off the extent of the entire world so that "all creatures of the sea and land were created" (571). All these texts behind the passage lend to Silko's title *Almanac* the sense of "record of the creator and his creation." The secret web of intertextuality stretches yet wider, for in its earliest recorded context, the Arabic-Spanish *almanakh* is a translation into local dialect of Greek *ephemerides* "daily" with the sense "a diary, a record of days"; and since the *Ephemerides ab Anno 1475–1506* was the astronomical calendar used by Columbus on his voyages of "discovery," Silko's *Almanac* is a palimpsest, or a "writing over" the almanac that steered the European destroyer to the plunder and rape of the "New World."

Finally, the three cities listed in the last item of the entry are current locations of ancient Mayan codices stolen from their indigenous sites to age idly in a foreign land.[26] The names of these cities, like Santa Fe ("Holy Faith"!), where Laguna grandmother-grandfather images lie naked in a museum case, locate secrets rendered powerless by theft and illegal sale. The sale of pages of the almanac itself is an appropriation of secrecy for profit, but what is stolen or sold has no force for the white who can neither read nor evoke its power (128). For the Indian, on the other hand, the names of these places call for reappropriation of both the physical objects and the stories they contain. If the stolen thing cannot be recovered—and even if recovered, their passage through enemy hands seriously weakens their power—their force must be regenerated in other forms. Since the enemy's own literary shapes are potential matrices for reempowerment, the European almanac has a form and content the American Indian can appropriate for his own use, and the arm of the enemy is the most appropriate tool for resisting him.

For the Euro-American reader, however, the word *almanac* evokes at least two familiar texts. The first is the famous *Almanach de Gotha* (1763), produced in Germany and written in French as a statistical annual with genealogical and diplomatic information on European royalty and nobility, though no numbers in that book are quite so telling as those in the end papers of Silko's *Almanac,* which count the American Indian dead between 1500 and 1600. The second is a product of Philadelphia (whose name-sense is ironic in the context of the history of American-Indian relations) and typifies what an almanac signifies to most Americans. This is Ben Franklin's *Poor Richard's Almanac,* which in its opening number in 1732 predicted the death of his major competitor, a prediction that not only attracted the curiosity of a reading audience but also contributed to the prophesied demise.[27] The concept of story as a weapon of death is not strange to the oral tradition of the Indian, like Momaday, who trusts in the real force of words.

The adaptation of the almanac tradition to the particularities of American climate and landscape, on the one hand, contrasts with the carrying eastward of the Mayan codices for no natural good and, on the other hand, imitates the translation of almanacs from an Indian linguistic matrix into Spanish on vellum. The translation that was a vector of loss is turned now into the directional force of rehabilitation. Yoeme understands the succeeding linguistic conversion from that Meso-American Spanish into English as "the sign the keepers of the notebooks had always prayed for" (130). As she transcribes its entries, Lecha comes to realize that the almanac, now in English, can exercise its power "to bring all tribal people of the Americas to retake the land" (569), recalling the words of Betonie's mother in *Ceremony* as she sent her son off to learn the white man's ways, "You have to know English too" (127–28).

The English of Silko's novel evokes that power not only with its title, but with the almanac of its story. The *Almanakh* entry in the notebooks is a thinly coded call for rescuing the Mayan codices from their European context as ethnographic artifacts and as exotic texts, and to return them as sacred story to the land that they nourished and that gave them force. This excerpt, then, signals the fictive intention of Silko's entire book. The *Almanac* as novel would reappropriate the secret force of the Mayan texts, for coding secrets in the oppressor's language turns the weapon of appropriation against him and makes new secrets he can read no better than he can read the signs of the land he has appropriated from the Indian.

While the white's own almanacs are manuals for reading natural signs, Silko's entire novel is a scathing indictment of the Euro-American's inability to read signs — other than those that indicate streets, cities, and nations — whether desert rocks and hills or the decay of the appurtenances of his culture, the signifying emblem of which is the city of Tucson. As Ku'oosh told Tayo in *Ceremony,* "the story behind each word must be told so that there could be no mistake in the meaning of what had been said" (37). Even names for whites are but banal indicators of people with little or no secret signifying power. "Once the whites had a name for a thing," old Mahawala tells Calabazas, "they seemed unable ever again to recognize the things itself" (1991, 224). The U.S. cavalry's inability to track down the man they called "Geronimo" comically proves the point, whereas an Indian's names — in both their native and European forms — are hidden texts of being. Alegría is Menardo's sexual and social "joy," which blinds him to her treachery. Iliana, Cazador, Zeta, Lecha, Rose, Mosca, and Popa have hidden story meaning in their names, which contrast with the sterility and waste in Anglo names like Root, Trigg, Roy, Peaches, Max, Sonny, and Bingo. The contrast reveals the extent to which the white is oblivious to name sense and power.[28] A stark example of ironic name appropriation identifies Bartolomeo ("son of the one abounding in furrows"), Alegría's Cuban revolutionary lover who enters the story one page after a reference to the "holy man Bartolomé de Las Casas" (277–78). The first scorns the Indians, while his sixteenth-century namesake wrote *New Laws for the Indians* (1544) to free them from slavery. Another example is El Feo, the Indian whose faith is true, and whose name contrasts with the name of the capital of New Mexico where sacred Indian artifacts are hoarded. There is ironic resonance in the name Popa, which in Spanish designates the stern, or poop, of a ship, and sounds like English "Pope," the title of the spiritual leader of the Christians who invaded the Americas. Both names echo Popé, the name of the San Juan Pueblo leader of the 1680 Indian revolt who, after the success of the revolt, ordered a purifying wash for every pueblo to remove the stains of Christianity. The point here is that the Anglo is no longer concerned with tapping the secret force in names, while the Indian carefully guards the story force in names, which can be marshaled at an appropriate moment.

The collaboration of reading, recalling, and retrieving the essence of word, name, and story — a crucial feature of the novel as a whole — is figured neatly by the account Yoeme gives of the old almanac.[29] In the early seventeenth century, when the Indian was at the edge of extinction, a Meso-American tribe sent away to the north its sacred story to save it from conquerors' eyes and hands. The old Yaqui Yoeme tells her granddaughter: "After all, the almanac was what told them who they were and where they had come from in the stories. . . . The people knew if even part of the almanac survived, they as a people could return someday," for it is "the book of all the days of their people. These days and years were all alive, and all these days would return again. The book had to be preserved at all costs" (246–47).[30] When the starving children began to chew pieces of the vellum, the eldest girl, who could neither read nor write, made mental images of the pages, and told the others: "'I remember what was on the page we ate. I know that part of the almanac. I have heard the stories of those days told many times.' . . . Each time a page had been memorized, they could eat it" (250). Yoeme continues: "The child had been told the pages held many forces within them, countless physical and spiritual properties to guide the people and make them strong" (252). Similarly, the cliff portrait of an elk holds its power as long as it is remembered (1977, 241–42).

Sterling, the exiled Laguna Pueblo Indian, has lost his native power and cannot see the figure of the snake in the rock exposed to the Hollywood crew, probably because his work on the flat railway line west of Laguna has blurred his vision of the land's configurations. Having been nourished by American pulp fiction and initiated into the deluxe delights of American whores, and having lost his way to Phoenix — another sign of lost bearings — he finds himself in Tucson where his involvement with the Cazador sisters and their entourage purges him of his American ways and restores his innate capacity to read the signs of his people's mythology. "He had never paid much attention to the old-time ways because he had always thought the old beliefs were dying out. But Tucson had changed Sterling" (762). Ultimately, like Tayo, he is rehabilitated for reintegration into his proper community, and when he finally sees the story in the snake form he becomes part of its story, just as Tayo had become part of the story of Ts'eh he tells the village elders in the kiva (269–70). Sterling quits drinking beer and has the postmaster let his subscriptions to his magazines lapse (763). "He knew now what the snake's message was to the people" (763); and since he can bring that message to Laguna, he is the prophet of the impending retrieval of the land appropriated by the white.[31] In short, renouncing the white's texts helps restore a power to read the sacred truths in natural forms.

What Sterling regains instinctively in Tucson is a capacity to read differences. His experience, which becomes ours in the reading, carefully traces two contrasting lines of secrets. The white's secrets are the perversity of his social experiences in sex, violence, and drugs. He also has a morbid curiosity about the secrets of the private lives of others, represented by the stories he once read. This is because, on the one hand, such secrets are entertainments and "innocuous" facts he can easily dispose of, and on the other hand, he has lost his innate sensitivity to real secrets his ancestor spirits guarded (604). As Calabazas puts it, the white cannot read differences, and "those who can't appreciate the world's differences won't make it. They'll die" (203). The novel's exposition of the white's lies, then, accumulate a force to destroy the liar. Tayo had entertained this thought in his musings after two Texan cowboys left him to track down a mountain lion: "Only a few people knew that the lie was destroying the white people faster than it was destroying Indian people. But the effects were hidden, revealed only in the sterility of their art . . . hollow and lifeless as a witchery clay figure" (1977, 213).

Since there is story in all things, the world itself is the dominant story that gives life and takes it away, though in Silko's world of sacred fiction only the Indian seems to care about the essential difference. In *Ceremony*, Betonie tells Tayo of the invention of the white by story when, after displays of magic in an all-tribal witches' conference, an unknown outsider announces "what I have is a story" and "as I tell the story / it will begin to happen" (141). His tale is of the white's discovery and use of uranium to kill. At the end, the others cry: "Okay, you win . . . call that story back" (145), but the story has been turned loose. Betonie says that the whites do not know the secret that they are products of the witchery power of story (162).[32] But could they read behind the superficial lies they perpetrate and see their theft, they could convert and join the Indian in the task of reclaiming the sanctity of the earth.[33] One who seems to do so in *Almanac* is the white woman Seese, who was a stripper and secret drug dealer before she "joined" the Yaqui community of Zeta and Lecha.

Almanac details the secret lies of the white that can't be called back: murder, pornography, sex change operations, abortions, and snuff films (102–3). Jamie, Ferro's secret cop lover, is an apt emblem of white America's secret perversions. Two tragic victims of it are Seese and her child Monty, who is stolen for vicious purposes. Judge Arne, representing white justice, is a secret zoophiliac. Max Blue, who deals in secret murder, leaves a business card on the scene of his crimes as a secret code for those who have hired him (354). His son Sonny takes up a secret trade in arms dealing with the Mexican Menardo (432), who makes secret his native origins behind the story of a broken nose. Trigg has a secret plan for a giant sex mall (381), and to finance it he operates a secret organ bank that he keeps full by killing wayfarers he picks up for sex. To support its own hidden designs, white authorities secretly protect the international drug trade (562). The upstart Mexican Menardo, who exemplifies the white drive for upward social mobility and prestige, masks a vicious view of life values. He rails against television revelations of police brutality because the bad publicity weakens his business links with corrupt authorities, and the television programming that shows affluent families incites theft from the rich by the poor. In self-serving fury, he exclaims with cutting irony: "That was the trouble! Television spoiled secrecy" (483). Keeping secrets in these contexts is inviting death instead of protecting life.

White perversions are crimes against the earth and, in failing to respect the earth as mother, whites bring about their own destruction. The earth, like the polar bear on Bering ice, turns against him, calling for blood.[34] In contrast, the Indian who shares the land with all its other residents without hierarchal distinction, speaks with the animals of earth, air, and water who still communicate with spirits: "The macaws had come with a message for humans, but it would take a while for Tacho to understand. The macaws had been sent because this was a time of great change and danger. The macaw spirits had a great many grievances with humans, but said that humans were already being punished and would be punished much more for their stupid human behavior" (476). Tacho's opal spirit transmits the secret message of the spirits of the mountains who call for their share of blood with the threat that they will tremble and shake (512).[35] Even the white's tools of mastery over nature turn against him: "Electricity no longer obeyed the white man. The macaw spirits said the great serpent was in charge of electricity. The macaws were in charge of fire" (512). The Indian, like his macaw "wives," can collaborate with that power. Lightning strikes Max Blue dead on a golf course because he fails to read its signs in the sky (751). Lightning is the mortal enemy of the Korean computer hacker Awa Gee (679), who controls the secrets of computer cryptology (689), and takes on identities of the dead to defraud the rich with secret numbers involved in international financial transactions (679–80). The Yupik Eskimo Rose and her old friend have telekinetic powers that can destroy the white's machines and bring down his airplanes.[36] Tuberculosis, smallpox and the flu are but a few of the other secret signs of the earth's vengeance.

Indian story collaborates with white story to destroy the liars. The Afro-American Clinton scours the public library to document a secret history of American slavery that he intends to reveal in a series of public broadcasts (415–16). The Vietnam veteran Roy (Rambo) recruits blood donors for Trigg with secret plans to organize an army of the homeless (399), and he makes secret lists of the real veterans to arm it. The Mayan Angelita La Escapía exposes a record of crimes against the Western Hemisphere and of Indian and slave resistance to it. Snakes, macaws, and other animals transmit story. So do artifacts like the Laguna stone snake, the grandparent creation bundle, and Tacho's opal eye. The most powerful secrets, like those in the notebook fragments hidden in the Potam family graves and recovered by Lecha (587–88), are those that the dead hold in trust for the living.[37]

It is this vital secret bond between living and dead that sustains Indians, while whites have lost it. When Lecha uses her innate powers for the police to find the shallow graves of the missing dead, she uncovers the Americans' secret propensity to kill.[38] Her ability to visualize the hidden dead (138, 142) is an ancestral gift to read the secret stories of people's lives: "Lecha had merely begun to tell the stories of the ends of their lives" (144), and those stories of the dead have power over what is to come. People send Lecha lists of facts about people out of which she can shape a narrative: "It didn't matter what the letters or messages said. Each story had many versions" (173). From collected miscellaneous data, Lecha produces her own "almanac of the dead," and sets her friend Seese to transcribe it as a sort of manual for reading death (174). In a very significant sense, the novel itself is the ancestral dead's prediction of the Euro-American's disappearance from the Western Hemisphere.

The story told by the spirits of the dead is the Indian's secret text of resistance, which actualizes its power in the process of translation out of its ancient matrix into new language and form. In explaining why translation is a propitious sign, Yoeme recalls listening to the language of snakes who hear the voices of the dead (130). As the snakes mediate between the living and the dead, so do Yoeme's notebooks in their English form. Voices of the dead, however, are muffled by witches and sorcerers allied with the Anglo. Yoeme explains that the white man is impotent against spirits (581), since he cannot understand the language of his own ancestral spirits, and therefore he cannot read their stories or transmit them to his children. Angelita La Escapía recalls that stories are essential to the life of the people because "the ancestors' spirits were summoned by the stories" (316). Ancestral secrets are transmitted by snakes, macaws, dreams, visions, and even the shoulder of Mosca, who can see the secret identity of curanderos and brujas and hear the language of wind spirits (601–3).

Transcribing the notebooks is an act of reactivating the secret power of the word, so that the transcriber's sequence of story accords with the sequence of life. When she decides to copy old Yoeme's book, Lecha tells her sister: "You could say 'her book,' but of course the book will be mine" (177). She means that its story, like a growing fetus, must find its nourishment in her being. When she was still alive, old Yoeme had hinted at this bond between myth and writer:

> I have kept the notebooks and the old book since it was passed on to me many years ago. A section of one of the notebooks had accidentally been lost right before they were given to me. The woman who had been keeping them explained what the lost section had said, although of course it was all in a code, so that the true meaning would not be immediately clear. She requested that, if possible, at some time in my life I should write down a replacement section.
>
> I have thought about it all my life. The problem has been the meaning of the lost section and for me to find a way of replacing it. One naturally reflects upon one's own experience and feelings throughout one's life. The woman warned that it should not be just any sort of words. (128–29)

Yoeme made the almanac her experience, and now Lecha's is conjoined with its cumulative life. Necessarily, then, the *Almanac* is a story of sequence and succession mediated by women; and stories of hidden things of the past and the future, like the life created and nourished in woman's womb, are the generic function of almanacs. All curative rituals and ceremonies are nourished in the womb of story (1977, 2).

In contrast, whites have conflicting agendas for the hidden future. Serlo, the Latino aristocrat, is a member of a secret multinational organization with a secret agenda for the entire world (545) with a secret alternative to atomic destruction in an Earth Module (542). He keeps a secret catalog of arms and materials for his la Finca "estate" (560). All the world powers have secret agendas for the future (549). The Arizona bubble biosphere is one phase of a secret plan for survival (728). There are even secret agendas to re-create the time long ago when the white still had a viable bond with the earth. As Awa Gee discovers when he breaks into the Eco-Grizzly secret "memo" code:

> Eco Grizzly and the others practiced what they called "deep ecology," and from what Awa Gee could tell, "Back to the Pleistocene" was their motto. Eco-Grizzly and the others genuinely wanted to return to cave living with the bears as their European forefathers had once lived. To Awa Gee such a longing for the distant past was a symptom of what had become of the Europeans who had left their home continent to settle in strange lands. (689)

Going backward is precisely what Yoeme realizes the Indian and his story must not do, for he who returns to a former cultural isolation will be rooted out or destroyed. Just as the old notebooks must be adapted and changed or have their sacred story wasted in an outmoded Meso-American Spanish idiom, the Indian must adapt or lose his distinctive being.

The point is fitting to *The Almanac of the Dead,* in which notebooks, diaries, and prophetic pronouncements shape an incremental repetition of loss and retrieval. All of these expose a compendious record of waste awaiting recycling of value. The almanac itself is the nucleate signifier for other "notebooks." It is a "conjoining" text,[39] a locus for converging old life with new by new story fashioned out of old with new tools. What is lost of old story is what has died of its former tellers, and the "replacement section" to be added is a revitalization with "one's own experience." Sacred story is to be told by those who enter into it; myth is regenerated when the performer of it engages his being within it. Its "true meaning" is realized by those like Tayo, Yoeme, and Lecha who succeed in speaking themselves into the texture of story. Renewing the almanac, then, re-empowers the life it embodies.

Reanimating the latent life in story by turning it into English has a double consequence. First, it effectively reappropriates the Anglo's wasted word while correcting the Indian's wasted sight. Technological computer codes and the white's reduction of words to banal designations lay waste "natural" powers to collaborate with the energy in things they signify. While the notebooks and the record of the story in the novel that takes place about their transcription comprise a text of retrieval and transformation of secret lore, they appropriate the sacred function of the Christian's biblical lore in the spirit of Michael

Horse, in Linda Hogan's *Mean Spirit*, who writes his own gospel as resistance and correction despite a Catholic priest's protest that "you can't do that" (273). In that story, when Michael completes his book and starts to read it to his people, a young woman wonders aloud why he doesn't just speak it in the traditional way instead of writing it. He replies: "They don't believe anything is true unless they see it in writing" (361).[40]

Second, Lecha's English within the novel and Silko's English of the novel revitalize the Anglo's own language, which like the Laguna creation bundle gathering dust in a museum, has been waning in power. The Indian's appropriation of English offers that language the ontological and epistemological particularities of the American Indian experience and fuses different realities into a new idiom. In this sense, Yoeme's almanac and Silko's *Almanac* are new and real stories that are susceptible to raise their truths out of narrow contexts and inform literature in English with something of sacred ceremonial force. The profit of the offer depends upon the Euro-American's willingness to discern, understand, and collaborate with things that do not conform to his habitual strait sense of "reality."

An axial hermeneutic emblem of an alternate "truth" is the messenger snake who mediates man's communication with the earth.[41] The snake's crucial role in the notebooks challenges the Anglo reader's Christian bias, which associates the snake with Satan's form. Silko deconstructs this association in her account of the parochial schooling of Angelita by nuns who called Marx the Devil, and who "had taught the children that the Morning Star, Quetzalcoatl [the feathered serpent] was really Lucifer, the Devil God had thrown out of heaven" (519). For the Indians in *Almanac of the Dead*, snakes are man's repository of secret story.[42] Yoeme talks to a bull snake, and when her grand-daughters want to know what the snake says, she explains that because snakes crawl close to the ground, "they heard the voices of the dead" (130), and they are privy to the secrets of criminals and to adulterous love trysts (131–32). Yoeme instructs the girls carefully how to communicate with snakes. Later, the first look the adult Zeta takes in Yoeme's bundles of loose notebook pages is upon a two-part snake entry, the first of which — from "the Snake's Notebook" — relates the story of Laguna's loss of the lake for which the pueblo is named and recalls the disappearance of the snake messenger from the Fourth World who inhabited it. Without the lake, which was emptied by foreigners, Laguna's name no longer has its natural logokinetic power (92). The second part is "Spirit Snake's Message," which is a gift to man of names and identities for days and years that qualifies him as the primal maker of the land's almanac whose stories protect the people. The last words of this entry are the snake's prophecy of the world's end (135). After the next entry predicts a new story to come (135–36), the word *almanac* is glossed with the etymological and historical references I scanned earlier. This sort of refiguration of European conventional iconography overlays Christian story with chthonic conceptions that undercut the Christian's dialectical opposition between the things of Caesar and the things of God. Alternate realities have alternate myths that do not so much challenge the white man's received "truth" as his ability to read differences.

The eminent figure of the snake pervades the non-European story of Silko's Americas. Clinton's notebooks recall the first black Indian medicine man Boukman ("bookman"?) "whose name meant 'spirit priest,'" and who consulted Ouidambala the Great Ocean Serpent about launching a revolution against the whites (418). A giant snake in a dream shows the Barefoot Hopi where to dig for a treasure (620). With the money he finds he finances revolution, the first stage of which is the dissemination to the oppressed of "stories about Corn Mother, Old Spider Woman, and the big snake" (619–20). An entry in the old notebooks reads: "Rain god sits on a coiled snake enclosing a pool of water: the number nine is attached. Nine means fresh, uncontaminated water.[43] . . . The snake god with the green symbol on the forehead means 'first time,' 'new growth,' 'fresh'" (574). The upstart hypocrite Menardo has a vague recurrent nightmare about reptilian skin, which is incited by Alegría's snakeskin shoes and purse. Tacho had told him that enemies could use your dreams to destroy you, so he decides to keep this one secret (321), but the snakeskin figures the bulletproof vest that Menardo wears dancing with Alegría (322) is the secret cause of his death (503–4). Domballah and Quetzalcoatl are the snakes of the vengeful gods (735).

As powers converge against white civilization, Sterling tells the story of the stone snake for the first time: "Religious people from many places had brought offerings to the giant snake, but none had understood the meaning of the snake's reappearance; no one had got the message. But when Lecha had told Zeta, they had both got tears in their eyes because old Yoeme had warned them about the cruel years to come once the great serpent had returned" (702–3). Telling the story of the snake whose public exposure causes Sterling's exile is a step in the process that leads to his return, where he completes the reading of the snake's gaze as the ultimate secret of the long-awaited and prophesied uprising. Sterling is now in communication with the snake. The one last test, or temptation, is to shake his head and think like a white: "The world was not like that. Tucson had only been a bad dream." What is nightmare in the epistemic reality of the Anglo is revelation in the chthonic realities of the American Indian, and it is the Indian readings of the snake that adhere in Sterling's mind. He rejects the snake's image as prophecy of the uranium mine's victory, because he knows now that man can only destroy himself and not the sacredness of the land (762).

To clean the terrain of the white's mundane debris, *The Almanac* historicizes evil in Anglo's acts and records of them. Exposing evil is, in one sense, only divulging information, but Silko's story is of power rather than of knowledge. Writing has the power to give life to the very evil it would destroy: only new story will defeat the effects of the older Indian story of the Gambler whose bag of tricks deprives the Indian of his vitality, and who haunts the world of the white who cannot see or resist him. All that is left to the Indian is the power of poetry, says Weasel Tail (714). Only new and vibrant story can destroy the lies and perverse secrets of whites which threaten to destroy the Indian as well as themselves. Silko's story would purge the earth of the white's bad story to make room for the good. Fly and Hummingbird made their plea to Buzzard in *Ceremony* to "Purge this town" (119). Decheeny's Mexican woman had told him that Indians must find the story that will lay whites low (157).

Silko has said that writing robs story from the telling that nourishes it, and living story must grow and change (Hirsch 1983, 152). Written story can also grow when it appropriates the contexts of oral telling, changing with each new performance.[44] *Almanac,* an open-ended and open-centered text, designed with strands of story forming a web that seems infinitely changeable, imitates oral performance. The sacredness of the text is ultimately in its variable organic and indeterminate shape, which engages the reader to enter it in the manner Yoeme enters the almanac. In this respect *The Almanac* conjoins its ideological stance with its aesthetic mode, its private vision with a public declaration that constitutes a dialectically fluid relationship between the text and its interpretation (Owens 1992a, 4).

The validity of Sterling's reappropriation of his powers to read and fuse differences is not confined to the American Indian. Whites can heed the message of the snake to the people and convert to indigenous realities of the continent they occupy — and hence join its residents — or return to where they have left their own ancestral spirits. While the novel can be read as a militant manual for Indian action, through the power of Silko's word, Sterling's predicament, like Tayo's, is transferred to the reader. It is *our predicament,* which is to say all of us are in need of retrieving a primal capacity to read differences and to arbitrate what is and should remain secret. The apparent incompatibility between white and Indian realities, between the white's cultural economy and the Indian's traditional healing, so poignantly illustrated by the experience of Tayo and Sterling, is an incompatibility that we must come to terms with in our reading if we are to understand their stories at all. It is the reader of whatever race who must mediate the transfer and relocate the problem to where it is most in need of being resolved.[45] In effect, he can do this only by reappropriating the secret story latent in himself and reclaiming what he can of his own abandoned and lost sense of being.

NOTES

1. I use "culture" in Wole Soyinka's sense as the "framework of [a] society's principles of reproducing itself, of sustaining and enhancing life" (1990, 111). I follow Louis Owens in preferring the designation "Indian" to "Native American" (1992a, 258 n. 43), and I attribute views to Indians in general in the same manner the Indian novelists and critics I cite do.

2. Owens 1994, 43. See also Mark Twain 1868, to General Grant: "Sir, do you propose to exterminate the Indians suddenly with soap and education, or doom them to the eternal annoyance of warfare, relieved only by periodical pleasantries of glass beads and perishable treaties?"

3. "Homoglossia" is a term Owens (1992a, 42 n.) borrows from Bahktin.

4. The archetypal guardian of secrets is the trickster messenger Hermes Trismegistus who has something to do with oracles and the "secret sense declaring itself only after long delay" (Kermode 1979, 1–2). Thus, hermeneutics—the art of reading—is the talent of tricksters who, like Christ with his parables, conceals the mystery already known to *insiders*. In this sense, Kermode notes, secrecy is the property of all narrative. Outsiders may see, but cannot perceive it. Insiders read and do perceive it (144). The Indian straddles the line between inside and outside.

5. Owens divides readers of Indian story into three groups: those with the same tribal affiliation as the storyteller, other Indians who share the same basic assumptions about story, and the whites who have an alien set of assumptions and values (1992a, 14). Such a categorization is arbitrary, of course, for there are Indians who are no more sensitive to the sacred truth in local story than whites who see no "truth" in their traditional folk tales.

6. As George Steiner observes, "the secrecy of the text stems from no esoteric knowledge, from no obstruseness of supporting philosophical argument. By themselves the words are nakedly simple. Yet they cannot be elucidated by public reference" (1973, 191).

7. Consider the current confusion over the extent to which a kachina doll *is* rather than *represents* a Kachina.

8. There is an analogy to this reshaping of story to fit new circumstances in the Nordic reaction to the appropriation of the pagan oral traditions and story vocabulary for Christian story and doctrine. Seeing his own native lore threatened with disappearance by the Christianization of his culture, the Icelander Snorri Sturluson carefully "recoded" the old lore by translating it out of oral poetic form into a written prose that might preserve its integrity. Sequoya approves of a cultural revitalization with tribal knowledge encoded in story that locates the identity of experience inside self rather than, as with the Anglo, outside (1993, 459–61). The

latter is what Descartes calls "adventitious epistemology." The former is factitious epistemology; produced within one's own mind. Owens uses the term *proprioception* for the Indian's particular "sense of being."

9. Anaya in his short story "B. Traven is Alive and Well in Cuernavaca" puts the case in terms pertinent to the American Indian: "In Mexico one never finds anything. It is a country that doesn't waste anything, everything is recycled . . . yesterday's Traven novel is the pulp on which tomorrow's Fuentes story will appear. Time recycles. . . . Time returns to the past" (1995, 127).

10. For the Indian trickster as disorderer and reorderer, see Babcock, " 'A Tolerated Margin of Mess.' "

11. Courlander 1971, 23.

12. Since the conception of divine force differs fundamentally between white and Indian, the notion of reward and punishment differs. A Sioux chieftain, in response to George Catlin's charges of Indian cruelty, refers to the white's prisons and tortures, and then, Catlin records, "he had heard also . . . that the Great Spirit of the white people was the child of a white woman and that he was at last put to death by the white people . . . 'The Indians' Great Spirit got no mother. The Indians no kill him, He never die'" (Gill 1987, 12–13).

13. There are Navajo and Apache, as well as Plains Indian beliefs in restless and malefic ghosts of the dead who have not been properly buried or fitted for their journey to the "other" world.

14. For example, Kopemah to Set, a bullsnake to Yoeme, So-at-sa-ki to Fools Crow, and el Viejo to Mundo Morales, respectively.

15. The Greek *sumiktos* is translated into Latin *commixticium*. From this comes *mixticius* [*de diversis gentibus* "of diverse birth"] the origin of the word *mestizo*. *Daidalos* means "harmer, cutter, inscriber," and the Indo-European root *del* lies behind English *tell*.

16. Owens dedicates his critical study *Other Destinies* "to mixedbloods, the next generation" and quotes Vizenor to the effect that "mixedbloods loosen the seams in the shrouds of identity" (1992a, vi).

17. "The Geographical Basis of History," *The Philosophy of History* (1821).

18. Niggli's *Mexican Village,* a Mexican novel written in English, merges the sociopsychological themes of *Winesburg, Ohio* with secrets of local lore.

19. The white's trite nomination of the mountain shames my own name. According to reliable Aztec chronicles, in C.E. 1425, Moctezuma I sent guides to search for Aztlán, the place of Aztec origins. For a comprehensive view of the story and its relevance to current conditions in the Southwest, see Michel Pina 1989, 14–48.

20. Tony Hillerman, who has earned an honorary identity as a Navajo, uses the topos in his mystery novel *Talking God* in which a Tano fetish, stored away in the Smithsonian, is incitement to political action. Louise Erdrich's and Michael Dorris's *Crown of Columbus* locates such a bundle lost in the Dartmouth Library.

21. Anaya in Johnson 1990, 420.

22. This process of a text's emergence has vague European counterparts in the "automatic writing" of W. B. Yeats and the archetypal imagery of Carl Jung.

23. Wole Soyinka characterizes reappropriation as "race retrieval" and defines it as

"the conscious activity of recovering what has been hidden, lost, repressed, denigrated, or indeed simply denied by ourselves — yes, by ourselves also — but definitely by the conquerors of our peoples and their Eurocentric bias of thought and relationships" (1990, 114).

24. In the front matter of *The Ancient Child,* Momaday carefully deconstructs received generic structures. After the cover and title page announce "a novel" and his foreword announces "a work of fiction," a motto quotes Borges on myth encapsulating literature, followed by a pointedly selective cast of characters, a new title page and a prologue consisting of the Kiowa story of Tsoai, another title page for "Book One," followed by a citation on astrology from *An Ethnographic Dictionary of the Navajo Language.* The "story proper" begins with a question in Spanish followed by the lyrics of a popular song.

25. This entry in the notebooks reproduces some of the entry for "almanac" in the *Oxford English Dictionary,* whose other etymological speculations are all pertinent.

26. Barnes 1983, 63–65, where Silko discusses the old Mayan almanacs and their refutation of the European's concept of linear time.

27. James Thorson reminds me that Franklin probably borrowed his ploy from Jonathan Swift, whose *Predictions* (1708) under the pseudonym Isaac Bickerstaff foretold the death of John Partridge, the author of an ill-favored almanac.

28. A primary nomination, Foucault has said, is given out of a sense of hope and promise. In Indian lore, a given name contains latent power. Nomen est omen is a commonplace, but Beaufrey, the homosexual lover of Serlo and David, and an accomplice in the killing of Monty, has a hybrid name whose etymological components render "beautiful love."

29. There is a wondrous circularity here, for Silko's novel contains a story of an almanac whose extension is the novel itself. The written text of the old almanac is committed to memory, which is expressed in oral recapitulation, which in turn, is written anew. The *Almanac of the Dead* is simultaneously a story of old notebooks of the Indian and a new notebook of the American. It is both a story of the dead and a story by the dead.

30. Mary Guerrero Milligan notes that the power of story to sustain life is magical (1993, 102). In D'Arcy McNickle's *Wind from an Enemy Sky,* the prophet Two Sleeps says that "an Indian can't tell what's on his mind until he tells a story" (125). Owens discusses the Indian power of language to speak things into being (1992a, 14).

31. Sterling's name-sense — "of persons: thoroughly excellent, capable of standing every test" [OED, def. 4] — is not inconsequential, considering that he was thrown out of Laguna as a bad penny.

32. In Hogan's *Mean Spirit,* the white women Martha Billy and China "convert" to the Indian way, and one man, the Catholic priest Father Dunn, is moving that way, having realized that the creatures of the earth are his brothers and sister. Mario Varga Llosa tells the story of a Peruvian Jew, Sául Zuratas, who becomes a member of the Machinguengas tribe, and then their storyteller. He is, effectively, born again, converting himself backward in tribal time from Spanish to Machiqueng, from reason to magic, and from agnosticism to animism (1988, 244).

33. "Witch" means different things to the white and to the Indian. For the white, Indian

ceremony is witchcraft, while to the Indian the culture that steals his well-being is witchcraft.

34. The earth's secret vengeance for crimes against life is an old popular European belief. The entry for A.D. 1137 in the Anglo-Saxon *Peterborough Chronicle* lists the crimes in the age of Stephen, and notes that no matter what husbandry man performed, "the earth bore no grain, for the land was all undone by such deeds."

35. According to the *Anales de Cuahtitlán*, Quetzalcóatl-Topiltzin refused sacrifice except for snakes, tortillas, flowers, and butterflies. The earth's cry for blood has an origin in the Aztec creation story in which Quetzalcóatl and Tezcatlipoca make heaven and earth out of the body of a goddess. Though they appease her with gifts, she produces life only when offered blood. This is one source of the legend of La Llorona, the woman crying for lost life. The other prominent story of La Llorona is based on the career of Malintzin, a figure of the Indian dispossessed of land and real being.

36. Sabine Ulibarrí's "He's Got a Cross and He Ain't a Christian" is the story of Camilo's voyage through the air in a tornado that gives him magical power over the electronic Anglo world, but he expends that power to save the plane carrying his mother to Albuquerque (1993).

37. While the ancestral spirits of the blacks have settled in America, claims Clinton (742), the white has lost his. Charles Johnson tells of the carrying of an African god to America, but when the ship sinks en route, it is not clear to which shore he swims (1990). The legends of Ulysses and Aeneas feature a channel of transmission of wisdom and prophecy for the dead, which the Synoptic Gospels and Dante appropriate for Christian thought. My colleague Jacqueline Cerquiglini-Toulet reminds me that book and cemetery are spaces for preservation that resist disintegration and dispersal, and that exist as memory banks that survive the passage of generations.

38. In *Ceremony*, even in face of the "enemy," Tayo resists shedding blood, though Emo, Harley, and Leroy boast of killing Japanese. Later, Tayo recalls that as an infant he witnessed the secret burial of a fetus in a blue rag and afterward cried at night when his mother left him (116).

39. "Conjoining" is putting together words with distinct meanings to produce new sense. In current French critical terminology, *conjointure* is an author's appropriation of a genre by adding something of his own to its scope.

40. In the recent film *Thunderheart*, Maggie Little Bear tells the Americanized Sioux Ray Lavoy that writing on paper isn't power; the wind, the river, and the land are power.

41. In *Ceremony*, Ku'oosh describes to Tayo the cave where snakes renew life (35). Later, Tayo sees a yellow spotted snake, which carries on its back the message of spring for his people (231).

42. Father Dunn, chastised by a snakebite that he survives, proclaims to the Indians: " 'The snake is our sister.' 'Yes, so what new thing did you learn?' asked one of the children. 'Don't be rude,' said his mother" (Hogan 1990, 262).

43. A written 9 is snake shaped, and nine months is the human period of gestation, but the secret number code here escapes me.

44. Readers of Indian fiction cannot fail to notice the marks of "orality" most of it displays, particularly in the form of stories told within story.

45. From a psychoanalytic point of view, Silko's *Almanac* is what Freudians and Laca-

nians call "countertransference," the transformation of a subject from the one who announces it to the one who receives it.

WORKS CITED

Allen, Paula Gunn. 1969. *The Woman Who Owned the Shadows*. San Francisco: Spinsters.

———. 1986.*The Sacred Hoop*. Boston: Beacon.

———. 1993. "The Sacred Hoop: A Contemporary Indian Perspective on American Indian Literature." In Hobson, 222–39.

———. 1990. "Special Problems in Teaching Leslie Marmon Silko's *Ceremony*." *AIQ* 15: 379–86.

Anaya, Rudolfo A. 1972. *Bless Me, Ultima*. Berkeley: Tonatiuh International.

———. 1976. *Heart of Aztlán*. Albuquerque: U of New Mexico P.

———. 1986. *A Chicano in China*. Albuquerque: U of New Mexico P.

———. 1987. *Lord of the Dawn*. Albuquerque: U of New Mexico P.

———. 1992. *Alburquerque*. Albuquerque: U of New Mexico P.

———. 1995. *The Anaya Reader*. New York: Warner Books.

Anaya, Rudolfo A., and Francisco Lomeli. 1989. *Aztlán: Essays on the Chicano Homeland*. Albuquerque: Academia/El Norte Publications.

Babcock, Barbara. 1985. " 'A Tolerated Margin of Mess': The Trickster and His Tales Reconsidered." *Critical Essays on Native American Literature*. Ed. Andrew Wiget. Boston: Hall. 153–84.

Barnes, Jim. 1982. *The American Book of the Dead*. Urbana: U of Illinois P.

Barnes, Kim. 1993. "A Leslie Marmon Silko Interview." In Graulich, 47–65.

Bloom, Harold, and David Rosenberg. 1991. *The Book of J*. New York: Vintage Books.

Courlander, Harold. 1987. *The Fourth World of the Hopi*. Albuquerque: U of New Mexico P.

Deloria, Vine. 1973. *God Is Red*. New York: Grosset and Dunlap.

Erdoes, Richard, and Alfonso Ortiz, eds. 1984. *American Indian Myths and Legends*. New York: Pantheon.

Erdrich, Louise, and Michael Dorris. 1991. *The Crown of Columbus*. New York: Harper.

Faiola, Anthony. 1995. "Disney Assailed for Pocahantas Portrayal." *International Herald Tribune*, 27 May.

Fernández Retamar, Roberto. 1971. "Calibán: apuntes sobre la cultura en nuestra América." *Casa de las Americas* 68 (Havana). Trans. "Caliban: Notes toward a Discussion of Culture in Our America." *Massachusetts Review* 15 (1974): 7–72.

Frye, Northrop. 1976. *Secular Scripture*. Cambridge: Harvard UP.

Gill, Sam D. 1987. *Native American Traditions*. Chicago: U of Chicago P.

González-T., César A. 1990. *Rudolfo A. Anaya: Focus on Criticism*. La Jolla: Lalo Press.

Graulich, Melody, ed. 1993. *"Yellow Woman"/Leslie Marmon Silko*. New Brunswick: Rutgers UP.

Hillerman, Tony. 1993. *Talking God.* New York: Penguin Viking.

Hirsch, Bernard A. 1993. "The Telling Which Continues": Oral Tradition and the Written Word in Leslie Marmon Silko's *Storyteller.* In Graulich, 151–83.

Hobson, Geary, ed. 1993a. *The Remembered Earth.* Albuquerque: U of New Mexico P.

———. 1993b. "The Rise of the White Shaman as a New Version of Cultural Imperialism." In Hobson, 100–108.

Hogan, Linda. 1990. *Mean Spirit.* New York: Ivy Books.

———. 1991. *Red Clay.* Greenfield Center, NY: Greenfield Review Press.

Johnson, Charles. 1990. *Middle Passage.* New York: Atheneum.

Johnson, David, and David Apodaca. 1990. "Myth and the Writer: An Interview with Rudolfo Anaya. In González-T., 414–38.

Kermode, Frank. 1979. *The Genesis of Secrecy.* Cambridge: Harvard UP.

———. 1983. "Secrets and Narrative Sequence." *Essays on Fiction.* London: Routledge and Kegan Paul. Reprinted from *Critical Inquiry* 7 (1980): 83–101.

Krupat, Arnold. 1989. "The Dialogic of Silko's *Storyteller.* In Vizenor, 55–68.

———, ed. 1993. *New Voices in Native American Criticism.* Washington, D.C.: Smithsonian Institution Press.

Llosa, Mario Vargas. 1980. *The Storyteller.* New York: Farrar, Straus and Giroux.

McNickle, D'Arcy. 1987. *Runner in the Sun.* Albuquerque: U of New Mexico P.

———. 1988. *Wind from an Enemy Sky.* Albuquerque: U of New Mexico P.

Milligan, Mary Guerrero. 1993. "Loterio." *Blue Mesa Review* 5: 98–103.

Momaday, N. Scott. 1969. *The Way to Rainy Mountain.* Albuquerque: U of New Mexico P.

———. 1989. *The Ancient Child.* New York: Harper.

Niggli, Josephine. 1994. *Mexican Village.* Albuquerque: U of New Mexico P.

Owens, Louis. 1992a. *Other Destinies: Understanding the American Indian Novel.* Norman: U of Oklahoma P.

———. 1992b. *The Sharpest Sight.* Norman: U of Oklahoma P.

———. 1994. *Bone Game.* Norman: U of Oklahoma P.

———. 1995. *Wolf Song.* Norman: U of Oklahoma P.

Pina, Michael. 1989. "The Archaic, Historical, and Mythicized Dimensions of Aztlán. In Anaya and Lomeli, 14–48.

Plato. 1972. *Collected Dialogues.* Ed. and trans. Edith Hamilton and Huntingdon Cairns. New York: Pantheon, Bollingen Series 31.

Sequoya, Jana. 1993. "How(!) Is an Indian?" In Krupat, 453–73.

Silko, Leslie Marmon. 1993a. *"Yellow Woman."* In Graulich, 31–43.

———. 1977. *Ceremony.* New York: Signet.

———. 1981. *Storyteller.* New York: Seaver Press.

———. 1991. *Almanac of the Dead.* New York: Simon and Schuster.

———. 1993. "An Old-Time Indian Attack Conducted in Two Parts." In Hobson, 211–16.

Soyinka, Wole. 1990. "Twice Bitten: The Fate of Africa's Culture Producers." *PMLA* 105: 110–20.

Starobinski, Jean. 1971. *Les mots sous les mots: Les anagrammes de Ferdinand de Saussure.* Paris: Gallimard.

Steiner, George. 1973. *After Babel.* London: Oxford UP.

Twain, Mark. 1992. "Concerning General Grant's Intentions." Open letter to the Tribune, 12 December 1868. *Mark Twain: Collected Tales, Sketches and Essays, 1852–1896*. Ed. Louis J. Budd 1992. New York: Literary Classics, 282–84.

Ulibarrí, Sabine. 1993.*The Best of Sabine R. Ulibarrí*. Albuquerque: U of New Mexico P.

Villanueva, Alma Luz. 1988. *The Ultraviolet Sky*. Tempe: Bilingual Press. Reissued by Doubleday, 1993.

Vizenor, Gerald. 1989. *Narrative Chance: Postmodern Discourse on Native American Literatures*. Albuquerque: U of New Mexico P.

Welch, James. 1974. *Winter in the Blood*. New York: Harper and Row.

———. 1986. *Fools Crow*. New York: Viking Penguin.

———. 1990 *Indian Lawyer*. New York: Viking Penguin.

NATIVE DESIGNS

Silko's Storyteller *and the Reader's Initiation*

Linda Krumholz

In a Tiffany's ad titled "Native Design," the famous New York jewelry store advertises 5"-x-7" frames for $300 apiece as part of their Native American Collection, with styles labeled "Hopi," "Iroquois," "Columbia," "Mississippi," "Mohawk," and "Pueblo."[1] This exemplifies the white American embrace and appropriation of American Indianness that makes it so difficult for American Indians to be heard in their own terms. Jimmie Durham, a Cherokee artist, describes a "Master Narrative" of American whites, a narrative that simultaneously erases, embraces, and consumes American Indians; a narrative that denies our colonial past, our colonial present, and the existence of contemporary colonized people. European settlers, according to Durham, want to *be* Indians but refuse to acknowledge the Indian voices that disrupt the Master Narrative and challenge the right of the United States to exist. The appropriation of Native American voices and Native American art is so pervasive that, Durham argues, "to accept any idea of ourselves as the subject matter for our art is a trap, potentially" (19). Leslie Marmon Silko, in her book *Storyteller,* resists appropriation by initiating the reader into a Native American reading practice that defies and subverts the Master Narratives. Rather than offering us a new "Native Design" for commodification, Silko has designs on her readers.

Nonetheless, any literary critical reading of *Storyteller* is an act of appropriation of the text for a predominantly white academic discourse. To contend with this problem, Larry Evers urges critics to work from an indigenous critical approach. He argues that an American Indian critical discourse is found in the stories themselves, that "performance of traditional stories and the criticism of those stories is really the same thing. Each time a storyteller tells a story he tells his own version of it. He gives his interpretation of it; he recreates it. If it works for others, they repeat it. Through his critical act it survives" (73). While Evers refers to *Ceremony* as this kind of critical act, *Storyteller* can certainly be read in the same way. In fact, *Storyteller* epitomizes a metacritical text; every piece can be read for the story it tells and for its story about storytelling and the role of stories.

But to designate *Storyteller* as a self-enclosed and self-explanatory system is to exclude it from the literary critical institutional practices that incorporate literary texts into the canon and the curriculum, to ignore the difficulties involved in reading a cross-cultural text, and to suggest it is not a part of contemporary literary production. James Ruppert argues that "[a]ny attempt to separate *Ceremony* from contemporary literature does a disservice to Native American literature and to American literature. My own belief is that critics must merge culturally and historically grounded approaches to such texts with contemporary theoretical approaches" (129). Ruppert uses Bakhtin's dialogics to describe the discursive shifts that make *Ceremony* a text that mediates between cultures. Ruppert's arguments and Bakhtin's theories of the novel are usefully applied to *Storyteller* to understand similar shifts in the reader's discursive ground. But Bakhtin explicitly rejects the use of sacred or mythic discourse, which he describes as antithetical to the socially transformative function of the novel.[2] Silko, on the other hand, emphasizes the transformative power of spirituality in her writing; the stories articulate a link between spiritual, discursive, and political transformations. As a ritual of initiation, *Storyteller* functions self-reflexively and intertextually. Rather than pose the approaches against one another, I suggest that dialogics and ritual complement one another in theorizing the reader's relations to Silko's text.

1. DIALOGICS IN *STORYTELLER*

Leslie Marmon Silko's *Storyteller* is a collection of stories that is also a highly self-conscious consideration of the processes of storytelling, an exploration into the ways the Laguna Pueblo society creates meaning and, subsequently, the ways cultures in general create meaning. *Storyteller* is a distinctively "readerly" text: the many stories, poems, and photographs are gathered into an apparently random "scrapbook" form, and it is left to the reader to construct connections between them. *Storyteller* is also a multicultural or cross-cultural text in which European-style short stories and traditional Laguna stories, "realistic" fictional characters, traditional characters (such as Yellow Woman, Coyote, and Spiderwoman), and Silko's family members are all brought together. The combination of an open "readerly" text and a cross-cultural text could leave the reception of the text "highly indeterminate," as Mary Louise Pratt argues is the case for "autoethnographic texts," texts in which the colonized merge their discourse and idioms with that of the colonizer in order to take back the power of self-representation while addressing both communities as audience (445–46). Yet Arnold Krupat argues that in *Storyteller* "for all the polyvocal openness of Silko's work, there is always the unabashed commitment to Pueblo ways as a reference point" ("Dialogic," 65).

In order to guide the reader's transformation within the polyvocal terrain of the text, Silko shifts the reader's discursive ground in two ways: she resituates the subject in the text and she redefines the power and position of the dominant discourse. Krupat and Hertha Wong argue that *Storyteller* should be read as a distinctively Native American autobiography in which Silko reconceives the autobiographical subject; she rejects the authoritative individual voice that represents Western concepts of the individual as defined by difference from all others and replaces it with a polyphony that indicates the Native American conception of the individual's story as part of the collective stories of the people. Krupat states, "There is no single, distinctive or authoritative voice in Silko's book nor any striving for such a voice; to the contrary, Silko will take pains to indicate how even her own individual speech is the product of many voices" ("Dialogic," 60). For Krupat and Wong, Bakhtin's dialogics connect to Native American autobiographies because multivocality is inherent in Native American concepts of the subject as defined within a social nexus. The Native American autobiographical subject is created amid a community of voices that relate, interact, and define one another — in dialogized speech.[3] Thus *Storyteller* is an autobiography in which the "I" has been recast as "the storyteller," one who finds her identity through her role for and in the community, which shifts the reader away from a traditional Western location of the "I" (as central and clearly differentiated) for author and reader. The location of the reader and storyteller as subjects who move within and between texts allows for an openness continually shaped by the Laguna Pueblo voices that compose and are composed by Silko.

Silko also shifts the textual ground in *Storyteller* through her construction of the "spheres of discourse" of the text. As noted, Ruppert uses Bakhtin's dialogics to describe Silko's novel *Ceremony* as a mediational text, a description that also applies to *Storyteller*. Ruppert writes: "Silko works with two different spheres of discourse, one of which is Native American and the other contemporary American. She must engage each sphere so that she can respond to previous and anticipated discourse, and yet turn that discourse around so as to make it express cross-cultural goals. She must restructure epistemologically two sets of perception and understanding. This is a process that I call *mediation*" (129). He concludes that the reader's "acts of mediation constitute Bakhtin's 'ideological translation of the language of the other' into a perspective on the text that merges the different spheres of discourse while continuing each" (134). In this same way, *Storyteller* is a novelistic work in which the convergence of competing cultural and ideological discourses enables the reader to "read" the Other across cultural differences.[4] But we can further define these spheres of discourse: rather than constructing the contemporary American discourse as a monolithic dominant discourse that is set against the Laguna Pueblo (or Native American) discourse, Silko presents the contemporary American discourse as an *already* multicultural, multilingual, "mixed" discourse.

Gloria Anzaldúa's *Borderlands/La Frontera* is another text that both describes and enacts a cross-cultural "mediation." This text is useful for comparison because of its similarities to *Storyteller,* because of its influence in "border" studies, and because it contrasts with Silko's text in its discursive approaches. *Borderlands,* like *Storyteller,* combines multiple genres, including poetry and autobiography, into a narrative of social and ideological transformation. Anzaldúa begins with descriptions of the borderlands as a division, a boundary, and a limbo containing "the squint-eyed, the perverse, the queer, the troublesome, the mongrel, the mulatto, the half-breed, the half dead" (3); she ends with a vision of the "new *mestiza*" at the "focal point or fulcrum . . . where the possibility of uniting all that is separate occurs" (79). Anzaldúa's "borderlands" and "*mestiza* consciousness" are positions of mediation and deconstruction, a place or consciousness from which the "mixed" and multiple discourses and social identities challenge oppositional structures of race, nationality, gender, and sexuality. The *mestiza* represents a multiple, antiauthoritarian, "in-between" position that deconstructs the monolithic, monologic power of the dominant society figured as white male patriarchal power. Anzaldúa states: "The work of *mestiza* consciousness is to break down the subject-object duality that keeps her a prisoner and to show in the flesh and through the images in her work how duality is transcended. The answer to the problem between the white race and the colored, between males and females, lies in healing the split that originates in the very foundation of our lives, our culture, our languages, our thoughts" (80). Despite Anzaldúa's avowed intention to dissolve dualities, her book creates a new duality; the "*mestiza*," multiple discursive position is formulated in opposition to a white male singular authoritarian discursive position. Thus, although the *mestiza* is described as the in-between position, the dialogics of the text leave us "in-between" the *mestiza* and the dominant discourses. The straight white male, or the white patriarchal system, is constructed as a powerful and oppressive force that needs to be deconstructed and destroyed.[5]

Instead of mediating between a dominant, normative discourse and a "marginal" discourse, Silko's *Storyteller* mediates between the Laguna Pueblo discourse and the "mixed" discourse of the United States that *already includes* both the white and the Native American. Silko shifts the power dynamic of the dialogic by marginalizing the dominant discourse. Although the preponderance of economic and political power in the United States is clearly still controlled by white Christian men, Silko's strategy begins with the assumption of a more equal power dynamic in the cultural, discursive, and spiritual realms. In many ways this fulfills the deconstructive impetus of "border" discourse as well, since the point is that there is no "pure" United States culture or language to begin with.[6] By redefining the discursive spheres that *Storyteller* mediates, Silko has already begun to bridge the cross-cultural space for the reader.

Within the "mixed" discourse of *Storyteller* there is also present an oppressive white discourse, but the power of white discourse to shape and define relations with the world is progressively marginalized in the book. For example, in the title story, which appears early in the collection, white discourse has the power to literally imprison dissenting discursive positions; as long as the Yupik girl refuses to conform her story to a sanctioned white version, which would mean a destruction of her entire sense of meaning and identity and, perhaps, of the world (apocalyptic imagery frames the story), she is branded crazy or criminal.[7] In "Lullaby," another story near the beginning of the collection, the white authorities have stolen everything and everyone that the old Navajo woman, Ayah, loved through their use of written language and her entrapment in their discursive system (she learns to sign her name, which becomes the authorities' way of sanctioning their theft of her children). Yet in the stories that appear later in the collection, white authoritative discourse is either excluded entirely or represented as thoroughly uncomprehending and unauthoritative (examples of uncomprehending white authority figures are the priest in "The Man to Send Rain Clouds" and Captain Littlecock in "A Geronimo Story"). Silko marginalizes and decenters the "dominant" white discursive position thereby leaving readers without what may be for many a normative discursive foothold.

Storyteller mediates between a "mixed" (partly Indian) discourse and a Pueblo (partly mixed) discourse.[8] The cross-cultural space, potentially a divide between self and Other, is traversed in part through the assumption of a shared cultural and discursive North American space in which only the monologic and oppressive white regulatory discourse is marginalized. As Krupat concludes in his essay, we must "see [*Storyteller*'s] art as a matter of values that are most certainly not *only* aesthetic" ("Dialogic," 65, emphasis added). Within this shared space, there is the assumption of a shared set of values through which an implied reader may be led to embrace Laguna Pueblo values and philosophies. The reader's process is a ritual of initiation; this ritual model helps to explain the narrative flow and structure of the text, and also connects the discursive shifts to the spiritual transformations that are central to a Laguna Pueblo understanding of the world.

2. RITUAL IN *STORYTELLER*

Rituals are formal events in which symbolic representations such as dance, song, story, and other activities are spiritually and communally endowed with the power to shape real relations in the world. Ritual is an indigenous idiom for many Native Americans, and it is a formal element in many contemporary Native American narratives. Paula Gunn Allen asserts that many contemporary novels by Indian authors "derive many of their structural and symbolic elements from certain rituals and the myths that are allied with those rituals" (79). The anthropologist Mary Douglas describes ritual as a form of communication that, like language, organizes and gives meaning to experience. Ritual communicates tradition, and thus it serves as transmitter and conservator of culture and the past.[9] But while ritual conserves, it also changes; Allen writes, "Ritual can be defined as a procedure whose purpose is to transform someone or something from one condition or state to another" (79–80). Ritual unites past and present, tradition and contemporary life, continuity and change. To emphasize the centrality of ritual in American Indian fiction, Allen compares it to white fiction: "Conflict is as basic to contemporary white fiction as ritual is to tribal Indian narrative" (78).

In *Storyteller,* Silko not only represents rituals, she simulates ritual processes to make her text function as a ritual for the reader.[10] Silko's novel *Ceremony* can be read as an adaptation of old ceremonies to new forms; *Storyteller* is also a "mixed breed" text, not simply because it uses writing and the English language (as opposed to oral forms and native languages) but also because it brings together the novel tradition (as a European-derived, colonial and postcolonial, global contemporary art form) and Native American ritual traditions. For instance, in *Storyteller* Silko employs techniques found in modernist novels, such as the use of multiple voices or narrative positions and the fragmentation of narrative. In modernist works, such as Virginia Woolf's *Waves,* T. S. Eliot's *Waste Land,* and Ernest Hemingway's *In Our Time,* these stylistic elements suggest the isolation and fragmentation of the individual psyche, the indeterminacy of truth, and the absence of any coherent cultural or religious meaning. For Silko, on the other hand, the fragmented narrative and multiplicity of voices represent an accretive, communal, and dialogic creation of meaning and truth in which meaning and truth are conscious and negotiable constructs, neither fixed nor indeterminate, but restricted by moral limits conveyed in stories. Thus these narrative strategies often associated with modernism are employed for much different purposes in Silko's book. Nonetheless, the readerly character of *Storyteller* and the ways in which the style *is* the content are familiar strategies to readers of Western modernist texts.[11]

Ritual functions in *Storyteller* as a theory of reading, as a discourse, and as a rhetorical strategy. As a theory of reading, ritual bears similarities to certain reader response theories that describe novels as sites of change. In fact, the definition of liminality, the central phase of ritual, proposed by anthropologist Victor Turner could describe an ideal reading practice.[12] He writes: "The liminal phase [is] . . . in the 'subjunctive mood' of culture, the mood of maybe, might-be, as-if, hypothesis, fantasy, conjecture, desire. . . . Liminality can perhaps be described as a fructile chaos, a fertile nothingness, a storehouse of possibilities, not by any means a random assemblage but a striving after new forms and structure, a gestation process, a fetation of modes appropriate to and anticipating postliminal existence" ("Are There Universals," 11–12). Turner's description of liminality as a space of potential, imagination, transformation, and a kind of birthing process fits well with Wolfgang Iser's theories of reading in which he argues that "there disappears the subject-object division that otherwise is the prerequisite for all knowledge and all observation, and the removal of this division puts reading in an apparently unique position as regards the possible absorption of new experiences" (66). While one could dispute whether objectivity is indeed the requirement of all other assumptions of knowledge, the idea of shifting subject positions within the reading experience has compelling implications. Iser quotes Georges Poulet, who writes, "Whenever I read, I mentally pronounce an *I,* and yet the *I* which I pronounce is not myself" (66). Iser considers this process transformative: "The production of the meaning of literary texts . . . does not merely entail the discovery of the unformulated, which can then be taken over by the active imagination of the reader; it also entails the possibility that we may formulate ourselves and so discover what had previously seemed to elude our consciousness" (68). While this idealized notion of the reading process leaves out issues of resistance as well as ideas of language as a transmitter of ideology, the notion of the literary work as a subjective, experiential mode of knowledge acquisition is similar to the processes of ritual.

As a discourse, ritual implies an unmediated relationship between language and the world. In many Western narrative theories, language acts are potentially transformative because they intervene in the cultural and ideological exchange of meaning production, but in Native American concepts of language, the word itself has a material reality that gives it direct power to transform the world. Brian Swann describes the generative power of language as a "sacrament," and he explains that "a truly sacramental sense of language means that object and word are so fused that their creation, the 'event,' is itself creative, bringing into this time and place the enduring powers which truly effect that which the event claims, and such action cannot be undone" (xii). The term "sacramental," with its religious echoes, conveys a spiritual concept in which a symbol becomes what it symbolizes — there is no gap between signifier and signified.[13] Thus the creative and transformative power of language connects linguistic acts to the transformative processes of ritual.

As a rhetorical structure, ritual functions as a vehicle or process for the transformation of the reader's imagination. In *Storyteller,* Silko arranges the stories into thematic sections; the reader is initiated into a Laguna Pueblo reading practice through the interplay of stories *within* thematic sections and through the organization of the sections into a narrative structure. Silko does not indicate sections explicitly in *Storyteller,* but Bernard A. Hirsch and Linda Danielson argue that Silko organizes her stories around themes. Danielson describes *Storyteller* as a web in which "thematic clusters constitute the radiating strands of the web" (21). The book can be coherently divided into six sections: Survival (1–53), Yellow Woman (54–99), Drought (100–155), Rain (156–86), Spirits (187–211), and Coyote (212–67).[14] The Survival section deals with the need for stories as a means of survival in an oral culture; it highlights the danger of white interpretations of Indian lives and stories. The Yellow Woman section focuses on women's roles and sexuality, and it sets up interactions between old and new stories, which suggest that change is part of Laguna Pueblo cultural processes and the oral tradition and not inimical to them. The Drought and Rain sections in the middle of the book reproduce the central ritual focus of Pueblo life in the arid Southwest. These stories begin with an emphasis on droughts and the disruptive forces that produce them, then shift to an emphasis on rain and the balances and creative forces necessary to perpetuate fertile relations with the world. Many of the stories in these two sections are also found in *Ceremony,* a novel shaped around a drought-to-rain ritual. The Spirits section carries the theme of change found in the Yellow

Woman section into a religious context of spiritual transformations in cycles of death and renewal. In the final section, the Coyote stories reconsider the Survival section, but now the Indian perspective and traditions pass judgment on the white world.[15]

Hirsch proposes that the process of reading within the thematic sections simulates the oral tradition; the reader learns by "the accretive process of teaching" in which the juxtaposition and compilation of stories create an interpretive context similar to the material context of the oral community (3). He argues that the abundance of stories and the multiple versions of stories within thematic sections work against the static nature of the written word and the absence of the oral community insofar as the many stories stimulate and shape the reader's interpretive play. He writes: "Successive narrative episodes cast long shadows both forward and back, lending different or complementary shades of meaning to those preceding them and offering perspectives from which to consider those that follow. Such perspectives are then themselves often expanded or in some way altered as the new material reflects back upon them. This kind of learning process is part of the dynamic of oral tradition" (3). Thus the stories create a context within which to interpret the other stories; in this way, Silko initiates the reader into a Laguna Pueblo interpretive practice.

The process of weaving meaning both within and between the stories also suggests certain cultural processes of meaning formation. First, the themat-ically grouped stories told in various ways (poetry, anecdote, short story, tradi-tional story) from various perspectives suggest that meaning is constructed communally, negotiated between voices and versions. Second, the process by which the many stories provide an interpretive context for each separate story also suggests a formation of meaning based on the establishment and under-standing of relationships. In other words, the "web" of interrelated stories is a metonym for the "web" of interrelationships that define life in a Native Ameri-can cosmology. Finally, the many traditional stories and the reappearance of characters such as Yellow Woman, Spiderwoman, and Coyote, along with the different interpretive contexts for these stories, point to the stories as sources of moral rather than etiological truths.

The compilation of stories in *Storyteller* also works to break down generic distinctions; Silko juxtaposes a variety of genres — traditional Laguna stories, Euro-American style short stories, poetry, family stories, gossip, and photo-graphs. The traditional Laguna stories convey the formal characteristics of the oral tales — repetitions, the storyteller's asides, the context of the stories, and the representation of human, animal, and spiritual characters with equal de-grees of agency and intelligence. Silko's Euro-American style short stories deal with Native American characters and situations using "realistic" conventions such as linear plot, conflict, character development, and denouement. Silko's poetry also blends Native American imagery and repetition with other modernist and poetic techniques of compression and lyrical complexity. The inclusion of family stories, as Krupat suggests, confuses the generic boundaries between fiction and autobiography. The gossip stories also break down categories, in this case erasing clear distinctions between sanctioned or mythic stories and popular communal stories, both of which help define one's position and meaning in the group. The photographs bring a visual aspect to the reader's experience; they convey a sense of place that is present in oral storytelling situations. The photographs also suggest that *Storyteller* is both a kind of personal "scrapbook" as well as a work of documentation — once again uniting the individual and communal memories and visions of Laguna life. This breakdown of generic boundaries challenges Western aesthetic categories and reading methods, thus the book resists easy appropriation to conventional reading methods while also creating a complex and dynamic reading process.

While the six thematic sections construct a dynamic intertextual reading process, they are also organized into a narrative structure — and a ritual structure — in the book as a whole. *Storyteller* begins with the Indian perspective in danger — disrupted, encroached upon, and subsumed under a white system of values and power — and it concludes by reinforcing Indian visions and values in vital interaction with the changing world. The narrative progressively marginalizes the dominant discourse and initiates the reader into an Indian reading of the world. The book also has a circular or mirror structure: the Survival and Coyote (first and last) sections treat the relations of storytelling and survival, the Yellow Woman and Spirits (second and fifth) sections focus on changes and the role of stories in change, and the Drought and Rain sections (in the center of the book) create a ritual within a ritual that demonstrates the fragile balances needed to maintain productive relations with and in the world. The progressive and reflective structures support each other. By progressing from stories of white power and domination to a humorous view of the illusions of white power, Silko deflates the "dominant" vision of a "dominating" system of power, but she also makes clear that both views — of Native American oppression and power — are necessary for a full understanding of power relations.

3. THE POLITICS OF SPIRITUALITY: A READING

Storyteller is a ritual of initiation that enables a transformation of consciousness and a shift in subject position for the reader, characterized by a new approach to "reading" the world and to "reading" oneself in the world. Silko's representation of spirituality, a vital part of this initiation, has radical political implications. In mainstream discourses of the United States, spirituality is often either compartmentalized away from daily life, derided as superstition, or manifested as a fundamentalism that mandates literal and rigid adherence to texts and religious dictates. In the Spirits section of *Storyteller,* Silko redefines spirituality and its social power. First, her presentation of spirituality infers connections between people, between people and the natural world, and between the living and the dead. The latter connection between the living and the spirits of the dead also deepens the bond between past and present; history is not a dead textual past but a living and tangible presence. Second, the validation of spiritual knowledge as a "true" and vital way of knowing challenges traditional U.S. epistemologies that posit truth and knowledge as scientific, empirical, and objective. Third, the representation of spirituality in and as story, and the intermixing of ritualized and sacred discourses within the indeterminacy of novelistic discourses, works against rigidities of textual and spiritual meaning. Stories are spiritual processes of creating and revising meaning in which meaning is fluid, shifting, relational, and in process. Finally, spirituality redefines power. Insofar as power is located not in technological, economic, or military domination but in the spiritual realm, the "dominant" society does not, in fact, dominate. This conception of power does not substitute for a material analysis of power but complements it.

In the Spirits section of *Storyteller,* Silko asserts the importance of spiritual relations in the transformation of the reader and the world. The Spirits section is composed of three photographs, five family reminiscences, six poems, one traditional story, and a description of the Deer Dance. Two photographs frame the section, each accompanied by a family story. The first photo is of Grandpa Hank, who figures prominently in this section. Beside a photo of her grandfather sitting and reading in an easy chair, Silko tells the story of Grandpa Hank's Navajo friend who came to the yearly Laguna Feast to exchange gifts and friendship. She tells of the last time the Navajo man came and learned Hank was dead. He cried, left, and never returned. Thus Silko expresses the sense of irretrievable loss at the death of those we love. The photo that ends the section is of Grandma A'mooh, Silko's great-grandmother, another abiding presence in Silko's life. She too sits in an easy chair, and she is tatting. Accompanying this photo is a story Grandma A'mooh heard as a child. After Navajos stole some Laguna sheep, the Laguna tracked and found the Navajos, but rather than harming the thieves the Laguna asked them why they had stolen the sheep. When the Laguna found out the Navajos had no food, they gave them some of the sheep and told them next time to ask and they would happily give them food. Silko concludes this story with a description of

Laguna Feast time when Navajos, like Grandpa Hank's friend, come to Laguna and are welcomed and fed.

These two photographs and their stories frame the section with Silko's family "spirits" who also represent the spirit of the Laguna Pueblo. Her great-grandmother's pride in the story of Laguna generosity, Grandpa Hank's friendship with the Navajo, and the Laguna Feast demonstrate the Laguna ethics that generate pride and power for Silko. These pieces also tie the ways of the Laguna to Silko's love for her deceased family members. She writes in a letter to James Wright:

> Death never ends feelings or relationships at Laguna. If a dear one passes on, the love continues and it continues in both directions — it is requited by the spirits of these dear ones who send blessings back to us, maybe with rain or maybe with the feeling of continuity and closeness as well as with past memories. . . . At Laguna, when someone dies, you don't "get over it" by forgetting; you "get over it" by *remembering,* and by remembering you are aware that no person is ever truly lost or gone once they have been in our lives and loved us, as we have loved them. (28–29)

The Spirits section is not only about those who are dead, it is also about the deepest feelings and desires, of love and loss, that one might call spiritual; it is about the cycles of death, loss, and change; and it is about the stories and rituals that evoke memories and bring renewal through the evocation of memories.

These cycles of death, loss, and renewal are intrinsic to the Deer Dance, as Silko describes it:

> In the fall, the Laguna hunters go to the hills and mountains around Laguna Pueblo to bring back the deer. The people think of the deer as coming to give themselves to the hunters so that the people will have meat through the winter. Late in the winter the Deer Dance is performed to honor and pay thanks to the deer spirits who've come home with the hunters that year. Only when this has been properly done will the spirits be able to return to the mountain and be reborn into more deer who will, remembering the reverence and appreciation of the people, once more come home with the hunters. (191)

The Deer Dance serves as a metaphor — for cycles of life and death, of love and loss — and as more than a metaphor, as a ritual that reenacts the relationship it represents.

In three poems — "Deer Dance/For Your Return," "A Hunting Story," and

"Deer Song" — the Deer Dance is used to combine the cycles of the hunt with cycles of sexual love and loss. The relationship of sacrifice and homage between the hunter and the deer is transformed into a relationship of love and desire modeled on the hunt: in the first two poems the speaker is the hunter as lover; in the third poem the speaker is the hunted deer as the lover. There is a dark irony in Silko's metaphor in these poems. The cycles of death, homage, and rebirth may create a hopeful analogy for the return of a lost lover, but in the Deer Dance death and sacrifice provoke the love. Thus the very act of love and desire, the hunt and possession of the loved one, kills the loved one. In these poems the beauty and power of desire is deepened by the sense of inevitable loss; the lover must kill what she loves to complete the cycle. Moments of tenderness and desire are inseparable from death. In "A Hunting Story" she writes: "I knelt above you / that morning / I counted the rattles / the last whistles / in your throat. / I put my mouth on yours" (194). In this combined imagery of lovemaking and death, the final gesture could be a lover's kiss or an attempt at resuscitation. In "Deer Song" she writes: "Do not think that I do not love you / if I scream / while I die. / Antler and thin black hoof / smashed against dark rock — / the struggle is the ritual / shining teeth tangled in / sinew and flesh" (201). The graphic imagery of the hunt adds a visceral quality to the long-standing analogy of sexual desire and death.

Although the cyclical nature of the Deer Dance signals a resuscitation of desire, the resuscitation is also the resumption of the hunt. Thus the ending is as ominous as it is exciting. For example, as "A Hunting Story" ends, the loved one returns as a deer in the final lines: "Up ahead / there is a small clearing / When you step out / into sight / I will be waiting" (197). Although the desire evoked throughout the poem moves the reader to desire this return, the hunter/deer analogy of the lovers and the idea of the rifle "sight" evoked in the penultimate line make the return as painful as the loss. Besides expressing a deep pessimism about sexual love relationships, these poems suggest that a belief in cyclical relationships, in death and renewal, and the performance of the corresponding rituals do not insulate one from the pain of loss and change.

The stories of familial love and loss, and of sexual love and loss, describe cyclical relationships that provide spiritual sustenance and spiritual anguish. But whether one experiences pain or pleasure, the cycles are beautiful because they weave our acts and our lives into the deep mesh of interrelationships that sustain the world. The next juxtaposed stories describe the role that stories and memory have in this sustaining process, while they also show how white concepts of death and knowledge can disrupt and imperil the cycles and, thus, the world. Because the poem "Where Mountain Lion Lay Down With Deer" is central to my discussion, I include it in its entirety:

I climb the black rock mountain
   stepping from day to day
      silently.
I smell the wind for my ancestors
    pale blue leaves
     crushed wild mountain smell.
Returning
  up the gray stone cliff
  where I descended
    a thousand years ago
Returning to faded black stone
where mountain lion lay down with deer.
It is better to stay up here
    watching wind's reflection
    in tall yellow flowers.
The old ones who remember me are gone
    the old songs are all forgotten
and the story of my birth.
How I danced in snow-frost moonlight
    distant stars to the end of the Earth,
How I swam away
    in freezing mountain water
    narrow mossy canyon tumbling down
      out of the mountain
      out of deep canyon stone
   down
     the memory
       spilling out
       into the world. (199–200)

The title of the poem clearly echoes biblical descriptions of Eden or Paradise, where the lion lay down with the lamb. The persona of this poem is in a mythic space where time and place merge — the speaker steps "from day to day." The speaker's mythic life span and its connection to the people — it smells the wind for its ancestors, it returns after a thousand years — suggest that it is the spirit of the people, the Laguna Pueblo or Native American people.

    The poem begins with an upward movement, the ascent up mountains and cliffs, also mimicking an ascent to Heaven "where mountain lion lay down with deer." The return upward, along with the biblical allusion, indicates a movement toward a timeless stasis, such as Paradise, outside the natural cycles of life and death, in the realm of the spirit according to Western cosmogony. Even though the spirit-character says "It is better to stay up here," the assertion is not convincing; it seems sad at being forgotten. But as the spirit remembers and retells its own birth it enacts it—the story and the memory *are* the spirit, and thus they are all simultaneously reborn in the world. The rest of the poem creates a downward motion both verbally and visually—the story told by the spirit-character re-creates in the reader the memory of the spirit, which becomes a physical manifestation, the creative water, flowing back "down / the memory / spilling out / into the world."

In this poem Silko takes the natural cycles—drought and rain, birth, death, and rebirth—and uses them to describe larger cultural cycles. Since Indians have been frequently described as extinct or part of the past, this poem has particular resonance as a refiguring of Indians and Indian culture, not only as alive and present, but as essential to the revitalization of America, naturally, culturally, and economically (if one thinks about economics as a balance of wealth, needs, and resources). The poem also implicitly contrasts Judeo-Christian and Native American spirituality. First, Silko takes away the taint of "superstition" from Native American religious beliefs, since Paradise is as "superstitious" and nonrational as any other religious belief. She also implies a connection between spiritual beliefs and ethics: the paradisiacal stasis connects to a Judeo-Christian ideal of an end point, a completion, a final Revelation or Apocalypse, in which the chosen find individual pleasure, satisfaction, and eternal rest; the choice of the spirit-character of the poem to reenter the spiritual and natural cycles suggests a continuing connection and responsibility to the earth and its inhabitants.[16]

This poem teaches us a great deal by itself, but the poem gains impact juxtaposed with the story about Grandpa Hank immediately preceding it. Written in poetic lines, Silko tells about Grandpa Hank's buggy and his job driving tourists around the Laguna-Acoma area. She tells about one particular job he had: "In 1908 when the Smithsonian Institution / excavated the top of *Katsi'ma*, Enchanted Mesa / Grandpa drove some of the archeologists / out there in his buggy" (198). After describing how the archeologists, with great enterprise, got on to the inaccessible mesa, she asks her grandfather what they found—"I had always been curious about what might be / on top of Enchanted Mesa" (198). She recounts for us a story of a blind woman and a baby trapped up there, as she asks her grandfather if there were any bones attesting to the story. Grandpa Hank replies that they packed everything in boxes too fast for him to see. The story ends with Grandpa Hank's words:

"You know
probably all those boxes of things
they took from Enchanted Mesa
are still just sitting somewhere
in the basement of some museum." (198–99)

In this brief poem-story, white disbelief in spiritual presences (as well as a conception of Indians as extinct relics to be captured and displayed in museums) essentially kills spirits by taking them out of the circulation of story and memory. Everything about Enchanted Mesa—its name, the photograph in *Storyteller* of a cliff wall looming into a mesa above the desert, its inaccessibility, and the stories attached to it—contributes to its power and mystery. The archeologists appear to see none of this. By collecting and boxing whatever was on top of *Katsi'ma,* they have rendered it meaningless, taking it out of the renewing cycles of the people, the land, and the stories, out of the cycles described and enacted in the poem "Where Mountain Lion Lay Down With Deer."

In "The Man Made of Words," N. Scott Momaday, the Kiowa author, writes: "an Indian is an idea which a given man has of himself. And it is a moral idea, for it accounts for the way in which he reacts to other men and to the world in general" (162). The archeologists represent here a kind of death that is not natural or cyclical, a death of the imagination. By juxtaposing these pieces, Silko leads the reader to interpret the archeologists' concept of knowledge, the collection and compartmentalization of information (the scientific method), as a spiritual death. The movement of the archeologists up and down Enchanted Mesa is repeated in the movement of the spirit up and down the mountain, but the latter is part of a recirculation of stories, knowledge, and the spirit of the place and the people, while the former ends that circulation. Together these stories teach us that the real threat to Indians—and to all of us—is not physical death but spiritual and cultural death; that the stories and the shared knowledge, as well as the imaginative and ethical power they convey and continue, is the essence of Indianness. To understand these stories, the reader is led to question the "white" beliefs in scientific truth, in knowledge as a thoroughly rational process, and in the finality of death.[17]

The last two juxtaposed stories in the section are complementary stories, or two versions of the same story, that shift attention from cycles of death and renewal to the spiritual transformations the living may undergo. These stories—about a boy's adoption by bears and his subsequent return, through a singer, to his human family—also describe, by analogy, the role of the storyteller in the spiritual initiation of the reader. The first piece, a poem called "Story from Bear Country," describes the allure of the bear's beckoning:

Their beauty will overcome your memory
like winter sun
melting ice shadows from snow
And you will remain with them
locked forever inside yourself
  your eyes will see you
  dark shaggy and thick. (205)

The loss of memory of one's humanness is an escape into the beauty of being a bear, and so the bear priests must sing songs of equal beauty to tempt the bear-person back to memories and humanity:

They will try to bring you
step by step
back to the place you stopped
and found only bear prints in the sand
where your feet had been. (206)

The use of second person in the poem makes the reader identify with the subject undergoing this transformation. Silko's poem is then identified as the song of the bear priest, the song meant to lure the "you," the bear-man (whose "wife and sons are waiting / back at the car"), back to humanity with the song's beauty. She writes: "But you have been listening to me / for some time now" (206). The poem situates the reader as the subject and the poet as the singer, as the poet brings us through a transformation process with her song and her love. In the end the voice of the poet becomes a communal voice:

Don't be afraid
  we love you
  we've been calling you
  all this time
Go ahead
turn around
see the shape
of your footprints
in the sand. (207)

This poem traces a double transformative process—from human to bear and back again. In the change to a bear-person, the "you" of the poem has accepted a wholly new perception and self-perception, a new subjectivity. Nonetheless, it would be a mistake to simply equate the beauty of the bear with the beauty of the Native American vision offered by the book, since our poet-singer is intent on luring us back to our humanity. The complexity of Silko's metaphor of transformation multiplies in juxtaposition with the second version of the story.

The second version is presented as a traditional story; it retains a narrative flow and the sense of an oral narrator but is broken into lyrical lines that are centered on the page. This version tells of a small boy who wanders off from his family and joins a bear family. His human family rushes for the medicine man who runs to call the boy back before he loses his humanity forever. The story explains that they must bring him back carefully: "They couldn't just grab the child. / They couldn't simply take him back / because he would be in-between forever / and probably he would die" (209). The story ends with the boy coming back to his human family, "but he wasn't quite the same / after that / not like the other children" (209). In this version the danger is that the boy will be lost, "in-between forever," but after he comes back he is never the same, so to some extent he is "in-between forever." In fact, as we see in *Ceremony* with the bear child Shush who helps Betonie with Tayo's ceremony, the bear child becomes the bear priest; the person who has been through the experience and moved in between the subject positions can guide another through the process.

Silko, then, is our bear priest, our singer. She is not donning the mantle of the shaman, but she is someone who has been in between and who can bring us through. Silko describes herself as "in-between" in a number of ways, as part of a mixed family living on the edges of the Laguna Pueblo, and as a Native American in the United States. In one interview she states simply, "I was born in the in-between" (Silko, Interview, 149). She describes the complexity of her "in-between" identity in her autobiographical note to her book *Laguna Woman*. She writes: "I suppose at the core of my writing is the attempt to identify what it is to be a half-breed or mixed blood person; what it is [to] grow up neither white nor fully traditional Indian. . . . I am only one human being, one Laguna woman" (35). Silko is both mixed (part Indian) and "one Laguna woman," an identity that is here inclusive of her mixed identity. Silko's multiple, "in-between" identity suits her to lead others "in between" subject positions. The "you" of "Story from Bear Country" goes where "your eyes will see you / dark shaggy and thick," where there were "only bear prints in the sand / where your feet had been" — the reader-persona sees herself or himself through bear eyes as a bear. Of course, the idea of walking in another's shoes (or footprints, in this case) is central to the ideal of literary identification. But in *Storyteller* Silko guides the reader, not through identification with a central character, but through a different sort of reading process, a process in which intertextual associations, the dissolution of generic categories, the shift of discursive ground, and the reformulation of the subject create a ritual of initiation.[18] To complete the analogy with the transformation of the bear-person, once the reader passes through this reading experience, she or he will never be quite the same.

The description of Silko's "in-between" status returns us to our earlier discussion of dialogics in which I argued that the competing discourses of the text were the mixed discourse (that includes the Laguna) and the Laguna discourse (that includes the mixed). At this point we can better define the discursive shifts in the book. Within the mixed discourse we find traces of the dominant discourse, already marginalized but still in need of refutation. We are all familiar with the terms of this discourse: science is true knowledge; Judeo-Christianity is religion, other beliefs are superstition; individualism (and its counterpart, private property) is the basis of all human freedom and justice; power comes from technology, military strength, and economic control. Silko's text does not directly address these definitions, but through the stories, the Native American discourse, and the initiation process these concepts are challenged and subverted.

Although the concept of dialogics helps to describe discursive shifts, it does not provide the language to describe spiritual changes. Central to Silko's representation of spirituality in the Spirits section is a concept of death as part of the cycles of nature; death as continuity rather than finality. Different concepts of death are central factors in distinguishing between many Western and non-Western beliefs, and these differences can be explained in part as different perceptions of time. Johannes Fabian argues that cultural concepts of time shape beliefs in the presence of ancestral spirits and the transformative, or magical, power of rituals and stories. Fabian writes:

> all temporal relations, and therefore also contemporaneity, are embedded in culturally organized praxis. . . . To cite but two examples, relationships between the living and the dead, or relationships between the agent and object of magic operations, presuppose cultural conceptions of contemporaneity. To a large extent, Western rational disbelief in the presence of ancestors and the efficacy of magic rest on the rejection of ideas of temporal coexistence implied in these ideas and practices. (34)

These differences in beliefs about time also create differences in beliefs about power. In fact, Silko rejects the term "magic" to describe the kinds of changes wrought by ritual and language; she prefers the word "power." Silko reserves the term "magic" to refer to deceptive tricks, such as those performed in the story of the Ck'o'yo magician, tricks that distracted the people from attending to their proper worship and the real sources of power, and thus brought about a drought (111–21). In this story, "magic" can be read to represent technology, the kind of "tricks" that appear powerful but do not take part in the "real" power found in connection to and facilitation of the creative cycles of the earth.

Throughout *Storyteller* Silko redefines power; she rejects the dominant connotations of the word as dominance, objectification, and manipulation, and rewrites it as a term conveying spiritual knowledge, profound interrelationships, and respect and responsibility for all things. The redefinition of power signals not only a spiritual and cultural change but a political change as well. Finally I want to insist that the reader's transformation is a political and moral transformation. The political implications of Silko's book must not be ignored, since, as Charles Bernstein warns, "Within the emerging official cultural space of diversity, figures of difference are often selected because they narrate in a way that can be readily assimilated—not to say absorbed—into the conventional forms of the dominant culture" (6). Rather than absorbing Silko's book, I have endeavored to trace processes by which the reader is absorbed by the book, not as a spiritual reconquest and embrace of Indianness, but as a challenge to the values and choices that allow that conquest to continue. To quote Bernstein again: "We have to get over, as in getting over a disease, the idea that we can 'all' speak to one another in the universal voice of poetry. History still mars our words, and we will be transparent to one another only when history itself disappears. For as long as social relations are skewed, who speaks in poetry can never be a neutral matter" (5). Silko's book presents aesthetic and political challenges to the reader. To learn a Laguna Pueblo reading practice is not a discovery of a universal Indian voice or spirit within us all. To learn the power of Native American stories and beliefs is not simply to be changed, but to begin to understand how we must act to change the world.

NOTES

Thanks to Jill Kuhnheim for her extraordinary support and her editorial skill.
1. *New York Times*, 3 August 1995, sect. A.

2. Bakhtin writes, "It is necessary that heteroglossia wash over a culture's awareness of itself and its language, penetrate to its core, relativize the primary language system underlying its ideology and literature and deprive it of its naive absence of conflict. . . . [S]uch external multi-languagedness strengthens and deepens the internal contradictions of literary language itself; it undermines the authority of custom and of whatever traditions still fetter linguistic consciousness; it erodes that system of national myth that is organically fused with language, in effect destroying once and for all a mythic and magical attitude to language and the world" (368–69). Bakhtin treats spiritual discourse as authoritative discourse, which attempts to reinforce a static or sacrosanct meaning from the past and thus cannot function within the discursive heterogeneity or fulfill the democratizing function of the novel (343–44).

3. Wong writes, "The Indian 'I,' in Bakhtinian fashion, is inherently polyvocal" (188). See also Krupat's *Ethnocriticism* and *The Voice in the Margin* for a more elaborate discussion of Native American autobiographies and Bakhtinian dialogics. Wong's work also challenges arguments by Krupat and others that autobiography is not an indigenous form (4). She argues convincingly that "[t]he roots of Indian autobiography . . . are not merely in the Western written tradition, but in the pre-contact Native American traditions of orality, art, and performance" (56).

4. "In describing *Storyteller* as an autoethnography and as an initiation for the reader, I will focus on the reader as outsider, the non-Laguna and non-Indian reader. What serves as an act of transformation for a non-Indian reader may serve as an affirmation for the Indian reader. But insofar as Silko engages with and challenges the dominant representations of Native Americans, she confronts the ideologies that all 'Americans' are subject to in varying degrees—many Native Americans have also been educated in Euroamerican schools, for example" (Krumholz, 91).

5. Anzaldúa is well aware of the limitations of this new oppositional position. She writes: "Because the counterstance stems from a problem with authority—outer as well as inner—it's a step toward liberation from cultural domination. But it is not a way of life. At some point on our way to a new consciousness, we will have to leave the opposite bank, the split between the two mortal combatants somehow healed so that we are on both shores at once and, at once, see through serpent and eagle eyes. Or perhaps we will decide to disengage from the dominant culture, write it off altogether as a lost cause, and cross the border into a wholly new and separate territory" (78–79).

6. Regarding the "mixed" heritage of the United States, see Ishmael Reed's essay "America: The Multinational Society," as well as other essays in the same collection.

7. See Vangen's essay on "Storyteller."

8. The Laguna Pueblo Indians have a long history of cultural exchange and the absorption of other Native Americans, Spaniards, and Euro-Americans. See Ruoff's essay for more information on this aspect of the Laguna Pueblo.

9. As Mary Douglas suggests, the United States has long fashioned itself as antitraditional, constantly breaking new ground, throwing off the old, and "making it new" (whether this self-description is true or not). But many cultural groups within the United States are interested in retaining and restoring traditions. As Henderson

writes, "For black and women writers [and, I would add, for Native American writers], such an avowal of tradition in the subdominant order, of course, constitutes an operative challenge to the dominant order" (20).

10. There are, of course, basic differences between reading a book and participating in a ritual especially between the primarily individual, intellectual experience of the former and the physical, spiritual, and communal focus of the latter.

11. While ritual has a particular relevance for Native American novels, the relationship of ritual to the novel is not wholly new either; in fact, many novels can be read as rituals of initiation for the reader in which the characters' lessons translate into a new interpretive practice for the reader. This reading can be applied throughout the canon, to conversion narratives such as Bunyan's *Pilgrim's Progress,* to slave narratives such as Douglass's 1845 *Narrative,* to social critiques such as Swift's *Gulliver's Travels,* and to bildungsromans such as Dickens's *Great Expectations,* Twain's *Huck Finn,* and Alcott's *Little Women.* A number of contemporary novels also consciously draw from ritual traditions, such as Toni Cade Bambara's *Salt Eaters,* Paule Marshall's *Praisesong for the Widow,* and E. M. Broner's *A Weave of Women,* to name a few.

12. Turner identifies three stages in rituals: rites of separation, rites of limen, or margin, and rites of reaggregation. For more information on ritual, see his work *Ritual Process.*

13. See also Barre Toelken, Kenneth Lincoln, and Hertha Wong regarding the creative power of Native American ritual language.

14. I got the first two categories and the very idea of thematic categories from Hirsch's article. Since by chance I read Hirsch's essay before Danielson's, I owe his work a greater debt, but I was gratified to discover that Danielson's divisions of *Storyteller* correspond to my own, which suggests that these designations are not entirely arbitrary.

15. For more about the structure of *Storyteller,* the content of the various sections, and an analysis of the Coyote section, see my essay in *Ariel.*

16. In *Ceremony,* Silko describes Christianity as a destructive element in Laguna society because it teaches people to seek salvation individually rather than as a group in harmony with the world.

17. It is interesting to note that in other contemporary novels, such as Toni Morrison's *Song of Solomon* and David Bradley's *Chaneysville Incident,* a reconceptualization of death in non-Western (in these cases African or African American) terms is central to the lessons the protagonist must learn to subvert constraining white definitions.

18. In Silko's novels, one can identify characters whose ritual or transformative process relates to the reader's process in the novel: in *Ceremony* there is Tayo, in *Almanac of the Dead* Sterling may play this role.

WORKS CITED

Allen, Paula Gunn. *The Sacred Hoop: Recovering the Feminine in American Indian Traditions.* Boston: Beacon Press, 1986.

Anzaldúa, Gloria. *Borderlands/La Frontera: The New Mestiza*. San Francisco: Spinsters/Aunt Lute, 1987.

Bakhtin, M. M. *The Dialogic Imagination*. Ed. Michael Holquist. Trans. Caryl Emerson and Michael Holquist. Austin: U of Texas P, 1981.

Bernstein, Charles. *A Poetics*. Cambridge: Harvard UP, 1992.

Danielson, Linda. "*Storyteller*: Grandmother Spider's Web." *Journal of the Southwest* 30.3 (1988): 325–55.

Douglas, Mary. *Natural Symbols: Explorations in Cosmology*. London: Barrie and Jenkins, 1970.

Durham, Jimmie. "Cowboys and . . . " *Third Text* 12 (autumn 1990): 5–20.

Evers, Larry. "A Response: Going Along with the Story." *American Indian Quarterly* 5.1 (1979): 71–75.

Fabian, Johannes. *Time and the Other: How Anthropology Makes Its Object*. New York: Columbia University Press, 1983.

Henderson, Mae Gwendolyn. "Speaking in Tongues: Dialogics, Dialectics, and the Black Woman Writer's Literary Tradition." *Changing Our Own Words: Essays on Criticism, Theory and Writing by Black Women*. Ed. Cheryl A. Wall. New Brunswick: Rutgers UP, 1989. 16–37.

Hirsch, Bernard A. " 'The Telling Which Continues': Oral Tradition and the Written Word in Leslie Marmon Silko's *Storyteller*." *American Indian Quarterly* 12.1 (1988): 1–26.

Iser, Wolfgang. "The Reading Process: A Phenomenological Approach." *Reader-Response Criticism: From Formalism to Post-Structuralism*. Ed. Jane P. Tompkins. Baltimore: Johns Hopkins UP, 1980. 50–69.

Krumholz, Linda J. " 'To Understand this World Differently': Reading and Subversion in Leslie Marmon Silko's *Storyteller*." *Ariel: A Review of International English Literature* 25.1 (January 1994): 89–113.

Krupat, Arnold. "The Dialogic of Silko's *Storyteller*." *Narrative Chance: Postmodern Discourse on Native American Indian Literatures*. Ed. Gerald Vizenor. Albuquerque: U of New Mexico P, 1989. 55–68.

———. *The Voice in the Margin: Native American Literature and the Canon*. Berkeley: U of California P, 1989.

———. *Ethnocriticism: Ethnography, History, Literature*. Berkeley: U of California P, 1992.

Lincoln, Kenneth. "Native American Literature." *Smoothing the Ground: Essays on Native American Oral Literature*. Ed. Brian Swann. Berkeley: U of California P, 1983. 3–38.

Momaday, N. Scott. "The Man Made of Words." *The Remembered Earth: An Anthology of Contemporary Native American Literature*. Ed. Geary Hobson. Albuquerque: Red Earth Press, 1979. 162–73.

Pratt, Mary Louise. "Art of the Contact Zone." *Profession 91*. New York: MLA, 1991. Rpt. in *Ways of Reading*. Ed. David Bartholomae and Anthony Petrosky. New York: St. Martin's Press, 1993. 442–55.

Reed, Ishmael. "America: The Multinational Society." *Multi-Cultural Literacy: Opening the American Mind*. Ed. Rick Simonson and Scott Walker. Saint Paul, MN: Graywolf Press, 1988. 155–60.

Ruoff, A. LaVonne. "Ritual and Renewal: Keres Traditions in the Short Fiction of Leslie Silko." *MELUS* 5.4 (1978): 2–17.

Ruppert, James. "Dialogism and Mediation in Leslie Silko's *Ceremony.*" *Explicator* 51 (winter 1993): 129–34.

Silko, Leslie Marmon. Interview. *Winged Words: American Indian Writers Speak.* Ed. Laura Coltelli. Lincoln: U of Nebraska P., 1990. 135–53.

———. *Laguna Woman.* Greenfield Center, NY: Greenfield Review Press, 1974.

———. Letters to James Wright. *The Delicacy and Strength of Lace.* Ed. Anne Wright. St. Paul, MN: Graywolf Press, 1986.

———. *Storyteller.* New York: Little, Brown, 1981.

Swann, Brian. "Introduction." *Smoothing the Ground: Essays on Native American Oral Literature.* Ed. Brian Swann. Berkeley: U of California P., 1983. xi–xix.

Toelken, Barre. "Life and Death in the Navajo Coyote Tales." *Recovering the Word: Essays on Native American Literature.* Ed. Brian Swann and Arnold Krupat. Berkeley: U of California P, 1987. 388–401.

Turner, Victor. *The Ritual Process: Structure and Anti-Structure.* London: Routledge and Kegan Paul, 1969.

———. "Are There Universals of Performance in Myth, Ritual, and Drama?" *By Means of Performance: Intercultural Studies of Theatre and Ritual.* Ed. Richard Schechner and Willa Appel. Cambridge: Cambridge UP, 1989. 8–18.

Vangen, Kate Shanley. "The Devil's Domain: Leslie Silko's 'Storyteller.'" *Dolphin* 9 (1984): 116–23.

Wong, Hertha Dawn. *Sending My Heart Back Across the Years: Tradition and Innovation in Native American Autobiography.* New York: Oxford University Press, 1992.

TO TELL A GOOD STORY

Helen Jaskoski

Even silence was alive in his stories.
SILKO, "A Geronimo Story"

The eight short stories that form part of the mixed-genre *Storyteller* were all previously published, some more than once, before *Storyteller* appeared in 1981. They are the author's first published fiction, and several were written for university creative writing courses. Their range of form and fineness of execution are thus all the more remarkable; the stories are framed in modes as various as allegory, pastoral elegy, tragic drama, comedy of manners. Diverse as they are in form and mode, they share a common thematic concern: the nature of language and its function in maintaining identity, especially in a world of conflicting cultures, values, religions, and idioms. Language as it functions in narrative is paramount. Through all her writings Silko has been engaged in developing a theory of story and storytelling as constitutive of human identity and community, and these short stories, metafictions on the nature of story, are some of her earliest meditations on this theme.

"Storyteller," the first short story to appear in *Storyteller,* seems an odd choice for a book that is permeated with loving familiarity with the American Southwest: "Storyteller" traces the thoughts and memories of a Yupik Eskimo woman as she waits in a remote Alaska jail to be interrogated regarding the death of a storekeeper. A brooding fatalism hangs over this tragic tale of cruelty, misunderstanding, and revenge; its anonymous characters seem fated to act out some archaic, unfathomable myth of the bleak Arctic world. Yet laid out in this harsh tale is the doctrine that one's language is the origin and guardian of the self, an assertion that all the remaining short stories in *Storyteller* interrogate.

"Storyteller" is also exemplary in its intense focus on a singular, interior point of view. Notwithstanding her intimacy with Laguna and other native oral traditions, Silko's short fictions are determinedly modern and impressionistic in their foregrounding of human consciousness and its apperceptions. With one exception all the stories are either related by first-person narrators or closely filtered through a single central consciousness. This narrative emphasis also makes for considerable ambiguity, many unanswered questions, and much potential for unreliability, and it is characteristic of these stories that at crucial moments in their plots they raise important and unanswerable questions.

The setting of "Storyteller" is the upper Yukon delta, where newcomers are all "Gussucks," a Yupik word derived from "cossacks" and reflecting early Russian colonization. The natural world of the story comes filtered through the liminal consciousness of the protagonist, whose awareness fixates on the apparently imminent disintegration of the whole of nature where "all the boundaries between the river and hills and sky were lost in the density of the pale ice" (19). The protagonist's vision of nature reflects her perception of the Gussuck world as a hostile, colonizing force bent on dissolving the outlines of her own identity, and that identity is bound up with language. This is the major lesson of her brief boarding school education: "The dormitory matron pulled down her underpants and whipped her with a leather belt because she refused to speak English" (19). The sadistic sexual implications of this incident reverberate later in the story in the woman's encounter with the Gussuck storekeeper, and her embrace of responsibility for his death serves to maintain the nexus of language, story, and sexuality that grounds her sense of her imperiled self.

The power of silence looms throughout this story, figured in the devouring cold on the brink of annihilating time itself. This story about being a storyteller alludes to many stories — they include the old man's story about the bear, the storekeeper's and grandmother's conflicting stories about the girl's parents, the stories that priest and lawyer want her to tell the court, the story she begins to tell at the end of "Storyteller" — yet few of these stories are actually told. A powerful, cold, devouring silence appears to swallow up these acts of origination, even as stories themselves — as seen in the case of the old man — have the power to devour their tellers. Indeed, "Storyteller" is as much about silence and the absence of story as anything else.

A refrain of horror and disgust at lying runs through "Storyteller." Yet silence reigns here as well, and at critical moments the content of the lie is withheld, ambiguous. The protagonist remembers that the old man "had lied about what he would do with her if she came into his bed" (20). He lied, but what the lie was remains ambiguous and problematic. Had he promised her sex, and then been unable to perform? Or had he cajoled her with promises of innocent caresses, and then turned to molest her? This is one of many silences at critical moments in the story.

Two things are important. One is the fundamental opposition between lying and story — not between lying and truth. "Truth" is not an issue: only once is the word used, when the protagonist recognizes that "what the old man said was true" (20), but in this instance — one among many — of absence as the only real truth, the text does not contain what the old man said. The other important issue is the relationship between the protagonist's vision of the natural world and her unyielding fidelity to her truth as the only truth, a resolution that corresponds to her equally rigid insistence on her own language. Maintaining impermeable boundaries of language is her means of maintaining her sense of self in this disintegrating world.

This monotone world lacking outline, perspective, or landmarks reflects the problematics of moral navigation in the story. The storekeeper pursues the woman to his death in order to violate her. Yet her attorney does not consider self-defense as a motive or reason for her involvement in the incident, but rather cites accident and her supposed confusion as her defense (31). Neither does she consider the idea of self-defense, but relates her actions to her hatred of this storekeeper on account of the death of her parents, which was evidently caused by the mendacity of a "storeman" who may or may not be the same one who follows her onto the ice. In keeping with the myth-like atmosphere of the story, individual Others lose all outline and distinction, coalescing into the allegorical, archetypal figure of Outsider, exploiter, colonizer, Gussuck.

A comedic companion piece to the tragic vision of "Storyteller" is "A Geronimo Story," in which language protects identity and assists survival. "A Geronimo Story" follows the reminiscences of an old man called Andy who recalls the time when, as a young boy, he rode with his uncle Siteye, Captain Pratt and other Laguna Regulars to scout the whereabouts of Geronimo for a certain Major Littlecock of the United States Army. In "A Geronimo Story" it is a white man, Captain Pratt, who invokes the protective value of language. The fatuous Littlecock makes a sexual slur, in English, against the Laguna men; Siteye responds in kind, in Laguna. Pratt deflects the potential hostility — by lying: "I'm sorry, Major, but I don't speak the Laguna language very well" (221). "A Geronimo Story" contrasts the uncompromising univocality and rigid horror of lying that centers "Storyteller"; the hapless Littlecock must recognize and yet accept Pratt's obvious prevarication. Above all, "A Geronimo Story" insists that "language" is more than lexicon, orthography, or grammar. Although Littlecock lectures Pratt on the many Indian languages he has mastered, he cannot grasp the information the Laguna scouts tell him in English about Geronimo's real whereabouts. The sly sexual implications in the major's name also reflect the easygoing comedy of this tale, in contrast to the sadism and perversion that underlie the ominous, bitter world of "Storyteller." The name suits this man, with its implication of a physical equivalent for his meanness of mind and character. It also resonates against the narrator Andy's description of his uncle Siteye, large and strong like an elk.

A sense of the amplitude of time emerges as an important value in "A Geronimo Story." The narration begins with a scene of haste, confusion, and urgency as Andy heads for the corral full of agitated horses to saddle his own and his uncle's mounts preparatory to their journey. The story ends in a contemplative stillness as the men sit on their horses "for a long time remembering the way, the beauty of our journey" (223). A generous sense of time belongs to the man who is mature, a full human being. Siteye is a compelling storyteller because he knows how to choose his words thoughtfully and pace his narration so that his words "followed each other smoothly to tell a good story. . . . [E]ven the silence was alive in his stories" (215). It is not merely Captain Pratt's tea drinking that Siteye admires, but the fact that "He has plenty of time" (215) for his brew.

This leisurely sense of time and the satisfaction of adjusting one's life and story rhythms to it contrast sharply with the conflicted apprehension of time in "Storyteller." The Yupik protagonist of the latter story undergoes a nihilistic vision of the disappearance of time and the end of life, movement and journey. The enervating frost that brings machines to a standstill and confines human beings indoors permeates "Storyteller," a tale driven by a centripetal energy that fragments and devours the many stories that leave only traces in the text. Andy, on the other hand, as the narrator of his Geronimo story, renders his story in accordance with the aesthetics he has outlined in it. His narration is deliberate, precise, replete with detail: he has plenty of time to describe the exact color of his first horse, his mother's sewing machine, a Pie Town woman who walks with a limp.

The stern and absolute resistance in "Storyteller" to any impingement on one's language and identity also contrasts with the polyglot tolerance of "A Geronimo Story." The rigid certitude and unconditional rejection of compromise, the disdain for any truth but her own, that mark the protagonist of "Storyteller" stand in pointed contradiction to the adroit manipulation of language that Andy admires in "A Geronimo Story." Nowhere is the contrast between the stories more evident than in the climactic event of each, the encounter of protagonist and river. In the context of Andy's initiatory journey, the visionary moment occurs when he stops to drink from a mountain stream: "Cold water — a snow stream. I closed my eyes and I drank it. 'Precious and rare,' I said to myself, 'water that I have not tasted, water that I may never taste again'" (223). Andy's virtual (if not physical) immersion both places him "in the moment," as the phrase is, and lifts him out of time for that epiphanic instant. The revivifying, Heraclitean stream he savors offers a powerful counterstatement to the engulfing Alaskan river of "Storyteller," a current that sweeps away anyone not defended by the strongest of icy barriers, physical and psychological.

The absence of Geronimo in what is announced as his story also complements the absence of story in "Storyteller." In "A Geronimo Story" Geronimo is present only in the tracings he leaves — his abandoned campsites (if they are his) and the stories told about him. Pursued by soldiers and scouts, he retreats forever in an infinite regress of language and story. Poor Littlecock, like an old soldier left without enemies, can only fade away: "His face had a troubled, dissatisfied look; maybe he was wishing for the Sioux country . . . If he hadn't killed them all, he could still be up there chasing Sioux" (223). This is the paradox of hunting and storytelling (and reading): success is defeat, for the object is to search — not find.

I have noted that one of the most remarkable aspects of Silko's stories, especially in view of their production as the first attempts of the author, is their variety and virtuosity of form and type. Tragic drama, pastoral elegy, and comedy of manners are represented in "Tony's Story," "Lullaby," and "Uncle Tony's Goat," respectively. The first of these, "Tony's Story," emphasizes in its title the metafictional qualities that connect it with "Storyteller" and "A Geronimo Story."

"Tony's Story" opens on a scene of amiable multicultural synergy. It is the feast of San Lorenzo, August 11, and the seasonal festival includes both the statue of San Lorenzo from the Catholic Church and the traditional Pueblo Corn Dance. However, it soon becomes clear that carnival festivities mask endemic hostility and violence. Overt conflict erupts between a non-Indian police officer and two young men of the pueblo, Leon and Tony, when the officer suddenly and without provocation attacks Leon and injures him seriously.

The policeman's behavior exhibits an irrational malevolence, and Leon and Tony represent, respectively, reliance on reason or on faith to understand and deal with evil. The ex-serviceman Leon possesses, on the face of it, better means to deal with the officer: he understands "rights," he is familiar with procedures, he believes in committees, meetings, and letters to higher authorities. Moreover, like the soldier that he has been, he is willing, when persuasion and rhetoric fail, to enforce his rights with his .30–30. He should be better equipped for this conflict than the shy, fearful Tony who believes the officer is a witch and who wears an arrowhead amulet as protection. The ending is ambiguous. The officer is shot, after all, with the gun that Leon insists on carrying in spite of Tony's doubt regarding its efficacy against witches.

Although use of first-person narration throws emphasis on internal monologue and the reliability of perception, "Tony's Story" is structurally the most dramatic of Silko's stories. After the initial stage setting and introduction of the two protagonists, the action proceeds through three "acts," each centered on an exchange between Tony and Leon and the unnamed officer. The story's symmetry invites a moral reading in terms of retributive justice: the officer's savage attack on Leon in their first confrontation eventually begets the brutality he suffers in their third meeting. Between these violent encounters occurs the only verbal interchange between the officer and the two Pueblo men he has been harassing, and in it language is the signifier for the ignorance and misunderstanding that underlie and reinforce distortions of power in a colonized world. The officer asks a question that is at the very least rude and that may be a demand for privileged information to which he has no right: "What's your name?" The officer's tone paralyzes Tony and renders him mute: "His voice was high pitched and it distracted me from the meaning of the words" (126). Leon then invents a language deficit to ameliorate the situation: "He doesn't understand English so good" (126). The response is well suited to appease a powerful adversary in such a context: it reduces the individual characterized as language-impoverished to a condition of immaturity or even subhumanity and implicitly plays into the paternalistic colonial paradigm.

Regardless of his assertion of rights and of being just as good as anybody else, Leon's statement offers an object lesson in the survival skills needed to negotiate the colonial experience. The explanation, of course, is false; the issue is not unfamiliarity with any specific language but the inadequacy of language itself. Tony's temporary loss of language, of logos, is a response to the fundamentally irrational — *illogical* — bind he is in as a reasonable person subjected to the demands of an unreasonable but powerful interrogator. He cannot speak because there are literally no words that are appropriate to his situation.

In its treatment of the theme of colonialism and its power relations "Tony's Story" is a companion piece to "Storyteller." In the arctic isolation of "Storyteller" the colonial enterprise manifests in the aggressive machines of corporate enterprise and the indifference of profiteering. "Tony's Story" by contrast depicts the colonial setup of ostensibly parallel governmental institutions:

tribal police parallel state police, the local Indian governor mirrors the federal Bureau of Indian Affairs, tribal prohibition statutes stand in place of state liquor regulations. The parallel breaks down, however, when it comes to the military: Leon has served in the United States Army, but there is no parallel Pueblo army. The absence is significant. Power is sham in the parallel colonial institutions: they are either impotent or they actually replicate and enforce the colonialist enterprise.

If "Tony's Story" offers tragic drama, "Uncle Tony's Goat" combines comedy of manners and initiation story in a seemingly transparent tale of pastoral nostalgia. The anonymous narrator serenely reconstructs a childhood perspective, and the aura of timelessness in the personal memory of life on the family's ranch coincides with the sense of timeless, pastoral life within the whole story. The narration suggests a verbal equivalent to the luminous placidity of Dutch genre painting, the vision of a world where time is the turning of the season, a September afternoon: "My uncle and my father were sitting on the bench outside the house when we walked by. It was September now, and the farming was almost over, except for bringing home the melons and a few pumpkins. They were mending ropes and bridles and feeling the afternoon sun" (172). It is a picture that suggests the timeless, traditional, "authentic" Pueblo world that artists like Georgia O'Keeffe and D. H. Lawrence sought in Taos and Santa Fe in the early twentieth century.

In classical comedy youth defeats age so that life can overcome death: the young and vigorous displace the old and impotent. "Uncle Tony's Goat" can be read as a miniature rite of passage, a wry, nuanced comedy of manners in which the family drama moves the narrator into a new position within a subtly altered dynamic. Decoding the gestures, asides, and throwaway lines reveals the subtext of sexual contestation, reversal, and reconciliation. When the children attack their families' female goats with their homemade arrows, more is at stake than the animals' annoyance, as both the narrator and the male goat are aware: "The billy goat never forgot the bows and arrows, even after the bows had cracked and split and the crooked, whittled arrows were all lost" (173). Never mind the inadequacy of their tools; the children's assault on the goats challenges the prerogative of their uncle and his close comrade, his powerful, lusty goat. So, the narrator recollects, it came as no surprise when the billy goat found his moment to attack.

The goat's assault on the narrator is the turning point in the story, an opening for the emergence of a female authority to balance the masculine contestation of power that is seen to have gotten out of hand when the child lies bleeding in the dirt of the goat pen. The narrator implies a subtle shift in the power coordinates of the household with indication of the force of his mother's decree that the goat must go and relates how the child and his mother watched Uncle Tony ride off on his old roan gelding after the missing goat.

In the end, the goat's escape satisfies everyone, and the contours of the classic comic design have been filled out. The (scape)goat has been released into the wilderness, taking along the onus of the narrator's guilt and the family's distress. The social order has been restored, even invigorated, as the comedic formula dictates, as Uncle Tony can now relish the thought of his virile comrade living wild and free. Far from being a loss, the goat's escape releases him into a new identity, contented hunter emerging from and replacing an erstwhile rather cranky shepherd.

A pastoral mood also infuses three of the remaining stories: "The Man to Send Rain Clouds," "Lullaby," and "Yellow Woman." The first of these, "The Man to Send Rain Clouds," is unique in its detached perspective and shifting point of view. It is possible to read this deceptively simple account of the burial of an old man as a critique of single-minded quests for authenticity and the pursuit of cultural survival through avoidance of contamination. The contrasting example of such essentialism occurs in "Storyteller," where we see the protagonist invest her identity solely in the avoidance of contamination, maintaining at all cost her exclusive monologue, "the story" that must be told "without lies." At the opposite reach from her is the totally assimilated Eskimo jailer who wants to speak only English. These two characters represent the extremes of identity politics: his embrace of compromise — politics — results in the erasure of identity, while any accommodation — any politics — is for her a mortal threat to identity. "The Man to Send Rain Clouds" offers, in contrast, a sense of culture not as a monologue whose purity must be maintained regardless of the cost, but as a dynamic process, a matter of strategic negotiations, respectful deliberation and consultation, a sensitivity to nuances of communication, and above all a sense of proportion regarding which things are matters of principles that must be maintained and which are secondary means that may be adjusted to suit the occasion.

The idea of cultural symbiosis evoked in this story emerges in the careful delineation of perceptions of time. During the day time is marked off in different ways. The body of the old shepherd Teofilo is found near daybreak under a cottonwood tree, a tree that figures in myths about the return of the sun; Teofilo's interment is completed as the sun disappears behind a mesa said to be the house of the sun. It is late March, almost time for the sun to set beyond that mesa at the point marking the equinox. Between these two events the people caring for the old man's remains take their noon meal marked by the ringing of the Angelus on "twin bells from the king of Spain" (184). The old man's relatives respond to the subtle markings of the passage of time. Louise's thoughtfulness for the old man's and the village's welfare extends to including the priest's holy water; her quiet mention of it sends Ken and Leon in their truck to fetch the village priest, Father Paul, to bless the grave. Here is an inclusiveness characteristic of the community whose vision can embrace ancient indigenous traditions, motor vehicles, Father Paul, holy water, and even the king of Spain.

In "Lullaby" and "Yellow Woman" the pastoral environment is a more conflicted place, a geographical and psychological space where a certain wariness, an edginess, and the constant potential for violence permeate the seemingly placid landscape. In "Lullaby" the constituents of pastoral elegy frame a painful story of exploitation, misunderstanding, and loss. The protagonist is an elderly Navajo woman named Ayah who waits one evening for her husband to emerge from a bar with their bottle of wine, then goes back, looks for him in the bar, finally finds him on the street, and walks up the road with him to wait, it appears, for death. During the short time, perhaps an hour or two, during which these banal events transpire, the narration follows her reverie as she recollects how much of her life has been lost to her and, in a process of grief and peacemaking, comes to terms with it.

Ayah has much to grieve for: the death of her eldest son, Jimmie, in a distant war; the deaths in infancy of other children; the forced removal and consequent alienation of her two remaining offspring; a long estrangement from her husband, Chato. Ayah's world has been contaminated and damaged by alien elements, which have entered her life by way of a language she has grown to hate. Proud of knowing how to sign her name, she had unwittingly signed the papers that removed her children from her. As she reflects on that loss she recalls how for many years she had blamed her husband for teaching her how to sign her name, thus giving her a weapon she had unwittingly used against herself and her children.

Finally, as the story ends, she appears to confront and accept her own death. The story portrays Ayah as realizing stages of grief identified in the literature of therapy for dying and grief: denial, anger, despair, and finally reconciliation and peace. The word "mourning" repeats like a melancholy refrain in the story accompanying these memories. On the day of the story, however, each recollection carries with it a sense of understanding and — finally — of peace. Consequent on the death of those nearest her is the more abstract but no less felt loss of heritage, culture, and way of life. There will be no children and grandchildren to teach and nurture in the way her mother and grandmother had educated and cared for Ayah, no infants to be lulled by the lyrics she sings to herself at the end of the story. Art, religion, language, natural history — all are being lost. The harshness and emptiness of present life correspond to the coldness of the alien society that surrounds the Navajo world.

Within the story Ayah confronts these hostile Others as she searches the bar for her husband. She feels that the Spanish-speaking patrons are looking at her "like she was a spider crawling slowly across the room. They were afraid; she could feel the fear" (48), and as she leaves, "She felt satisfied that the men in the bar feared her" (49). In the view of the non-Indian drinkers the comparison with a spider might inspire irritation or contempt for a creature denigrated as a common pest. Ayah's view of the matter is completely different. The spider, called Grandmother Spider or Spider Old Woman, is a revered figure of wisdom for all the peoples of the Southwest. She is the creator, spinning the world from her body, and she inspires abject fear and obedience. A weaver like Ayah, Spider Woman can help her children out of dangerous situations by giving them stern warnings and good advice; she is benevolent but terribly powerful, death to her enemies and those who ignore or disobey. The episode is a moment of truth for the reader of the story as well: the informed reader will understand the importance of Ayah's comparison to the spider, while those who remain outside Ayah's field of communication, like the men drinking in the bar, will think they see only a delusional old woman.

Forming a triad with "Storyteller" and "Lullaby," a third female consciousness emerges in the story titled "Yellow Woman." The narrator, a young mother living a placid if boring existence with her family in an unnamed Pueblo village, elopes with a handsome, masterful stranger who calls himself Silva. She experiences the fulfillment of wishes familiar to readers of romantic novels, playing out in her brief interlude the fantasy of an exciting anonymous encounter unburdened by guilt or consequences. The story follows the narrator's internal process of interpreting and making sense of her escapade, and the model she finds to rationalize her predicament is the traditional Laguna figure of Yellow Woman. The protagonist explains her adventure to herself as a process of becoming part of the tradition that lives in the Yellow Woman stories.

"Yellow Woman" has elements of a romantic idyll, yet even within its erotic escape there may be unpleasant contact, full of misunderstanding and the potential for violence. Silva is a cattle rustler, and the disintegration of their sweet interlude begins when the couple encounters an irate rancher on an isolated trail. This is a critical moment in the story as much for its representation of the narrator's point of view as for the moment of imminently violent confrontation. Language difference is multilayered. Silva speaks the narrator's language, the language of Yellow Woman's people, presumably to protect her from the rancher's pursuit. She then attributes the rancher's anger to his inability to understand their language: "The white man got angry when he heard Silva speak in a language he couldn't understand," and moments later offers a complicated analysis of his inner state of mind: "The rancher must have been unarmed because he was very frightened and if he had a gun he would have pulled it out then" (61). Certitude like this about events beyond knowing is characteristic of the unreliable narrator and paradoxically moves this abrupt confrontation with the prosaic real world into a realm less certain than the dreamlike, magical lovers' encounter. Ambiguity clouds the outcome of the confrontation as well: "I think four shots were fired—I remember hearing four hollow explosions that reminded me of deer hunting. There could have been more shots after that, but I couldn't hear them" (61). Who or what was shot, or even if there really were gunshots, is part of the already receding liminal world the protagonist is leaving behind to return to the certainties of husband, mother, grandmother, and the making of Jell-O.

N. Scott Momaday has said many times that we are who we imagine ourselves to be, and that the greatest of gifts is to imagine oneself richly. "Yellow Woman" is about a young woman who is engaged in imagining herself richly. All the events of the story are portrayed as they come filtered through the consciousness of the first-person narrator, and much of the story's ambiguity and open-endedness results from this filtering. The protagonist's inner monologue weaves together different planes of reality: game or story, everyday prosaic existence, and magic, myth or the supernatural as she engages in a process of speculation, attempting to interpret and define the reality she has entered and to understand the new self that her interpretations have created.

As a study in the work of the imagination "Coyote Holds a Full House in His Hand" forms a companion piece to "Yellow Woman." Both stories associate their protagonists with figures from powerful myths: Yellow Woman and Coyote. The central character of "Yellow Woman" is otherwise anonymous, while the only name attributed to the protagonist of "Coyote Holds" is Sonny Boy, the nickname his mother had called him. Like the avatar of Yellow Woman, Sonny Boy also engages in imagining himself richly.

Although the story lacks the voice of a first-person raconteur, the diction that renders the protagonist's central consciousness suggests internal monologue. The passage relating the protagonist's analysis of the village postmistress is exemplary of Silko's rendering of local diction and also emphasizes the ambiguity inherent in this protagonist's interpretation of events.

The Mexican woman thought Pueblo men were great lovers—he knew this because he heard her say so to another Mexican woman one day while he was finishing his strawberry soda on the other side of the dry goods section. In the summer he spent a good number of hours there watching her because she wore sleeveless blouses that revealed her fat upper arms, full and round, and the tender underarm creases curving to her breasts. They had not noticed he was still there leaning on the counter behind a pile of overalls; " . . . the size of a horse" was all that he had heard, but he knew what she was talking about. They were all like that, those Mexican women. That was all they talked about when they were alone. "As big as a horse" — he knew that much Spanish and more too, but she had never treated him nice, not even when he brought her the heart-shaped box of candy, carried it on the bus all the way from Albuquerque. He didn't think it was being older than her because she was over thirty herself — it was because she didn't approve of men who drank. That was the last thing he did before he left town; he did it because he had to, because liquor was illegal on the reservation. So the last thing he did was have a few drinks to carry home with him the same way other people stocked up on lamb nipples or extra matches. She must have smelled it on his breath when he handed her the candy because she didn't say anything and she left the box under the counter by the old newspapers and balls of string. The cellophane was never opened and the fine gray dust that covered everything in the store finally settled on the pink satin bow. The postmaster was jealous of the letters that were coming, but she was the one who had sent him into the arms of Mrs. Sekakaku. (257–58)

Like the rest of "Coyote Holds" this paragraph is notable for its length, as it meanders from the protagonist's memory of eavesdropping on a conversation in Spanish while loitering in the general store to generalizations about all Mexican women to recollections of the box of candy to rationalizations regarding his drinking to observations on last-minute provision purchases and finally to the supposed jealousy of the postmistress.

The passage is rich in metafictive possibility. The sketching out of the protagonist's interpretive strategies as he analyses the postmistress serves as a cautionary model for the reader approaching the whole story — and for the reader approaching American Indian literature generally. Indeed, Sonny Boy listening to the Mexican women gossip is not too unlike the reader encountering native texts in translation, although he does have an advantage in being able to understand some Spanish. He hears a single phrase, which is repeated in altered wording: first, "the size of a horse" and then "As big as a horse." The postmistress's actual words in Spanish are absent (as are the originals for most "original" American Indian texts in translation), and it is impossible to know what she "really said"; all the reader is left with is an ambiguous interpretation

shaped to the libidinous requirements of Sonny Boy's fantasy. Similar tempta-
tions to fill out the fragments of dictated stories and lyrics have beguiled many
a critic into wonderfully fantastic readings of native texts in translation, notwithstanding the absence of any knowledge of the originals.

The cellophane-wrapped candy gathering dust under the post office counter
is an emblem for the series of substitutions, displacements, and deferrals that
constitute the protagonist's adventure. His gratification consistently involves a
high degree of self-textualization, and Sonny Boy's most satisfying encounters
with the world tend to occur by means of textualized displacements: his amo-
rous letters to Mrs. Sekakaku, his preference for correspondence school, most
poignantly his habit of carrying photographs of himself in his wallet so "he
could tell people about himself while they looked at the photos in the plastic
pages of his wallet" (260). The photographs, it turns out, are pictures that
strangers have taken of him in front of upscale bars and restaurants that he has
never entered. Even the climax of his physical encounter with the Hopi women,
in which tactile gratification finally replaces voyeurism, is described in terms of
distancing and displacement in the image of a hawk circling over its prey.

Not surprisingly in a story alluding to the exploits of Coyote, sexual gratification is often figured in animal associations, beginning with the inferences
on horses in his post office reverie. The drollest as well as the most highly
developed of these animal tropes in the story is Mrs. Sekakaku's pet dog. As in
"Storyteller," the way in which a dog is connected with sexuality is key to the
story's atmosphere and tone. The rage and depravity that pervade the tragic
world of "Storyteller" are figured in the impotent oil driller's talisman of
potency, a picture of a woman copulating with a dog, and for all his sense of
his superiority to the Gussucks who keep dogs in their houses, the old man of
that story links his and the protagonist's sexual appetites with the urges of the
village dogs. Standing in vivid contrast is the comic air of "Coyote Holds,"
simultaneously bemused and priapic, summed up in the vignette featuring
Mrs. Sekakaku's little dog, which Sonny Boy at first mistakes for a big rat
when he sees it emerge from her outdoor oven. Sonny Boy immediately recognizes the erotic dimension of this vision as he reflects that "Only lonely widows
let their dogs sleep in the bread oven," and promptly addresses the possessive
canine with an announcement of his intention to displace the tyrannical
pooch: "Not much longer little doggy" (261). Mrs. Sekakaku confirms his
view of the dog as his sexual rival when she signals her invitation to him after
the ceremony at Aunt Mamie's house by kicking the dog and blocking up the
oven with an orange crate. True to his usual practice, however, the narrator
declines this invitation to direct instead of displaced gratification. The story
ends as he is en route back to Laguna — as Coyote is always "going along" in

his stories—where he anticipates the superior pleasure of a male bonding ritual in which he can hold the "full house" of ladies in his snapshot before the admiring gaze of his fellows. This indeed is the triumph of storytelling: to find in narration a pleasure superior to sex.

Modern literature in English is rich in short fiction, and particularly rich in collections of short fiction that create the atmosphere, values and texture of particular communities. Joyce's *Dubliners, The Golden Apples* of Eudora Welty, the short story collections of Faulkner and Hemingway spring immediately to mind. Some might argue that their short fiction represents the finest work of these authors. The short stories of Leslie Marmon Silko, splendidly crafted, nuanced, lovingly detailed, belong in this company.

SPINNING A FICTION OF CULTURE

Leslie Marmon Silko's Storyteller

Elizabeth McHenry

S peaking at a meeting of the English Institute in August 1979, Leslie Marmon Silko warned her audience about the structure of the presentation they were about to hear:

> For those of you accustomed to a structure that moves from point A to point B to point C, this presentation may be somewhat difficult to follow because the structure of Pueblo expression resembles something like a spider's web—with many little threads radiating from a center, criss-crossing each other. As with the web, the structure will emerge as it is made and you must simply listen and trust, as the Pueblo people do, that meaning will be made.[1]

This warning applies equally well to *Storyteller,* whose patterning is not readily apparent to those unfamiliar with oral stories in Pueblo society. *Storyteller* sits in seeming defiance of the very written English tradition in which its author chooses to work: in it, Silko creates a text governed not by the standards of the European literary tradition but by a mixture of written genres, written transcriptions of conversations and internal memories, and photographs.

At the outset, this difference is not apparent. Apart from *Storyteller*'s rather atypical physical shape, the publication trappings of Silko's text suggest that, as a literary object, *Storyteller* follows the traditional conventions of bookmaking. The book's front cover, title, and acknowledgment pages contain information that maintains the usual communication between publisher and book buyer; the back cover is complete with an appropriate "blurb" about the "magical spell" Silko "weaves" into her text. In keeping with these mandatory publication elements, Silko's name appears in many places as the book's author.[2]

Beyond these standard introductory pages, however, everything about the text and the presentation of *Storyteller* suggests Silko's denial of conventional authorship. Following *Storyteller*'s title pages, Silko seems to reclaim from the world of Western publishing houses and traditional rites of publication the interior of her book for her own objectives. The result is an overall design and textual construction that is distinctly nontraditional: inside, among the mixture of genres presented, are no numbered divisions, no chapter headings. Silko does not introduce each piece or "announce" the connections between her autobiographical, fictive, or mythic stories. Instead, the "space" where chapter headings might be is filled by four-leafed symbols that merely suggest division. The table of contents appears at the back—not the front—of the book. Only the pagination remains of the usual published book features. Effectively refusing to be categorized according to recognizable dimensions, the book is off-sized. Neither paperback-size nor picture book–size, *Storyteller* quite literally does not "match" any standard book on the shelf.

Silko's ultimate subversion of these trappings of literary publication is significant, but her seeming independence of vision and desire to see anew her work and community in the midst of established forms of presentation should not be mistakenly associated with "experimental" literature. Rather, it is more accurate to consider that Silko's nonlinear form of narrative appears as it does because she sees it as the only appropriate vehicle of expression that will contain the transcription of her fragmented and collective experience. Readers trained to identify the single generic classification of a literary work will be stumped by *Storyteller*, which is as much an autobiography as it is a collection of poems or annotated photographs. But the text is not simply a multigeneric work composed of previously published short fiction and poetry, personal narratives, pictures, memories, and retellings of traditional stories and legends. Although all these elements are present in the book, Silko combines these genres to create "a single form, a new thing which grows naturally out of [these] other forms of experience and expression."[3]

"[A]lways . . . curious about narrative being combined with visual images" (Lace, 62), Silko punctuates the unorthodox *Storyteller* with family photographs. *Storyteller* begins with Silko relating autobiographically that "[p]hotographs have always had special significance / with the people of my family and the people at Laguna"; she establishes a crucial connection between the "hundreds of photographs" in the "tall Hopi basket" and the "stories as she remembers them."[4] As the "imaginative heart" of the text, the pictures provide important visual aids to allow readers to "see" the specific people and places about which stories are told (Lace, 67). Silko explains that "[t]he photographs are here because they are part of many of the stories / and because many of the stories can be traced in the photographs" (ST, 1). She sees the pictures — from posed portraits to haphazard snapshots — as a vital part of the text as a whole.

Silko's positioning of these photographs in *Storyteller* figures strongly in what she sets out to do and ultimately accomplishes. In a series of letters to poet James Wright written while in the process of composing *Storyteller*, Silko debates whether it is a "wise decision" to use snapshots, which are potentially "inarticulate" or worse, "boring or meaningless if one doesn't have an identity of sorts for the person or places in them" (Lace, 65). The frequency with which Silko's letters to Wright during this time focus on and return to the question of whether to include photographs in her new publication suggest the extent to which Silko was virtually haunted not only by her artistic decision but also by the pictures themselves. Indeed, the photographs Silko remembers from the Hopi basket and reprints in *Storyteller* do more than simply evoke relatives or remind her of past events: "I am interested now," she writes, "in the memory and imagination of mine which come out of these photographs — maybe I am more affected by what I see than I had heretofore realized. Strange to think that you *heard* something — that you heard someone describe a place or a scene when in fact you saw a picture of it, saw it with your own eyes" (Lace, 65).[5]

In *Storyteller*, the family photographs Silko was shown and looked at throughout her life act as puzzle pieces that let in partial images of the past: the process of restoring pictures to their narrative contexts provoked questions never before asked or answered about Silko's sense of self, family, immediate community, and the larger myths and legends of her region. Through these images, Silko introduces her own entirely new discursive system, one that tests the value of recent claims by social scientists and humanists that the stories of literary writers often function as effective vehicles for recording ethnography in twentieth-century America. Increasingly aware of their failure to bridge the gap between the richness of lived experience and the paucity of the professional written product, anthropologists and other social scientists have been among the first to flag the important confluence of fiction, autobiography, and ethnography toward recording cultures and identities.[6] The resulting "Literature of Culture" demands attention in two significant ways: as a model for the analysis of culture and identity and as a source of information or "data" on the diversity of experience in twentieth-century America.

FAMILY TIES

Silko begins *Storyteller* with her own story. It is a story that cannot be told exclusively in words: she relies on pictures of her family and the place they are from to recall and reestablish essential contexts. The opening photograph is of Silko's great-grandparents, Robert G. Marmon and Marie Anaya Marmon; they are "holding [her] grandpa Hank" (ST, 2, 269). The next photograph, three pages later, is of Silko herself as a small child with her Aunt Susie. Throughout *Storyteller,* members of Silko's immediate and extended family "become" specific individuals through their visual introduction. In the book's third photograph, Marie Anaya Marmon reappears in the less formal and more familiar form of Grandma A'mooh; she is reading a story to Silko's sisters, Wendy and Gigi. Later in the text, a photograph of Grandpa Hank shows him as an adult with his automobile, a 1933 Auburn; Grandpa Hank's son, Silko's father, is shown in the desert with his camera. Something of the particular landscape and community is revealed through the photographs, as well as family rituals. Silko's explanation of a picture of five dead deer suggests one such ritual: "My uncle Polly and I have just finished arranging the bucks on the porch of the cabin so they can have their pictures taken" (ST, 78, 270).

The photographs through which Silko tells the story of her own genealogical context provide not only the literal frame for the text of *Storyteller* but situate her in a continuous generational line of Laguna storytellers. The last three photographs in the book bring the story of Silko's family full circle. The first is of Silko herself as an adult, taken where she now lives "in the Cottonwood Wash below Wasson Peak in the Tucson Mountains, Arizona" (ST, 266–67, 274). The second is of Grandpa Hank as a young man. The third picture includes the three generations that precede her own: her father as a boy, Grandpa Hank's brother, and her great-grandfather. By arranging the photographs at the beginning and the end of the book, Silko deemphasizes the strictly autobiographical dimension to *Storyteller* by subordinating an isolated view of herself as the text's sole creator and subject to a view of herself in the context of her family and community and their culture.

Silko's position in *Storyteller* is firmly established as a link in the ongoing process of remembering the stories of her family in order to further the survival of their personal, communal, and cultural history. Her responsibility in this chain is clear: "As with any generation," Silko explains early in *Storyteller,* storytelling "depends upon each person / listening and remembering a portion / and it is together — / all of us remembering what we have heard together — / that creates the whole story / the long story of the people" (ST, 7). Silko's contribution to this process is *Storyteller,* in which she uses her voice to revoice

Aunt Susie, Grandma A'mooh, Grandpa Hank, her father (Lee Marmon), and others, humbly admitting "I remember only a small part [of the whole story of the people]. / But this is what I remember" (ST, 7).[7]

A great deal of what she remembers and what becomes the written rendition of *Storyteller* relies on her relationship and experiences with these various members of her family. Growing up in Laguna, Silko's childhood memories revolve around stories of her ancestors and older relatives, most of whom lived in close proximity. It is in the medley of these older, familial voices that Silko came to learn about her culture and herself; she is figuratively nourished and instructed by her family's stories. Examples of this abound in Silko's presentations of members of her family: Silko's Aunt Alice provides an especially touching one of how important family stories were to her education and development. Silko's metanarrative voice sets the story up: "Aunt Alice told my sisters and me this story one time when she came to stay with us while our parents had gone up to Mt. Taylor deer hunting. I was seven years old the last time I had to stay behind. And I felt very sad about not getting to go hunting. Maybe that's why Aunt Alice told us this story" (ST, 82). The story Aunt Alice tells on this disappointing day sets the sisters up with the promise of possibilities. "You know," Aunt Alice tells them, even though this information will be a part of the story, "there have been Laguna women / who were good hunters / who could hunt as well as any of the men" (ST, 82). Aunt Alice's story is about a girl-hunter, Kochininako, who overcomes the unexpected obstacles she encounters: she is a "young laguna girl / who was a fine hunter / who hunted deer and rabbits / just like the boys and the men did" (ST, 82).

Aunt Alice's story is entertaining, but it also offers perspective. Laguna women have always been hunters. And the girls will not always be left behind: by emphasizing that young girls can be clever and courageous hunters — better hunters, often, than young boys — Aunt Alice builds their self-esteem.[8] When they are allowed to go on hunting trips, they will remember that all hunters meet with unexpected dangers from time to time. Such obstacles, however, may be overcome with calm and clever thought. The end of Aunt Alice's story, which merges legend with the physical reality of the Laguna landscape, provides perhaps the most important part of the story's lesson. The girl-hunter who has been threatened by an insatiable creature calls on her brothers to help her finish him off. Together they cut out the creature's heart and throw it as far as they can: Aunt Alice reports that the heart landed "right over here / near the river / between Laguna and Paguate / where the road turns to go / by the railroad tracks / right around / from John Paisano's place — / that big rock there / looks just like a heart /" (ST, 87–88). By identifying a very real and ordinary rock as a part of the story, Aunt Alice turns an unremarkable aspect of the girls' landscape into a landmark. The story and the land become connected: each time they pass the rock, the Marmon girls will be reminded of their limitless possibilities.

Silko's inclusion of Aunt Alice's story suggests how she began to discover her own identity through the storytelling of her relatives. Aunt Alice contributes to Silko's developing sense of self by telling a story in which Silko is able to see herself. In a *Sun Tracks* interview, Silko explicitly comments on this crucial value of the stories she heard growing up: "People tell those stories about you and your family or about others and they begin to create your identity. In a sense, you are told who you are, or you know who you are by the stories that are told about you."[9] True to Aunt Alice's prediction, Silko does eventually have her own hunting story to tell. Although it appears earlier in *Storyteller* than Aunt Alice's story to her nieces, Silko's own story of a hunting trip on which she is the girl-hunter filled with curiosity and fear makes a deep impression on her. Her sighting of a real or imaginary "sleeping, not dead" bear takes its place with the other family hunting stories (ST, 79).

In *Storyteller,* Silko acknowledges the centrality of these family stories to her own childhood while also signaling the changing forms of storytelling in the community. Her memory of Aunt Susie early in the text suggests that both oral and, more recently, written storytelling are essential to the passing on of knowledge. Although Aunt Susie "was of a generation, / the last generation here at Laguna, / that passed down an entire culture / by word of mouth / an entire history / an entire vision of the world / which depended on memory / and retelling by subsequent generations" (ST, 6), Silko's first memory of her is at work at "her kitchen table / with her books and papers spread over the oil cloth" (ST, 4). In Aunt Susie, Silko identifies an important mix: although she "took time from her studies and writing / to answer [my] questions / and to tell [me] all she knew on a subject . . . she had come to believe very much in books / and in schooling" (ST, 4). Silko establishes the importance of a continuing oral and a newer but necessary written tradition in part through Aunt Susie's understanding of her changing culture:

> She must have realized
> that the atmosphere and conditions
> which had maintained this oral tradition in
>   Laguna culture
> had been irrevocably altered by the European
>   intrusion —
> principally by the practice of taking the children
> away from Laguna to Indian schools,

taking the children away from the tellers who had
in all past generations
told the children
an entire culture, an entire identity of a people. (ST, 6)

Aunt Susie's stories reflect her awareness of the changing obligations of the storyteller through her obvious sensitivity for the role. At the heart of one of these is a little girl who wants her mother to fix her some "Yashtoah," an unfamiliar word and cultural item for her young modern audience. But Aunt Susie's telling of the story includes explanation: " 'Yashtoah' means / it's sort of curled-up, you know, dried, / just as mush dries on top" (ST, 8). Aunt Susie's (and Silko's own) narration continues throughout the text of the story, as they together explain the meanings of words such as "bun'yah'nah" ("west lake"), and concepts such as that of entering a Pueblo house from the top instead of the bottom floor or carrying firewood — with the help of "yucca thongs" — on one's back.[10]

In *Storyteller*, Silko is picking up — through her written storytelling — where her Aunt Susie left off: although she acknowledges the great differences between oral and written storytelling she is, like her Aunt Susie, neither unrealistic nor sentimental about the changes in oral transmission or the communal changes that have increased the importance of writing stories down.[11] Equally conscious of her own expanded and nonpresent audience, Silko emphasizes that cultural transmission involves more than just the retelling of stories; the entire context in which the transmission takes place must be re-created. Again and again throughout *Storyteller*, Silko's introduction of family members and the animation of their lives through pictures and precise details indicates her belief that to tell a story correctly involves bringing those reading the text into a position similar to that of the original audience of the story: they must be brought into the very presence of the storyteller. Silko must somehow allow us to "see" and to "sense" something of the storyteller, to be familiar with the teller's history, and finally to see and hear them tell their stories. Of Aunt Susie's telling of the "Yashtoah" story, for instance, Silko says "[s]he had certain phrases, certain distinctive words / she used in her telling." Silko insists that we hear these features because they are central to her understanding of the stories: "I write when I still hear / her voice as she tells the story" (ST, 7).

Silko's comments that frame Aunt Susie's telling not only distinguish her Aunt Susie's storytelling from that of all other tellers by the quality of her voice but also introduce the importance of how the story is told. The metanarration that surrounds the story of the little girl lets the reader in on the setting of the story's telling in a way an ethnographer's literal translation would not. Silko's interest lies in the telling as an event, and she intends to reveal fully Aunt Susie's discourse. Thus, the memory of the "great tenderness and great feeling" (ST, 15) of Aunt Susie's telling, which Silko includes in her metanarrative closure of Aunt Susie's story, adds to her reassessment of the early stories as well as her emphasis on narration. Also important is the proper acknowledgment of Aunt Susie's language: it is not altered to contribute a sentimental quality to the text but remains faithful to a vocabulary that moves between her own memories of stories she heard and that of the "books and papers" on the kitchen table.

Silko's assessment of the difficulty of conveying what was traditionally oral cultural material and stories is expressed again and again in the text. In one episode, Silko records a conversation with her friend Nora, whose grandchildren had found "a library book [with Silko's] 'Laguna Coyote' poem in it." "We all enjoyed it so much," Nora's critical voice begins, "but I was telling the children / the way my grandpa used to tell it / is longer." "Yes, that's the trouble with writing," Silko responds, "You can't go on and on the way we do / when we tell stories around here. / People who aren't used to it get tired" (ST, 110). As Bernard A. Hirsch has observed in his analysis of Storyteller, Silko uses this short passage to identify at least two problems with written storytelling. First, writing seemingly eliminates the life from a story by freezing it on the page and removing it from its storytelling context: confined to the printed "version," the story is no longer allowed to expand or change. Second, the writing of stories potentially removes them from the living and present storytellers, the people who, in their telling of the story, nourish it and supply it with meaning.[12]

But from Silko's perspective, despite the "trouble with writing," what Nora does with this written version of the story is cause for great celebration. Out of the experience of reading with her grandchildren Silko's written form of a traditional story, Nora creates a new occasion and context for oral storytelling by telling her grandchildren her grandfather's version of the story. Silko's written poem thus becomes an important contribution to the oral tradition despite its printed form. This presentation supports the new realities of Native American life, while providing some explanation of the old ones.[13]

COMMUNITY TIES

Nora's voice is only one of the communal though nonfamilial voices that build and nourish Storyteller. Indeed, the text that bears Leslie Marmon Silko's name is a prime linguistic and literary example of theorist Mikhail Bakhtin's observation that "[a]ll there is to know about the world is not exhausted by a particular discourse about it."[14] Although Bakhtin posits in *The Dialogic Imagination* that the genre of the novel specifically provides the closest literary example of dialogic discourse, it is more useful in relation to *Storyteller* to consider a less genre-specific idea of "novelized discourse." The basis for Bakhtin's novelized discourse is a consideration of human language as "heteroglossic, polyvocal": the speech of each human being is enabled not so much by language as a system as by the actual speech of other individuals. "What is realized in the novel," Bakhtin writes, "is the process of coming to know one's own language as it is perceived in someone else's language, coming to know one's own belief system in someone else's system" (DI, 365). Silko presents *Storyteller* as such a polyphonic text, taking great pains to acknowledge and insist that even her own voice is a product of many voices. She retells tales and myths in relation to other tellers and their different versions and differing ways of telling stories. By prefacing her own tellings "[t]his is the way Aunt Susie told the story" (ST, 7), or " 'Uncle Tony's Goat' is from a story Simon [Ortiz] told me when he called one morning about 4 A.M." (ST, 170), Silko's text implies its communal authorship: it acknowledges the other voices on which her voice is dependent and a part while also leaving the story open to future tellings and other versions.

In this sense, Silko's work in *Storyteller* is consistent with the need Bakhtin identifies to "uncover the multiplicity of languages in a cultural world" (DI, 367). As many critics have noted, Bakhtin's distrust of monological power and his preoccupation with the representation of nonhomogeneous wholes must spring in part from his experience with totalitarian Stalinism. Such monologism is comparable in literary terms to forms of written discourse that act to subordinate or suppress other voices toward the imposition of a single, authoritative, and absolute voice. Silko's attempt to represent her own self-definition — her own origins and her story — in relation to the pluralism of her environment insists that there is no such thing, in Silko's *Storyteller,* as an "absolute form of thought" (DI, 367). In Bakhtin's terms, the text works to record the changing and contestable conditions and the dialogical interplay of voices that surround its author.[15]

To encompass and represent an entire range of human possibility, Silko must rely not only on her own experience but also on her creativity. In *Storyteller,* Silko implies that stories — whether fact or fiction, "true" or mythical — are essential to both art and ethnography. Even Silko's fictional stories in *Storyteller* are presented without the connotation of falsehood: they are something fashioned, as all truths are. In *Storyteller,* fictional stories serve to emphasize that all cultural and historical stories are more accurately described as "partial truths" than "fact" or "fiction." Rather than standing in opposition to truth, fiction takes its place with other forms toward the representation of culture. "Storyteller," the title story of the collection, illustrates the extent to which fiction makes a unique contribution to this effort. In "Storyteller," Silko steps outside her native pueblo, setting the story instead among another native people, the Inuit, on the shores of the Kuskokwim River near Bethel, Alaska. The story tells of three Eskimos, an old couple and a girl, the woman's grand-daughter, all of whom live in a shack near a village where white (Gussuck) oil workers are employed.

Although Silko has said that "Storyteller" is about "the dimensions of the process" of storytelling, this overriding theme is somewhat difficult to see at first.[16] "Storyteller" is immediately preceded by a short vignette on Silko's great-grandfather Marmon's experience in an Albuquerque hotel with his two young sons. Upon entering the hotel, Robert Marmon, who was white and married to an Indian, was told by the hotel manager "he was always welcome / when he was alone / but when he had Indians with him / he should use the back entrance to reach the café" (ST, 17). Like many of the other brief introductions to family members in Storyteller, this episode is reported not only for its own value but by way of introduction to the tales that follow. In this case, the discrimination Grandpa Hank experiences is recast as one of the central themes of "Storyteller."

The central character of the story is a girl who, in her adolescence, is exposed to white systems of education, religion, and sexual relations. At the "big school where the government sent all the other girls and boys," the girl is beaten for speaking her native language and not knowing the ways of white culture; to the authorities at the school she is one of "[t]hose backward village people" who was "kept" until she was "too big to learn" (ST, 19, 20). She returns home to a white priest who reports her grandmother's death but is not observant or involved enough to know that the old man with whom the grandmother lived is lecherous and not the girl's grandfather. Her relationship with the old man quickly becomes sexual but unfulfilling. Boredom and her curiosity about "Gussucks" leads her to an experimental sexual relationship with a white oil field worker that proves equally empty: to him, she is simply something to supply the appropriate physical sensations to a picture of a woman engaged in intercourse with a dog.

The girl is left with the old man and her memory of the old woman, who together gradually lead her toward a certain peace through their passing on of vital information and the old ways. Obsessed with the retelling of one story over and over again as if his life depends on it, the old man stays in bed all the time "smelling of fish and urine" (ST, 19), repeating "the story [of a bear chasing a hunter over the frozen tundra] all night in his sleep" (ST, 26). It is her relationship with her grandmother, however, that finalizes her absorption of her culture and discovery of an integrity of self that defies the discrimination of white culture. The wolfskin parka the girl wears, which "her grandmother had worn . . . for many years," comes to represent the protective "equipment" her grandmother provides toward her survival.[17] With the information about her own parents' death her grandmother gives her before she dies and her understanding of the grandmother's words to the old man about his incessant storytelling, the girl understands and insists on the integrity of her own story.

"It will take a long time, but the story must be told. There must be no lies" (ST, 26). With this vital instruction, the girl plots her revenge against the white cultural and discursive system: in essence, she is incorporated into and becomes the bear of the old man's story. Because her parents were killed by drinking bad alcohol bought from an opportunistic storekeeper, she lures the present storekeeper out onto weak ice, which he falls through and drowns. Remembering the old man's telling, the girl maintains the integrity of her story, ensuring that the truth is told and that there are "no lies." In telling her own version of the story, she insists she occupy the privileged position of the definer rather than that of the defined. The girl refutes the liberal white lawyer's efforts to argue her case with another "version" of the story. "I intended that he die," she maintains. "The story must be told as it is" (ST, 31).

Taking control of the story pattern, telling the story "as it is" and finding the delicate balance that results is not easy in a world dominated by cultural systems, language, and religious or ceremonial beliefs that are not her own. In "Storyteller," it is not only that the educational system or the priest are ineffectual: they fail to understand, to make connections, and they are unable to accept the girl or the grandmother or the old man as who they are. At the close of "Storyteller," the girl is sitting on the edge of the bed repeatedly telling her story almost as a way of being: "she did not pause or hesitate; she went on with the story, and she never stopped" (ST, 32). The instructions the two old people leave her about storytelling and the content of her story become her means of survival: telling and retelling her story is a strategy of portraying herself and documenting her perspective.

Although "Storyteller" appears early in the collection, its themes of discrimination, misunderstanding, and the necessity of telling one's own story in a changing and unaccepting world that is not one's own are repeated with such frequency in subsequent stories that they can almost be seen as retelling themselves. Although these stories are to some extent individual stories, Silko's exploration of the position of Native Americans in relation to the surrounding white culture is clearly a matter of community and national concern. Silko's retellings clarify the ways individuals as well as whole communities have been pushed aside under the influence and "guidance" of white culture — and how and at what cost they have survived as well. By incorporating multiple perspectives into her stories, Silko is able to reevaluate the historical and political "truths" that traditional anthropologists and ethnographers as well as historians and government representatives have previously recorded.

PERSONAL TIES

While the work of critics such as Benjamin and Lyotard lament the fact that, in Western societies, the traditional role of the storyteller no longer serves a clear or essential role, this is not true of the culture out of which Leslie Marmon Silko writes. On the contrary, Silko grew up as a part of a culture in which the conventional storyteller played a central role by participating, in a communally sanctioned manner, in the development of group identity. When Silko titled her collection *Storyteller* and dedicated it to "the storytellers / as far back as memory goes and to the telling / which continues and through which they all live / and we with them," she identified herself as within this tradition of tellers and located her stories within a sequence of tellings. This implied positioning is in keeping with what Silko herself said about *Storyteller* upon completing the manuscript: "I see *Storyteller* as a statement about storytelling and the relationship of the people, my family and my background to the storytelling — a personal statement done in the style of the storytelling tradition, i.e., using stories themselves to explain the dimensions of the process" (LMS, 35).

As Silko lays it out in *Storyteller,* the dimensions of the process and, by extension, the dimensions of her own self-positioning as *Storyteller*'s "teller," are quite complex; Silko's effort to make us hear and see the various languages and voices that constitute her world is a political as well as aesthetic or artistic endeavor. Her absolute denial of individual authorship throughout *Storyteller* insists her readers rethink the very idea of "story" and the concepts of authorship and ownership as well. If Silko claims to be the vehicle through which versions of traditional stories and the stories of others are voiced, is she then these stories' author or their transcriber? *Storyteller* seems to tackle this very question, and with it the questions that have surrounded the "authorship" and authenticity of American Indian texts throughout history.

In a Western culture and literary world that insists on the establishment of authorship and thus, ownership, before a work can be considered critically, Silko's suggestion that authors do not possess stories but rather, stories "belong" to their tellers, questions the nature of authorship in important ways.

Although *Storyteller* is copyrighted in Silko's name, at its very core is a celebration of the extensive oral tradition of storytelling on which Silko is dependent for her written material. Silko's stance in *Storyteller* insists that her readers accept a collectivity of authorship that is antithetical to traditional Western literary study.[18]

Although Silko's respect for what the exchange of stories can do for families and communities is evident in all her work, nowhere is the influence of storytelling on the individual more apparent than in the story of the creation of *Storyteller*. The form as well as the content of *Storyteller* underlines the extent to which Silko believes in the ability of narratives to create the "chains" needed to link generation to generation and community to community; to stories she attributes the vital dynamic of "bringing and keeping the people together."[19] The story of the making of *Storyteller* asserts Silko's conviction that the telling of stories is also the primary mode by which individuals regenerate themselves. *Storyteller* contains only fragments of two letters Silko wrote to poet James Wright, but the letters as they appear in the text do not begin to express the depth of Silko's friendship with Wright or the importance of their correspondence between August 1978 and March 1980 to the composition of *Storyteller*. The first fragment that appears in *Storyteller* is from a letter early in their correspondence; it is in fact the first time Silko addresses Wright as "Dear Jim" instead of "Dear Mr. Wright." In a true storyteller's style, Silko's introduction of the story of a feisty rooster establishes an intimacy and a working relationship in which they exchange ideas about their writing and their lives. Because Silko was in the midst of putting together the "'new' book—the collection of short writings I call *Storyteller*" (Lace, 35), it is insight into this collection that she shared in her letters to Wright. In turn, Wright quickly stepped into an important role in Silko's life: he became, during their relatively short relationship, the "[listener] who made it possible for the storyteller to go on" (Lace, 41).

Silko's correspondence to James Wright made it possible to "go on" about aspects of her life beyond the eventually unlucky rooster. *Storyteller* was composed at an especially difficult time in Silko's life; she was in the midst of her "second divorce, while Laguna is just now learning about divorce at all" (Lace, 60), and a custody battle over her children, which during the course of the letters, she loses. Silko tells Wright: "Isolation is so overwhelming at these times—I could feel myself lying deeper in it until I could not talk, literally, until I did not want to talk to anyone—my mother, my sisters—about anything. I still only write letters to you. . . . I realize now how the telling at Laguna was meant to prevent the withdrawal and isolation at times like this" (Lace, 68).

She frequently emphasizes the importance of stories and sharing stories in difficult times: "[I]t is in the sharing of stories of our grief that we somehow make sense out — no, not make sense out of these things. . . . But through stories of each other we can feel that we are not alone, that we are not the first and the last to confront losses such as these" (Lace, 68). Because Silko shares her story she finds that she is not alone: their letters show that the story of Wright's own divorce and the estrangement of one of his children touched Silko with "grief and love and compassion" and made her "happiest that you and I have these letters to each other. With you to write to," Silko continues, "I go through the day with a certain attention that I might not always have" (Lace, 74).

Although emotionally closed off from other people, Silko reaps the benefits of the power of sharing and shared stories during this period in two ways: through her actual exchange with Wright and through the conception and completion of *Storyteller,* the text in which she is both the ultimate listener and teller of tales. "[I]n this scheme of things," Silko wrote to Wright in the summer of 1979, "every story that is remembered has at least some reassurances for you" (Lace, 69). It is through the process of remembering and writing down, in such loving detail, what she remembers that Silko found in *Storyteller* a way to feel as if she were not alone. Although most of *Storyteller*'s poems and prose stories were not "new" material, *Storyteller* led her to see and set them in a new context. Silko's increasing conception of the process of remembering and recording stories as a necessary medicine for herself and for her community is clarified in her letters to Wright:

> I am happy to have *Storyteller* in the works even if it really isn't a 'big piece,' like *Ceremony* was. I think that putting it together gave me a great deal — that I discovered a great deal in making *Storyteller.* I think it is the book I was worried about, the book I felt I should do; the night before I had the emergency surgery three years ago now, my greatest and I think my *only* regret about my life was that I hadn't yet written all the stories that needed writing. Anyway, Jim, this book removes that burden. (Lace, 88)

Although she refers to *Storyteller* as not a "big piece," the importance of Silko's juxtaposition of her family, cultural, and regional origins and her own position and role in that matrix is evident in the final content and construction of the manuscript. Through the process of composing *Storyteller,* Silko quite literally comes to understand the way the stories of others illuminate her own story. Of her Aunt Susie's story of the girl and her "yashtoah," Silko confides to Wright: "I heard this story years ago, but didn't write it down until this past winter. Even then I didn't know why I was remembering it after all that time. But today, Jim, thinking about your letter and what you said [about his own divorce and children] suddenly makes it very clear" (ST, 71). Taking its place in the context of the other stories of Silko's life, Aunt Susie's story begins to make sense. Certainly this is a different "sense" of the story than that which Silko understood as a young girl. But Silko's retellings emphasize that, from generation to generation, telling to telling, the stories and their perceived meanings must change to meet the different needs of the changing circumstances of the people.

SOMETHING TO LIVE BY:

"Sound, however faint or fickle, is essential to survival."
(COOK-LYNN 1983)

In his introduction to *These Are Our Lives,* a collection of oral histories of American southerners, W. T. Couch articulated the historical urgency of the 1930s writers' project when he insisted that "the people, all the people, must be known, they must be heard. Somehow they must be given representation, somehow they must be given voice and allowed to speak."[20] Something of this era's urgency is captured in the work of Leslie Marmon Silko: in Silko's hands, storytelling is an act that generates more telling and places in contradistinction different versions of experience. In *Storyteller,* she relies on a confluence of autobiography, fiction, and ethnography to record the experience of her culture as she remembers and understands it. *Storyteller* explains that the real history of a given community cannot be recorded in an absolute way but only sensed in each generation's understanding and use of the vital images of their culture.[21] Although Silko is the first to admit "we cannot dictate or predict which stories will be 'the ones,'" *Storyteller* celebrates her belief that "[a]ll we can do is . . . remember, and . . . tell with all our hearts, not hold anything back, because anything held back or not told cannot continue on with others" (Lace, 69).

By recording history and representing culture from this perspective, Silko's text forms one response to poet Elizabeth Cook-Lynn's pinpointing of the shortcomings of what she calls the "literal history" of the American Indian. "Literal history," explains Cook-Lynn, has had its own special way of describing the tragedy of the American Indian, and it has taken on a substance of its own as all histories do. In one sense, that kind of history is valid and real, of course, but in another it is a cruel distortion, like concentrating in sorrow on the traceless disappearance of winter snow without the telling of nourishment for early spring fertility. This distortion comes about, I believe, because the traditions of literal men suffer a weakness, a flaw—a silence if you will, which makes them seem deaf. Literal history, you see, has no sound. Yet sound, however faint or fickle, is essential to survival.[22]

For Native American communities and communities of indigenous people throughout the world, finding effective strategies of representing not only past history and culture but also present vitality is a matter of great importance. In *Storyteller*—as well as her other major publications, *Ceremony* and more recently *Almanac of the Dead*—Silko forges such a strategy by walking a fine line: she functions as both artist and ethnographer. Blurring the boundaries between art and social science, she is able to introduce her readers to the fullness and fragmentation of her own private life and the life of Laguna culture. She introduces narrative strategies and structures that allow her stories to reveal the complexity of the lives and circumstances of the people. Although *Storyteller* captures again and again the difficulty of such representation, it simultaneously stands as proof that only through such difficult telling will we come to understand that recording culture is a complex (and perhaps perpetually failing) enterprise, inevitably compromised and enriched by the relations of power in which both writer and "subjects" are enmeshed.[23]

Storyteller's challenge to aesthetic and literary conventions is a tribute to the politics as well as the poetics of innovation. Silko's diverse storytelling comes together to result in a text that refutes Paula Gunn Allen's observation that "any typeset version of traditional materials is distorting."[24] Although *Storyteller* is a written archive of Native American storytelling, it does not attempt to be an absolute form. Rather, the interplay of what Silko has pieced together and the holes that remain result in a written text that alters its reader's perception of the project of writing culture. Quoting Fritz Kaufmann's 1969 article "Art and Phenomenology," Barbara Babcock explains that "any significant new form reconstructs cultural reality, causing a dislocation in the economy of representation: 'A work of art does not substitute, but institutes an original awareness of existence, on the whole; it does not so much reproduce as produce and present a total experience.'"[25] A coordination of artistic and social innovation, *Storyteller* provides such a dislocation in order to expose the dynamics and potential of telling stories.

NOTES

1. Leslie Marmon Silko, "Language and Literature from a Pueblo Indian Perspective," 54. The text printed in this volume is a transcription of an oral presentation; Silko purposely did not "write" a paper, and her remarks were intended to be heard, not read.
2. In *The Spoken Word and the Work of Interpretation,* Dennis Tedlock's discussion of the trappings of written texts, which he sets up toward a comparison with Zuni oral storytelling, raises useful ideas about the framing devices of Silko's *Storyteller* as well as her other texts. He lists the "framing devices" that are a part of the written tradition. "A book begins with a cover," Tedlock writes, "and this is followed by some or all of the following features: flyleaves . . . , title page (with the title, in former times, taken from the opening lines of the text proper), foreword (by someone other than the author himself), table of contents, chapter heading, and finally, the work itself" (163). As Linda Danielson notes, "[a]s a product of Bureau of Indian Affairs (B.I.A.) schools and mainstream American university education," Silko would have understood "what constitutes a book and conventions about how one speaks as an author. But like many other contemporary women and tribal men writers, Silko subverts and transforms these inherited traditions, appropriating the making of books to her own purposes" (329).
3. James Wright to Leslie Marmon Silko, *The Delicacy and Strength of Lace,* 67. All further references to this edition will be flagged "Lace" and cited parenthetically in the text.
4. Leslie Marmon Silko, *Storyteller,* 1. All further references to this edition will be flagged "ST" and cited parenthetically in the text.
5. The distinction between what constitutes a photograph and what constitutes a snapshot is hotly debated in art circles. Although in her letters to Wright, Silko uses the terms photograph and snapshot interchangeably, she does attempt to articulate her understanding of the difference between the forms: "I suppose that's the nature of the snapshot — it needs words with it. Photographs which speak for themselves are art" (Lace, 65).

    Many of the photographs in *Storyteller* were taken by Silko's father, Lee Marmon, who pursued a career as a commercial photographer after learning photography in World War II.
6. Of the body of recent work challenging the divide between literature and ethnography, those that have been particularly useful to my thinking on this issue include Boon (1982), Marcus and Fischer (1986), Clifford and Marcus (1988), and Clifford (1988).
7. The authorial stance in *Storyteller* is comparable to that implied in Silko's first novel, *Ceremony.* In the novel's opening poem, Thought-Woman, the spider, "is sitting in her room / thinking of a story . . . / I'm telling you the story she is thinking" (2). Arnold Krupat offers a particularly cogent assessment of Silko's voice in *Storyteller:* "There is no single, distinctive or authoritative voice in Silko's book nor any striving for such a voice; on the contrary, Silko will take pains to indicate how even her own individual speech is the product of many voices. *Storyteller* is presented as a strongly polyphonic text in which the author defines herself — finds her voice, tells her life, illustrates the capacities of her vocation — in relation

to the voices of other native and nonnative storytellers, tale tellers and book writers, and even the voices of those who serve as the (by-no-means-silent) audience for these stories" (60).

8. Linda Danielson's reading of this scene is especially to the point. She argues that this story can be read in ways "that will satisfy both the ardent feminist and the traditional purist. As portrayed by Silko, Aunt Alice states at once that Kochininako is a fine hunter — no apology, no qualification — and that she brought deer and rabbits to her mother and sisters. . . . The listeners are not cautioned about girls overreaching themselves as hunters" (339–40).

9. Silko, "A Conversation with Leslie Marmon Silko," 29–30.

10. Bernard A. Hirsch argues that Silko's inclusion of these explanatory details, rather than reflecting the changing needs of the audience, echoes aspects of and indicates a continuum with traditional storytelling. He writes: "She . . . provides several italicized expository passages to evoke the digressive mode of traditional storytellers and the conversational texture of their speech" (7). Hirsch's article offers a cogent reading of the continuity between oral and written storytelling traditions in Silko's *Storyteller;* he calls this aspect of Silko's work the "structural and thematic basis of *Storyteller*" (1).

11. In a review of *Storyteller,* Priscilla Wald described Silko as the "self-acknowledged, self-appointed heir" of her Aunt Susie's work (19). Silko herself refers to Aunt Susie's contributions to her storytelling in a 1981 interview: "It was Aunt Susy [sic] who told me a lot of the stories, and who in some sense trained me, if that's what you want to call it, helped me to love the stories and to learn them." See Per Seyersted, "Two Interviews with Leslie Marmon Silko," 28.

12. Hirsch, "'The Telling Which Continues,'" 1.

13. In her study of *Storyteller,* A. LaVonne Ruoff argues the very strength of Indian tradition for Leslie Marmon Silko is located in this merging of traditions: rather than rigid adherence to the old ways, Silko advocates the creative incorporation of new elements.

14. Bakhtin, *The Dialogic Imagination,* 45. All subsequent references to this edition will be flagged "DI" and cited parenthetically in the text.

15. In his "Dialogic of Silko's *Storyteller,*" Arnold Krupat reads *Storyteller* similarly against a backdrop of Bakhtinian ideas of language as an example of Native American autobiography in what he calls the "dialogic mode" (64). Krupat argues that in *Storyteller,* Silko reconceives the very idea of autobiography by replacing the authoritative individual voice commonly associated with Western autobiography with a polyphony that indicates the Native American concept of the individual's story as a part of the collective stories of the people. Among other valuable contributions made in Krupat's article, one of the most significant is his effort to trace Silko's other, previous tellings of stories that appear in *Storyteller.* Krupat points out the different forms these episodes have taken in various publications.

16. Quoted in Per Seyersted, *Leslie Marmon Silko,* 38. All subsequent references to this edition will be flagged "LMS" and cited parenthetically in the text.

17. Danielson's reading of the girl's relationship to both the old man and her grandmother is especially helpful here. Noting that the girl "always seems to choose freely in her relationship with the old man," Danielson argues that "the real significance of [that relationship] may be to suggest her absorption into her culture. This, for Silko,

overrides the implied oppressiveness of the relationship" (334). She compares the girl's relationship to the old man with her inheritance of her grandmother's clothing: each offers her something of themselves (bodies, stories of the past) that contributes to her understanding of herself and the tradition to which she belongs.

18. This lesson is not only important to the study of works by Native American authors. Because Western scholars have traditionally put the establishment of authorship of a work before any discussion of the work itself, issues of "authenticity" remain at the heart of the study of ethnic American literatures today. Perhaps the most well-known example of this issue of authenticity in contemporary literary circles is the treatment of slave narratives: the debates that raged over the "true" authorship of *Incidents in the Life of a Slave Girl* are particularly interesting. Jean Fagan Yellin's persistent scholarship resulted in the recent acceptance of Harriet Jacobs as the text's sole author. Because of her pivotal work to uncover the authorship of Jacobs's work, Yellin's introduction to the Harvard University Press edition of *Incidents* is most useful to anyone interested in these issues.

19. Silko, "A Pueblo Indian Perspective," 59.

20. W. T. Couch, preface to *These Are Our Lives,* xiii–xiv.

21. Arnold Krupat considers that "the present 'blurring of genres,' . . . in both the social sciences and in the arts, is actually a return to a time when the line between history and myth was not very clearly marked." In this context, he would consider Silko's *Storyteller* in keeping with tradition rather than as something new: this "blurring of genres" is "the way things have always been for Native American literatures" (59).

22. Elizabeth Cook-Lynn, *Then Badger Said This,* 33.

23. My perspective on Silko's *Storyteller* as "literature of culture" is enhanced by Linda J. Krumholz's insightful reading of the text as one that functions in and negotiates what Mary Louise Pratt has called the "contact zone." According to Pratt, the "contact zone" describes the "social spaces where cultures meet, clash, and grapple with each other often in contexts of highly asymmetrical relations of power, such as colonialism, slavery, or their aftermaths as they are lived out in many parts of the world today" (Pratt, qtd. in Krumholz, 89). Krumholz uses this idea to define Silko's *Storyteller* as "an autoethnographic text, a book that engages with the dominant representations of Native Americans in order to appropriate and transform these representations" (90).

24. Allen, *The Sacred Hoop,* 243. Although *The Sacred Hoop* was published after *Storyteller,* none of Allen's essays touch on Silko's achievement in it.

25. Fritz Kaufmann, "Art and Phenomenology," in *Essays in Phenomenology,* ed. W. Natanson (The Hague: Martinus Nijhoff, 1969), 144–56. Qtd. in Babcock, "At Home, No Womens [*sic*] Are Storytellers," 359–60.

WORKS CITED

Allen, Paula Gunn. *The Sacred Hoop: Recovering the Feminine in American Indian Traditions.* Boston: Beacon Press, 1986.

Babcock, Barbara. "'At Home, No Womens Are Storytellers': Potteries, Stories, and Politics in a Cochiti Pueblo." *Journal of the Southwest* 30 (1987): 356–89.

Bakhtin, Mikhail. *The Dialogic Imagination: Four Essays by M. M. Bakhtin.* Ed. Michael Holquist. Trans. Caryl Emerson and Michael Holquist. Austin: U of Texas P, 1981.

Benjamin, Walter. "The Storyteller." 1936. Rpt. in *Illuminations.* Trans. Harry Zohn. New York: Schocken Books, 1968. 83–109.

Boon, James. *Other Tribes, Other Scribes: Symbolic Anthropology in the Comparative Study of Cultures, Histories, Religions, and Texts.* Cambridge: Cambridge UP, 1982.

Clifford, James. *The Predicament of Culture: Twentieth-Century Ethnography, Literature, and Art.* Cambridge: Harvard UP, 1988.

Clifford, James, and George Marcus. *Writing Culture: The Poetics and Politics of Ethnography.* Berkeley: U of California P, 1986.

Cook-Lynn, Elizabeth. *Then Badger Said This.* Fairfield, WA: Ye Galleon Press, 1983.

Couch, W. T. Preface. *These Are Our Lives As Told by the People and Written by Members of the Federal Writers' Project of the Works Progress Administration in North Carolina, Tennessee, and Georgia.* Chapel Hill: U of North Carolina P, 1939.

Danielson, Linda L. "Storyteller: Grandmother's Spider Web." *Journal of the Southwest* 30.3 (1988): 325–55.

Hirsch, Bernard A. " 'The Telling Which Continues': Oral Tradition and the Written Word in Leslie Marmon Silko's *Storyteller.*" *American Indian Quarterly* 12.1 (1988): 1–26.

Krumholz, Linda J. " 'To Understand This World Differently': Reading and Subversion in Leslie Marmon Silko's *Storyteller.*" *Ariel* 25.1 (January 1994): 89–113.

Krupat, Arnold. "The Dialogic of Silko's *Storyteller.*" *Narrative Chance.* Ed. Gerald Vizenor. Albuquerque: U of New Mexico P, 1989. 55–68.

Marcus, George, and Michael Fischer. *Anthropology as Cultural Critique.* Chicago: U of Chicago P, 1986.

Ruoff, A. LaVonne. "Ritual and Renewal: Keres Traditions in the Short Fiction of Leslie Marmon Silko." *MELUS* 5.4 (1978): 2–17.

Seyersted, Per. *Leslie Marmon Silko.* Boise: Boise State UP, 1980.

———. "Two Interviews with Leslie Marmon Silko." *American Studies in Scandinavia* 13 (1981): 17–33.

Silko, Leslie Marmon. *Almanac of the Dead.* New York: Penguin, 1991.

———. *Ceremony.* New York: New American Library, 1977.

———. "A Conversation with Leslie Marmon Silko." Ed. Larry Evers and Denny Carr. *Sun Tracks: An American Indian Literary Magazine* 3:1 (1976): 28–33.

———. *The Delicacy and Strength of Lace.* Ed. Anne Wright. St. Paul, MN: Graywolf Press, 1986.

———. "Language and Literature from a Pueblo Indian Perspective." *English Literature: Selected Papers from the English Institute, 1979.* Ed. Houston A. Baker Jr. and Leslie A. Fiedler. Baltimore: Johns Hopkins UP, 1981. 54–72.

———. *Storyteller.* New York: Seaver Books, 1981.

Tedlock, Dennis. *The Spoken Word and the Work of Interpretation.* Philadelphia: U of Pennsylvania P, 1983.

Wald, Priscilla. "Review of Leslie Marmon Silko's *Storyteller.*" *Studies in American Indian Literature* 6.4 (1982): 17–26.

Yellin, Jean Fagan. Introduction. *Incidents in the Life of a Slave Girl.* By Harriet Jacobs. Cambridge: Harvard UP, 1987. xiii–xxxiii.

SHIFTING PATTERNS, CHANGING STORIES

Leslie Marmon Silko's Yellow Women

Elizabeth Hoffman Nelson and Malcolm A. Nelson

Yellow Woman (Kochininako) stories have been a part of the Keres Pueblo oral tradition since time immemorial, and every time a Yellow Woman story is told, it changes, it is new. Leslie Marmon Silko once said in an interview, "And no matter how carefully I remember, memory gets all mixed together with imagination" (Barnes, 51). Changing tradition is a perilous enterprise, yet change can be creative and renewing. Silko's short story "Yellow Woman," originally published in Kenneth Rosen's anthology *The Man to Send Rain Clouds* (1974), was later included in *Storyteller* (1981), a collection of Silko's stories, photographs, reminiscences, and poems. In *Storyteller*, Silko retells the Yellow Woman stories in various styles and voices.

The traditional Yellow Woman stories involve a young woman who wanders away from the pueblo and either goes with, or is abducted by, a ka'tsina-spirit from the mountains. Sometimes she is killed by the ka'tsina or her husband; sometimes she returns to the pueblo with a renewed spirit, and the tribe benefits from her encounter (Graulich, 11). Silko makes her Yellow Woman a modern woman, with all the confusion and bewilderment a contemporary person would feel if thrust into the middle of an ancient story.

Silko once again borrows the story of Yellow Woman for use in her 1977 novel, *Ceremony*. Ts'eh is a Yellow Woman who helps the protagonist, Tayo, finish his ceremony and become a whole, healed person again. But

Ts'eh is not the only Yellow Woman in *Ceremony*. In the spirit of a storyteller who uses memory and imagination to tell (and, therefore, change, re-create, renew) the stories, Silko has created a new kind of Yellow Woman. When studied in conjunction with Silko's "Yellow Woman," Tayo, in *Ceremony*, plays a role similar to the unnamed narrator in that short story; similar in that both find a new identity through a new relationship with tradition, the spirits, the land, and themselves.

Is Tayo a Yellow Woman? In her essay " 'The Belly of This Story': Storytelling and Symbolic Birth in Native American Fiction," Mary Chapman states that in *Ceremony*, Silko gives us two ideas: "language can engender life, because a story can 'bear' a culture like a woman bears a child, and men, through language, can have access to what might otherwise be considered a female power to create" (4).[1] Chapman believes that the link between language and male creative power is "pervasive in Native American 'stories,' from traditional myths of creation to contemporary fiction, in which gender is less important than language" (4). Tayo, through language, through storytelling, creates life — a new life for himself. We believe that Tayo is a Yellow Woman.

In *Ceremony*, Ts'eh is a Yellow Woman, but she goes beyond her traditional role. Silko empowers Ts'eh and gives her, more than anyone else in *Ceremony*, more even than the medicine man Betonie, the ability to heal Tayo with her body, mind, and spirit. In *Ceremony*, Ts'eh's role approaches that of a ka'tsina spirit, and Tayo, as a Yellow Woman, follows Ts'eh.

It is useful to look at some of the other ways of interpreting the relationship between Tayo and Ts'eh. In his book *Other Destinies: Understanding the American Indian Novel*, Louis Owens explains that the involvement of Tayo, Ts'eh, and the Hunter (Ts'eh's companion on the mountain) is a reenactment of a traditional myth in which Winter (i.e., the Hunter) and Summer (i.e., Tayo) fight for the right to marry Yellow Woman (i.e., Ts'eh). The resulting preparation for battle ends with an agreement that Summer and Winter shall share Yellow Woman (each having her for half the year). According to Owens, "A reader familiar with the traditional paradigms of the story will recognize what is happening to Tayo and will know, of course, the outcome of the story. If he renders his role accurately, 'remembers the story,' Tayo will succeed in restoring balance to his world" (187). Owens says that a reader "familiar" with this "time immemorial story" will understand why Tayo finds Ts'eh instinctively at the beginning of summer. "If the story is told correctly, with whatever variations the storyteller may effect, it will always end this way" (187).

Silko, as storyteller, has made variations on the original. Tayo and the Hunter are not angry and feel no need to battle for Ts'eh's affections. Tayo and

Ts'eh do meet again after the winter ends, but *Ceremony,* like a lot of stories, is open-ended; we don't know if Tayo will see Ts'eh again next summer.

In her essay "Kochinnenako in Academe: Three Approaches to Interpreting a Keres Indian Tale," Paula Gunn Allen discusses the same Yellow Woman story. Her mother's uncle, John Gunn, gathered information and stories from the Laguna people he lived among, and then wrote them in a book called *Schat Chen: History, Traditions, and Narratives of the Queres Indians of Laguna and Acoma* (1917). The story is called "Sh-ah-cock and Miochin or the Battle of the Seasons." Allen says, "In the end, the tale I have analyzed is not about Kochinnenako or Sh-ah-cock and Miochin. It is about the change of seasons and it is about the centrality of woman as agent and empowerer of that change" (244). Silko gives her Yellow Women this same kind of empowerment. Ts'eh and Tayo, and the narrator of "Yellow Woman," are the central agents of change in their respective lives and futures.

In *Ceremony,* Silko takes Laguna myths, breaks them up, and places them incrementally throughout the prose. This work is obviously meant to be told and heard. The introduction of the mythic poetry introduces Silko, the storyteller, as she weaves her tale — and the reader becomes the listener. The central myth involves the Ck'o'yo medicine man/magician. One large section of this myth appears just before Tayo meets Ts'eh for the first time, suggesting a mythic parallel.

This medicine man is also called Kaup'a'ta, or the Gambler, who lived high in the mountains where he would gamble with passersby and take everything they owned; he tricked them into eating blue cornmeal with human blood in it. "They were in his power" (*Ceremony,* 171). Once he even captured the stormclouds, creating a devastating drought. The clouds' father, the Sun, with some help from Spiderwoman (the creatrix), gambled with Kaup'a'ta and won. Sun Man cut out the Gambler's eyes and these became the autumn stars — the Pleiades and Orion. Sun Man's success ensured the end of the drought and the salvation of the people, land, and animals.

Edith Swan, in "Laguna Symbolic Geography and Silko's *Ceremony,*" places this myth in context: "The narrative in *Ceremony* portrays Tayo as an analog of Sun Man. . . . Tayo, like Sun Man, must free the rains" (238).[2] And Tayo, with Ts'eh's (i.e., Spiderwoman's) help, is able to do just that. Ts'eh instructs Tayo in the art of gathering plants and roots that have the color of rain in them and planting them in drought-stricken places. The Hunter and the Gambler share a role in this analogy. Both men live in the mountains, and both wear "strings of turquoise" from their ears (*Ceremony,* 170, 207). But the Hunter is much less violent and destructive. He never hurts Tayo, and Tayo never has any cause to injure him. The stars (i.e., the Gambler's eyes) are the same ones Betonie

prophesied, and they are also seen by Tayo the night he faces the destroyers —
Emo and the boys. "But he saw the constellation in the north sky. . . . [T]he
pattern of the ceremony was in the stars. . . . [H]is protection was in the sky, in
the position of the sun, in the pattern of the stars" (247).

Silko makes this analogy plain, readily available to most readers. The myths
and prose work together to tell the story. We need not be experts on Pueblo
mythology to make the connections. Edith Swan, like Louis Owens, recognizes the mythic parallels between Tayo/Ts'eh/Hunter and Summer/Yellow
Woman/ Winter, and she takes it a step further: "Silko's permutation on the
parable of Yellow Woman, who is married to Winter and Summer, shows Tayo
as a Yellow Man joined to Winter and Summer aspects of the same woman"
(Swan, 245–46). We agree that Silko has radically altered the story. Tayo *is* a
man who has many of the characteristics, actions, feelings of the contemporary Yellow Woman of Silko's short story. A closer look at "Yellow Woman"
will help to put Tayo's transformation into perspective.

The Yellow Woman of Silko's story of that name is a modern Pueblo
woman. She is a daughter, wife, and mother, but when she meets a strange
man by the river, she puts her responsibilities aside to follow him. Silko endows her unnamed narrator with a complex problem. This Yellow Woman is
familiar with the traditional Yellow Woman stories her grandfather used to
tell her, and this familiarity adds to the confusion and ambiguity she feels
when she realizes she is now becoming a part of these stories.

"Yellow Woman" is also a story of discovery. The narrator finds within
herself an unknown passion, a deep, sensual desire that is fulfilled through her
sexual encounter with Silva, the stranger. And with the narrator's search for
identity and sexual freedom, comes a growing awareness of the land around
her (and her place in it) and a further understanding of the importance of the
stories.

In "Yellow Woman," Silko uses first-person narration. This gives the reader
a better sense of how this Yellow Woman feels and what she thinks. Her
narrator does not tell us her name, thereby seeming to accept her role, her
identity, as Yellow Woman. This ambiguity of her identity reinforces Silko's
emphasis on the question of what is real and what is not, rather than on the
events of the story. Silko adds a sexual dimension to her Yellow Woman by
opening the story with an intimate moment: "My thigh clung to his with
dampness," dampness mirrored in Silko's extensive use of water imagery
("Yellow Woman," 54). Yellow Woman is associated with the life-giving rain.
"The loss of these Yellow Women portends loss of rain, of livelihood" (Allen,
Spider Woman's Granddaughters, 210).

Yellow Woman meets Silva by the river on the outskirts of the pueblo, and their first sexual encounter takes place on the riverbank. She leaves her village willingly; Silva does not kidnap her. The following morning she "tried to look beyond the pale red mesas to the pueblo," and she knows even though she cannot see it, it is still there ("Yellow Woman," 54). She must believe it is real. Soon she wakes Silva to tell him she is leaving. He laughs. He knows she is Yellow Woman and she must stay with him. She has yet to accept it: "But I only said you were him and that I was Yellow Woman — I'm not really her — I have my own name and I come from the pueblo on the other side of the mesa. Your name is Silva and you are a stranger I met by the river yesterday afternoon" (55). She tries to reassure herself of who she is not. She is not Yellow Woman — is she? — but she does not give her real name, suggesting she likes her new identity or at least the freedom that the ambiguity gives her. She confronts Silva with the unreality of being part of a story, and knowing it: "the old stories about the ka'tsina spirit and Yellow Woman can't mean us" (55). She recalls how her grandfather loved to tell the Yellow Woman stories the best, and because of this love, she is aware of her predicament. (In many tribes, the oral traditions are dying and people might not know if they were suddenly a character in a story.)

As the narrator's confusion grows, so does her desire for Silva: "I was wondering if Yellow Woman had known who she was — if she knew that she would become part of the stories. Maybe she'd had another name that her husband and relatives called her so that only the ka'tsina from the north and the storytellers would know her as Yellow Woman. But I didn't go on; I felt him all around me, pushing me down into the white river sand" (55–56). She decides to give in. "This is the way it happens in the stories, I was thinking, with no thought beyond the moment she meets the ka'tsina spirit and they go" (56). Her use of the present tense ("happens") signals the reader that she understands that oral tradition is alive — the stories are alive. Yet she is still so unsure of what being a Yellow Woman means to her that she tries to convince herself (with the modern Indian reality of pickup trucks) that it isn't happening: "I will see someone, eventually I will see someone, and then I will be certain that he is only a man — some man from nearby — and I will be sure that I am not Yellow Woman. Because she is from out of time past and I live now and I've been to school and there are highways and pickup trucks that Yellow Woman never saw" (56).

Silva, the ka'tsina, takes her away from the present, takes her north to his home in the mountains. She wonders what her family is thinking about where she went. Yellow Woman tries to get Silva to confess that, yes, he is the ka'tsina and that he has done this type of thing before. She tells him that she does not believe the old stories could happen today. He sadly shakes his head and says, softly: "But someday they will talk about us, and they will say, 'Those two lived long ago when things like that happened'" (57). The narrator is part of the story now — the story she is telling us and the stories people will tell about her in the future. She belongs to the Yellow Woman tradition.

Thus far into the story, Silva has appeared nonthreatening; but the ka'tsinas who abduct Yellow Women are often evil. They make the women perform difficult tasks and often kill them. Silva becomes increasingly dangerous. He matter-of-factly tells Yellow Woman that he is a cattle thief. When she and Silva make love again, Silva laughs at her and she turns away from him. "He pulled me around and pinned me down with his arms and chest. 'You don't understand, do you, little Yellow Woman? You will do what I want.' And again he was all around me with his skin slippery against mine, and I was afraid because I understood that his strength could hurt me. I lay underneath him and I knew that he could destroy me" (58). She knows the traditional Yellow Woman stories and their outcomes — if she is a Yellow Woman, Silva could kill her. Her fears are diminished by the attraction she feels for Silva (and the danger is part of it) and the freedom he brings from the monotony of pueblo life. The next morning, Silva is gone, yet she doesn't try to escape. She takes her time, eating, drowsing, soaking up the landscape. Yellow Woman again thinks of her family and her new identity; she comes to accept that she will be part of the story one day. She asserts that she was an involuntary participant: "Silva had come for me; he said he had. I did not decide to go. I just went" (59). Her new identity as Yellow Woman is taking shape, perhaps taking her over as well, and she seems quite content with it.

Her opportunity to escape has passed. Silva and Yellow Woman go toward Marquez to sell the beef he has stolen. On the ride, she sees everything — mesas, trails, flowers. The cactus flowers are of every color: "the white ones and the red ones were still buds, but the purple and the yellow were blossoms, open full and the most beautiful of all" (60). She is this most beautiful yellow flower — open and full. As Yellow Woman, she has discovered another self — sensual and free.

The beauty of this moment is abruptly ended by a white rancher who accuses Silva of being a cattle rustler. Silva orders Yellow Woman to go back up the mountain, and then he pulls his gun on the rancher. "I turned my horse around and the rancher yelled 'Stop!' I looked at Silva for an instant and there was something ancient and dark — something I could feel in my stomach — in his eyes" (61). Like many Yellow Woman stories, this one turns violent. The narrator is forced to recognize that Silva, the man she feels such passion for, is, in part, an evil ka'tsina. She hears four shots but is never sure who fired them or who may have been injured or killed. Because Yellow Woman is uncertain of the outcome, she believes she may meet Silva again—and that prospect pleases her. "Yellow Woman" ends with the narrator by the same riverbank where she met Silva, feeling sad at having to leave him: "I saw the leaves and I wanted to go back to him—to kiss him and to touch him—but the mountains were too far away now. And I told myself, because I believe it, he will come back sometime and be waiting again by the river" (62).

She believes she is Yellow Woman. All the confusion and doubt about her identity and her place in the stories is over; she believes. "As she reaches her home, she is brought back to the realities of her own life by the smell of supper cooking and the sight of her mother instructing her grandmother in the Anglo art of making Jell-O" (Ruoff, 78). She returns home with a new self, and a new role in the community—not only is she part of the Yellow Woman stories now, she is now also a storyteller: "I decided to tell them that some Navajo had kidnaped me, but I was sorry that old Grandpa wasn't alive to hear my story because it was the Yellow Woman stories he liked to tell best" ("Yellow Woman," 62).

Silko gives us a multilayered story. The narrator was told stories about Yellow Woman by her grandfather, and then became a Yellow Woman herself, part of a new (and renewing) set of stories. When she returns from her adventure with Silva, *she* is the storyteller. Yellow Woman finds a new self—she breaks away from the routine of daily village life and discovers a free, open, passionate, sensual, spiritual self. Silko has created a strong, new Yellow Woman. Readers can identify with all her emotions—confusion, desire, fear, and delight at who she has become. Silko's Yellow Woman seems more real than in the traditional stories—partly because the language and settings are so clearly pickup truck, bar lingo contemporary ("Have you brought women here before. . . . [D]o you always use the same tricks?" [57]); partly because she tells her own story, with all the power and all the ambiguity that that implies.

When we look for Yellow Women in Leslie Marmon Silko's *Ceremony* there is one obvious choice—Ts'eh. She wears "a man's shirt tucked into a yellow skirt that hung below her knees. Pale buckskin moccasins reached the edge of her skirt. The silver buttons up the side of each moccasin had rainbirds carved on them" (177). Add to that her ocher eyes and her agelessness and, clearly, she is a Yellow Woman. Ts'eh embodies Yellow Woman characteristics—the color yellow surrounds her; she is linked with the rain; she has the Hunter as her companion part of the year. But does she behave as other Yellow Women?

Later she tells Tayo her name—Ts'eh Montaño. Ts'eh, she tells him, is a nickname; it is short for Tse-pi'na, the Laguna name for Mount Taylor. She also tells Tayo about her siblings: "I have a sister who lives way down that way. She's married to a Navajo from Red Lake. . . . Another lives near Flagstaff. My brother's in Jemez" (223). "She is a mountain spirit, like her brothers and sisters — sacred mountains all" (Smith and Allen, 140). Her surname 'Montaño' means mountain in Spanish. Traditionally, Yellow Women are Pueblo women who are taken by spirits who live in the mountains. Ts'eh's name seems to state the opposite — she is identified with sacred mountains.

Ts'eh's role in *Ceremony* is not that of a traditional Yellow Woman. Her history is unclear, but she does not seem to be held against her will by the Hunter. She is not given impossible tasks to do by her "captor." Silko has given her freedom and power that most traditional Yellow Women lack. Silko has taken the ideas from "Yellow Woman" and shifted them across gender lines to create a wholly new story. In this new version — which is at the very heart of *Ceremony* — the sexual desire, passion, confusion, and love are the same; only the people have changed. Tayo takes on the role of the ingenue, the Yellow Woman, and Ts'eh, the ka'tsina/mountain spirit. Ts'eh "takes" Tayo and enables him to discover a new/renewed self through oneness with her, with Mother Earth, and with the stories.

The similarities between Tayo and Silko's "Yellow Woman" narrator are many. The settings and actions correspond. Both protagonists stay with their mountain spirits in the mountains, far removed from their Pueblo homes. The passion and sexual encounters, and the characters' increased awareness of the land around them, are similar. The unnamed narrator first makes love with Silva at the river. Tayo and Ts'eh's first lovemaking takes on an ethereal, spiritual quality, and Tayo likens it to being on a riverbank. Tayo has completed Betonie's ceremony, but he is still unsure of himself and his place in the world. The scene Silko describes is passionate and erotic, and ultimately healing for Tayo:

> He eased himself deeper within her and felt the warmth close around him like river sand, softly giving way under foot, then closing firmly around the ankle in cloudy warm water. But he did not get lost, and he smiled at her as she held his hips and pulled him closer. He let the motion carry him, and he could feel the momentum within, at first almost imperceptible, gathering in his belly. When it came, it was the edge of a steep riverbank crumbling under the downpour until suddenly it all broke loose and collapsed into itself. (*Ceremony*, 181)

On the morning after, Tayo smiles: "being alive was all right then: he had not breathed like that for a long time" (181). After their initial interaction with Silva and Ts'eh, the unnamed narrator and Tayo, respectively, think back to their villages and their people, and Silko intertwines their thoughts with a new appreciation for the land. Tayo leaves Ts'eh to go find Josiah's spotted cattle. He is not held prisoner as Yellow Women are, but the reader gets the distinct feeling that he and Ts'eh will meet again. The woman in "Yellow Woman" does not flee Silva — some power greater than she keeps her with him. For both characters that power seems to be passion, and the controllers of that are Ts'eh and Silva.

While on the mountain searching for the cattle, Tayo thinks about time. Like the "Yellow Woman" narrator, he is learning that time is not linear. "The ride into the mountains had branched into all directions of time. He knew then why the oldtimers could only speak of yesterday or tomorrow in terms of the present moment: the only certainty; and this present sense of being was qualified with bare hints of yesterday or tomorrow, by saying, 'I go up to the mountain yesterday or I go up to the mountain tomorrow'" (Ceremony, 192). Silva tells the unnamed narrator the same thing; "What happened yesterday has nothing to do with what you will do today, Yellow Woman" ("Yellow Woman," 55). At a Writers and Books master class in Rochester, New York, in January 1993, Silko told us in no uncertain terms that "Linear time is a complete fiction." Her writing clearly demonstrates this. The protagonists of both "Yellow Woman" and Ceremony are confused by time and its seeming lack of relationship to reality but, as their journeys continue, they come to understand how to "be here now." As Tayo continues on his journey, he doubts himself and the ceremony he is participating in: "all that was crazy. . . . [I]t was all superstition" (Ceremony, 194–95). These doubts are similar to those of the narrator of "Yellow Woman"; she often questions her new identity. In the end, however, both Tayo and the narrator grow to understand, accept, and be pleased with who they've become.

The Hunter in Ceremony can be viewed as an obstacle on the road to proving Tayo's "Yellowness." If he is the evil ka'tsina who is holding Ceremony's Yellow Woman (Ts'eh) captive, he doesn't act it. He is friendly toward Tayo, jokes with him about Ts'eh, and never stands in the way of either Ts'eh or Tayo's going about their business, even if it is sexual. If the Hunter is not the evil ka'tsina, who is?

Ts'eh is not an evil person — she opens her heart, body, and spirit to help Tayo heal. But she does seem dangerous, powerful, when Tayo asks if she thinks the Texans will come looking for Josiah's cattle.

> She shrugged her shoulders, unconcerned.
> "They won't come down here," she said.
> "Why not?"
> She gave him a look that chilled him. She must have seen his fear

because she smiled and said, "Because of all the snow up there. What else?" She was teasing again. He shook his head. (213)

That look can be read two ways — one, she has power great enough to prevent anyone from stealing the cattle back, and two, Tayo should have more sense than to question her. Ts'eh is not an evil ka'tsina in the traditional sense, but she is a powerful, even dangerous, spirit.

Tayo, like the "Yellow Woman" narrator, leaves the ka'tsina spirit and goes back to the pueblo. Tayo's love for Ts'eh, like the narrator's passion for Silva, is undiminished. He dreams of her. "He was overwhelmed by the love he felt for her; tears filled his eyes and the ache in his throat ran deep into his chest. He ran down the hill to the river, through the light rain until the pain faded like fog mist. He stood and watched the rainy dawn, and he knew he would find her again" (217–18). Tayo and the narrator both long to see these spirits who have power over them, and they both believe they will see them again. For Tayo it comes true; for the narrator, it is unclear, but the hope is there.

On his way north, before he meets Ts'eh again, Tayo is surrounded by the color yellow: the sun, a yellow snake, yellow pollen from sunflowers, yellow sandstone (221). The ceremonies have brought Tayo in touch with Mother Earth and all her gifts. In these yellow objects he sees himself, as the narrator did in the yellow cactus flowers. And there is Ts'eh: "She turned to him as soon as he saw her, as if she had been waiting" (221). Ts'eh reveals herself to Tayo as Silva does to his Yellow Woman.

As with any Yellow Woman story, things do not remain eternally happy. The white rancher intrudes upon Silva and his Yellow Woman's journey, and violence ensues. Ts'eh's and Tayo's healing time and love are interrupted by the witchery. (Betonie had warned Tayo of the dangers of the witchery — a power loosed upon the world by Indian witches.) Uncle Robert comes to tell Tayo that Emo is still after him — the possibility of a confrontation with Emo becomes a reality for Tayo. Ts'eh knows of the danger Tayo is in and prepares him for the destruction he may face at the hands of Emo. When she reveals untold details of Tayo's past and future, he understands how she knows. "She could see reflections in sandrock pools of rainwater, images shifting in the flames of juniper fire; she heard voices, low and distant in the night" (232).

Even though both Ts'eh and Silva are ka'tsina spirits, they have different reactions to the danger and violence, the witchery. Ts'eh gives Tayo a great gift — knowledge. Tayo knows the importance of the stories and the old ways, and if he resists Emo's witchery, the witchery will be destroyed (or, at least, sent to California). Silva sends his Yellow Woman away to a safe place, and then pulls a gun on the rancher. Shots are fired, but the violent outcome is not part of Silko's story. The violence does not happen directly to either of the Yellow Woman figures — the narrator is saved by Silva, and Tayo's knowledge saves him. They both return home to their villages.

One final similarity between Silva and Ts'eh — perhaps the most important — is their shared understanding of the significance, the power, of the newly created stories. Silva tells the narrator that someday people will tell stories about the two of them. Part of the knowledge Ts'eh gives Tayo is the necessity of the story being finished without the witchery's influence: "The end of the story. They want to change it. They want it to end here, the way all their stories end, encircling slowly to choke the life away" (231–32). She tells Tayo that as long as he remembers what he has seen, then nothing is gone: "As long as you remember, it is part of this story we have together" (231). This is the thread that ties together Silko's entire novel: "You don't have anything if you don't have the stories" (2).

The "Yellow Woman" narrator is about to become a storyteller at the end of her journey. Tayo becomes one too. He defeats the witchery and returns home to the kiva where he tells his story to the elders. Part of the traditional Yellow Woman stories is the benefit to the community after her return home. In "Yellow Woman," she has become a storyteller, and she will keep her grandfather's traditions alive. Tayo benefits his community by helping to end the drought. Some things do stay the same: Tayo's Auntie is still a grumpy martyr; old Grandma still shivers by the stove; and there will always be Jell-O to make. Yet the conclusion of *Ceremony* still has a positive tone.

Ceremony ends with old Grandma remarking that "It seems like I already heard these stories before . . . only thing is, the names sound different" (260). Exactly, Grandma. The names have changed, and so have the genders. The one who returns to the community bringing health and fruitfulness is no longer the one with the womb — it is Tayo, he who cursed the rain and brought the drought. The one who takes us out of ourselves to find new fruitfulness and new selves is no longer Silva or the evil ka'tsina or even Betonie — it is Ts'eh. And the one who tells us all about how to heal ourselves is no longer old Grandpa — it is Leslie Marmon Silko.

The Yellow Woman stories in *Ceremony* and "Yellow Woman" are the same. The names, places, times, details, and genders have changed, and that change is vital. As Betonie says:

At one time, the ceremonies as they had been performed were enough for how the world was then. But after the white people came, elements in this world began to shift; and it became necessary to create new ceremonies. I have made changes in the rituals. The people mistrust this greatly, but only this growth keeps the ceremonies strong. . . . [T]hings which don't shift and grow are dead things. They are things the witchery people want. Witchery works to scare people, to make them fear growth. But it has always been necessary, and more than ever now, it is. Otherwise we won't make it . . . if only in the aging of the yellow gourd rattle or the shrinking of the skin around the eagle's claw, if only in the different voices from generation to generation, singing the chants. You see, in many ways, the ceremonies have always been changing. (*Ceremony,* 126)

NOTES

1. See also Jude Todd's "Knotted Bellies and Fragile Webs: Untangling and Re-Spinning in Tayo's Healing Journey," *American Indian Quarterly* 19:2 (spring 1995): 155–70.
2. See also Claire R. Farrer's response to Edith Swan: "The Sun's in Its Heaven, All's NOT Right with the World: Rejoinder to Swan," *American Indian Quarterly* 14.2 (1990): 155–59. This is followed by Swan's "Answer to Farrer: All Is Right with the Word as Laguna Notions Speak for Themselves," *American Indian Quarterly* 14.2 (1990): 161–66. And finally, Farrer's re-rejoinder: "Reprise of Swan's Song and Farrer's Chorus," *American Indian Quarterly* 14.2 (1990): 167–71.

WORKS CITED

Allen, Paula Gunn. "Kochinnenako in Academe: Three Approaches to Interpreting a Keres Indian Tale." *The Sacred Hoop: Recovering the Feminine in American Indian Traditions.* Boston: Beacon, 1986. 222–44.
———, ed. *Spider Woman's Granddaughters: Traditional Tales and Contemporary Writing by Native American Women.* New York: Fawcett Columbine, 1989.
Barnes, Kim. "A Leslie Marmon Silko Interview." *Journal of Ethnic Studies* 134 (1986): 83–105.
Chapman, Mary. " 'The Belly of This Story': Storytelling and Symbolic Birth in Native American Fiction." *Studies in American Indian Literature* 7.2 (summer 1995): 3–16.
Graulich, Melody, ed. Introduction. "Remember the Stories." *Women Writers — Texts and Contexts: "Yellow Woman": Leslie Marmon Silko.* New Brunswick: Rutgers UP, 1993. 3–25.
Owens, Louis. *Other Destinies: Understanding the American Indian Novel.* Norman: U of Oklahoma P, 1992.
Ruoff, A. LaVonne. "Ritual and Renewal: Keres Traditions in Leslie Silko's 'Yellow Woman.'" In Graulich, 69–81. Rpt. of "Ritual and Renewal: Keres Traditions in the Short Fiction of Leslie Silko." *MELUS* 5.4 (winter 1978): 2–17.
Silko, Leslie Marmon. *Ceremony.* New York: Viking, 1977.
———. "Yellow Woman." *Storyteller.* New York: Seaver Books, 1981. 54–62.

Smith, Patricia Clark, and Paula Gunn Allen. "Earthy Relations, Carnal Knowledge: Southwestern American Indian Women Writers and Landscape." In Graulich, 115–50. Rpt. from *The Desert Is No Lady: Southwestern Landscapes in Women's Writing and Art.* Ed. Vera Norwood and Janice Monk. New Haven: Yale UP, 1987. 174–96.

Swan, Edith. "Laguna Symbolic Geography and Silko's *Ceremony.*" *American Indian Quarterly* 12 (summer 1988): 229–49.

ANTIDOTE TO DESECRATION

Leslie Marmon Silko's Nonfiction

Daniel White

Leslie Marmon Silko has established herself as a leading voice among contemporary Native American writers through her poetry and fiction, particularly *Ceremony* (1977), her widely read first novel, and *Almanac of the Dead* (1991). But until recently, Silko's major contribution to the nonfiction genre consisted of the essay "Landscape, History, and the Pueblo Imagination."[1] The essay's effective encapsulation of Pueblo philosophy and its reprinting in dozens of anthologies served to establish the piece as essentially Silko's creed. In *Sacred Water* (1993), which combines photographs with nonfiction prose and Pueblo mythology with autobiography, Silko creates a powerful sequel to the earlier essay, though one available only in a self-published limited edition. Thus many readers have yet to discover the later volume. In Silko's most recent book, however, most of her periodical pieces, along with an expanded version of "Landscape" retitled "Interior and Exterior Landscapes: The Pueblo Migration Stories," have been collected into one readily accessible volume, *Yellow Woman and a Beauty of the Spirit: Essays on Native American Life Today* (1996).[2]

At a glance, Silko's essays cover a broad range of disparate topics — from the historical patterns of abuse in federal Indian policies to the contemporary issues of immigration and the United States Border Patrol, from the marriage of literature and photography to the relationship between the southwestern landscape and Pueblo mythology — all focused through the lens of Silko's autobiography. Yet the *Yellow Woman* essays and *Sacred*

Water ultimately dovetail toward one controlling question: as our modern world spirals downward on intensifying cycles of greed and violence, can we find a better way to live? To Silko, prevailing Eurocentric values and the governments that sustain them are not merely corrupt; they desecrate and destroy whatever they touch; they are "serial killers of life on earth" (*Yellow Woman and a Beauty,* 95).

The human race may have one chance to save itself. In a letter to Laura Coltelli, Silko specifically describes *Sacred Water* as "a soothing, healing antidote to the relentless horror loose in this world" ("Silko's *Sacred Water,*" 26). This "relentless horror" cannot be attacked directly, at least not successfully. It must be gradually eroded away. In an interview, Silko says, "I believe in subversion rather than straight-out confrontation. I believe in the sands of time" (Coltelli, *Winged Words,* 147). Subversion is the active ingredient of Silko's antidote to the poison of Euro-American culture. Just as Tayo in *Ceremony* turns away from the madness and death that are symptomatic of his exposure to mainstream America and its war, we, *the people* — regardless of heritage — must reject Euro-American values. And just as Tayo finds his salvation in an intricate ceremony associated with the land beneath his feet and the people who have lived on and with it for centuries, so we must accept the antidote she offers not only in *Sacred Water* but also throughout *Yellow Woman and a Beauty of the Spirit,* asserts Silko. We must absorb and act upon the wisdom of the ancient Pueblo worldview.[3]

Passed down through successive generations by the oral-storytelling tradition, the Pueblo worldview recognizes that our continued existence depends upon a complex web of relationships that must be kept in balance. Classifying components of the philosophy can be misleading, as Silko describes attempts by anthropologists to categorize individual tales. But for the sake of convenience and discussion, two general types of lessons can be delineated — those about how people should relate to each other and those about how they should relate to the earth — though these cannot be separated in practice.

"WE ARE ALL SISTERS AND BROTHERS"

In the introduction to *Yellow Woman,* Silko reveals how her awareness of the conflicting value systems developed. She credits her family background, "a mixture of Indian, Mexican, and white," with making her "acutely aware of the inherent conflicts between Indian and white, old-time beliefs and Christianity" (17). The Laguna Pueblo of her childhood was a society steeped in centuries of tradition, yet troubled by the increasingly pervasive influence of modern Euro-American culture. During Silko's generation, the pueblo had arrived at a sort of crossroads, and Silko could feel the opposing influences operating upon her: "Life at Laguna for me was a daily balancing act of Laguna beliefs and Laguna ways and the ways of the outsiders" (17). Silko's mixed bloodlines placed her in a singular position among Laguna children. She experienced how outsiders — primarily white tourists — responded to her skin color, for example, but just as significantly, how the younger Pueblo people were beginning to adopt similar prejudices.

In the title essay, "Yellow Woman and a Beauty of the Spirit," Silko expands upon the theme of prejudice as one clear contrast between Euro-American and Pueblo values. Yet Silko sees this distinction becoming blurred at Laguna: "Younger people . . . seemed to look at the world in a more modern way. The modern way included racism" (61). Silko suggests that the way for all people to combat racism is to embrace the beliefs of Grandma A'mooh (her great-grandmother) and the "old-time people": "For them, a person's value lies in how that person interacts with other people, how that person behaves toward the animals and the earth. . . . The Pueblo people believed this long before the Puritans arrived with their notions of sin and damnation, and racism" (61). The ancient Pueblo people realized that the strength of a society lay in its cohesiveness, the willingness of its people to work cooperatively. Survival depended upon a communal effort, and individuals achieved respect in proportion to the value of their contributions.

Racism, on the other hand, leads to divisiveness, confrontation, and ultimately, self-destruction. But it is only one of the many poisonous by-products of a Euro-American culture that finds beauty — and status — in superficial appearances: "People no longer hide their face-lifts and they discuss their liposuctions because the point of the procedures isn't just cosmetic, it is social. It says to the world, 'I have enough spare cash that I can afford surgery for cosmetic purposes'" (65). Silko deplores the value system that reduces "people" — mainly women, of course — to such a ridiculous level of competition. Since, as she argues, "most of the definitions of beauty in contemporary Western culture are really codes for determining social status," one can understand how women have lagged behind men, whose competitions traditionally have been economic, in acquiring power and respect.

Again Silko promotes the egalitarianism within ancient Pueblo philosophy as the sane alternative to sexism: "In the view of the old-time people, we are all sisters and brothers because the Mother Creator made all of us" (63). The phrase "sisters and brothers" suggests that men and women exist on equal terms. Actions determine worth, regardless of gender, and the greatest deeds are those that help sustain life — producing healthy children, for one. Thus "strong, sturdy women [are] most admired" (66), and beauty becomes a matter of good health and "a feeling of harmony" (65). These are the desired qualities to be passed down to the next generation. Consequently, the concept of a "Mother Creator" celebrates the power of female sexuality and fertility, allowing women to serve "as often as men in the old stories as hero figures" (70).

Silko cites Kochininako, or Yellow Woman, as her favorite "hero" and recounts several examples of tales in which "Kochininako's vibrant sexuality benefits her people" (71). Clearly, Silko admires Yellow Woman's combination of sensuality, resiliency, and cunning, as is evident from the prominent role she plays in Silko's fiction. The most notable example is, of course, "Yellow Woman," perhaps Silko's best-known short story, in which a young Laguna wife and mother becomes a not-too-unwilling captive of Silva, a cattle rustler of mysterious origin, and wonders if she may actually be Yellow Woman and Silva a ka'tsina, or mountain spirit, as in the old stories. Her identification with Yellow Woman stems, in part, from her recollections of these tales as told by her grandfather: "it was the Yellow Woman stories he liked to tell best" ("Yellow Woman," 45).

The story suggests that Pueblo men and women admire Kochininako, but women have a special affinity for her. As Paula Gunn Allen notes, "In many ways Kochinnenako [Gunn's spelling] is a role model. . . . She is, one might say, the Spirit of Woman" (88). Melody Graulich adds, "Kochinnenako is a liberating figure, especially for young women" (12). In Yellow Woman, Leslie Silko finds a source of power and inspiration: "Kochininako is beautiful because she has the courage to act in times of great peril, and her triumph is achieved by her sensuality, not through violence and destruction. . . . Yellow Woman and all women are beautiful" (72). Silko implies that the true potential of "all women" is revealed in the Kochininako stories, not on the plastic surgeon's table.

It is also telling that Silko specifically disassociates Kochininako from "violence and destruction." These, she argues, are the provinces of Euro-American culture's two most powerful and corrupt institutions: religion and law. While these institutions convey the appearance of invulnerability, both, according to Silko, show signs of imminent collapse.

Describing European religion in the essay "Tribal Prophecies," Silko writes, "Torture and death have been the centerpieces of Christianity in the Americas from the beginning" (147). Having "arrived fresh from the . . . Inquisition," European Christians were especially ill-prepared to understand Native American spirituality (147). The Christian religion acknowledged one divine being, and "for Europeans, it was quite unimaginable that Quetzalcoatl might ever share the altar with Jesus" (177). Yet it is just such sharing that, in Silko's view, elevates Pueblo spirituality to its privileged position. Whereas Christians must invest all their faith in a single deity, "Pueblo cultures seek to include rather than exclude. The Pueblo impulse is to accept and incorporate what works, because human survival in the southwestern climate is so arduous and risky" (177). While Christianity tends to disconnect its followers from the earth with promises of an otherworldly Heaven, Pueblo religion reinforces the people's ties to each other and to the land. And while Christianity has been used to justify atrocities ranging from the Spanish Inquisition to slavery in the American South, Pueblo religion teaches that "all things, even rocks and water, have spirit and being" and thus are deserving of respect (64).

Through her discussion of Pueblo spirituality, Silko makes it clear that rescuing the continent from the evils of Christianity is no mere pipe dream. She believes that just as ancient Native American prophecies predicted the European invasion of America, so too, do they foretell a period of "great turmoil and suffering," after which "all things European will gradually disappear" (147).

Undoubtedly, one of the first things Silko would like to see disappear from America is its "barbaric legal system" (20). She was introduced to the system as a young child when Laguna Pueblo sued the state of New Mexico over "six million acres of land the state wrongfully took" (18). The pueblo spent twenty years and $2 million fighting for the return of "the land they cherished," and in return, the United States Court of Indian Claims awarded the Lagunas twenty-five cents per acre (19). The lawsuit left "a great and lasting impression" on Silko (19), who understood that it typified the kind of justice Native Americans had come to expect. Indeed, government confiscation of Indian lands has become a familiar refrain in American history. In a brief essay entitled "Auntie Kie Talks about U.S. Presidents and U.S. Indian Policy," Silko creates a platform for the local expert on "the history of Indian treaties and Indian law" to sum up the damage: "On the day the pilgrims washed up on the East Coast shore, the tribal people of this continent had 1,905,000,000 acres of land. By 1871 the Indians had 140 million acres left. And today, we have 92 million acres, 40 million of which are in Alaska. That's about 5 percent of what we started with, and most of this land is what the white people didn't want" (80–81). Auntie Kie's dynamic speech revitalizes the old story of broken treaties and outright theft. With relish, she exposes the hypocrisy of a nation that claims to value "liberty and justice for all," while practicing "fraud, armed robbery, and murder" to appease its appetite for exploitable land (81–82).

Ultimately, Silko arrives at the essential motivation for such depraved behavior and the defining characteristic of Euro-American values: utter greed. In Silko's view, the dominating Euro-American culture hoards every available parcel of land, along with its concomitant natural resources. Historically composed of white males, its power structure reacts defensively and almost instinctively to members of the other sex or different races who threaten to divide the spoils. The usual result has been the oppression of minority groups as a means of stifling competition. Elaborate, draconian mechanisms must be unleashed to keep these potential economic rivals in check. In the American Southwest, the ultimate symbol of oppression, Silko argues, is the Border Patrol.

With virtually unlimited powers to restrict citizens' freedom of movement, she charges in "Fences against Freedom," the Border Patrol has created a "police state . . . in the southwestern United States. No person, no citizen is free to travel without the scrutiny of the Border Patrol" (111). Silko supports her accusations, in part, by recounting several personal confrontations with the agency, including one particularly chilling incident in southern New Mexico:

> It was nearly midnight on New Mexico State Road 26, a dark lonely stretch of two-lane highway between Hatch and Deming. When I sat up, I saw the headlights and emergency flashers of six vehicles — Border Patrol cars and a Border Patrol van blocked both lanes of the road. . . .
>
> I will never forget that night beside the highway. There was an awful feeling of menace and of violence straining to break loose. (109)

The Border Patrol has the authority to stop and detain anyone regardless of probable cause, but they target people of color. Silko states, "It was clear that my appearance — my skin color — was the reason for the detention" (108). As long as politicians are allowed to exploit economic anxiety by pinning the blame for unemployment and other ills on illegal immigrants, such overtly racist harassment will continue, charges Silko, and will probably worsen. Indeed, we may already have begun "the inexorable slide into further government-mandated 'race policies' that can only end in madness and genocide" (114).

But there is hope. As always, Silko believes the solution lies with the will of the people and their power to overthrow oppression through the gradual subversion of authority. "Fortunately," Silko declares, "the people of the United States are far better human beings than the greedy elected officials who allegedly represent them" (107). And in "The Border Patrol State," her second essay on this subject, Silko goes further, concluding that, regardless of what occurs north of the border, the Border Patrol's efforts are doomed to failure: "It is no use; borders haven't worked, and they won't work, not now, as the indigenous people of the Americas reassert their kinship and solidarity with one another. . . . The great human migration within the Americas cannot be stopped" (122–23). I noted previously that Silko looks toward the impending collapse of Christianity and every remaining vestige of Euro-American culture, as forecast in the ancient prophecies. Here, she expresses her confidence that Native Americans are already positioning themselves to fill the resulting void with "kinship and solidarity." Silko plants the idea that, as Native Americans reclaim their lands, a state of natural harmony may once again evolve and prevail.

"HUMAN BEINGS DESECRATE ONLY THEMSELVES"

Any recent collection of "nature writing" is replete with references to Native American culture and philosophy. Indeed, pleas for a saner way of living — ecologically and otherwise — run like a river current through nature essays and frequently echo the traditional values of Native Americans. In acknowledging this influence, Barry Lopez, for example, offers the following advice to readers interested in the genre: "I would suggest, first, the anthropological work that records with respect and fidelity the *other* visions of North America, those of the native people" (297). As one classic example, Lopez cites Richard K. Nelson's *Make Prayers to the Raven,* concerning the Koyukon people of Alaska's boreal forests. Lopez himself has introduced native legends to his readers and has often emulated the style of Indian mythology. Clearly, nature writers approach native ideas with deference and noble intentions. Yet there is something subtly disturbing in the fact that nature writing enjoys a wealth of anthropologists, but suffers a poverty of Native American writers to tell their own stories.

Robert Finch and John Elder, editors of *The Norton Book of Nature Writing* (1990), describe how they were "struck" by this realization: "although the figure and experience of the Native American come into much early American nature writing, examples of nature writing by Indians in English have not often been available until our day" (26). Even in "our day," examples beyond Silko and N. Scott Momaday do not come readily to mind. Thus, their works take on added significance in view of the relative scarcity of other voices. At a glance, Native American writers, with cultural ties to the land dating back centuries, would seem to fit perfectly into the nature-writing genre. But as Lee Schweninger observes, "whereas the Euro-American tradition considers nature writing as a special genre, Native Americans 'write nature' regardless of genre" (49). To many Native American authors, the nature-essay form may imply an artificial division between the human and nonhuman compartments of the world.

While the nature-writing genre can be traced back to Linnaeus's systems of classification, contemporary American nature writing essentially was fathered by a New Englander, Henry David Thoreau. Thoreau hiked out of Concord to commune with nature at a local pond; the result, of course, was *Walden,* a fact-based personal account, manipulated artfully. He undertook a number of other "excursions," as he called them — most notably to Cape Cod and to Maine — writing about these, too. The pattern has become familiar: John Muir trekking off to the Sierra Nevadas, Edward Abbey to the Colorado Plateau, Barry Lopez to the Arctic, and on and on. By contrast, traditional native peoples have never needed to leave town to seek out an experience in nature; nature *is* their town. As Finch and Elder suggest, the dearth of Native American writers publishing nature essays "may . . . reflect the fact that a certain kind of intense and self-conscious awareness of nature follows from a loss of integration between society and nature" (26).

Silko seems acutely aware of this "loss of integration." She perceives it to be a primary affliction of Euro-American culture as well as a growing threat to young Native Americans. "Interior and Exterior Landscapes," with its creed-like invocation of *integration,* presents one of Silko's strongest arguments in favor of the ancient Pueblo worldview as model. In this portrait she paints "from a high arid plateau in New Mexico," Silko reveals how the seams connecting the older Laguna people to the land are as natural and unobtrusive as the ecotones that connect one type of landscape to another. The people "all originate from the depths of the earth," which is "the Mother Creator of all things." And when they die, they "become dust, and in this becoming they are once more joined with the Mother" (27). Silko has elevated her message — literally — by speaking from this plateau, as a minister from a pulpit. She speaks with a quiet confidence designed to assure her readers that they, too, can reestablish ties to "the Mother." Her words, backed by the wisdom of centuries, ring with authority, but not with superiority.

Silko acknowledges, as did her Pueblo ancestors, that all humans are fallible. Indeed, Pueblo teachings depend upon an awareness of such shortcomings, and Silko's goal is to exhibit how her people have heeded the lessons from their mistakes. They had to, or they would have perished. Pueblo wisdom is gained from trial and error in an arid, unforgiving land where even the tiniest mistake can be fatal. An individual transgressor may not be the only one at risk; the harmful actions of one may have dire consequences for all.

Thus cautionary themes are ubiquitous within the oral tradition. Just as humans must display cooperation with and respect for each other, so for example, must they treat the "Antelope People" who feed them: "Waste of meat or even the thoughtless handling of bones cooked bare will offend the antelope spirits. Next year the hunters will vainly search the dry plains for antelope" (26–27). Obviously, food is a precious resource on the "dry plains," so Pueblo youth must be taught to cherish and protect the delicate balance between beings who depend on each other for survival.

Another key example of the dangers of upsetting natural processes is the story of the Gambler, a malicious spirit who steals the rain clouds. In a dry land, nothing is more valuable than rain, so the Gambler hopes to reap a huge financial gain from his theft. What occurs instead is a drought that endangers everyone. Silko sums up the moral: "greed, even on the part of only one being, had the effect of threatening the survival of all life on earth" (29–30). These stories serve as constant reminders, particularly to each new generation, of the people's responsibilities to the earth and, consequently, to each other.

In his essay "Remembering the Sacred Family," John Daniel muses, "Our own European cultures must once have carried similar stories with similar themes, but we have for the most part left those stories behind, along with our sense of responsibility" (162). One of the self-imposed duties of the nature writer is to raise awareness of our "responsibility," something that traditional native peoples have practiced as naturally as breathing. Silko presses the same issues from the Native American perspective. In so doing, she is not merely instructing other cultures; she is taking a stand in defense of her people and, by extension, the earth.

Her plateau perspective may be elevated, physically and ethically, but it is isolated and surrounded — a fortress under siege, with the invaders even more numerous and powerful than the Apache raiders or Spanish conquistadors of centuries past. A few miles east of Laguna lies the water-guzzling urban sprawl of Albuquerque. Jets and helicopters from Kirtland Air Force Base rip through the skies and shatter the silence hanging over the Swahnee mesa where two of Silko's ancestors died in an Apache ambush (33–34).

In the original version of "Interior and Exterior Landscapes," Silko seems content with offering a sensible alternative to contemporary techno-industrial culture. Her expanded version, however, reflects a deepening anxiety, a darker vision. She describes how a uranium mine north of Laguna village has despoiled the land: "The Jackpile Mine is an open pit that has been blasted out of the many hundreds of acres where the orchards and melon patches once grew" (44). Silko notes that its opening inspired "apocalyptic warning stories," yet the mine advocates pushed forward (44). Now the mine is mingled with history. For Silko, the Jackpile Mine is a cautionary tale in the making; uncertainty hangs over its ending.[4] Meanwhile, Silko moves from the story of the mine to one of her own short stories.

In the final section, "Landscape as a Character in Fiction," Silko summarizes "Storyteller" and emphasizes the active role the Alaskan landscape plays in her story. Nature, in the form of a frozen river, helps a "young Yupik Eskimo woman" exact vengeance on a white trader who is a murderer and "a parasite, exploiting not only the fur-bearing animals and the fish but also the Yupik people themselves" (45). His actions are symptomatic of a dominant white world whose defining characteristics are exploitation and waste, anathema to the Pueblo worldview. He believes in the invincibility of his technological gadgets and brute strength: "The white man had reckoned with the young woman and determined he could overpower her. But the white man failed to account for the conjunction of the landscape with the woman" (45). The Yupik woman uses her intimate knowledge of the river, the brittle ice, and the "blinding white" canvas of the entire landscape to destroy the oppressor and restore balance to her world (46). An ironic twist in this story is that the legal system could work in her favor—if she denies the truth and goes along with describing the incident as an accident. But in her mind, she must take responsibility for the trader's death. She will not allow the corrupt system to corrupt her or her special relationship with the land.

Silko concludes the essay by moving from this consideration of her story, with its theme that landscapes can avenge themselves, or at least serve as willing accomplices, to an explicit warning: "When humans have blasted and burned the last bit of life from the earth, an immeasurable freezing will descend with a darkness that obliterates the sun" (47). With these final words, Silko seals and delivers her own apocalyptic vision.

The question then becomes what an individual does in the face of such potential devastation. *Sacred Water* portrays Silko confronting this struggle on a personal level. In a ranch house on the outskirts of Tucson, she is physically removed from Laguna Pueblo, but she continues to draw strength and resolve from her heritage. Her major theme is the sanctity of water, as the title indicates, and the lack of respect for it manifested by urban encroachment and the wasteful attitudes that ensue.

Early in the book, Silko looks to her childhood in establishing the cautionary tone of the book: "We children were seldom scolded or punished for our behavior. But we were never permitted to frolic with or waste fresh water. We were given stern warnings about killing toads or frogs. Harm to frogs and toads could bring disastrous cloudbursts and floods because the frogs and toads are the beloved children of the rain clouds" (6). These "beloved children of the rain clouds" are indicators of rain or "fresh water." In the desert, they are like cottonwood trees—symbols of life.

But not all cultures have valued the water, the creatures, or life. As an example, Silko describes how the Spaniards misinterpreted petroglyphs depicting coiled snakes: "The Spaniards thought the snake glyphs pointed to buried treasures the Indians had hidden" (29). In reality, the snakes point out the direction of a freshwater source: "The Spaniards did not understand: fresh water is the treasure" (29). They had not yet come to terms with this desert landscape and the premium it placed upon commodities that, in Spain, were taken for granted. Besides, they were obsessed with gold, and they valued the accumulation of wealth above all else.

In short, Silko argues, the Spaniards failed to grasp the obvious. More recently, the perceptive abilities of U.S. government officials have been no more acute. By comparison, Silko remembers her childhood neighbor, Felipe, who prudently collected rainwater runoff for irrigation, which simultaneously protected homes from flood damage. His handmade "stone check dams" were "subtle, and conformed to the natural contours," whereas years later, after Felipe's death, the federal government sent in its engineers to address the situation. With typical inefficiency and overkill, the engineers "spent months and many thousands of dollars to install giant storm drains that dump the run-off into the river" (47).

Silko sees this conflict — between the thrift and sanity of the Pueblo world-view and the waste and arrogance of the techno-industrial forces — epitomized by Tucson life. The city is dependent on " 'fossil water' " from an ancient "aquifer which has receded so far that the two hundred year old cottonwood trees along the Tanque Verde wash are dying" and which can no longer be pumped in certain areas because it is contaminated with "trichloroethylene and other industrial chemicals" (52). Silko responds by looking back to Felipe's example and saving the rainwater. Her ranch house "has a similar rain water catchment system which routes all rainwater from the roof into a concrete pool," where it is stored along with "run-off from a gravel-covered slope" (52). This pool becomes the focus and symbol of Silko's struggle to maintain a respectable life in a world that is indifferent at best — and often overtly hostile — to her values.

Myriad forces converge to assault the pond. First are thoughtless and careless individuals (reminiscent of the Gambler). The life force of Silko's pond is represented by its thriving population of Sonoran red-spotted toads: "Hundreds of toads used to sing all night in magnificent choruses with complex harmonies" (63). Silko writes, "used to sing" — past tense. She made the mistake of inviting the wrong man to dinner. His sons took their dog outside after the meal, and Silko describes the unforeseen consequences: "A few minutes later, when the man and I joined the boys, we found them with the dog by the rain water pool. Strewn all around the pool were the remains of toads smashed flat by the boys and the dog" (64). She "managed to keep [her] composure" and adds, without elaborating, that she "never saw them again" (66).

But thoughtless individuals are not the only threat, nor the worst. The rain itself may not always be benign. The toad population was slow in making a comeback, and Silko poses the subsequent Chernobyl disaster as a potential explanation.[5] Whether the actual culprit is radioactive fallout or some other techno-industrial by-product such as acid precipitation, the toads function as an indicator species for the pond habitat. Their decline alerts Silko that the ecosystem and its ability to sustain all life remain under attack by powerful and mysterious forces. As Sheila W. Polson reports in her article on ongoing scientific investigations into plummeting amphibian populations worldwide, "If a frog or toad population is hurting, say scientists, the chances are good that some other living thing or natural system is also askew" (39).

The next signal to Silko that the "natural system is . . . askew" arrives when "a strange red algae with the texture of mucous" invades the pond (68). It blankets the water, kills the aquatic vegetation, and lures animals to a death by drowning. At this point, Silko nearly surrenders: "I considered destroying the pool" (70). She even begins to fill it in with crushed rock, but then discovers that she has stumbled onto the beginnings of a possible solution. The rock "created a natural escape ramp" for the wildlife and "acted as a natural filter" that seemed to weaken the algae (70). Bolstered by this limited success, she renews her efforts.

Searching for a natural solution rather than a technological one, she discovers the water hyacinth. Often considered a pest species due to its clogging of navigable waterways, the hyacinths nevertheless beat back the algae and rejuvenate Silko's pond: "The water in the pool began to clear and smell cleaner because water hyacinths digest the worst sorts of wastes and contamination . . . even lead and cadmium" (72). Silko has clearly gained the upper hand in her struggle for life. As Laura Coltelli observes, "The story of this water purified from the devastating invasion of red algae by means of water hyacinths indicates — as for Tayo in *Ceremony* . . . — the route towards a genuinely regenerative ceremony" ("Leslie Marmon Silko's *Sacred Water*," 26). Silko finds this "regenerative" force at work beyond the pond water itself; she discovers that "last summer the pool had polly-wogs again, the descendants of the red-spotted toads which had survived fall-out and the boys with the dog" (66).

Silko's personal triumph is reassuring, but the hope provided by her model is tempered by another warning. Unfortunately, winning the battle of the pond, while a good omen if we heed its message, does not represent an unqualified victory in the war for continuing existence. She points out that "only the night-blooming datura . . . sacred plant of the Pueblo priests . . . has the power to purify plutonium contamination" (75). But will enough people wake

up and heed the wisdom of the Pueblo priests — as channeled through Silko —
and consume the antidote, or will too many of us continue to smash toads and
poison ourselves? Silko's outlook in the final words of *Sacred Water* may be
less bleak than her conclusion to "Landscapes," but only slightly:

> Across the West, uranium mine wastes and contamination from under-
> ground nuclear tests in Nevada ruin the dwindling supplies of fresh water.
> Chemical pollutants and heavy metals from abandoned mines leak mer-
> cury and lead into aquifers and rivers. But human beings desecrate only
> themselves; the Mother Earth is inviolable. Whatever may become of us
> human beings, the Earth will bloom with hyacinth purple and the white
> blossoms of the datura.

There may be some solace in Silko's assertion that "human beings desecrate
only themselves." She has faith that the earth will survive, that the hyacinth
and datura will flourish, even if we no longer exist to enjoy them.

NOTES

1. The essay first appeared in a special edition of *Antaeus* 57 (autumn 1986): 83–94.
   The expanded version included in *Yellow Woman* was first published in George F.
   Thompson's anthology *Landscape in America* (Austin: U of Texas P, 1995).
2. One work that was not included deserves mention. "In the Combat Zone" (*Hungry
   Mind Review* [fall 1995] 44, 46) addresses the topic of violence against women.
   Silko argues that whereas most women (meaning Euro-American women) learn to
   "be self-sacrificing, passive victims," her upbringing at Laguna, where she became a
   skilled hunter, enables her to protect herself if threatened. She advocates that all
   women "learn how to take aggressive action individually" to "destroy the myth that
   women are born to be easy targets."
3. Silko provides a note to define "ancient Pueblo people": "I mean the last generation
   or two, which included my great-grandmother, just barely. Their worldview was still
   uniquely Pueblo" (203).
4. Silko discusses some recent developments in "Fifth World: The Return of MA AH
   SHRA TRUE EE, the Giant Serpent" (124–34). She describes a "giant stone snake
   formation" discovered by two of the miners and its apparent connection to stories of
   "a giant snake who is a messenger for the Mother Creator" (126). Silko suggests that
   the snake could be a warning of ominous consequences if the harmony of the earth
   continues to be disturbed by the mine.
5. A recent Associated Press report out of Tucson verifies that some two dozen of
   Arizona's native amphibian populations are on the decline "in a pattern similar to
   one scientists are seeing worldwide." In Arizona, the main factor appears to be the
   destruction of riparian habitats, but "environmental pollution in the form of acid

rain and ultraviolet radiation are also reasons for the decline" (*Daily Lobo,* 29 January 1996).

WORKS CITED

Allen, Paula Gunn. "Kochinnenako in Academe: Three Approaches to Interpreting a Keres Indian Tale." *The Sacred Hoop: Recovering the Feminine in American Indian Traditions.* Boston: Beacon, 1986. Rpt. in Leslie Marmon Silko. *"Yellow Woman"/ Leslie Marmon Silko.* Ed. Melody Graulich. Women Writers: Texts and Contexts. New Brunswick, New Jersey: Rutgers UP, 1993. 83–111.

Coltelli, Laura. "Leslie Marmon Silko's *Sacred Water." Studies in American Indian Literature* 8.4 (1996): 21–29.

——. *Winged Words: American Indian Writers Speak.* Lincoln: U of Nebraska P, 1990.

Daniel, John. *The Trail Home: Essays.* New York: Pantheon, 1992.

Finch, Robert, and John Elder. Introduction. *The Norton Book of Nature Writing.* New York: Norton, 1990. 19–28.

Graulich, Melody. Introduction. *"Yellow Woman"/Leslie Marmon Silko.* Ed. Melody Graulich. Women Writers: Texts and Contexts. New Brunswick, New Jersey: Rutgers UP, 1993. 3–25.

Lopez, Barry. "Natural History: An Annotated Booklist." *Antaeus* 57 (1986): 295–97.

Polson, Sheila W. "Amphibian Assault." *National Parks* (May–June 1997): 38–41.

Schweninger, Lee. "Writing Nature: Silko and Native Americans as Nature Writers." *MELUS* 18.2 (1993): 47–60.

Silko, Leslie Marmon. *Sacred Water.* Tucson: Flood Plain Press, 1993.

——. "Yellow Woman." *The Man to Send Rain Clouds: Contemporary Stories by American Indians.* Ed. Kenneth Rosen. New York: Viking, 1974. 33–45.

——. *Yellow Woman and a Beauty of the Spirit: Essays on Native American Life Today.* New York: Simon and Schuster, 1996.

SILKO'S BLOOD SACRIFICE

The Circulating Witness in Almanac of the Dead

David L. Moore

In a crucial sense, Leslie Silko's *Almanac of the Dead* precedes her earlier novel *Ceremony* by magnifying its climactic narrative moment and theme of witness, and by recirculating its distinct traditional impulse. *Almanac* reopens the literary ceremony through a ritual, analogical reenactment of a specific tradition that shapes not only *Ceremony* but also *Storyteller,* her multigenre narrative of Laguna life. The latest novel amplifies originary aspects of the former texts, circling back and replaying a pivotal gesture in Tayo's healing and Estoy-eh-muut's quest, like the refrain in a drum song. *Almanac*'s cyclic return to the precarious balance of an extended autumnal equinox replays the axial night at the Jackpile Mine in *Ceremony,* radiating its toxins and its cures into the world. "The days, years, and centuries were spirit beings who traveled the universe, returning endlessly" (*Almanac* 523). The oppositional forces that *Ceremony* works to heal in Tayo and in the land, and that Estoy-eh-muut senses as "a fear for all of us" (*Ceremony* 142) when the Kunideeyahs work their evil, reveal themselves in *Almanac* to be larger still. As Joy Harjo suggests, "*Almanac of the Dead* is an exploded version of the same text *[Ceremony],* only now the terrain encompasses all of America" (209). Thus the healing process must be repeated over and over with more intensity. *Storyteller,* like *Ceremony,* places the Estoy-eh-muut/Arrowboy story at its typographic and geographic core, and expands it beyond *Ceremony*'s treatment by juxtaposing Arrowboy directly to the grand witchery tale of "white skin people . . . Killing killing killing

killing . . . Whirling / whirling / whirling / whirling" (*Storyteller* 133–36). In all three of these texts, it is Arrowboy's task to witness and thus undo this cyclic killing. *Almanac* thereby moves into and out of the heart of *Ceremony* through the dynamic silence in *Ceremony*'s final witchery scene where Tayo, in a modern role of Arrowboy against the witches, gazes from the boulders and triumphs by restraining himself from fighting with the destroyers.

For many readers witnessing that amplified witchery in *Almanac* on a larger scale, the novel's breadth and complexity are as daunting as are its graphic brutalities, but its arduous elements are specifically dictated by its purpose as an account of complex forces in the world, by its Arrowboy dedication to witness history. My preliminary commentary does not attempt an overview, but highlights a few threads in the novel's vast tapestry. Other features of the novel might occupy the careful reader, notably the giant stone snake, or the "shallow graves," or the presence of rocks, or the prophetic progress of certain characters like Sterling, Lecha, or Tacho, but I forego these textual and textural features for a somewhat more contextual approach. That is, the interpenetration of text and context in Silko's work pushes the fictional form to extremes by the ways she structures relations between text and reader, and through the reader as witness, between text and history. Thus this discussion focuses on two refrains in *Almanac* that echo and amplify *Ceremony* and *Storyteller*: the witness of death, through the trope of the Tayo/Arrowboy myth, and the narrative of circulation of life and death, through the trope of blood itself.

I

Narrative Witness: "The Thing Itself"

Let's first look at a ritual of the reader in *Almanac* by which Arrowboy's gaze defeats the witchery, "for now." The interactive dynamics of Silko's oral tradition structure this literary process of witness, so that author and reader witness, elude, and neutralize destruction, as in *Ceremony:* "Something is wrong," [the witchman] said. / "Ck'o'yo magic won't work / if someone is watching us" (259). In *Storyteller,* because Estoy-eh-muut watches the witches trying to shape-shift into animals, "Nothing happened. / 'Something is wrong,' the leader said . . . 'go and see / if an outsider is spying on us'" (146). That "someone," the "outsider," in *Ceremony, Storyteller,* and *Almanac* is of course, first, Silko. Yet her earlier books also have constructed a reader(ship) who may watch like Arrowboy, if they have learned the ritual lessons of *Ceremony* and *Storyteller,* and are ready for her next ritual, *Almanac of the Dead.* As James

Ruppert writes in his essay on "mediational texts," frequently Silko and other contemporary American Indian writers, "construct implied readers through the textual perspective presupposed and through the narrative competence required, but also, because they are moving from one world view to another, implied readers require certain epistemological competence at various points in the text. The writers hope that the readers will assume these roles" (10). One particular epistemological competence required for *Almanac* is a recognition of *Ceremony*'s complex ethos of not fighting with the destroyers. As Betonie says early in the ceremony, "And the desire is strong to make things right, to take back what was stolen and to stop them from destroying what they have taken. But you see, Tayo, we have done as much fighting as we can with the destroyers and the thieves: as much as we could do and still survive" (134). Instead, the role to which Silko tries to fuse her reader is that of witness to the witchery, through the powerful silence of Arrowboy that Tayo learns by the end of *Ceremony*. Testing the reader's competence as witness, Silko measures her reader against the textual brutality of *Almanac*. Whatever Silko's own sacrifices might have been in her nearly ten years of labor on these topics, she leads her readers through the personal ritual of *Ceremony* to sacrifice their egos, their epistemologies, and their ideologies on the rebuilt altar of history in *Almanac*. By assuming the role she builds for them and bearing witness to a different history, recognizing "that theirs was a nation built on stolen land" (*Ceremony* 199), they may effect a different reality.

Revisionary history that is unabashedly political and idealistic has become a positive force among contemporary American Indian writers. Gerald Vizenor's editorial choice for an epigraph to *Narrative Chance* underlines the significance that contemporary Native writers such as Vizenor and Silko give to the revisionary power of the witnessing process that saturates their work. For both ethos and aesthetic in a strategy of self-representation, they write as a way of gaining access to stories that history makes inaccessible. Vizenor quotes Wolfgang Iser: "Representation as aesthetic semblance indicates the presence of the inaccessible. Literature reflects life under conditions that are either not available in the empirical world or are denied by it. Consequently literature turns life into a storehouse from which it draws its material in order to stage that which in life appeared to have been sealed off from access" (v). Iser's notion that representation is itself a performance underlines Silko's ethical presence as witness in this modern Arrowboy myth.[1] What then are the dynamics of witness?

RADICAL PATIENCE Not surprisingly, the steps to *Almanac* as a "prequel" to *Ceremony* are not linear. Over and over again as it recounts its horrors, this expansive novel spirals back to the witches' fire that is still warm in *Ceremony's* uranium mine scene, "a black mark on the ground where the fire had been" (266). *Ceremony* emphasizes the defeat of the witchery, "It is dead for now" (274), while *Almanac* emphasizes the qualifier "for now." The structure of *Almanac* pesters and recirculates its own thematic content of witness, emphasizing how cyclic and temporary that victorious ceremony may be, requiring constant vigilance by the keepers of the almanac. This vigilance is why, indeed, *Almanac* seems to many readers to be a step backward, so grim, so muddled and pessimistic after the luminous healing of *Ceremony*. If that was a ceremony bringing life back to the land, is this a ceremony of death? Does the textual brutality mean the witchery has won over Silko's powers of mythic storytelling? Where is the text of regeneration?

As we shall see through Silko's complex circulation between death and life, the land cannot die. It is less pessimism or cynicism than anxious faith in the power of witness, a faith spurred by anger, which leads the narrative into such an inferno of fear. Each horrific or numbing episode of *Almanac* takes place metaphorically in that narrative hiatus within the momentary climax of *Ceremony*, just when Tayo steps back among the boulders in silent refusal to fight with the destroyers, as he watches the witches, Emo and Pinkie and Leroy, even Harley, turn on each other. We find in *Almanac,* however, that the power of cultural regeneration has been more than in Tayo's not fighting the destroyers; it resides also in the very act of witnessing, the watching. Rather, the potency of "not fighting" is equated with witnessing, with "someone is watching." Thus witnessing is a double power circulating in the silent power of sight, a necessary event that precedes the power of telling.

To briefly review this crucial dynamic in the (anti)climax of *Ceremony*, it must be said that the blank space on the page of the final witchery scene is one of the most resonant silences in modern literature. Silko leads the protagonist, along with the reader, to witness and hence undo oppositional evil, or evil as oppositionality itself. At the culmination of his arduous ceremony, after struggling to find himself on his mythic Laguna landscape, Tayo, in horror and anger, has been watching his enemies enact the witches' ritual. "He was certain his own sanity would be destroyed if he did not stop them and all the suffering and dying they caused" (264). In his panicked stream of consciousness, the narrative has built toward a violent confrontation, yet the momentum in that direction shifts abruptly amid the grisly details of "bleeding chunks of human skin." Instead of advancing to fight the witches, "Tayo stayed on his knees in the shadows" (265). An extra empty space on the page separates not only the paragraphs but the world-shaping choice between fighting and not fighting the destroyers. "The moon was lost in a cloud bank. He moved back into the boulders." The narrative then continues with an explanation of the different potential outcomes: "It had been a close call. The witchery had almost ended the story according to its plan; Tayo had almost jammed the screwdriver into Emo's skull the way the witchery had wanted, savoring the yielding bone and membrane as the steel ruptured the brain. Their deadly ritual for the autumn solstice [sic] would have been completed by him" (265).

Tayo remains in the outwardly passive stance of a witness, but his invisible action is in fact a triumph in the battle over an evil defined in *Ceremony* as witchery's racist and classist lie of oppositionality "united by a circle of death" (258).

> The liars had fooled everyone, white people and Indians alike; as long as people believed the lies, they would never be able to see what had been done to them or what they were doing to each other. . . . [T]hey would never know that they were still being manipulated by those who knew how to stir the ingredients together: white thievery and injustice boiling up the anger and hatred that would finally destroy the world: the starving against the fat, the colored against the white. The destroyers had only to set it into motion, and sit back to count the casualties. (199–200)[2]

The witchery's blood-soaked racism has honed those lines of opposition to a razor's edge, as Emo tries to draw Tayo out of hiding in the boulders with a raging display of Harley's blood on his own hands: "Look at this, you half-breed! White son of a bitch! You can't hide from this!" (264) *Almanac* is a testimony to the power of Emo's words, an attempt to face that blood, and to show by witness a different response, like Tayo's, to such polarized violence in the world.[3]

This different response amounts to a radical patience that, especially among the elders in *Almanac*, sustains the thematic core of the text: "they must not shed blood or the destruction would continue to accompany them" (712). (This particular note of caution comes via even the young, militant Angelita's skeptical voice.) The respect in such care to not shed blood allies itself imagistically with the circulating power and the inexorably cyclic purposes of blood. For instance, in a section of *Almanac* entitled "How Capitalists Die," Tacho, the most unassuming prophet, ruminates humorously on the larger powers at work that allow patience to be the ethos of revolution. His role, with no subversive effort, in pulling the trigger at his corrupt boss's own request to test a "bulletproof" vest in a sales pitch for "security," makes him laugh at the irony of Menardo's pointlessly "active" efforts to defend against the forces of a revolution powered by the spirit. "Tacho thought it really was funny: he, Tacho, had been in his way the most loyal, and yet, look what had happened. Nothing could have saved Menardo" (511).

The epic patience in Tacho's performance of witness relies, as we shall see, on the ostensibly passive forces of time, land, and dreams. Because a response of witness seems passive, Silko's narrative of witness works to undermine the common opposition of active versus passive responses to colonial pressure, what James Clifford refers to as the "pervasive dichotomy" of absorption or resistance in stories of cultural contact (343). Elaine Scarry suggests in her critique of legal theories of medicine, matrimony, and nationality that "active and passive are so mystified in consent that the phenomenon of consent actually calls into question the reality or usefulness of the categories of passive and active" (883). While Scarry's purpose is to show how ostensibly passive bodies in fact retain political agency, her critique amplifies the dynamic that Tayo performs in silence. His very presence as witness and his silent refusal to consent to violence transform the event through his dreaming alliance with the forces of space and time: "He had seen them now and he was certain; he could go back to tell the people" (262).

By replaying at length *Ceremony*'s moment of witness, *Almanac* articulates the witchery's grisly rituals of opposition in order to name them and thus redirect their power toward a different history. Through the equation of witchery with oppositional thinking, Silko subverts the ideology of colonialism, founded on the historical opposition between the European as Self and the Native as Other. Arnold Krupat maps that subversive history in his discussion of *Almanac* as "a powerful example of anti-imperial translation." He describes the metaphorical power of the novel's border crossings, and especially its vision of a great march from Chiapas in the south, as a forceful revision of the east-to-west history of manifest destiny: "Silko's insistence upon the primacy of north-south/south-north movement contests and quite literally seeks to displace the privileged east-west directionality of the hegemonic American master narrative" ("Postcoloniality" 175). A radical patience that finds its time to displace the demographics of manifest destiny draws on forces larger than colonial ones.

TIME Even more than the dramatic march north, Arrowboy's ostensibly passive strategy of watching but not fighting the destroyers changes the colonial story of destruction. A silent efficacy is one reason why that more "active" and dramatic march remains offstage, located "after" the novel itself whose witness effects the real change. The history of opposition would have the First Nations fight a fool's fight, like Tayo against Emo. Instead, the wide-ranging narrative of *Almanac* describes teachings of the elders who valorize patience over violence because of the cyclic power of time. As Old Pancakes says of the aging warrior Cochise, equating passive with active and contrasting strategic patience with ineffectual violence, "Guns and knives would not resolve the struggle. He had reminded the people of the prophecies different tribes had. In each version one fact was clear: the world that the whites brought with them would not last. It would be swept away in a giant gust of wind. All they had to do was wait. It would be only a matter of time" (235). An alliance with time itself allows the patience of the elders to stand against bloodshed: "Tacho recalled the arguments people in villages had had over the eventual disappearance of the white man. Old prophets were adamant; the disappearance would not be caused by military action, necessarily, or by military action alone. The white man would someday disappear all by himself. The disappearance had already begun at the spiritual level. . . . The forces were harsh. A great many people would suffer and die. All ideas and beliefs of the Europeans would gradually wither and drop away" (511). Such historic restraint underlies the macabre stories of neo-colonial brutalities, and it is founded on a peculiar transcendent toughness that does not bifurcate experience into good and evil: "the forces were harsh" on everyone. The function of the guardians of the almanac is to witness and tell every story, including blood sacrifices, perverse or otherwise. Even more than marching, the keeping of the stories holds a sustaining power over time: "Yoeme had believed power resides within the stories; this power ensures the story to be retold, and with each retelling a slight but permanent shift took place" (581). This power becomes time itself, embodied in the spirits of the days. Joy Harjo emphasizes this point: "The main character in *Almanac of the Dead* is Time itself. . . . It's as if the days were ancestors of themselves, much as humans" (209), and the mission of the keepers of the almanac is to attend to those ancestors, a timeless act, or an act in circular time.

Radical patience knows that as blood circulates, so does time, erasing boundaries of past and future, and erasing even the ego structures built on linear, mechanical time. In one example, Clinton, a black and Indian organizer of the homeless army, "had listened to the Barefoot Hopi, and he had talked day and night with the African. Both had preached patience, the patience of the old tribal people who had been humble enough not to expect change in one human lifetime, or even five lifetimes" (741). This humility, allied also with a circulating sense of life and death, which is the engine of cyclic time, takes on power. (My analysis will discuss that ultimate circulation at the end.) The voice of witness enters the thoughts of a prophet: "The Hopi knew he might work to make preparations the rest of his life, yet never see the day when prisons and jails all over the U.S. were hit with riots and strikes simultaneously. But that didn't discourage the Hopi. One human lifetime wasn't much; it was over in a flash.

Conjunctions and convergences of global proportions might require six or seven hundred years to develop" (618).

While *Almanac of the Dead* elaborates *Ceremony*'s theme of not fighting with the destroyers, it dramatically complicates it as well. Opening the text into prophetic possibilities, it articulates the drama of revolution with voices of righteous violence, whose relation to time is marked by revolutionary impatience: "Angelita did not believe in leaving the people or the twin brothers defenseless, even if the spirit macaw had said the end of the Europeans in the Americas was inevitable" (712). Angelita's will to violence is a necessary openness in the narrative, a descriptive turn to complicate the plot, without the prescriptive force of the elders' voices: "All money went for food; the people were protected by the spirits and needed no weapons. The changes might require another hundred years, until the Europeans had been outnumbered and the people retook the land peacefully. All that might be okay for Wacah and El Feo, but Angelita had plans of her own" (710). In fact, her impatience and her violence, like that of the witchery, is embedded in a mythic context: "But Wacah did say the pilgrims would be protected by natural forces set loose, forces raised by the spirits. Among these forces there would be human beings, warriors to defend the religious pilgrims" (712), warriors like Angelita. Indeed, La Escapia voices much of Silko's own anger at a world where, as Silko writes in a recent essay, "money and power deliver 'justice' only to the rich and powerful; it cannot do otherwise" (*Yellow Woman*, 20). Silko's autobiographical essays reinforce the political commitments of her presence as witness in her fiction. Unlike Angelita's focus on the power of the sword, Silko herself has chosen the power of the word for very similar political purposes. She writes about having given up on law school after three semesters because she "realized that injustice is built into the Anglo-American legal system. . . . I wanted nothing to do with such a barbaric legal system. . . . I decided the only way to seek justice was through the power of the stories" (19–20). This, according to *Almanac,* is a slower but surer strategy.

Silko's own persona as witness derives partially from the heteroglossia of the text itself. This quality, moving through so many voices, has the reflective effect of foregrounding the author as performer (of negative capability). That is, when the contents are both so fluid and so fluctuating, there is a tendency to note the container. One technique by which she amplifies the heteroglossia is to write direct quotes both without quotation marks and with the speaker in the third person. Much of the book is thus the "transcribed" words or thoughts of characters from widely divergent angles of the cosmic battle between witchery and witness, but these thoughts are delivered as narrative exposition, as though the narrator / author is speaking. For instance, in the chapter ironically entitled, "Rapture of the Plain," Beaufrey's musings about the perverse delights of ruthless capitalism, delivered as a verbal diatribe to the neo-Nazi, Serlo, while Beaufrey photographs and commodifies David's corpse, are punctuated as straight narrative. They follow directly on David's narrative thoughts as he rides his horse to suicide, and they are followed directly in the next section, "The Foes," by the unpunctuated narrative consciousness of Lecha, a keeper of the almanac and thus a witness to David's and Beaufrey's evil. The reader bouncing among the fragments of these narrative voices, from victim to victimizer to witness, all in third rather than first person, is forced to stand back as witness in order to salvage some coherence. The reader's act must remark at the artistry, the witnessing skill, the presence or persona of an author who sacrifices the reader on the altar of her historical imagination to make the reader witness, endure, and untangle these events.[4]

The circulation of time and text is made explicit in the novel through the notion of the spirits or gods of the days, the source for the almanac as a voice of those spirits: "The only true gods were all the days in the Long Count, and no single epoch or time of a world was vast enough or deep enough to call itself God alone. All the ancestors had understood nothing stayed fixed in the universe" (257–28). The almanac both recounts and invokes the activities of these gods who are the days themselves, the most concrete units of time, and this witnessing function, as the originary impulse of Silko's work, runs from the title to the not-so-final period. An "almanac" is precisely an accounting, a witnessing of days of the year, each endowed, in the oral traditions, with a spirit, sometimes a bloodthirsty one.[5] The patience of the old ones becomes the patience of counting those days, assuming neither that one can hold them static nor that one can count them all. As El Feo, the prophet twin of Tacho / Wacah, affirms, "Politics didn't add up. In the end only the Earth remained, and they'd all return to her as dust. . . . El Feo himself did not worry. History was unstoppable. The days, years, and centuries were spirit beings who traveled the universe, returning endlessly. The Spirits of the Night and the Spirits of the Day would take care of the people" (523).

LAND If time is on their side, a strategy that the young like Angelita have yet to learn, the land also upholds the elders' power of patience, a power tied in cultural and historical ways to the seemingly passive power of the land as an ally. As Silko writes in *Sacred Water,* "But human beings desecrate only themselves; the Mother Earth is inviolable" (76). Echoing *Ceremony*'s affirmations of the land, "The mountain outdistanced their destruction, just as love had outdistanced death" (*Ceremony* 234), *Almanac*'s strategy of witness is powerful because both time and space conspire on the land against "all things European." As

Calabazas reminisces, "Strategists for both the Yaquis and the Apaches quickly learned to make use of the Europeans' inability to perceive unique details in the landscape. . . . The trick was to lead the chase to rocky terrain cut by narrow, deep arroyos. The longer the soldiers rode up and down the steep terrain, the more exhausted and afraid they became" (225). Waiting became a cycling balance of space and time, of geography and history, of land and legend, of arroyos and stories of arroyos. Like Tacho's patience with Menardo, the only thing these Yaqui and Apache warriors had to do was to witness and wait for the soldiers to put themselves into the hands of death. Like these warriors, Silko and her readers have only to witness the blindness of a nation as it destroys itself by its "inability to perceive unique details" in the strength of native presence on the land.[6] They must write and read the almanac of these days.

If the spirits of the days and of the land are both embodied and summoned in the almanac, we begin to understand its prophetic power: "Despite all of Yoeme's lying and boasting, the 'almanac' was truly a great legacy. Yoeme and others believed the almanac had living power within it, a power that would bring all the tribal people of the Americas together to retake the land. . . . Without the almanacs, the people would not be able to recognize the days and months yet to come, days and months that would see the people retake the land" (569–70). Recognizing, seeing, watching, keeping count become the key to that repatriation.

DREAMS To achieve this subversive prophetic agenda of witness, the strategic dynamic of the elders is visionary rather than revolutionary in the usual sense. "The macaws said the battle would be won or lost in the realm of dreams, not with airplanes or weapons" (475). Inwardly active, the revolutionaries perform in the unseen world of the psyche. "The Barefoot Hopi's entire philosophy was to wait; a day would come as had not been seen in five thousand years. On this day, a conjunction would occur; everywhere at once, spontaneously, the prisoners, the slaves, and the dispossessed would rise up. The urge to rise up would come to them through their dreams. All at once, all over the world, police and soldiers would be outnumbered" (617).

But what does it mean to work in the realm of dreams? How does such a politic avoid cooptation in the name of pacifism? Silko's text is clear that this political philosophy engages the techniques of storytelling, the "mythification of lived experience," as Paul Zumthor says of the poetic function in oral traditions (100).[7] Witnessing retells and thus rewrites the story of colonial history to defeat the witchery over time. This is the aesthetic and ethic of the keepers of the notebooks: the power of witness translates into the story of time itself. As one of the novel's street people of Tucson considers the process,

Mosca had not actually seen one of the Hopi's letters, but he knew the Hopi wrote to the prisoners about their dreams. The Hopi worked only in the realm of dreams; the Hopi's letters made no mention of the strikes or uprisings; instead the letters had consisted of the Hopi's stories about the Corn Mother, Old Spider Woman, and the big snake. The black convicts and the Hopi talked about African spirits. Even redneck bikers ate up the Hopi's stories, but that was because the Hopi had already infiltrated their dreams with the help of the spirit world. (620)

In league with spirit helpers, the aesthetic of storytelling proceeds in *Almanac* from the famous lines of *Ceremony:* "You don't have anything / if you don't have the stories. . . . The only cure / I know / is a good ceremony, / that's what she said" (2–3). The crowded and decaying notebooks of the almanac, like Betonie's hogan in *Ceremony,* collect the medicinal detritus of the world to bear witness to those curative energies. Among the ominous rags, roots, twigs, herbs, newspapers, metropolitan telephone books, and old calendars gathered from his travels into his medicine hogan, Betonie tells Tayo, "All these things have stories alive in them. . . . I brought back the books with all the names in them. Keeping track of things" (127). The aesthetic of *Almanac* as a novel is the ethic of Betonie's hogan as a ceremonial site. Since the stories reside in the objects of the world, the medicine people, like the keepers of the almanac, stand as witness to those stories, and influence the retelling, the reliving. The Barefoot Hopi refocuses the collective mind on the ancient stories reworking their way through the world. Keeping the stories alive, even as they change with the ceremonies, storytellers help the people survive change. Taken together, *Ceremony* and *Almanac* are one long story dreaming "about the Corn Mother, Old Spider Woman, and the big snake."

ojo These circulating elements in patient witness of time, land, dreams, and stories focus together to make powerful the single function of sight in the witness. A passive yet potent sight of witness contrasts in *Almanac* with the intrusive, voyeuristic, parasitic, homicidal sight of *mal ojo,* the evil eye. Voyeurism finds its prominent role in the novel largely because of its significance as the converse of witnessing. Silko's invocation of Arrowboy's witness, drawing on ancient Keresan tradition in its balanced strategies against more traditional witchery, has been recycled throughout *Ceremony* and *Almanac* to offset the evil eye of postcontact witchery, which itself has been intensified by the sometimes hysterical Christian dualism of dogmatically oppositional good and evil.[8]

The power in vision itself is suggested in *Almanac*'s "death-eye" passages, intimating the power of both prophetic witness and colonial *mal ojo* in the "Death-

Eye Dog" section. As Menardo, who eventually will succumb to this evil, re-members, "It was then he [the old man] bragged the ancestors had seen 'it' all coming, and one time I interrupted to ask what 'it' was, and he waved his hands all around the shady spot where we were sitting and he said, 'The time called Death-Eye Dog'" (257). Among the layers of connotation for this label, tied to precontact pictographic symbolism, the novel's own contexts of white supre-macist and pornographic snuff flicks suggest that Death-Eye is a complex voy-eurism, the evil eye that can kill both the colonial and the sexual object.[9] "Some knew it as 'The Reign of Fire-Eye Macaw,' which was the same as saying 'Death-Eye Dog' because the sun had begun to burn with a deadly light" (257–28).

This power of vision turned to witchery's purposes in *mal ojo* finds its most striking narrative thread in Beaufrey and his decadent, racist compadres. Their mercenary fascination with the blood-drenched pornography of suicide, homi-cide, and infanticide connects them directly to witchery's delight in destruction, to those who are "secretly . . . thrilled by the spectacle of death" (475).[10] In the following passage, Silko ties their voyeurism directly to colonial ideology and its most extreme capitalist extensions. This is the rotting heart of the beast that the keepers and readers of the almanac must witness. The Lacanian notion, in Terry Eagleton's words, that "all desire springs from a lack, which it strives continually to fill" (168), barely begins to convey the force of vacuum pressure sucking all life into this nihilistic void of death and capital. It does suggest, however, by the equations in the novel, the specular dynamics of desire in colonial capitalism, racism, voyeurism, and finally torture, propelled by intense lack, in contrast to the specular dynamics of witness and radical patience mov-ing with the forces of time, land, and dream.[11]

A resonant passage of voyeurism, briefly mentioned earlier in reference to narrative voice, follows Beaufrey's thoughts as he photographs the mutilated corpse of his jealous lover, David, himself a renowned photographer of death scenes like "the Eric series," and whose own child Beaufrey has kidnapped and featured in a snuff film. David, in sharp contrast to Tayo, has been driven by his own implication in this horror to involuntary suicide on horseback. Beaufrey, camera in hand, is speaking (in third person) to Serlo, his neo-Nazi lover, and the echoes of Emo's murderous witchery in *Ceremony* are clear. Beaufrey's empty heart of witchery drinks the blood of this death, and it feeds his fantasies of global power:

David was worth more dead than he had been worth alive. The Eric series would appreciate in value, and even pictures of David's corpse would bring good prices. . . . [H]ere was what gave free-world trade the edge over all other systems: no sentimentality. Every ounce of value, everything worth anything, was stripped away for sale, regardless; no mercy. Serlo and his associates feared the rabble were about to seize control of the world, but Beaufrey knew the masses in the United States and England were too stupid to turn on their masters; all slaves dreamed of becoming masters more cruel than their own masters. Serlo and the others had to realize the best policy was to allow the rabble their parliaments, congresses, and assemblies; because the masses were soothed and reassured by these simulations of "democracy." Meanwhile, governments followed secret agendas unhindered by citizens. (565)

Beaufrey sees himself in command of those secret agendas, a simple extension of mercantilism to protect and pamper the wealthy whites. The almanac, however, sees his external control as a projected form of surveillance that masks his internal desire in voyeurism. Because of the emptiness, the lack in that desire, he is ultimately vulnerable, in spite of his global, conspiratorial power base, and must succumb to his own blood lust. As Janet St. Clair characterizes the equation, "Vicious, manipulative homosexuality and injurious — even murderous — sexual perversion become relentless metaphors of the insane self-absorption and phallocentric avarice of god-forsaken Euroamerican culture" (86). Beaufrey's deadly light of evil vision contrasts with the elders' and prophets' dream visions of mythic storytelling.

The reader finds by contrasting Beaufrey and, say, the Barefoot Hopi, or Menardo and Calabazas, or General Crook and Geronimo, or a host of other possible pairings in the novel, that voyeurism seeks to define, to claim, to possess the truth of the other, while witnessing seeks to parry, to elude, or to triangulate and set the other off balance. Voyeurism erases difference; witnessing asserts difference. The one is a compressing and capturing, the other an expansion and releasing. The one wants closure, the other wants openness, as in the novel's recounting of three — or is it four? — Geronimo stories. Witnessing recognizes its own implication in the other, which it sees, while voyeurism, which is blind to the other, leaves the other in its own separation. Voyeurism commodifies and dehumanizes; witnessing recognizes and humanizes. Voyeurism crystallizes; witnessing circulates.

The focus on vision in the text aims at the very last line, which turns away from the voyeuristic vision of closure and affirms the ultimate witness's vision of an open future, eclipsing Beaufrey's plans of manifest destiny: "The snake was looking south, in the direction from which the twin brothers and the people would come" (763).

RITUAL OF THE READER Through vision, the ritual circulation of these passive powers of time, land, and dreamed stories gradually interpellates the reader of *Almanac* as witness. The reading eye watches torture as a perverse exercise of colonial pressure on the human psyche. In Arrowboy's context, this watching becomes a strategy of undoing. The dynamic functions ritualistically, "a good ceremony" for the reader to test her or his responses against Arrowboy's ethos: am I a witness or a voyeur? am I a protester or a participant in this violence? The difference bears all the personal-as-political weight of colonial history and psychology.[12] James Ruppert makes it clear that this ritual reckoning is the purpose of such literature: "A mediational text attempts to maneuver readers into taking a series of regenerated socio-political positions. An ideological translation takes place, though not a physical transmutation. However, real readers may be ready to act because they perceive things differently" (16). Silko's cyclic translations between colonialism, voyeurism, pornography, and homicide are so disturbing exactly because they unveil "the lies" of American ideology.

Throughout *Almanac,* Silko offers the reader a profusion of chances to practice these distinctions. *Ceremony*'s trope of witness coalesces in this ritual of the reader with *Almanac*'s trope of blood, which circulates fiction and reality, myth and history, all within the gaze that measures itself against the destruction of the world. As Ruppert summarizes the ethical dimensions of an aesthetics of mediation, "Briefly, texts aspire to change readers. The more complete the fusion between the implied reader and the real reader, the more complete the change" (13–14).

That fusion can be dangerous. Proximity to evil requires a further ethical operation in the reader's ritual of *Almanac.* As in the healing of Tayo's perspective in *Ceremony,* " 'It all depends,' she said. 'How far you are willing to go' " (*Ceremony* 240). Entering this close to the blood pulse, to witness the distorted horrors of the world, is dangerous work. In spite of the fierce wisdom of the keepers of the almanac, their role, like the reader's, remains risky: "A few of the keepers had fallen victim to delusions of various sorts" (569–70). That danger, in a necessary vulnerability, proves to be the living heart where the power of the witness resides.[13] The task of the witness is to keep her own heart alive. This is why the witchery wants, most of all, the victim's beating heart for the witchery's ritual. As Ts'eh warned Tayo, "Their highest ambition is to gut human beings while they are still breathing, to hold the heart still beating so the victim will never feel anything again. When they finish, you watch yourself from a distance and you can't even cry — not even for yourself" (240). The witness must remain alive to the sensitive connections that animate the world, but in order to do this, he or she must die to boundaries that defend against those connections.

A Hopi version of the Arrowboy myth (a widely distributed oral tale among the Southwest tribes), describes the witness's danger of proximity to the evil powers extending as far as a transformative death.[14] In "Powaq-wuuti," or Witch Lady Story, a figure parallel to the Keresan Estoy-eh-muut is transformed as he helps to defeat the witchery. As Helen Jaskoski analyzes the tale, "The husband, the hero/questor of the comedy, undergoes a symbolic death in the witches' ritual, with a subsequent rebirth on the mountain top followed by a process of education and empowerment" (5). Tayo's story, following so closely that pattern in the oral traditions, must become the reader's story in *Almanac,* if Silko's project is to be fulfilled. Just as the unfolding narrative relies on openness in history, the unfolding narrative voices rely on openness in the listener to effect a transformation. The fact that the many versions of this widely distributed oral tale involve Arrowboy's or the witness/husband's dangerous engagement as a spy in the activities of the witchery itself sets the stakes in the oral tradition for the literary witness: the dangers of Tayo's camaraderie with Harley and Emo in *Ceremony;* the perilous balancing act on "a ledge so narrow / he could not move in any direction" in "Estoy-eh-muut and the Kunideeyahs" (*Storyteller* 149); the reader's engagement with the author in the horrors of *Almanac.*

The witness's deep involvement in the witchery again blurs the boundaries between good and evil, while emphasizing the focus on the communal values in mind and heart of the "outsider," as a protection against cooptation in the dark heart of the battle. Jaskoski writes, "Witches can control those who unwittingly come in contact with them, yet the story makes clear that the husband reflects and chooses, eventually deciding to deceive them. . . . The text dwells on the humaneness of his decision in electing not to take human life" (15). This intense implication in the violence of witchery, a proximity to bloodshed, proves to be an integral part of the traditional hero/protagonist's "death and rebirth" or his "quest to locate, and if possible eradicate, some hidden evil" (Jaskoski 5, 14). In Silko's retelling, this proximity makes the reader's ritual a "blood sacrifice."

Because the witness is blood-deep in the events, implicated by silent presence at the destruction, the energy of that destruction becomes diffused, deflecting off the victim and onto the witness as teller or reteller of the tale, like a keeper of the almanac.[15] How does Arrowboy's witnessing stop the witchery from working? By exploding, opening, triangulating the binary of victim and victimizer, the witness creates a circulation of the blood energy among three poles — and then many in the telling — rather than between an oppositional two. In Bakhtinian terms, the witness makes a dialogic polyglossia out of a dialectic monoglossia.[16] The energy is freed from oppositionality as the witness harnesses her own vulnerability.

2

Narrative Circulation: "Blood Madness"

In addition to circulation between text and reader, Silko constructs a relation between text and history unique in the literature. By initiating a circulating system of myth and history, fiction and reality, text and context, she creates such interplay that those categories, like active and passive, break down. Harjo, writing of Silko's "border consciousness," suggests that in *Almanac*, "There ultimately is no boundary between event and story" (208). Contemporary history enters in through the perverted perpetrators of neocolonialism and capitalism in the witchery's pawns: Max Blue, Menardo, Beaufrey, Judge Arne, General J. These are undercut by the quiet persistence of the witnesses, in the people: Calabazas, Clinton, Root, the Army of the Homeless; in the keepers of the almanac: Lecha, Zeta, and their allies, even Sterling; and in the prophets: Tacho, El Feo, the Barefoot Hopi. Silko's open form makes this contemporary and mythic literary content intersect with history. Her strategy of firing Arrowboy's gaze at the destruction through these characters and their stories requires a technique that I call narrative circulation. Its prophetic power derives from the blood of circulation between death and life, and such circulation bends and twists linear time. The following four sections describe such elusive bends and twists.

PROPHECY Compared to the relative ceremonial closure of Tayo's narrative, by which his and the land's healing and the defeat of the witchery are finished, "for now," *Almanac*'s narrative remains open to the historical moment that Silko invokes, precisely by avoiding narrative closure. (A nonlinear narrative structure, like *Ceremony*, may yet retain a sense of closure, like Spider Woman's web coming full circle.) Constructing less closure in *Almanac* is actually a way of opening the text to material power by blurring the boundaries between fiction and reality. Unlike European expectations of narrative (which have been broken steadily each century since the novel began), *Almanac*, while it suggests "realities" in intense detail, leaves the plot open, allowing narrative gaps and leaving them unfinished. This open-endedness emerges not only in the anecdotal technique of juxtaposing narrative vignettes, but especially in the finale and in the Geronimo sequences. The novel thus unfolds into a reciprocal, circulating relation to emerging material events. The recent Zapatista movement in Chiapas, launched January 1, 1994, and aimed on that opening date of the North American Free Trade Agreement to resist American corporate colonialism, followed the same north-south/south-north axis suggested by Krupat as the axis of *Almanac*.[17] One effect of these events, three years after publication of *Almanac*, was that Silko's narrative circulation had reached a chillingly prophetic flow to the future. This is not merely a novelist's good luck, nor the result of skillful marketing on the part of her publisher's promotion staff. The linkage between the narrative of Silko's novel and the historic eventualities in Chiapas that followed her work is made possible by her narrative structure.

In the novel's thematic terms this remarkable achievement begins by the circular dynamic of the almanac itself, whereby days past return in present and future form, allowing prophetic assertions to the keepers of the almanac. As one of the "fragments from the ancient notebooks" explains, "An experience termed *past* may actually return if the influences have the same balances or proportions as before. Details may vary, but the essence does not change" (574). "Memory" in this system is not relegated to past representations, nor, in such a narrative circulation between fiction and reality, is myth relegated to fantasy. Instead, the almanac sees, "Narrative as analogue for the actual experience, which no longer exists; a mosaic of memory and imagination" (574). This mosaic suggests a mechanism of prophecy. In the novel's structural terms, *Almanac*'s epistemological openness, perhaps its most radical element contrasting with colonial notions of time and space, creates the dynamics of that prophetic power in relation to material history. Comparing Silko's transformation of the North American novel to that of the "magical realists" for South American literature, Harjo writes, "Silko's work in the north opens the form to new possibilities. Silko isn't a magical realist but she too radicalizes the novel. . . . The foreground becomes the earth and the peoples of the Americas" (208). The Zapatistas of Chiapas merely stepped out onto that stage. What began lyrically in *Ceremony,* as an opening for "the indigenous soul" of America, according to Harjo, explodes in *Almanac,* and indigenous explosions in the political realm then propel that textual explosion across the boundary between fiction and reality.

The contrast in closure between the novels is due in part simply to *Ceremony*'s plot location in the post–World War II past and to *Almanac*'s location in the millennial present and near future. The circulation between a story of the past and history becomes relatively limited by received notions of time. *Almanac,* however, by ending with the Native armies of the poor marching north toward a promised climax, leaves its own finale to a silence that only future history can fill. Yet even Silko's treatment of the past in *Almanac* can be comically open-ended, as in the story of the three — or is it four? — Geronimos. This section of the novel performs the evasive magic initiated in her early "Geronimo Story," first published in 1974, three years prior to *Ceremony.*[18] If Geronimo is a recurring theme in Silko's published works (Betonie mentions him when Tayo first arrives to begin the ceremony, he reappears in *Storyteller*), we find out in these Geronimo sequences of *Almanac* why his story weaves so intricately into the larger fabric of her work. In fact, her storytelling devices echo the representational tactics of "the warrior of prominence" who "had not been a warrior but had been trained as a medicine man," and whose "specialty had been silence and occasionally, invisibility" (225). By Silko's sleights of hand, the Geronimo stories create a textual past as open as the future, allowing events and revisionary history to play into the text. The resonances of her treatment of Geronimo in *Almanac* bear so directly on the dynamics of witness and narrative circulation in her work that it is worth a closer look to explicate some of those dynamics. Geronimo is the paradigm of her revisionary history.

GERONIMO?! Silko's hilarious performance of semiotic play in the multiple and conflicting Geronimo stories provides an analogue in the oral traditions for the framing novel's unconfined structure and for an epistemology that seeks not to decode all the mysteries of its own texture. The Geronimo joke, threading through several chapters, plays especially on colonial projections. Each of its several angles is a voice, often in contradiction, suggesting in this microcosm of the novel a polyvocality of Bakhtinian proportions. A handful of narrative angles play into the joke: the source of "Geronimo's" name in Mexican soldiers' battlefield prayer to St. Jerome, mistaken by U.S. soldiers; European blindness that sees all Apaches as the same; the whites' thus mistaking several Apache warriors for the one they want to label "Geronimo"; the U.S. Army's preposterous investment in capturing "Geronimo"; the mercenary Apache scouts' heavy investment in maintaining the ruse of a single "Geronimo" so that they are not "court-martialed and hanged" (227) for concealing and so prolonging the confusion; the competition among white soldiers and among journalists for the honor of "Geronimo's" capture in body or photograph; the confusion over journalistic photographs of the various real Apache warriors mistaken for "Geronimo"; and, the punch line, the identical image of "Geronimo" in each of these photographs of different warriors: "The image of this [unknown] man appeared where the faces of the other Geronimos should have been" (228). Beneath the Geronimo image, which might be a projected "Apache face white people identified as Geronimo" (228) or a spirit protector, "an ancestor, the soul of one long dead who knew the plight of the 'Geronimos'" (232), there remain a number of separate identities, like the voices weaving the tale.

The complexities of this ludic storytelling play on all the cultural differences that Silko represents as so brutally destructive elsewhere in the novel, but there is one additional element in her presentation of the Geronimos that I want to highlight for its investment in narrative fluctuation and play, in circulation between fiction and reality. Without accounting for the differences, Silko repeatedly misrepresents, or rather un- or re-represents, the exact number of historical Geronimos in the tale, now four, now three, now four again, effectively breaking up any semblance of order in the telling, and letting the joke reach farcical intensity.

The gag begins by setting the aesthetic terms in the oral tradition for the joke and for the novel. Calabazas' old aunt recounts the tale, "Of course the real man they call Geronimo, they never did catch. The real Geronimo got away. . . . Old Mahawala started out, and then the others, one by one, had contributed some detail or opinion or alternative version. The story they told did not run in a line for the horizon but circled and spiraled instead like the red-tailed hawk" (224). While this simile describes *Almanac*'s nonlinear structure and the structure of the joke, it also launches the joke's tricks, because as we soon find out, there was no "real man they call Geronimo," or rather there were three, or perhaps four, of them. No wonder Calabazas, the reteller of this tale, "had looked at each face trying to determine in an instant if this was a joke or not. Because if it was a joke and he appeared to take it seriously, they would have him. And if it wasn't a joke, and he laughed, they would have him too. But when Calabazas realized the old ones were serious about this Geronimo story, he had given in" (224). Silko's joke is that the serious story that is not a joke *is* her joke on the reader. By it she tests and refines the reader's ritual.

Why else would Calabazas himself seven pages later finish the old people's story, which he, and Silko, first pretended he didn't know: "'And what do you think?' old Mahawala had said, pointing her arthritic finger so it nearly touched Calabazas's forehead. . . . They had all been grinning at Calabazas, waiting for him to pick up where old Mahawala left off. Calabazas opened the last beer and began" (231), and he concludes Old Pancakes's pitiful climax to the tale. As Calabazas finished, "Old Mahawala gave a grin as wide as a full moon," and said [incongruously speaking to the teller of the tale's finale], "'There . . . you have heard that one again.' Calabazas had nodded. A lot of Yaqui stories about Apaches were not so good or amusing" (232). This is an exercise in comic relief that probes the roots of colonial representation.

Almanac may be a most careful and imaginative accounting of a certain history, but we find in the Geronimo sequence that it never pretends to an accurate count or definition. A different relation to accounting and representation *is* its revisionary power. The novel takes this approach directly to emphasize a spirit of knowing and perceiving, an epistemology of witness, different from a European colonial fascination with names and numbers (which today finds its sanguine expression, for instance, in federal and tribal disputes over Indian identity and blood quantum — the very currency of spirit in *Almanac*). The narrative critique in the voices of the "old ones," which frames the narrative farce, proceeds to mark that difference in valuing names as a fatal one: "The tribal people here were all very aware that the whites put great store in names. But once the whites had a name for a thing, they seemed unable ever again to recognize the thing itself. . . . The elders used to argue that this was one of the most dangerous qualities of the Europeans: Europeans suffered a sort of blindness to the world. . . . The Europeans . . . could often be heard complaining in frightened tones that the hills and canyons looked the same to them" (224–25). A looser relation to definitions, at the core of Silko's treatment of Geronimo, allows a more alert perception, freeing the witness from her own filtering categories, from the illusion that the sign is the signified.

The attention to see and hear the life in nature stands close, for instance, to the heart of Calabazas's culture, a Yaqui way, in contrast to a Euro-American commodification, colonialization, and demonization of nature and the people of the desert. Indeed, Calabazas, in his own subversive context of drug-running across the border, sets the ground for the Geronimo story, itself set in a section with the telling title "Indian Country," to direct the reader toward this primeval kinship. Calabazas uses an oldtimer's timeless present tense: "We don't believe in boundaries. Borders. Nothing like that. We are here thousands of years before the first whites. . . . We know where we belong on this earth. We always moved freely. . . . We pay no attention to what isn't real. Imaginary lines. Imaginary minutes and hours. Written law. We recognize none of that" (216). Old Calabazas elucidates the seditious side of this culturally different relation to signs, the difference that sustained Geronimo and his followers. "We have always had the advantage because this country is ours—it's our backyard. We know it in the black of night. We know it in the July heat of hell" (218).

Describing the sacred spirit of signification in that Yaqui way (which Silko clearly links to Calabazas's profane enterprises to dissolve the sacred/profane boundary), Larry Evers and Felipe Molina write in *Yaqui Deer Songs/Maso Bwikam,* "Yaquis have always believed that a close communication exists among *all* the inhabitants of the Sonoran desert world in which they live: plants, animals, birds, fishes, even rocks and springs. . . . Yaquis regard song as a special language of this community, a kind of 'lingua franca' of the intelligent universe'" (18). Euro-American blindness to that community would set them outside "the intelligent universe," in the eyes of those whose very purpose is to remain in close communication through that lingua franca. "There was one who could hear the sounds of the tree" (35). Evers and Molina emphasize Yaqui attention to this natural language. "In fact, deer songs often take the form of dialogues in which *saila maso* [little brother deer] and others in the wilderness world speak with one another or with the deer singers themselves. It is in this way, according to deer singer Miki Maaso, that 'the wilderness world listens to itself even today'" (18). Now this acute perception marks colonial survival,

"In that sense deer songs are regarded as one of the most essential expressions of what it is to remain Yaqui after four and one-half centuries of attempts to destroy their communities and to dissolve them as a people" (19). Silko's looser relation to definitions suggests in this Yaqui context not indifference to language but circumspect awe, an intense respect for the sign, for the power of words and songs to shape realities, as words directed the fate of the soldiers frightened by their own definitions of the land and of the Apaches.[19]

This double relation to signification, respecting and thus distancing the definitive power of words, underlies the sequence of the counts in the Geronimo story. The following discrepancies do not represent a copy editor's oversights, but are much more interesting as traces of a skillful authorial evasion, in the spirit of Geronimo, of historical definitions. The first mention, as Mahawala begins, is of four Geronimos (emphasis added): "In time there came to be at least *four* Apache raiders who were called by the name Geronimo, either by the Mexican soldiers or the gringos" (224). Yet the end of the very next paragraph offers a different count: "To whites all Apache warriors looked alike, and no one realized that for a while, there had been *three* different Apache warriors called Geronimo who ranged across the Sonoran desert south of Tucson" (224–25). The next entry is an ambivalent view: "So the Apache warrior called Geronimo had been *three, even four* different men" (225). Then the narrative oscillates again: "The old Yaquis liked to tell stories about the days when their beloved mountain canyons used to shelter the *four* Geronimos" (225). Two sentences later, the count shifts back: "First they had settled back over mutton ribs supplied by the youngest of the *three* 'Geronimos.'" (225). In the middle of the next paragraph, the count continues: "At the meeting of the *three* Geronimos, naturally there had been a discussion of photographic images" (226). The brief swing toward continuity then is offset by another speculation in the note that the whites' Indian scouts, to save their own credibility and their necks, could not divulge the possibility that there were "*three or maybe even four* Apache warriors called Geronimo" (227). The account returns without comment to reaffirm a last count of four: "The discussion of the photographic image centered upon the group photograph . . . and Calabazas knew they were nearing what they considered to be the heart of the story of the *four* Geronimos" (227).

The final joke, that photographs of each of the four, or three, Geronimos all came out with an identical face, plays against the voyeuristic blindness of colonialism to which "the hills and canyons looked the same," a historical barb against the cliché of blindness in which "all Apache warriors looked alike" (225). The jumbled stories of Geronimo in this re-re-revisionary historical prank are punctuated by points of cultural critique that elucidate the difference between Arrowboy's witnessing power and the whites' cultural blindness. The

Geronimo sequence begins and ends by questioning the expense of the pitiful military boondoggle in simple financial terms: "How many years had the U.S. Army garrisoned five thousand troops in Tucson to chase one old Apache man, twenty-five or thirty teenagers, and fifty women and small children?" (220–21). "For more than fifteen years, five thousand U.S. troops, costing $20 million, had stomped through cactus and rock to capture one old Apache man more sorrowful than fierce" (231). It proceeds by marking the metaphorical nature of this episode: "The U.S. soldiers had misunderstood just as they had misunderstood just about everything else they had found in this land" (224).

Observations of cultural blindness are emphasized by an extended discussion of semiotics from a desert hunter's point of view. The "heart of the story of the four Geronimos" (227) proves to be a commentary on cultural semiotics in the function of witness. It emerges from "a lot of thinking and looking at these flat pieces of paper called photographs" (227) on the part of Wide Ledge, one of the warriors mistaken for "Geronimo." Examining the "little smudges and marks like animal tracks across snow or light brown dust," Wide Ledge said, "these 'tracks' were supposed to 'represent' certain persons, places, or things. . . . But invariably . . . these traces of other beings and other places preserved on paper became confused even for the white people, who believed they understood these tracks so well" (227). That the discussion echoes Derrida's "trace" and the slippery signs of poststructuralism is probably no coincidence. Wide Ledge, one of those nonmetaphysical presences signified by the colonial sign "Geronimo," theorizes about the Euro-American's photographic, and by extension textual, semiotics. Silko is playfully applying the critical theory of postmodernism to a distinctly nonpostcolonial moment.[20]

After her shell game of signification, after these pointed critiques, after pages of play with the reader, Silko's narration unravels the semiotic comedy and dismisses the question of Geronimo as an abstraction that obscures the heart of the issue: power. The Geronimo joke eventually plays with another frontier cliché, derived ignorantly by tourists from traces of tribal beliefs, about Natives fearing capture of the soul in photographs, itself a power issue in who controls the image.[21] Silko gives us a scene in which three of the four so-called Geronimos dismiss the pseudoethnographic-pseudotheological debate about this question of soul-capture on film. Such metaphysical speculation, we find, proves as fruitless as trying to track the signified by the sign, or the real Geronimo by the photograph: "Why bother with speculations and arguments over whether the crystal always stole the soul or only did so when white men harbored certain intentions toward the person in front of the camera. The point was, Sleet reminded Wide Ledge and Big Pine, whites on both sides of the border were hunting the Apache called Geronimo" (228). Sleet asserts that raw military power is the issue, not merely signification. His material point, in its contrast with the abstract debate over photographic images, forecasts Angelita's focus on shoulder rockets and her contrast with Wacah's and El Feo's focus on dreams.

Yet Silko, who obviously is concerned with signification, may have pulled off a final joke even in this denial of the significance of rhetorical legerdemain, for in fact there has been a loose pattern to her use of three and four Geronimos. In subtle shifts of narrative point of view, she has used three Geronimos when speaking about confusion on the subject of Apache warriors from a white perspective grounded in corrupt Tucson, while she has used four (though sometimes three) Geronimos when speaking from an Indian perspective about white blindness to three Apache warriors plus the impostor Old Pancakes. At no time does the white perspective consider four Geronimos; only the Native view allows that number. By generally presenting four when giving the Indians' view and three when giving the whites' view, she evidently is playing on differences in the founding numerologies of Euro-American and some Native American worldviews between the trinity and the four directions. This difference subtly structures the telling. For all of Silko's mythopoetic seriousness, the Geronimo sequence is sparked by radical humor while retaining its mythic dimensionality.

To mark the mythic, prophetic seriousness of the joke, what follows directly on this Geronimo story are those prophecies of the end of "all things European," as Calabazas remembers the old promises: "the world that the whites brought with them would not last. . . . All they had to do was to wait. It would be only a matter of time" (235). Against the context of Geronimo's subtle elusiveness, the greatest European projection of all, its own manifest destiny over colonized Native peoples, collapses like the slippery signs of European projections onto Geronimo. Because of the European fascination with their own projections, what Vine Deloria Jr. calls "the American fantasy" (Bataille and Silet ix), even manifest destiny must self-destruct. The structure of loose play of signification with the past now opens up prophetic possibilities for the future.

DEATH/LIFE The structural circulation of reader and text, past and future, reality and fiction, history and myth, as it eludes narrative closure in *Almanac of the Dead,* is rooted ultimately in a thematic circulation between life and death, a warrior's evasion of the final closure. As Old Yoeme, a keeper of the almanac, describes it, "The energy or 'electricity' of a being's spirit was not extinguished by death; it was set free from the flesh. . . . and all the time, the energy had only been changing form, nothing had been lost or destroyed" (719). Deloria, in *God Is Red,* generalizes about this belief:

> The Indian ability to deal with death was a result of the much larger context in which Indians understood life. Human beings were an integral part of the natural world and in death they contributed their bodies to become the dust that nourished the plants and animals that had fed people during their lifetime. Because people saw the tribal community and the family as a continuing unity regardless of circumstance, death became simply another transitional event in a much longer scheme of life. (171)

While the theme of death as circulation resonates with *Ceremony's* understanding of "no boundaries, only transitions through all distances and time" (258), it takes on a peculiar dramatic force in *Almanac.* Death, like the blood that is its marker, evidently must be seen as cyclic for the reader/witness to survive the witchery's violence, as blood is also a marker for life: "The unborn baby drank the mother's blood; unborn chicks grew from delicate halos of blood inside the egg. The spirits of the mountains had to have their share. . . . Blood: even the bulletproof vest wanted a little blood. Knives, guns, even automobiles, possessed 'energies' that craved blood from time to time" (512). The novel's repeated focus on blood, and its many seemingly confused manifestations in death and life, "blood madness," "vampire capitalists," "plasma donors," "sangre pura," plays out the struggle between witchery and witness for the direction of that "energy or 'electricity.'" Gradually the blood imagery emphasizes the circulatory relationship between life and death. The logical affirmation of life per se, which cannot be destroyed by death, underlines the affirmation of Native ways that cannot be destroyed by "all things European." If life circulates with death, and if circulatory systems prevail rather than linear ones, then life, in that sense, defeats death. Similarly, if colonial European culture is identified with death, Native culture is identified with life.

The identification of Europeans with death links Silko's books as intimately as does the role of witness, whose function is to account specifically for the death waged by Europeans. In *Ceremony* that equation is established in the Ck'o'yo witches' "whirling whirling" creation of the whites, as they "set in motion now / set in motion by our witchery / set in motion / to work for us. / They will take this world from ocean to ocean / they will turn on each other / they will destroy each other" (144). As I mentioned, *Storyteller* features that witchery myth at its physical center, again juxtaposed with the fuller telling of "Estoy-eh-muut and the Kunideeyahs" to emphasize the witness's power. The equation of whites with death continues in *Almanac* in legendary terms parallel to the Ck'o'yo myth:

> Yoeme alleged the Aztecs ignored the prophecies and warnings about the approach of the Europeans because Montezuma and his allies had been sorcerers who had called or even invented the European invaders with their sorcery. Those who worshiped destruction and blood secretly knew one another. Hundreds of years earlier, the people who hated sorcery and bloodshed had fled north to escape the cataclysm prophesied when the "blood worshipers" of Europe met the "blood worshipers" of the Americas. Montezuma and Cortés had been meant for one another. Yoeme always said sorcery had been the undoing of people here, and everywhere in the world. (570)[22]

Grouping Europeans with death in the novels through witchery does not merely switch colonial agency from Europe to the Americas, any more than it switches it from Cortés to Montezuma, though it does equalize.[23] Nor does it suggest unconscious Europeans passively manipulated by Native sorcery. On the contrary, from either side of the ocean, "blood worshipers" are represented as potent, indeed actively desirous. A focus on the erotic element in violence and colonialism drives *Almanac* to amplify Emo's bloody fantasies with corpses and keepsakes into the enormities of Beaufrey, Trigg, and the other conspirators for sangre pura: "The people had always feared the Destroyers, humans who were attracted to and excited by death and the sight of blood and suffering. The Destroyers secretly prayed and waited for disaster or destruction. Secretly they were thrilled by the spectacle of death" (475). The almanac marks these intimacies as the pornographic pulse of the witchery's history of exploitation in order to witness ways in which the precious circulation between death and life may be corrupted by the voyeuristic, commodifying eye.

Thus the sinister shadow of witchery and colonial destruction, with all their evil associations, generates a peculiar oppositional connotation between life and death through corrupt commodification of sacred blood. A major theme of the novel is to transcend that oppositionality, to maintain the living energies in these two universals, beyond and even within destruction. As Janet St. Clair suggests, "despite its ghastly brutality, *Almanac* is ultimately less an ethnocentric attack on cultural decay than an attempt to understand and then transcend the fear and loathing that such decay inspires. The almanac, timeless chronicle of recurring histories, becomes a symbol of hope and continuance" (88). The mixed sense of horror and hope circulates in *Almanac* through the trope of blood itself.

BLOOD General J., the sadistic security chief, is "so anxious to talk about sex and blood" that he concocts sociohistorical fantasies, elaborate invocations of destruction, as "he speculated that the sight and smell of blood naturally excited human sex organs. Because bloodshed dominated the natural world, those inhibited by blood would in time have been greatly outnumbered by those who were excited by the blood. Blood was everywhere" (337). As General J. moves through his fantasies, he moves through the novel in a sinister object lesson of the fundamental principle: "Blood was powerful, and therefore dangerous. Some said human beings should not see or smell fresh blood too often or they might be overtaken by frightening appetites" (336). His sexual appetites link General J. to historical forces, for instance to an ancient Mexican priest in the "Transcriptions from the Old Notebooks" who "leans over the boy- / sacrifice / a lovely young prince. The young sacrifices eat their last meal / together . . . the sound of their soft breathing sends aches of desire down / the old priest's legs" (593). The intimate vitality of blood humanizes history and mixes binaries.

Mixed meanings of blood proceed, for instance, from the voice of the Native chauffeur and prophet, Tacho. Before he emerges as the quiet twin prophet, Wacah, he relates the spiritual history of blood to the co-opted capitalist, the rich Menardo, as they drive in the limousine. Blood as an energy in this account is a power that may be turned to good or evil:

> Blood fed life. Before you had anything you had the blood. The blood came first. At birth there was blood. Blood and its power had been misused by sorcerers. Long before Europeans ever appeared, the people had already disagreed over the blood and the killing. Those who went North refused to feed the spirits blood anymore. Those tribes and people who had migrated North fled the Destroyers who delighted in blood. Spirits were not satisfied with just any blood. The blood of peasants and the poor was too weak to nourish the spirits. The spirits must be fed with the blood of the rich and the royal. (336–37)

Tacho is not only threatening Menardo indirectly, "The spirits must be fed with the blood of the rich," but the passage also delineates different approaches to blood, suggesting a right relation: "Those who went North refused to feed the spirits blood anymore."

The passage touches on a key question for readers of *Almanac:* what is the difference between the destroyers' secret love of bloody death and the angry spirits' appetite for blood sacrifice? The question gets at the heart of the difficulty of reading the book. The violence at times seems indiscriminate, perpetrated by both "the good and the bad." Violence seems to be the currency of both the spirit macaws protected by militant Indians and the torturous racist police, protected by their own power even as it destroys them. By the end, the old traditionals El Feo and Wacah are clearly nonviolent. Their militant supporters, La Escapia and Zeta, however, are clearly violent. (Note that the male twins are the pacifists; the women are the militants.) Does it all go together for the spirits' inexorable purposes?

Perhaps Silko's general notion of blood sacrifice, "All the spirits ate blood that was offered to them" (512), is a way to explain the suffering of the innocent, to distinguish her apocalyptic vision from a Christian rapture where only the holy will be saved, where the innocent do not suffer. Here the death is indiscriminate and realistic, but purposive nonetheless. This is, after all, the *Almanac of the Dead,* and "[t]he forces were harsh." Further, the spirits' insistence on "the blood of the rich and the royal" allies those spirits' appetites with the hunger of the poor for justice. It suggests, like Tacho's veiled threat to Menardo, that this blood flows in a revolutionary sacrifice to balance injustice. The trope of blood as energy deconstructs the binary of life and death, so that in a certain sacrifice even death becomes a making sacred, a giving rather than a taking of life. "At birth there was blood" (336). Again, "all the time, the energy had only been changing form, nothing had been lost or destroyed" (719).

Blood thus does not *mean* a particular thing in the symbolic structure of this novel; it is not an allegory for life or death or good or evil or unity or witchery. It is simply "powerful, and therefore dangerous," being both a sign and a signifier, a trope for the circulation of all these energies, for the ways in which the days contain all of this complexity. The almanac is the witness of this circulation of power, a circulation that moves, like the novel, without closure, without demarcation between innocent and evil, or between life and death. Circulation operates, the text is explicit here, because of the "electricity" in everything, whether mountain, egg, weapon, or bulletproof vest, and blood becomes the currency for the exchange of those energies. Energy and blood in fact are a single phenomenon in this system. Blood has become the metaphor for energy, which is a metaphor for spirit, whether benevolent or sinister. Adding time to the equation, Silko arrives at the spirits or gods of the days, whose story is the almanac. "The Spirits of the Night and the Spirits of the Day would take care of the people" (523), as long as they make their blood sacrifice.

Around these alternate relations to blood, established when Emo flaunted his bloody hand and Tayo simply "moved back into the boulders," *Almanac* has become an extended performance of *Ceremony*'s climactic moment, set in the next generation. Rather than apologizing for its graphic violence and brutality, *Almanac* is an extended witnessing gaze on contemporary witches' fascination with blood and death, while juxtaposing linkages between blood and life. Witches' pawns like Emo, Max Blue, and Trigg destroy themselves while they attempt to destroy others because of blood's dangerous power. In their bloodshed they cut themselves off from the life-giving energies of blood, and in their fetishism with body parts they reveal belief in a commodified and ultimate death rather than in a death circulating with life.

The novel's ontology of blood and the circulation of "energies" of life and death shapes both its circulating narrative structure and its historical theme of the ultimate transcendence by the land and the land's people over colonialism. Silko's blood sacrifice becomes the ritual of the reader's circulation as a witness to all of these horrific events. The specular power of that witness flows through the narrative voices, reshaping the stories, as the narrative itself circulates in and out of history. This performance reenacts the story of native cultural survival itself with unprecedented fierceness. History, which could become another name for the almanac, must circulate its own blood as well, and the novel identifies the veins and arteries that link history with the powers of radical patience in contemporary Native American cultures.

NOTES

1. While this paper focuses on the literary side of the oral-literary continuum between text and context in Silko's work, another analysis focusing on oral dynamics of performance as they play through these literary dynamics would make a fascinating study. For background in some of those oral dynamics, see Hymes, Kroeber, Swann, and Tedlock in the works cited.
2. In a recent videotaped interview, Silko's statement on the witchery is as concise as her notion of the efficacy of witnessing: "My notion of the witchery is that which takes delight in destruction and suffering and destroying. I like to feel a little bit with these stories and narratives that I'm working to confront these destructive impulses, and more than to confront them, to sort of turn them back upon themselves" (Interview).
3. For a fuller discussion of ways that Native American writers elude binary thinking, see my "Decolonizing Criticism" and my "Myth, History, and Identity in Silko and Young Bear."
4. Silko's own performance as witness might be seen in the contemporary contexts of certain other Native novelists' profound investments in the personas generated by their texts and their collateral personal investments in rewriting contemporary time in mythic dimensions. Gerald Vizenor encourages a trickster persona for himself as author and reader on the lecture circuit, embodying the "trickster discourse" of his novels. N. Scott Momaday's autobiographical works and paintings mark his identification with the bear as Rock-Tree Boy, a central motif in his fiction. The auto-

biography often follows the literary productions, as those productions follow oral traditions of trickster, bear boy, or Arrowboy. If there is a pattern of "persona-fication," it suggests an autobiographical aesthetic close to the core of these writers' work, but the notion is complicated by ways that their textual productions seem to reconstruct their autobiographical personas. The topic suggests contextual questions for further study. For example, Silko is less explicit about her persona as witness than Momaday is about his bear boy persona, or certainly than Vizenor is about his trickster persona. Does Silko's own regenerative textual performance subsume her persona more thoroughly than Vizenor's or Momaday's because of a gender difference in these performances? Does Silko move toward more engagement of the reader as participant and less toward the author as focus of the performance? That different engagement of the reader may suggest a different political strategy, which then is implicated in the radical patience of *Almanac*'s notion of cyclic time.

5. Among the many conjectures cited in the *Oxford English Dictionary* for the etymology of "almanac," which trace *al-manakh* to an Iberian Arabic usage of the thirteenth century but to no certain Arabic roots prior to that, the first etymological speculation the *OED* deems "worthy of notice" links the word to a sense of accounting, an act of measured witness: "Explanations have been offered of *manakh* from Semitic sources, as Arab. *manay* to define, determine, *mana* measure, time, fate; Heb. *manah,* to allot, assign, count; Arab. *manaha* to present, *minhat* a gift, all of which fail in form or sense or both." These plausible sources do point to the almanac's potent usage as an accounting of time, and to the ancient sources of Silko's act of witnessing in these "notebooks." As to the uncertain geolinguistic roots of the word, perhaps we would do as well to combine the revisionary forces of Silko's *Almanac of the Dead* with Gerald Vizenor's *Heirs of Columbus* to suggest that the original Mayan keepers of the almanac brought the term with them to the Mediterranean when they colonized the European continent in ancient times.

6. Fergus M. Bordewich, in *Killing the White Man's Indian,* asserts that "tribes are destined to play increasingly important and self-determined roles on the national scene" and "that Indians and other Americans share not only a common history but a common future as well" (20).

7. See Paul Zumthor, *Oral Poetry: An Introduction.* Silko's practice in her prose contradicts some of Zumthor's conclusions in his fascinating discussion of relations between literature and reality. He establishes differences between narrative and lyric as, respectively, "dramatic" and "gnomic": "the 'narrative' tends to exhaust the signified within the signifier, the 'lyric' rejects it" (105). This notion that a definitive narrative, against a more fragmented, impressionistic lyric, tends to try to tell the whole story, in a totalizing gesture that Lyotard would equate with "meta-narrative," is precisely what Silko's narrative tries to elude. Perhaps because of the metanarrative of colonial history, with its epistemology of linear and dualistic hierarchy, her revisionary historical narratives never try to "exhaust the signified within the signifier." Translating Zumthor's terms into Silko's terms of textual openness to material history, as a strategy for eluding colonial metanarratives, I suggest that *Almanac* represents a defeat of narrative and a lyric triumph of history. When a "fragment from the ancient notebooks" affirms "[n]arrative as analogue for the actual experience, which no longer exists; a mosaic of memory and imagina-

tion" and then connects that analogue to the actual return of an "experience termed *past,*" that narrative analogue becomes history, as the signifier becomes the signified (574). Again, history emerges through the text itself.

8. This intensified oppositionality, the theme of *Ceremony,* may have developed as a historical phenomenon after missionary contact. Marc Simmons, in *Witchcraft in the Southwest,* describes this colonial influence on Native witchery: "For the Indians, be they the Aztecs of Mexico or the Pueblos along the Rio Grande, a strict division of the universe into opposing forces of good and evil was incomprehensible. They viewed evil as a shadowy negative force present to some degree in every man and god and an immutable part of life one simply endured. That the new priests placed such emphasis upon evil and that their creed looked toward its total elimination was a matter evoking astonishment and dismay. . . . This preoccupation with sin, evil-mongering, idolatry, and witchery soon infected the impressionable Indians and they too became engrossed in the contemplation of iniquity and the black side of supernaturalism. From here it was but a short step to an obsession with witchcraft" (13–14). "Other aspects of Spanish practice included . . . the evil eye *(mal ojo).* The latter belief, that a mere gaze can produce the most diabolical evil, existed throughout the Old World and was rapidly picked up by the Indians of Mexico" (Gifford). Elsie Parsons adds a more interactive and dynamic explanation to Gifford's and Simmons's patronizing one: "The padres encouraged witchcraft beliefs by stigmatizing as witchcraft what they disapproved of. The unbaptized became witches; all who practice non-Christian rites are wizards. Witchcraft was the nearest approach to the Catholic conception of sin that was made by the Indians and the padres took advantage of it" (251).

9. "[T]he time when peninsulars [Iberian conquistadors and colonists] could simply take any native American woman they wanted is more or less past. And yet, social power is still constructed by the repression of the defenseless, whether they be boys or men, girls or women" (Trexler 174). Richard C. Trexler's recent discussion in *Sex and Conquest* deromanticizes the history of Mexican conquest on the intimate level of sexual practice, suggesting that in both hemispheres "in much of antiquity, males as well as females were . . . sometimes punished through sexual means" (7) and that colonial repression of New Spain, "the hellhole to which the Iberian exploitation exposed" Native Americans on the largest scale (9), was an oppression different in degree, but not in kind, from "a world of penetrative penality" associated with indigenous patterns of military and civil discipline (7). Such a perspective is useful in reading Silko, whose myth of witchery also deromanticizes the Native American past and present as profoundly implicated in oppressive and destructive, even murderous, sexual practices.

10. Silko's undiluted representations of homosexuals as murderous degenerates in *Almanac* poses a significant problematic beyond the scope of this paper. She is equally excoriative of heterosexual and homosexual exploitation, especially in the colonial and racial frame, and her focus, in Richard Trexler's context, is power relations in sex and conquest.

11. The photographic medium Silko explores so thoroughly in *Storyteller* and *Sacred Water,* two works that bracket her publication of *Almanac of the Dead,* is clearly a central element in her aesthetic. "The Indian with a camera is an omen of a time in the future that all Euro-Americans unconsciously dread: the time when the indige-

nous people of the Americas will retake their land" (*Yellow Woman* 178). In fact, some of her own camera work coincides with her writing of *Almanac*. "In the early 1980s, as I was beginning to write *Almanac of the Dead* . . . I had also begun to take photographs of the rocks in the big wash by my house" (*Yellow Woman* 13). Her father Lee H. Marmon's work as a photographer influences her forms, as her own ethical concerns with social and ecological justice in turn influence her visual aesthetic to draw the contrast between colonial voyeurism and American Indian self-representation. *Almanac*'s explorations of pornography then stand in contrast to her own efforts as photographic witness. She valorizes David Seal's "point that the spiritual integrity of the person behind the camera matters most" (*Yellow Woman* 183). She even attributes *Almanac* to inspirations from "glyphs" developed by images of "stones and driftwood" in her own photographs of "the dry wash below my ranch house": "Most of these narratives were constructed from the images of the 'glyphs' I 'saw' in the debris at the bottom of the arroyo" (*Yellow Woman* 181).

12. See Eduardo Duran and Bonnie Duran, *Native American Postcolonial Psychology,* for a treatment of the complex psychological effects of colonial history.

13. I have minimized the autobiographical dimensions of Arrowboy's role of witness in relation to Silko, and I prefer not to speculate on this topic beyond my discussion of narrative persona. Joy Harjo, who knows Silko, describes in her essay review of *Almanac* a certain danger to the witness that confirms my analysis of the reader's ritual: "It took Silko ten years to write *Almanac of the Dead*. In those years we were in danger of losing her to the story. The story became larger and more real than anything else, and it took her over. . . . I was truly worried for her life when she ventured into the Mayan calendar of days searching out the stories that would form her novel. I knew she was risking her life. I knew of the danger which came in dreams to form story fragments were warnings *[sic]*. These pieces of the story wound their way through the dream world. I was relieved when I finally saw her one day on the streets of Tucson a few years ago. She too had been concerned she wouldn't be released, that once and for all the story would bypass the storyteller, tangling her in the story. I'm not sure that it won't happen some day. It wouldn't surprise me if Silko disappeared into the pages of one of her novels, became the most provocative character of all. I think it's possible" (210).

14. Toby Langen's article "Estoy-Eh-Muut and the Morphologists," with an ironic title playing on Silko's "Estoy-eh-muut and the Kunideeyahs" in *Storyteller,* traces some of the patterns of this widely distributed story in the oral tradition.

15. In informal answer to my Internet discussion question about *how* Arrowboy's gaze defeats the witchery, critics Helen Jaskoski and Robert Nelson agree on the dynamics of this power of the witness to neutralize the witchery's power. The passage in *Ceremony* where the witches' transformation cannot take place because "someone is watching us," has to do, as Jaskoski writes, with, "non-believers contaminating a process that requires faith" (Helen Jaskoski, Internet posting, Nativelit-L, 5 February 1996). Nelson writes, "Tayo's becoming self-consciously a part of the Event that is presenting there 'northwest of Canyoncito,' where in time immemorial that first Ck'o'yo Witch put the Big Whirling Darkness ceremony into motion and where in time present the ck'o'yo kiva they call the Jackpile Mine has been opened, 'contaminates' the otherwise purely destructive motive that is the spirit of whatever Emo's up to there. Unable to suck Tayo into the whirling dark-

ness, it can only spiral in on itself" (Robert Nelson, e-mail correspondence to DLM, 13 February 1996). Karen Provost, in this intriguing discussion on the Internet, added that the " 'evil' magic not working when someone is watching" makes "sense in terms of community and communal ethics or standards. In other words, isolation, being outside the community and community standards, is one way witchery/ 'evil'/destruction creeps in. When 'someone is watching,' there is a community . . . other eyes/hearts/souls/minds/experiences that both witness and potentially judge one's actions. Pressure from community values/ethics (and perhaps also the love/ connectedness that being in a community can provide) may help keep witchery at bay" (Karen Provost, Internet posting, Nativelit-L, 5 February 1996). Jaskoski, in her article "The Witch Lady Story," suggests that community-connection is a measure of the right use of power: "Hence, human beings can reach and use awesome power beyond the scope of ordinary reason. The individual may choose to use power to benefit the community, or selfishly for profit at the expense of a victim. A person who uses spiritual power selfishly may be a witch" (7). These formal and informal comments confirm my notion of triangulation as the dangerous dynamic of witnessing.

16. Bakhtin's notion of heteroglossia suggests the latent power in language and stories, as "passive" witness, to shape reality. For fuller discussions of Silko's work in relation to Bakhtinian dialogics, see Krupat's "Dialogic of Silko's *Storyteller*," Louis Owens's chapter " 'The Very Essence of Our Lives': Leslie Silko's Webs of Identity" in his *Other Destinies,* and my "Myth, History, and Identity in Silko and Young Bear."

17. For a discussion of the history, economics, and culture of the renewed Zapatista movement, see Barreiro in the works cited.

18. "A Geronimo Story" was first published in Kenneth Rosen, ed., *The Man to Send Rain Clouds: Contemporary Stories by American Indians* and then reappeared in *Storyteller* in 1981.

19. Much has been written about ways that contemporary Native American writers reflect the high value placed on the power of language in different oral traditions. N. Scott Momaday's "Man Made of Words" is the contemporary manifesto of this notion, and Silko's emphasis on the power of stories is a strategic extension of this central feature of a Native epistemology.

20. For an incisive discussion of the questionable applicability of the term "postcolonial" to Native American literatures, see Arnold Krupat's article "Postcoloniality and Native American Literature."

21. In her short essay "The Indian with a Camera," Silko writes, "The Pueblo people did not fear or hate cameras or the photographic image so much as they objected to the intrusive vulgarity of the white men who gazed through the lens" (*Yellow Woman* 175). In addition to glosses on Sleet's insights, another essay, "On Photography," in this collection provides a glimpse of Silko's fascination with photographic developing and the physical potential for an ancestral "Geronimo" to influence the plates: "The more I read about the behavior of subatomic particles of light, the more confident I am that photographs are capable of registering subtle electromagnetic changes in both the subject and the photographer" (180). This suggests further semiotic questions of radically slippery signification in the photographic dimensions of her Geronimo story.

22. Simmons affirms Montezuma as an "amateur dabbler in witchcraft" (12), referring to Valliant, 231–33.
23. An absolute switch of agency would be absurd, although the satirical nature of such an absurdly revisionary history is not lost on other writers, such as Gerald Vizenor, whose novel *Heirs of Columbus* pivots on this very reversal of colonial power in history. This difference, Vizenor's willingness to play with historical absurdities and Silko's unwillingness, develops in important ways in their texts and contexts. Some readers, of course, would call them both absurd.

WORKS CITED

Barreiro, Jose, ed. *Chiapas: Challenging History*. 11.2 (Summer 1994) of *Akwe:kon: A Journal of Indigenous Issues* (recently retitled *Native Americas*).

Bataille, Gretchen M., and Charles L. P. Silet, eds. *The Pretend Indians: Images of Native Americans in the Movies*. Ames: Iowa State UP, 1980.

Bordewich, Fergus M. *Killing the White Man's Indian: Reinventing Native Americans at the End of the Twentieth Century*. New York: Doubleday, 1996.

Clifford, James. *The Predicament of Culture*. Cambridge: Harvard UP, 1988.

Deloria, Vine, Jr. Foreword. "American Fantasy." *The Pretend Indians: Images of Native Americans in the Movies*. Ed. Gretchen M. Bataille and Charles L. P. Silet. Ames: Iowa State UP, 1980: ix–xvi.

——. *God Is Red: A Native View of Religion*. Second Edition. Golden, CO: North American Press, 1992.

Duran, Eduardo, and Bonnie Duran. *Native American Postcolonial Psychology*. Albany: State U of New York P, 1995.

Eagleton, Terry. *Literary Theory*. Minneapolis: U of Minnesota P, 1983.

Evers, Larry, and Felipe S. Molina. *Yaqui Deer Songs/Maso Bwikam: A Native American Poetry*. Tucson: U of Arizona P, 1987.

Gifford, Edward S., Jr., *The Evil Eye: Studies in the Folklore of Vision*. New York: Macmillan, 1958.

Harjo, Joy. "The World Is Round: Some Notes on Leslie Silko's *Almanac of the Dead*." *Blue Mesa Review*. 4 (Spring 1992): 207–10.

Hymes, Dell. *"In Vain I Tried to Tell You": Essays in Native American Ethnopoetics*. Philadelphia: U of Pennsylvania P, 1981.

Jaskoski, Helen. "The Witch Lady Story: Narrative Art in a Hopi Tale." *Native American Literatures*. Ed. Laura Coltelli. Pisa: SEU, 1989. 65–80.

Kroeber, Karl, ed. *Traditional American Indian Literatures: Texts and Interpretations*. Lincoln: U of Nebraska P, 1981.

Krupat, Arnold. "The Dialogic of Silko's *Storyteller*." *Narrative Chance: Postmodern Discourse on Native American Literatures*. Ed. Gerald Vizenor. Albuquerque: U of New Mexico P, 1989. 55–68.

——. "Postcoloniality and Native American Literature," *Yale Journal of Criticism*. 7.1 (1994): 163–80.

Langen, T. C. S. "Estoy-Eh-Muut and the Morphologists." *Studies in American Indian Literature* 2d series, 1.1 (1989): 1–11.

Momaday, N. Scott. *The Ancient Child*. New York: Doubleday, 1989.

——. "The Man Made of Words." *Indian Voices: The First Convocation of American Indian Scholars*. Ed. Rupert Costo. San Francisco: Indian Historian, 1970. 49–84.

——. *The Names: A Memoir*. 1976. Tucson: U of Arizona P, 1987.

——. *The Way to Rainy Mountain*. Albuquerque: U of New Mexico P, 1969.

Moore, David L. "Decolonizing Criticism: Reading Dialectics and Dialogics in Native American Literatures," *Studies in American Indian Literatures*. 6.4 (Winter 1994): 7–35.

——. "Myth, History, and Identity in Silko and Young Bear: Postcolonial Praxis," *New Voices: Critical Essays on Native American Literatures*. Ed. Arnold Krupat. Washington, DC: Smithsonian Institution Press, 1993. 370–95.

Owens, Louis. *Other Destinies: Understanding the American Indian Novel*. Norman: U of Oklahoma P, 1992.

Parsons, Elsie Clews. *Mitla, Town of the Souls, and Other Zapotec-speaking Pueblos of Oaxaca, Mexico*. Chicago: U of Chicago P, 1936.

Ronnow, Gretchen. "Tayo, Death, and Desire: A Lacanian Reading of *Ceremony*." *Narrative Chance: Postmodern Discourse on Native American Literatures*. Ed. Gerald Vizenor. Albuquerque: U of New Mexico P, 1989. 69–90.

Ruppert, James. "Mediation in Contemporary Native American Writing." *Native American Perspectives on Literature and History*. Ed. Alan R. Velie. Norman: U of Oklahoma P, 1994: 7–23.

Scarry, Elaine. *The Body in Pain: The Making and Unmaking of the World*. New York: Oxford UP, 1985.

Silko, Leslie Marmon. *Almanac of the Dead*. New York: Penguin, 1991.

——. *Ceremony*. New York: Signet, 1977.

——. "A Geronimo Story." *The Man to Send Rain Clouds: Contemporary Stories by American Indians*. Ed. Kenneth Rosen. New York: Random House, 1974. 128–44.

——. Interview. "Leslie M. Silko." Native American Novelists Series, FFH 5348. Princeton, N.J.: Films for the Humanities and Sciences, 1995.

——. *Sacred Water: Narratives and Pictures*. 2d edition. Tucson: Flood Plain Press, 1993.

——. *Storyteller*. New York: Seaver Books, 1981.

——. *Yellow Woman and a Beauty of the Spirit: Essays on Native American Life Today*. New York: Simon and Schuster, 1996.

Simmons, Marc. *Witchcraft in the Southwest: Spanish and Indian Supernaturalism on the Rio Grande*. Lincoln: U of Nebraska P, 1974.

St. Clair, Janet. "Uneasy Ethnocentrism: Recent Works of Allen, Silko, and Hogan," *Studies in American Indian Literature*. 6.1 (Spring 1994): 83–98.

Swann, Brian, ed. *Smoothing the Ground: Essays on Native American Oral Literature*. Berkeley: U of California P, 1983.

Swann, Brian, and Arnold Krupat, eds. *Recovering the Word: Essays on Native American Literature*. Berkeley: U of California P, 1987.

Tedlock, Dennis. *The Spoken Word and the Work of Interpretation*. Philadelphia: U of Pennsylvania P, 1983.

Trexler, Richard C. *Sex and Conquest: Gendered Violence, Political Order, and the European Conquest of the Americas*. Ithaca, NY: Cornell UP, 1995.

Valliant, George C. *The Aztecs of Mexico.* Baltimore: Penguin, 1944.
Vizenor, Gerald. *Heirs of Columbus.* Hanover, NH: Wesleyan UP, 1991.
———, ed. *Narrative Chance: Postmodern Discourse on Native American Literatures.* Albuquerque: U of New Mexico P, 1989.
Zumthor, Paul. *Oral Poetry: An Introduction.* Minneapolis: U of Minnesota P, 1990.

MATERIAL MEETING POINTS OF SELF AND OTHER

Fetish Discourses and Leslie Marmon Silko's Evolving Conception of Cross-Cultural Narrative

Ami M. Regier

In *Almanac of the Dead,* Leslie Marmon Silko adapts the Mayan almanac as an indigenous source for a contemporary Native American novel tradition concerned with lost material histories in the Americas. Yet her reclamation emphasizes the expansive, compendious nature of the almanac form rather than emphasizing the purity of a past set of formal practices. Further extending a genre originally elaborated in discontinuous collections rather than in linear narratives, Silko's almanac-based narrative includes elements of genres as diverse as North American contemporary talk show discourse and melodrama.[1] Silko utilizes the multiple plot lines and exaggerated dramatics characteristic of these genres to engage a broad range of characters and cultural issues in extremis. The various characters include a Laguna exiled from his tribe, mestizas who transport guns and anthropological artifacts illegally across the U.S. border, drug dealers, land-grabbing real estate agents, politicians with bestial sexual practices, and international crime figures. At first such characters seem to provide inauspicious perspectives for a study of cross-cultural issues, but the plots associated with them reveal in a melodramatic form the cultural consequences of a history of colonial encounter. Like the recent works of Chicana writers Ana Castillo and Denise Chávez, which meld the tradition of the Latin American historical novel with the Mexican *telenovela* (soap opera), *Almanac of the Dead* draws upon international women's genres and historical sources indigenous to the Americas.[2]

Silko dramatizes the recovery of the almanac as a contemporary form of historiography in a subplot involving the twins Lecha and Zeta and their grandmother Yoeme, all mestizas from Mexico. Yoeme develops a life commitment to translating an ancient almanac. The story of passing on her life work to Lecha as well as her collection of notebooks and fragments of glyph manuscripts is introduced within the same context as, but in contrast to, Zeta's occasional business involvements with the contraband importation and selling of ethnographic artifacts (*Almanac*, 128). In the world of Silko's novel, characters are often placed according to their attitudes toward sacred texts and objects, and the politics of the transmission of those objects would seem to extend beyond individual lives. Silko's expansive narrative might thus be said to follow materialist histories through the complicated politics of the histories of artifacts rather than following a logic of the narratives emerging from character development. Along these lines, Silko has commented in an interview about *Almanac of the Dead* that she wished to give "history a character" rather than working through conventional character development (Interview, 10). Within the novel, the reclamation of indigenous textual production and the merchandising of artifacts are only two of many kinds of collection practices; key to many subplots are objects that become touchstones of personal and cultural identities, as well as touchstones in the proliferation of multiple plots. While the Western novel has long been described in terms of its commitment to deep character development, Silko's almanac builds a novel structure by eliciting narratives from the otherwise silent artifacts of the anthropological past and from contemporary objects as diverse as kitchen utensils and computers.

Silko's narrative practice in this novel thus reflects a number of evolutions from her previous novel, *Ceremony* (1977): the narrative focus has expanded from the elaboration of Laguna storytelling to hybrid Native American and popular cultural forms and from one particular cultural setting, the Laguna Pueblo, to a pantribal survey of the Americas. Similarly, in contrast to the staging of conflicting tribal and Anglo viewpoints within one character's central consciousness, *Almanac of the Dead* has no protagonist. Rather, Silko shifts the narrative ground from a centered subject to multiple persons and, often, their various obsessively valued object collections that in turn signify belief systems and cultural histories. Within the context of her development of a hybrid narrative form, I describe Silko's narrative development as a somewhat curious shift from a centered subject to multiple objects. This turn toward objects can be seen as a key part of her development of a comparative narrative form drawing upon tribally based narrative and Eurocentric histories affiliated with theories of fetishism.[3] Objects in many recent literary and theoretical works function as a materialist metaphor for the condition of colonized people existing as the object of the Western subject's gaze and as the object of investigation by Western anthropologists. However, Silko's narrative poses a second stage to this critique. Silko investigates "objecthood" for its dialectical potential as a material meeting point of self and other, not as the colonized opposite of "subjectivity." Object collections thus are central to Silko's evolving conception of cross-cultural narrative. Through her treatment of object collections as highly charged sites of cross-cultural politics Silko develops a "contaminated" narrative form appropriate to the history of colonial encounter. Rather than posing a narrative reclamation of precontact epistemologies, spiritualities, and discourses in pure or "authentic" form, this hybrid narrative form represents both the dilution of Native cultural presence in the Americas and ongoing, transformative aspects of significant pantribal cultural presences.[4]

I begin with a discussion of "fetishism as cultural discourse" in the Americas.[5] I then turn to Silko's engagement with such discourse in *Almanac of the Dead*. Whereas Silko uses fetishism in *Ceremony* to define Anglocentric viewpoints, more recently she reconfigures fetishism as an impure, culturally comparative discourse that is usable by tribal cultures for undermining Anglocentric cultural assumptions. In a final section I discuss Silko's development of a pantribal coalitional identity through fetish discourse and object collections that revise traditional subject-object and self-other relations.

HISTORICIZING FETISHISM IN THE UNITED STATES

Fetishism arose as a discourse within the earliest moments of organized anthropology in the United States. Frank Hamilton Cushing appropriated the term to describe Zuni practices in the article "Zuñi Fetiches" (1882) as the first material he published from his study of the Zuni pueblo between 1879 and 1882 for the newly formed [American] Bureau of Ethnology.[6] He presents the word *fetish* as a direct English translation of Zuni practices. The translation, however, is necessarily an idiomatic one, if not a creative mistranslation; the etymology of the English word *fetish* has been exhaustively traced to the intercultural pidgin developed on the African Gold Coast.[7]

Cushing's translation is surprising because rather than using fetishism to define "deviant" social values, or even to define a necessarily syncretic discourse that addresses the clash of radically differing social values, he diverges from precedent, using it to define an internally consistent metaphysics within

Zuni culture. Cushing's imprecise translation might be best characterized as an example of what Emily Apter describes as a "semantic disjunction" that typically becomes productive as "the word *fetishism* is displaced from language to language, discipline to discipline, and culture to culture" (*Feminizing*, 4). She argues that "it is precisely this process of creative mistranslation that endows the term with its value as a currency of literary exchange, as verbal token" (4). Critics such as Apter have tended to focus only upon European displacements of the term, given its genesis in a Euro-African encounter, and its later elaboration by Europeans such as Marx and Freud.

However, Cushing's use of fetishism in the Americas also productively poses cultural disjunctions; his elaboration of fetishism as an integral, consistent element of a cultural system diverged from American anthropological discourse of the 19th and early 20th centuries. More typically, broad descriptions of indigenous populations' tendencies to collapse human consciousness into a thing (as opposed to the Western philosophical tradition of positing a radical difference between self and thing) was used to show the lack of cultural development in those populations. In descriptive surveys, the term *fetishism* demarcated broad time scales in the "development" of increasingly sophisticated civilizations in the Americas, particularly during the rise of Darwinism in the Victorian era. The collapsed distinction between subject and object was sometimes described as an inability to think in terms of symbolism; symbolism, in opposition to fetishism, came to function as a marker of "civilized" religions.[8] Animism was the favored 19th century anthropological term, created by Edward Burnett Tylor and later applied by Hartley Burr Alexander, as a catchall for various Native American practices that "conceptually instill[ed] life into a universe that was essentially inanimate" (Vecsey, 2).

Tylor was a major influence on Cushing; Green notes his use of Tylor's vocabulary of the "confusion of the subjective with the objective" as a structural characteristic of Zuni fetishism (Cushing, *Cushing at Zuñi*, 21). However, rather than using this characteristic of a civilization to show that it hadn't evolved to the level of culture (unitarily conceived), Cushing uses this notion to develop the internal consistency and complexity of a highly evolved indigenous culture.

Whereas Europeans historically regarded African fetishes as indexes of culture-specific irrationality, recent appropriations of Cushing's anthropology in Anglo-American discourse tend to treat fetishism as an index of rationality.[9] For example, fetishism as a discourse arises in recent mystery fiction attempting to factor in the detective's traditional reliance on rationality with untraditional approaches to cross-cultural knowledge. In Tony Hillerman's 1973 mystery novel *Dance Hall of the Dead,* Navajo policeman Joe Leaphorn's understanding of Zuni fetishism, within Zuni religious practices, is the key to a rational explanation for the murder of two children (one Navajo, one Zuni) by a white anthropologist. From the perspective of the Navajo detective (who is also an anthropologist in the sense that he is seeking to understand both Zuni and white cultural assumptions in order to solve a crime), fetishism is a notion that describes a complexly ordered worldview. It is a foil to white values that often seem irrational to Leaphorn.[10]

A second type of legacy emerging from Cushing's use of fetishism has to do with anthropologists' personal relations to their object of study. Cushing's defense of Native American "confusion" of subjective and objective resonates with his own commitment to a highly personal methodology. In 1895 Cushing wrote the following in his defense of his own always partly autobiographical method of ethnography for a talk he gave at the American Association for the Advancement of Science:

> If I am at times seemingly too personal in style of statement, let it be rememberd [sic] that well-nigh all anthropology is personal history; that even the *things* of past man were personal, like as never they are to ourselves now. They must, therefore, be both treated and worked at, not solely according to ordinary methods of procedure or rules of logic, or to any given canons of learning, but in a profoundly personal mood and way. (*Zuñi: Selected Writings*, 17)

Cushing elsewhere describes his "personal equation" as a principled commitment to attempting to identify, and work from, the indigenous point of view as part of his notion of the correct methodology for the Anglo anthropologist.[11] Fetishism in his case is proper both to the task of describing an indigenous population's practices, and to describing the white anthropologist's encounter with, and attempt to internalize, the worldview of an indigenous population.

A recent example of this legacy occurs when James Clifford describes the process of recovering artifacts in such a way as to change the relationship of self to cultural "others" as a species of intimate fetishism: "At a more intimate level, rather than grasping objects only as cultural signs and artistic icons . . . we can return to them . . . their lost status as fetishes—not specimens of a deviant or exotic 'fetishism' but *our own* fetishes. This tactic, necessarily personal, would accord to things in collections the power to fixate rather than simply the capacity to edify or inform" (229). Looking for a more progressive form of collecting—rather than a practice of containing specimens of the Other—in his notion of fetishism, Clifford proposes thinking of collecting artifacts as creating a syncretic relation of self to culture through the intensity of obsession: to move the object ever closer to the self, so that it affects the self and has some power over it, means that the self can no longer be singular nor exist easily within a monocultural setting.

Fetish discourse in the United States arises out of the anxieties produced by the interaction across cultures that increasingly defines contemporary America, particularly within the vexed task of writing cross-cultural literature in areas as diverse as anthropology and mystery fiction. Fetishism as a category of discourse offers a particularly useful basis for Silko's narrative tracing of a history founded in colonial contact because it indexes an evolving history of Eurocentric conceptions of aboriginal cultures and less Eurocentric anthropological methods of interacting with non-Western perspectives. Far from deploying fetishism as a form of naive anthropological nativism, Silko presents fetishism as a problematized touchstone of cultural difference where tribal and European points of view are laden with histories of cultural politics.

In *Almanac of the Dead,* there is one central object that is explicitly called a fetish. A large opal with mysterious origins in the possession of two Peruvians captured by border police, it plays a prophetic role in an indigenous plot to retake lands in the Americas. The characteristics of this object are similar to those of Zuni fetishes: it is "dressed," or wrapped with string and feathers (478), is accompanied by a pinch of cornmeal to feed it, and has been packed with coca leaves, which the narrative also identifies as religious objects (480). The opal becomes a source of revelation for Tacho, who by seeing prophetic images in it becomes a coleader of a revolutionary band of Indians: "The fetish suffered night sweats, and one morning Tacho had found a puddle of urine at the foot of the bedroll. Tacho had been afraid to disturb the bundle since then. . . . Tacho worried the police had killed the bundle's Peruvian caretakers and the bundle had been angered and desired revenge" (*Almanac,* 502). Other objects affiliated with commodity culture rather than tribal religions also gain the human ability to "desire revenge"; in the course of the narrative, fetishism spreads infectiously. In a closely linked subplot, the sweating, urinating fetish begins to bleed. Tacho's employer, Menardo, is a mestizo from Tuxtla Gutiérrez who, rather than embracing a polyglot cultural identity, rejects *mestizaje* in order to enter Anglo circles of power. Having become a gun runner and a target of a South American revolutionary group, Menardo becomes obsessed with his bulletproof vest; its technological complexity becomes an index to him of the separation he creates between his Indio heritage and his perception of his growing affiliation with Western technology and culture. Eventually Menardo asks Tacho, his Indian chauffeur and (unbeknownst to him) an infiltrator from the South American group, to shoot him when he is dressed in his vest. Ironically, the vest fails to protect him and he dies: Tacho sees blood at the base of the fetish at this time and suggests that even high technology can participate in the animation often associated only with sacred objects in an indigenous tradition (512). It is this charged and changing relationship between sacred objects and "impure," nonsacred objects now affected by tribal belief systems, whose politics of transmission occur through infection, that most defines a politically operative fetishism offered in *Almanac of the Dead*.

The more "pure" sacred tribal objects in the novel, such as the Laguna stone figures called the "little grandparents" in the chapter "The Stone Idols," are not described as fetishes per se, but similarly are part of a larger pattern of an infectious fetishism. Having been stolen and then put into the collection of an ethnographic museum, the history of these sacred objects offers testimony to the invasion of local tribal beliefs. For example, the subplot of the stolen figures, the little grandparents, is not resolved through the history of the crime and the recovery of the items. Rather, the story of the stolen figures is linked to the contemporary emergence of the giant stone snake, a figure that mysteriously erupts into existence near the uranium mine opened much earlier, in 1949. The plot events concerning the character Sterling emerge from his failure, according to tribal elders, to absolutely protect the snake from contact with an Anglo filming crew (35). Far from being made ineffective by impure contact, and becoming the vehicle of another narrative of loss, the snake becomes the final harbinger of revolution. The novel ends with the image of the snake "looking south, in the direction from which the twin brothers and the people would come" (763). In contrast to the little grandparents, the snake never had been a "pure" sacred object: it had appeared next to the mountainous piles of mine tailings, looking "as if it might be fleeing the mountains of wastes" to some tribal observers (762). However, the snake's origin might also be the accumulation of uranium tailings themselves; the plot structures proliferating out of the snake shrine scenario are necessitated by the question of impurity. While the reclamation of the sacred objects of the little grandparents gestures toward the reclamation of the past, the powerful figure of the impure object gestures toward a changing future.

Similarly, Lecha's involvement in psychically locating lost persons hinges upon a rhetoric of lost objects and the contaminated materiality of memory. Her psychic searches for signs of murdered or lost loved ones is interwoven with her project of translating the ancient manuscripts of her ethnic past (see, for example, the chapter "Shallow Graves," 172–77). The two plots develop from each other and interrupt each other; the noncontinuous, fragmented nature of many chapters similarly tends to position the narrative structure within the economy of material fragments, lost objects, and the always-already contaminated recovery of the past.

This object economy best described as a category of fetishism also generates the dynamics of Anglo plots in the novel. Within the narrative of Alegría's near death, emeralds become touchstones of the symbolic death of Alegría's emotional life when she is abandoned in a desert south of the U.S.–Mexico border (678). Similarly, Seese uses a kilo of cocaine as a kind of charged object equivalent to her missing child to try to intervene in a scenario of addiction and loss. These confusions of subjects and objects in turn offer the instrumental means for the novel's unifying theme of indigenous revolution. The revolution begins to develop by the novel's end through the structures of obsession and the circulation of culturally charged objects within them.

WESTERN INFECTIONS OF FETISHISM

In *The Transparency of Evil,* Jean Baudrillard uses a rhetoric of infection across an axis of tribal and technological systems when he speculates about the subversive effect that aboriginal cultures may have upon Western culture:

> It is not even remotely a matter of rehabilitating the Aboriginals, or finding them a place in the chorus of human rights, for their revenge lies elsewhere. It lies in their power to destabilize Western rule. It lies . . . in the way in which the Whites have caught the virus of origins, of Indianness, of Aboriginality, of Patagonicity. We murdered all this, but now it infects our blood, into which it has been inexorably transfused and infiltrated. The revenge of the colonized is in no sense the reappropriation by Indians or Aboriginals of their lands, privileges or autonomy. . . . Rather, that revenge may be seen in the way in which the Whites have been mysteriously made aware of the disarray of their own culture. . . . This reversal is a worldwide phenomenon. It is now becoming clear that *everything* we once thought dead and buried, everything we thought left behind forever by the ineluctable march of universal progress, is not dead at all, but on the contrary likely to return — not as some archaic or nostalgic vestige (all our indefatigable museumification notwithstanding), but with a vehemence and a virulence that are modern in every sense — and to reach the very heart of our ultra-sophisticated but ultra-vulnerable systems, which it will easily convulse from within without mounting a frontal attack. Such is the destiny of radical otherness. (*Transparency,* 137–38)

Silko treats the return of ancestral lands and the recovery of indigenous histories as important and legitimate components of a revolutionary agenda in

Almanac of the Dead, in contrast to Baudrillard's claims of their irrelevance. However, Baudrillard's description of a non-nostalgic, pervasive return of indigenous origins outside the narrow confines of the museum is an apt metaphor for further revolutionary strategies enacted in Silko's novel. The axis of relationship between sacred objects and technology hints that the reestablishment of Native American communities and rights may be one form of "museumification," where tribal culture is contained in its ethnographic past. Silko pushes the role of sacred objects toward another level of broader cultural influence when, in one of many visions of revolution posed by various characters, fetish objects inspire high technology to participate in a large-scale invasion of infrastructure. In this view, the communications, power, and transportation systems will simultaneously crash and enable the reconquest of lands and reveal the powerful presence of indigenous spiritual systems. Tacho reflects upon the vulnerability of Western technological culture to tribal belief systems in the following terms:

> Blood: even the bulletproof vest wanted a little blood. Knives, guns, even automobiles, possessed "energies" that craved blood from time to time. Tacho had heard dozens of stories that good Christians were not supposed to believe. Stories about people beaten, sometimes even killed, by their own brooms or pots and pans. Wise homemakers "fed" goat or pig blood to knives, scissors, and other sharp or dangerous household objects. Even fire had to be fed the first bit of dough or fat; otherwise, sooner or later, the fire would burn the cook or flare up and catch the kitchen on fire. Airplanes, jets, and rockets were already malfunctioning, crashing and exploding. Electricity no longer obeyed the white man. (*Almanac,* 512)

A logic of the fetish animates this vision of revolution, spreading from objects contextualized in tribal belief systems to the technological objects of postindustrial capitalism.

The invasion most fully realized within the novel may be limited to the disarray of which Baudrillard speaks; for Silko represents, in particular, the fetish's ability to "infect" mainstream culture, especially in the return of indigenous worldviews, which were thought to have been sacrificed to "progress." The novel portrays such a return or infection in various capitalists who become subject to the power of the objects they covet; they fall victim to a destabilizing realization that objects are not necessarily so separable from their own subjectivity as they would like to believe. Menardo's death collapses the distance between subject and object, between the man of Western capitalism and his ultimately uncontrollable possession. The larger implication in the narrative is that the distance between the Western subject and the Other collapses, and the Other can no longer be held at bay. Thus, Menardo's story is not limited to the vengeful destruction wreaked upon those who privilege Anglo cultural constructs, but is also part of an attempt to articulate a non-Western mode of subject-object relations.

In *The Transparency of Evil* Baudrillard presents the object as the ultimate symbol of cultural difference to Western eyes: "In the end, all figures of otherness boil down to just one: that of the object" (172).[12] This view of the object is new in his work as well as in many cultural studies. Previously, fetishism had represented all that was wrong with structuralist thought, according to his highly influential formulation: "[F]etishism is actually attached to the sign object, the object eviscerated of its substance and history, and reduced to the state of marking a difference, epitomizing a whole system of differences" (*For a Critique*, 93). An analogous trajectory occurs in Silko's work, as objects increasingly become key elements in her critique of Western history. Her earlier novel is critical of fetishism, but *Almanac of the Dead* indicates an embrace of a fetishist metaphor precisely in order to confront the problem of the evisceration of history from objects and people. In *Ceremony* one of Tayo's symptoms of psychosis is his vomiting.[13] Tayo vomits to evacuate knowledge and history from his body, yet he cannot. In one telling episode, he faints in a train station and when he awakens he hears Japanese voices. He questions whether Japanese Americans have been released from American relocation camps; he thinks he sees his cousin Rocky's face in the face of one of the Japanese American children: "He could still see the face of the little boy, looking back at him, smiling, and he tried to vomit that image from his head. . . . He couldn't vomit any more, and the little face was still there, so he cried at how the world had come undone" (*Ceremony*, 18).

In *Ceremony* the issue of historical loss is focused upon the bodily person, but in *Almanac* the issue is embodied in objects. In this more recent novel, the fetish objects excrete and bleed. The night sweats, urine, and blood of various fetish objects are revelations of and reactions to historical knowledge; fetishes, like the body, are anything but evacuated of historical knowledge. Fulfilling their oracular function, the fetish objects know more than humans. An oracular, religious fetish should know its history; however, I suggest that Silko's fetishes do not represent a naive religious belief system but rather forge a meeting point between tribal religious fetishism and commodity fetishism. Silko's syncretic fetishes are responsive to the concerns voiced by Baudrillard regarding the erasure of historical inscription upon the object and to the specific polemics of commodity fetishism originating in Marxist thought.

Marx based his notion of commodity fetishism upon a comparison of "primitive" or tribal object worship to the operations of capital, both of which, he claimed, mystify history:

> A commodity is therefore a mysterious thing, simply because in it the social character of men's labor appears to them as an objective character stamped upon the product of that labor. . . . In order, therefore, to find an analogy, we must have recourse to the mist-enveloped regions of the religious world. In that world the productions of the human brain appear as independent beings endowed with life, and entering into relation both with one another and the human race. So it is in the world of commodities with the products of men's hands. This I call the Fetishism which attaches itself to the products of labor, so soon as they are produced as commodities (77).

By means of this formulation, Marx articulates the broad processes whereby socially constructed values and meanings come to disguise the imprint of human labor and, more broadly, human experience, on the object.[14] While Marx's theory of commodity fetishism describes the problem of the cover-up of labor through socially constructed "mists" or representations, it does not, in its original formulation, reveal such cover-ups.

There is some debate, therefore, whether the concept of commodity fetishism can be reappropriated as a tool for the critique of capital beyond the level of a definitional apparatus. While much effort has been exerted recently by materialist cultural critics to revive the Marxist commodity fetish, Laura Mulvey has noted that it is difficult to use it as a revelatory instrument because what commodity fetishism so powerfully explained in its original formulation was "false consciousness," or the disguise of the operations of capital and political power ("Some," 12).[15]

For these reasons, a religious, tribal fetishism is an easier type of fetishism to politicize than commodity fetishism. Nevertheless, Silko chooses to present fetishism comparatively, rather than defining tribal, religious fetishism as a discrete practice. I suggest that Silko links the oracular fetish to the commodity fetish in order to problematize Marx's comparison of capital's operations to tribal fetishisms; instead of covering up social constructions of value and meaning, her comparatively presented fetishisms reveal their operations.

Marx's commodity fetishism becomes an explicit point of reference in the narrative of *Almanac of the Dead* when an activist working for the return of Indian lands in the United States must explain her interest in Marx to fellow Native American activists who feel uncomfortable using European theoretical sources. This activist, Angelita la Escapía (the Meathook), argues that Marx had tribal models in mind for the communal values represented in his texts, however much he misunderstood and misrepresented them from a European perspective:

> Marx understood what tribal people had always known: the maker of a thing pressed part of herself or himself into each object made. Some spark of life or energy went from the maker into even the most ordinary objects. . . . Marx of the Jews, tribal people of the desert, Marx the tribal man understood that nothing personal or individual mattered because no individual survived without others. . . .
>
> Marx, tribal man and storyteller; Marx with his primitive devotion to the workers' stories. No wonder the Europeans hated him! Marx had gathered official government reports of the suffering of English factory workers the way a tribal shaman might have, feverishly working to bring workers a powerful, even magical, assembly of stories. (*Almanac,* 520)

In this passage, Angelita affirms Marx's underlying concept of the inscription of human experience onto objects. While Marx argued that any such personal inscription was erased by a social hieroglyph written over it, Angelita sees the fetish object at the very least as a palimpsest of meaning. In her view, the fetish is not a mere sign-object eviscerated of historical content, as it appeared to Baudrillard in his early work ("Fetishism and Ideology").[16] To Angelita, objects are not empty; rather, they are full of stories that contain history and a "magical" power to transform lives through knowledge.

Whereas Silko uses Angelita to articulate a repoliticized, comparative tribal and commodity fetishism in *Almanac,* her earlier novel had defined commodity fetishism as a tool of capital and historical evil, completely opposed to tribal fetishistic practices. There, Tayo goes to Betonie to be healed after his war experiences. Betonie is a nontraditional medicine man who adapts the old ways to contemporary social settings and who, like Tayo, is of mixed blood. Betonie tells a story of witchcraft creating whites and evil in which whites are described in terms that Alan Wald has argued diagnoses commodity fetishism as the root of their evil (25):

> They see no life
> When they look
> they see only objects.
> The world is a dead thing for them. (*Ceremony,* 135)

The healing ceremonies involve learning to animate the environment. Throughout the novel, perceiving subjectivity in the environment is presented as a Native practice in opposition to the white, capitalist mode of objectifying the environment. Tayo's cure at first seems focused upon his return to nature through a healing relationship with a very earth-motherish woman and his recovery of lost cattle. However, beyond this return to nature, Tayo eventually must understand the relationship of technology to the environment and, by extension, the relationship of war and human evil in a larger creation. Tayo has an epiphany about the nature of his illness while he is on the site of a uranium mine and is thinking about the U.S. government's nearby production of bombs; he recognizes in the physical site of the mine a large-scale pattern of destruction and cultural imperialism. This site becomes for Tayo a physical point of convergence in which local religious objects and the natural landscape are drawn over by technological markers:

> Los Alamos, only a hundred miles northeast of him now, still surrounded by high electric fences and the ponderosa pine and tawny sandrock of the Jemez mountain canyon where the shrine of the twin mountain lions had always been. There was no end to it; it knew no boundaries; and he had arrived at the point of convergence where the fate of all living things, and even the earth, had been laid. . . . [T]he lines of cultures and worlds were drawn in flat dark lines on fine light sand, converging in the middle of witchery's final ceremonial sand painting. (*Ceremony*, 246)

Technology marks the pattern of evil overlaying the environment in *Ceremony* while technology can be seduced to assist the revolution in *Almanac of the Dead*. This difference can be described in terms of the treatment of commodity fetishism in the two novels; while commodity fetishism is a central part of the problem in *Ceremony*, a revisionist notion of commodity fetishism is part of the solution in *Almanac of the Dead*. A creeping commodity fetishism animates technology as a weapon in an indigenous, rather than a capitalist, cause.

Silko's development of fetish objects with functions that parallel those of the human body, both in terms of consciousness *and* gross bodily functions, as well as her attempt to merge Native American and Marxist ideas of human imprint on objects, represents a significant intervention in debates over whether Marxist discourses of commodity fetishism can be a tool of social criticism or must be only a tool of capital. By locating history in both the human body and the object, *Almanac* complicates Western humanism's polarization of subject and object. Marx's humanism contributed to that polarization by locating history only in the worker and not in any accessible way in the object. By connecting person and object, Silko's revisionist use of commodity fetishism suggests a productive intersection in posthumanist methodology and the engaged politics of Marxism. In *Almanac of the Dead* the overt movement between body and object — and, implicitly, between human subjectivity and objects of culture — suggests that engagement with fetishist metaphors does not have to represent a nostalgic or impossibly humanist desire to recover an unalienated subject. Rather, such an engagement provides a mode of representing the subject's split constitution in culture and ideology without relinquishing its material, historical grounding.

Silko's materialist discourse of commodity fetishism, with its play between bodies and material objects, thus suggests an allegory of humanism and materialism. Donna Haraway has argued in another context that fetishism precludes a "dialectical interplay of human beings with the surrounding world" (8). Yet in Silko's narratives, the fetish remains the dialectical object — precisely the mediating presence through which such dialectical interplay occurs, quite literally, with the surrounding world.

PANTRIBAL IDENTITY AND FETISHISM

If fetishism emerges as fundamental to the politics of indigenous histories in the course of Silko's novels, it also becomes a mode of articulating a substantive tribal identity in a technological, contemporary society. Fetishism as an overall category of belief in the consciousness of objects — natural and technological — becomes a rallying point for the consciousness-raising of many groups of tribal peoples. Silko's merger of person and technology represents a challenge to the stereotype of the Native naturalist. Wald has pointed out that Native American literature is often misperceived as constructing "an impossible return to an idealized, pre-technological existence" (25). In this sense Silko's experiment with tribal and Marxist fetishisms participates in a tradition of Native American literature that understands human ties to the environment to be close; yet this experiment broadens the definition of the environment to include the technological in order to render tribal identity a productive, active, and viable presence in a nonpastoral world.[17]

Silko's vision of a revolution of indigenous peoples revolves around a coalition of the dispossessed. The armies of the revolution include the indigenous by heritage, international peoples of color, various political subgroups, and homeless and imprisoned populations of the United States. Clinton, a homeless Vietnam War veteran, intends to be a leader of such an army of the dispossessed. Interested in tracing meeting points between African and Native American histories in the public libraries where he goes to wash, he practices an object-focused religion with connections to Haitian Voudoun practices and to both African and South American Damballah. Of African and Cherokee ancestry, Clinton attributes syncretic tribal religious powers to a knife that he feeds and for which he keeps an altar (after it once partially deflected shrapnel from his body). He feels it "had power all its own," and he argues that his family's traditional regard for knives "was a remnant of old African religion" (413). Clinton discusses the meaning of his knife blade in the context of his radio broadcasts, in which he works out the history of religious aspects shared among peoples of color:

> From the beginning [of African slave importation to replace Caribbean Indian slaves in Haiti], Africans had escaped and hid in the mountains where they met up with survivors of indigenous tribes hiding in remote strongholds. In the mountains the Africans had discovered a wonderful thing: certain of the African gods had located themselves in the Americas as well as Africa: the Giant Serpent, the Twin Brothers, the Maize Mother, to name a few. Right then the magic had happened: great American and great African tribal cultures had come together to create a powerful consciousness within all people.
>   . . . Clinton did not think of the knife blade itself as Ogou. He did not think the tribal people had confused the gentle, huge snakes at the shrines for the Great Damballah or his wife. The spirit of God had only been manifested in the blade and in the giant snakes. God might be found in all worldly places or things. (*Almanac*, 416–17)

Clinton's development of his broadcast language seems to anticipate an accusation of fetishism in the distinction he carefully draws between object and deity. Nevertheless, he defends his own object-based religious practice because it is materialist evidence of remnant and migratory cultural presence attesting to cultural survival. The material histories are key to the forging of pantribal consciousness; he situates his practice among a number of traditions of "ancestor spirits" with inclusive beliefs and rituals associated with them. Clinton gives particular emphasis to Ogou[n]. Ogoun refers to one of the primary West African deities of war that later appeared in Haiti; as Clinton suggests, the importations of Africans to Haiti included groups from many West African states. Haiti becomes Clinton's central example because it is a syncretic culture made of composite histories of the dispossessed, in Joseph Campbell's words, "a congeries of displaced persons, ravished from various African homelands to the Caribbean hell of Hispaniola, where Spain had already all but annihilated the native Indian population" (xi). Maya Deren describes Voudoun as a composite sort of religion, and as such it is uniquely suited for the coalitional purposes articulated by Clinton. Deren writes that it is "a monumental testament to the extremely sophisticated ability of the West African to recognize a conceptual principle common to ostensibly disparate practices and to fuse African, American Indian, European and Christian elements dynamically into an integrated working structure" (56).

Deren's research would also indicate that Silko's notion of revenge enacted through a coalition of tribal peoples has affinities with the struggles punctuating Haitian history beginning with the arrival of the Spanish in the late 15th century and continuing with the establishment of a French sovereignty in 1677. By this time Indian peoples were almost extinct, but Deren argues that runaway African slaves made contact with the few remaining Arawakan tribes in hiding in the hills. She further notes that, over the years, the infusion of Arawakan Carib militancy into the more gentle African spirituality contributed to the African slave revolt of 1790–1804, which culminated in the establishment of Haiti as the second independent democracy in the Western Hemisphere after the United States (Deren, 62).

> What emerges . . . is the fact that the African culture in Haiti was saved by the Indian culture which, in the Petro cult, provided the Negroes with divinities sufficiently aggressive (as was not true of the divinities of the generally stabilized African kingdoms) to be the moral force behind the revolution. In a sense, the Indians took their revenge on the white man through the Negro. (Deren, 11)

Silko's treatment of African-Caribbean history closely parallels Deren's argument that these cultural links occurred in Haiti (*Almanac,* 415–18).

The figure of Ogoun, so central to Clinton's thinking in Silko's text, forms a powerful part of the linking of cultures described by Deren. Ogoun originally was a Nigerian deity associated with power and militancy and affiliated with ironworkers and warriors. Hence "[p]ower resides, too, in the saber or machete which is sacred to Ogoun" (Deren, 133). Deren claims that today's Ogoun has evolved with changing circumstances to become associated more with political power than actual war, and therefore with verbal craft (134). The combination of Clinton's involvement with radio, his militant leadership, and his knife ritual reflects the evolution of Ogoun. Thus Clinton's interests in technological communication and Haitian syncretic religion give material, contemporary expression to his African American and Native American heritages. In this sense, Clinton represents a further transformation of the motif of storytelling as a central element of Native American identity, as Silko's previous works, *Storyteller* and *Ceremony,* exemplify.

All physical objects in *Almanac of the Dead,* including the knife blade, the opal, and various technological instruments, thus forcefully contribute to Silko's project of both articulating multiple forms of substantive indigenous identity in a cross-cultural setting and presenting a weapon for indigenous people to use in the revolution against their domination by Anglo capitalist culture. Silko describes as fetishes those objects that anthropologists such as Frank Hamilton Cushing have associated with tribal belief systems and describes other object-related practices with the vocabularies proper to them, such as Voudoun. I emphasize the aspects of fetishism involved because, as Pietz writes, "[i]n Marxist terms, one might say that the fetish is situated in the space of cultural revolution" ("Problem, 1" 11). As defined by Jameson, cultural revolution only occurs in a comparative, cross-cultural scenario when "the coexistence of various modes of production becomes visibly antagonistic, their contradictions moving to the very center of political, social, and historical life" (95). It is in this context that Silko's *Almanac of the Dead* presents the fetish as revolutionary. Within the novel, fetishes are indexes of the clash of specific Native American and African belief systems with an Anglo-controlled North American culture. By deploying a comparative object discourse that includes a revisionist fetishism, Silko links tribal histories, reformulations of identity, and cultural change.

NOTES

1. Inga Clendinnen, for example, describes Mayan almanacs in terms of the accumulation of dispersed "fragments of history" and "echoes of local events" (135). The almanac of the title refers to the many ancient manuscripts primarily written before the first Spanish colonial contact with the Americas. These books or codices record the history, cosmology, calendrics, and astronomy of various groups of indigenous peoples. The almanacs are not overtly specified in *Almanac of the Dead,* and thus the term "almanac" exists in the narrative as a pantribal grouping of indigenous writings from various periods and tribal groups. The almanacs that are currently known come from Mayan-speaking peoples living in the area stretching from the Yucatán Peninsula of Mexico to El Salvador and Honduras. Four precontact codices "are known to have survived the Spanish Conquest" and are continuing to undergo translation (Love, xv). Additionally, various Mayan works were written in the Latin alphabet between the late 15th century and approximately 1880, such as the *Popol Vuh* and the books of *Chilam Balam* (the sacred books of "the jaguar prophet").

2. Chávez' *Face of an Angel* blends almanac discourse with soap opera plotting in the story of a waitress who writes a book of advice (a form deriving from the Mayan *Libro del Consejo*). See also Castillo's novels *Sapogonia* and *So Far from God*. Melodrama itself has become of increasing interest to feminist theorists who argue that its dramatic excesses, far from representing only apolitical sentiment, often express the rage and emotions of women who experience and recognize patriarchal oppression: Laura Mulvey writes that "[i]deological contradiction is actually the overt mainspring and specific content of melodrama. . . . [S]exual difference under patriarchy is fraught, explosive, and erupts dramatically into violence within its own private stamping-ground, the family" (*Visual,* 39). Silko's *Almanac* brings the question of cultural difference to this context, connecting political violence in the "private" venue of the family to political violence in the Americas.

3. When discussing the politics of the anthropological study of aboriginal bones in *Crossbloods,* Gerald Vizenor blends postmodern narrative theory with tribal narrative practice. By reminding readers that "[t]ribal narratives are located in stones, trees, birds, water, bears, and tribal bones" (65), he, like Silko, moves narrative from the subject to multiple objects. He compares this tribal conception of narrative to European narrative theory, pointing to Roland Barthes's suggestion that the writing voice "loses its origin" when narratives are "distributed amongst different substances — as though any material would fit to receive man's stories" (qtd. in Vizenor, 65). While Vizenor is more amenable to postmodern theory than Silko (see her "Here's an Odd Artifact" and Pérez Castillo) his use of objects as both comparative and Native offers a precedent for the objects in this most hybrid novel of Silko's body of work.

4. See Diana Brydon's discussion of literary strategies of contamination. See also Renato Rosaldo's reflections on finding significant cultural presence among the Ilingots despite the catastrophic history of a "brutal, all-too-familiar, apparently transparent process of land grabbing, exploitation, and 'incorporation' into the nation-state" (209). He argues that classic anthropological conceptions of authentic culture need to be jettisoned in favor of notions of culture that take into account mundane and seemingly inauthentic discourses.

5. I borrow this phrase from a collection of essays by this title edited by Emily Apter and William Pietz. Whereas Apter and Pietz trace the interdisciplinary uses of fetishism as a trope and a critical tool in Marxist and psychoanalytic approaches to European literatures and arts, I see my essay as a provisional beginning point in exploring the potential uses for interdisciplinary and cross-cultural fetish discourse in the Americas. I do not touch on Freudian fetishism in this essay, because of the European sources of that discourse. However, Silko comments that she read all of Freud's writings in the process of writing *Almanac of the Dead* (Interview, 10). A further issue that indeed could be productively pursued is the role of psychoanalytic fetishism in this novel. Fetishism was central to Freud's theorization of sexual difference and is related to his thinking on cultural difference. See Laura Mulvey's "Some Thoughts on Theories of Fetishism" for a discussion of fetishism as a "haunted" construct revealing cross-cultural ideologies of gender, and Roger Dadoun for a discussion of the ethnographic underpinnings of Freud's theory of fetishism.

6. Cushing's contact with the Zunis was part of the first expedition organized by the Bureau of Ethnology in 1879. Although Jesse Green has done much to reevaluate

Cushing's anthropological legacy, Cushing's work on fetishism specifically has received little scholarly attention (see Green's introduction to Cushing, *Zuñi: Selected Writings*).

7. The etymology of the term begins with the Portuguese *feitiço* of the late Middle Ages, meaning "magical practice" or "witchcraft." *Feitiço* shared a common Latin root ("factitious") with the Spanish term *hechizo,* which also was used to designate a wide range of witchcraft practices. The pidgin term *fetisso* arises from the Portuguese on the African coast between 1436 and the 1590s, when it is well established; the time frame spans the arrival of the first Portuguese traders in 1436 and their subsequent ouster by Dutch Protestant traders 1642 (Pietz, "Problem 2," 39). In the Americas, various first-contact conquistadors and friars consistently employed a vocabulary of "idolatry" *(ydolatria)* rather than fetishism or its antecedents *feitiço* and *fetisso.* For example, Olga Lucía Valbuena cites the use of *hechizo,* the Spanish term that developed from the same root as the Portuguese *feitiço,* in a trial record of an accused adulteress and sorceress in New Granada in 1568 and translates the term variously as "spell" and "fetish" (217–18).

8. For example, "unsymbolic art," as found in nude female figurines described as fetishes, is a main identifying feature for the "archaic horizon" in Herbert J. Spinden's 1928 study for the American Museum of Natural History, *Ancient Civilizations of Mexico and Central America.*

9. Pietz describes early European-African conflicts over the social valuations given to objects in these terms: "All other meanings and values attributed to material objects were understood to be the culture-specific delusions of peoples lacking 'reason'" ("Problem 2," 36).

10. In contrast, Marcia Muller's 1990 mystery novel *Trophies and Dead Things* describes fetishism as the locus of irrational desire, rage, and misogyny in the context of white, professional San Francisco; an artist-hobbyist who describes his sculptures as his fetishes is killed by someone who uses one of them as a murder weapon. While the detective, Sharon McCone, is puzzled by the chain of events, the fetishes of the dead man loom large in her imagination as symbols of all that seems out of control. However, as she is able to discern a pattern of cause and effect, the imagery of the fetishes no longer troubles her and indeed the fetishes, as well as the possibility of a crime of passion or any other marginally nonrational explanation, drop out of the plot. Of these two divergent definitions and contexts of fetishism (as the locus of rationality or irrationality in the context of race and gender) Muller's represents by far the most common use of the histories of fetishism.

11. In his unpublished notes, Cushing wrote that "the day is fast approaching when it will be demonstrated that the personal equation is the supremely essential thing in such researches as this, provided it has been abundantly [saturated] with the primitive elements it is dealing with — has absorbed at all points practical, sensational or emotional" (qtd. in Eggan, xii; see also Green's introduction in Cushing, *Zuñi: Selected Writings,* 23).

12. His treatment of the object in this recent work represents an evolution in his thinking on fetishism. Previously, Baudrillard argued that fetishism allows no meaningful treatment of history in relation to objects. In his 1970 essay "Fetishism and Ideology," in *For a Critique of the Political Economy of the Sign,* Baudrillard argued that tribal fetishism in "other" cultures may have operated there as a sub-

versive form of value and as an alternative to rationalistic social rules. However, he continued, such fetishism cannot function as a useful critique of culture for contemporary Marxist thinkers. He gave two reasons: first, that tribal fetishisms involved positing an autonomous, nonalienated self not possible in capitalist cultures. Second, he argued against the possibility of associating a materialist history with objects. Rather, he argued, focusing upon objects was a matter of reading the ideological meanings attached to them under structuralist sign systems. The key problem, according to Baudrillard, was the erasure of the historical dimension of any object under a structuralist paradigm of culture. Thus it is something of a surprise when Baudrillard hints that he would now reattach history to the (non-museum) object and bring tribal worldviews into conversation with capitalism in *The Transparency of Evil.*

13. Tayo is a Laguna Pueblo "half breed" veteran of the Korean war suffering mental illness. His Anglo doctors treat his illness as a problem limited to an individual, but Tayo and a medicine man, Betonie, understand his illness as a part of a larger pattern of history (*Ceremony,* 125–26).

14. Labor, to Marx, produces the bodily and personal aspects of human identity and thus is most expressive of the humanism that is central to his work. Marx presented commodity fetishism as capitalism's central mode of naturalizing ideology in the worker (and thus dehumanizing the worker), by making unreadable the signs of human experience that the process of labor inscribes on its products (Baudrillard, *For a Critique,* 88).

15. Andrew Ross writes that "[f]or the most part, the materialist analysis of ideological relations has based itself on various extensions of Marx's discussion of commodity fetishism" (366). For example, William Pietz argues that Marx's commodity fetishism makes the object of analysis actual transactions and conditions rather than making the object the question of the functioning of sign systems ("Fetishism," 150). Elsewhere Pietz has argued that a "discourse of fetishism represents the emerging articulation of a theoretical *materialism* quite incompatible and in conflict with the philosophical tradition" ("Problem 1," 6, my emphasis), rather than, as Baudrillard argued in his earlier work, the epitome of philosophical systems.

16. See Pietz, "Fetishism," for the argument that Marx's comparative method overrides his use of tribal religion as a negative term. Pietz finds Marx's critique of bourgeois culture to be stronger than his critique of indigenous practices and argues that there is a consistent "twinning" of the proletarian and the tribal "fetishist" throughout the development of Marx's thought.

17. See Lee Schweninger's article in which he understands Native American writing to be fundamentally concerned with the environment. Christopher Vecsey, in a related context, has argued that Marxism provides one strain of thinking to ground Euro-American philosophy stressing ecological values; he sees a 'natural' connection (and some problematic points) between Native American beliefs regarding the environment and Marxism: "Karl Marx wrote in 1844: 'nature is (1) his [humanity's] direct means of life, and (2) the material, the object, and the instrument of his life-activity. . . . That man's physical and spiritual life is linked to nature means simply that nature is linked to itself, for man is part of nature" ("Economic and Philosophic Manuscripts of 1844," *Marx-Engels Reader,* ed. Robert C. Tucker

[New York: Norton, 1972]: 61). However, "even Marx saw a sharp cleavage between humans and the rest of the natural world. His view of nature was of inorganic matter, not living being" (Vecsey, 35).

WORKS CITED

Apter, Emily. *Feminizing the Fetish: Psychoanalysis and Narrative Obsession in Turn-of-the-Century France*. Ithaca: Cornell UP, 1991.

Apter, Emily, and William Pietz, eds. *Fetishism as Cultural Discourse*. Ithaca: Cornell UP, 1993.

Baudrillard, Jean. *For a Critique of the Political Economy of the Sign*. Trans. Charles Levin. St. Louis: Telos Press, 1981.

——. *The Transparency of Evil: Essays on Extreme Phenomena*. Trans. James Benedict. London: Verso, 1993.

Brydon, Diana. "The White Inuit Speaks: Contamination as Literary Strategy." *Past the Last Post: Theorizing Postcolonialism and Postmodernism*. Ed. Ian Adam and Helen Tiffin. New York: Harvester Wheatsheaf, 1991.

Campbell, Joseph. Foreword. In Deren, xi–xiii.

Castillo, Ana. *Sapogonia*. Tempe, AZ: Bilingual Press/Editorial Bilingüe, 1990.

——. *So Far from God*. New York: Norton, 1993.

Chávez, Denise. *Face of an Angel*. New York: Farrar, Straus, and Giroux, 1994.

Clendinnen, Inga. *Ambivalent Conquests: Maya and Spaniard in Yucatán, 1517–1570*. London: Cambridge UP, 1987.

Clifford, James. *The Predicament of Culture: Twentieth-Century Ethnography, Literature, and Art*. Cambridge: Harvard UP, 1988.

Cushing, Frank Hamilton. *Zuñi Fetishes*. 1883. Las Vegas: KC Publications, 1990.

——. *Zuñi: Selected Writings of Frank Hamilton Cushing*. Ed. Jesse Green. Lincoln: U of Nebraska P, 1979.

——. *Cushing at Zuni: The Correspondence and Journals of Frank Hamilton Cushing, 1879–1884*. Ed. Jesse Green. Albuquerque: U of New Mexico P, 1990.

Dadoun, Roger. "Fetishism in the Horror Film." *Enclitic* 1.2 (1977): 39.

Deren, Maya. *Divine Horsemen: The Living Gods of Haiti*. London: McPherson, 1953.

Eggan, Fred. Foreword. In Cushing, *Zuni: Selected Writings*, xi–xiv.

Haraway, Donna. *Simians, Cyborgs, and Women: The Reinvention of Nature*. New York: Routledge, 1991.

Hillerman, Tony. *Dance Hall of the Dead*. New York: Harper Collins, 1973.

Jameson, Fredric. *The Political Unconscious: Narrative as a Socially Symbolic Act*. Ithaca: Cornell UP, 1981.

Love, Bruce. *The Paris Codex: Handbook for a Maya Priest*. Austin: U of Texas P, 1994.

Marx, Karl. *Capital: A Critique of Political Economy*. Vol. 1. Trans. Samuel Moore and Edward Aveling. Ed. Frederick Engels. New York: International, 1984.

Muller, Marcia. *Trophies and Dead Things*. New York: Warner Books, 1990.

Mulvey, Laura. "Some Thoughts on Theories of Fetishism in the Context of Contemporary Culture." *October* 65 (1993): 3–20.

———. *Visual and Other Pleasures*. London: MacMillan, 1989.

Pérez Castillo, Susan. "Postmodernism, Native American Literature, and the Real: The Silko-Erdrich Controversy." *Massachusetts Review* 32 (1991): 285–94.

Pietz, William. "The Problem of the Fetish, 1." *RES* 9 (1985): 5–17.

———. "The Problem of the Fetish, 2." *RES* 13 (1987): 23–45.

———. "Fetishism and Materialism: The Limits of Theory in Marx." In Apter and Pietz, 119–51.

Rosaldo, Renato. *Culture and Truth: The Remaking of Social Analysis*. New York: Beacon, 1989.

Ross, Andrew. "The New Sentence and the Commodity Form: Recent American Writing." *Marxism and the Interpretation of Culture*. Ed. Cary Nelson and Lawrence Grossberg. Urbana: U of Illinois P, 1988. 361–80.

Schweninger, Lee. "Writing Nature: Silko and Native Americans as Nature Writers." *Melus* 18.2 (1993): 47–60.

Silko, Leslie Marmon. *Almanac of the Dead*. New York: Penguin, 1991.

———. *Ceremony*. New York: Viking, 1977.

———. "Here's an Odd Artifact for the Fairy-Tale Shelf." Rev. of *The Beet Queen*. *Impact/Albuquerque Journal* 8 (1986): 10–11.

———. Interview. "Narratives of Survival." By Linda Niemann. *Women's Review of Books* 9 (July 1992): 10.

———. *Storyteller*. New York: Arcade, 1981.

Spinden, Herbert J. *Ancient Civilizations of Mexico and Central America*. 1928. New York: Biblo and Tannen, 1968.

Tylor, Edward Burnett. *Religion in Primitive Culture*. New York: Harper and Bros., 1958; originally published as chapters 11–19 of *Primitive Culture*, 1871.

Valbuena, Olga Lucía. "Sorceresses, Love Magic, and the Inquisition of Linguistic Sorcery in *Celestina*." *PMLA* 109 (1994): 207–24.

Vecsey, Christopher. "American Indian Environmental Religions." *American Indian Environments: Ecological Issues in Native American History*. Syracuse: Syracuse UP, 1980. 1–37.

Vizenor, Gerald. *Crossbloods: Bone Courts, Bingo, and Other Reports*. Minneapolis: U of Minnesota P, 1990.

Wald, Alan. "The Culture of 'Internal Colonialism': A Marxist Perspective." *Melus* 8.3 (1981): 18–27.

CANNIBAL QUEERS

The Problematics of Metaphor in Almanac of the Dead

Janet St. Clair

As much as readers were prepared to embrace Leslie Marmon Silko's *Almanac of the Dead,* many were repelled by its apparent homophobia. The novel is admittedly full of savage white homosexual men who prey on weak and unsuspecting victims to feed their insatiable lusts for sex, money, and power. The brutal homosexuality of *Almanac,* however, should not be interpreted as a bigoted travesty of a legitimate expression of human sexuality but rather as a metaphor of the insane solipsism and androcentric avarice that characterize the dominant culture. Western philosophy is founded on the primacy of the individual and subsequent objectification of anything outside the ego; on the acquisition of private property by those powerful enough to seize and amass it; and on the devaluation, commodification, and exploitation of women and people of color. Silko's homosexual characters incarnate these tenets. In addition, their equation of carnal gratification with viciousness and their gynephobic sexual self-absorption emblematize the egocentric, phallocentric, and misogynistic savagery that Silko sees as endemic to Western culture.

Homosexuality as metaphor is amplified through the emblem of cannibalism, which figures the insatiable greed that inevitably attends undisciplined individualism and amoral objectification. These bestial men, ravenous for blood, stalk and devour whatever titillates their jaded appetites. Twisted by crimes of unchecked egomania, Silko's characters are not intended to portray gay men, but malevolent and voracious monsters.

Nevertheless, the trope of cannibal queers is in some senses unfortunate. Surely Silko was not attempting to malign gay culture or sexuality in her use of the metaphor: there is only one minor homosexual character in her novel who is not fabulously monstrous in his arrogance, greed, and viciousness. And surely she did not intend to imply that normal male homosexuality is characterized and driven by phallocentric self-adulation and crazed misogyny nor that its expression is typically brutal, rapacious, and loveless. The gay character Eric is portrayed as gentle, compassionate, and noble, but he too is destroyed and devoured by the malevolence of Silko's cannibal queers. Except for Eric, who is victimized for and by his capacity to love, her homosexual characters are deliberately fantastic caricatures designed to condense the persistent injustices of Western culture into tightly concentrated emblems. Many are not even strictly homosexual: they will sexually use whomever they wish to consume. And yet, these freaks that she has created as metaphors of collective trespasses unfortunately tap into the traditional negative stereotypes that have defaced male homosexuality for at least the last fifty years.

During the 1940s, homosexuals were commonly regarded as mentally deranged psychopaths. Allen Bérubé, in his book *Coming Out Under Fire* (translated in 1994 into an award-winning documentary film by Arthur Dong) unmasks the brutal purges of homosexuals in the U.S. military late in World War II because of the victims' alleged unspeakable depravity. Postwar psychoanalytic theory legitimized homophobia, reiterating well into the 1970s that male homosexuals are narcissistic, promiscuous, predatory, exploitative, amoral, and malicious psychopaths. The stereotypes persist, and Silko — however unwittingly — might fairly be charged with perpetuating these distortions in her portrayals. Even if it were charitably argued that she is deliberately exposing Euro-America to its own bigoted contagions, the fact remains that only the oppressed are injured by it.

Her use of the metaphor of cannibal queers engages the reader in a thorny dilemma. Mired in negative stereotype, it offends. On the other hand, the metaphor works. It elegantly exposes the most heinous attributes of a stumbling ideology taken to its conceivable extremes. The novel is far more likely to nurture the continuing fruitful critique of America's foundational values than to support ignorance and malice: it is too hard a book to read for those seeking merely to titillate their bigotries, and judgmental ignorance and malice are under unrelenting attack throughout the novel. It is difficult to imagine, in fact, a reader who might come away from the work with prejudices intact. To that extent, Silko's use of the metaphor is perhaps vindicated. Discomfort with the social morality of the figure nonetheless persists.

The characters of Beaufrey, Serlo, and Trigg are only three of literally countless male homosexuals in *Almanac of the Dead*. But these three, taken together, amply illustrate Silko's skillful construction and implementation of her complex metaphor of cannibal queers. In each case, Silko's focus on the characters' psychotic self-absorption rather than on their sexual gratifications reiterates in various specific ways her use of homosexuality as an elaborate figure of speech.

Beaufrey, international broker in pornographic videos of sexual torture and mutilation, figures the predictable end result of unexamined moral relativism: he is utterly devoid of conscience. "He had always loved himself, only himself," Silko writes. "Others did not fully exist [for him] — they were only ideas that flitted across his consciousness then disappeared" (533). Chronically bored in his insular egomania, he diverts himself by bending handsome young men to his insidious will. Because there is no reality beyond his own ego, Beaufrey sees other humans merely as game pieces, or puppets in his "one-man theatre experiments" (543). His victims are themselves too self-involved to see they are only "toys, little trifles" whose destruction Beaufrey choreographs to relieve his haughty ennui. The young men, dazzled by Beaufrey's power, money, and savoir faire, are easy sexual conquests — too easy. Soon, they bore him. And "when the young men bored Beaufrey" he destroyed them, because "Beaufrey became aroused watching the young men break down" (560).

Fresh meat was never his object, anyway. Convinced that "the words *unavailable* and *forbidden* did not apply to aristocrats" such as himself, Beaufrey requires, rather, the fresh blood of dead meat (535). He gets it by manipulating his boy toys into histrionic suicides. "Beaufrey loved the theatre," Silko writes. He "was the director and author; he was the producer," and "players . . . were a dime a dozen" (537). His video productions of sodomy rape, strangulations, genital mutilations, and tortures that "progressed conveniently into the 'autopsy' of the victim" leave him unaroused (538). Only his own live psychodramas can stir his jaded passion.

The egocentric brutality that emblematizes for Silko the male-dominated individualistic Euro-culture might be evident in Beaufrey's sexual scenarios alone. But the author underscores her metaphorical interpretation of his homosexuality by deemphasizing the importance of both the sexual act and his sexual partners and emphasizing, rather, his isolate self-gratification. Beaufrey wears two condoms, one over the other, as well as clothes or pajamas during sex with faceless, nameless partners. He "did not allow himself to be seen or embraced or touched. He ignored his partners," and "he never altered his behavior for others" (533, 552).

If the emblematic significance of homosexuality is established by the indifferent contempt with which he regards his male lovers, it is even further strengthened by his undisguised misogyny — a quality shared by virtually every man and acknowledged by virtually every woman in the novel. Beaufrey's fear and loathing of women is culturally representative, according to Silko: near the end of the novel, after countless horrific examples, the character Zeta "still had to marvel at the hatred white men harbored for all women, even their own" (704). Beaufrey started, he recalls, "by hating his mother; hating the rest of them was easy" (102). Although he feigns indifference to women, "he enjoyed conversation that upset or degraded them" (102). He seeks to destroy Seese, the only woman with whom he comes into contact in the novel, because she distracts their mutual lover David from David's otherwise complete psychological enslavement to Beaufrey.

Beaufrey's metaphorical cannibalism is obvious: he sees other people as consumables. Silko again emphasizes the figurative significance by making his interest in the subject chillingly literal. Since childhood Beaufrey had been fascinated with the Long Island cannibal Albert Fish. At the age of eight, he recalls, "He had felt Albert Fish and he were kindred spirits because they shared not only social rank, but complete indifference about the life or death of other human beings. As Beaufrey had read European history in college, he had realized there had always been a connection between human cannibals and the aristocracy" (534–35). His recollections of Bluebeard that immediately follow this quotation reveal Silko's skillful splicing of literal and figurative. "Bluebeard hung his 'wives' from meat hooks in the tower," Beaufrey gloats; "the 'wives' had been the brides of serfs raped by the master on the evening of their wedding night" (535). So rich aristocrats "might crave roasted human flesh," he muses. "What of it?" (535).

Beaufrey's methodical destruction of his lover David serves as metaphorical case study of the egocentric arrogance, ruthless objectification, and cannibalistic greed that characterize Western culture in Silko's estimation. Seeking a new "plaything," he uses Seese as a "decoy" to lure the bisexual David into a pathological homosexual triangle with Beaufrey and his naive young lover Eric (544). He is drawn to David, a handsome young photographer, because "[a]rtists were quite exciting to destroy. Because they participated so freely" (537). Imagining the possibilities for his own fiendish amusement, Beaufrey indulges "the great hunger, the greed to have all of David" (59). Setting the three young people against each other in his private self-indulgent theatrical production, he "felt the thrill" of "watching Eric, David, and Seese waltz one another closer to suicide" (550). He is delighted when Eric "made his suicide a sort of visual event . . . which Eric had somehow known would be irresistible," and "intrigued by the process of deterioration" in David that promises yet another garish melodrama (537–38).

When Beaufrey fails to coerce Seese into a second abortion, the vainglorious David becomes narcissistically fixated on his little likeness, baby Monty. After Beaufrey kidnaps the baby and disposes of it, he "got really hot" during sex with David, "because David never even suspected what had happened to the infant, something terrible; nothing got Beaufrey hotter" (561). Soon bored again, he allows David to see the photographic proofsheets of his slaughtered baby. Minutes later, grinning in satisfaction, he bends over David's corpse snapping commercially valuable photographs while extolling the glories of free-market trade. Throughout, his ruthless self-indulgence emblematizes in every aspect a culture of what Silko calls Vampire Capitalists—a society gone rotten under an ideology that scorns women and rewards egotism, manipulation, exploitation, and amorality.

Beaufrey's friend Serlo is another character whose deviant sexuality figures the phallocentric avarice and arrogant egomania of racist and sexist Western cultural traditions. Again, Silko suggests a metaphoric rather than literal interpretation of the character's sexuality by virtually dismissing the carnal to focus sharply on moral deviance. Serlo is not actively homosexual, but he abhors women and associates socially only with homosexual men. Steeped in the fiction of his own genetic and social superiority, he detests a world that is being "overrun with swarms of brown and yellow human larvae called natives" (545). Everything, he knows, is rightfully his; the masses must, quite simply, be exterminated. Smug and insolent in his impenetrable arrogance, Serlo suffers only his own kind—the European *sangre pura*—and even they must maintain a deferential distance. He lives alone with his staff of silent and invisible servants on a vast family estate, needful, he believes, of no one.

He is as egomaniacal sexually as he is socially: no one touches him but himself; he is intact and indivisible in his own perfection. Having learned from his pedophilic grandfather that "sexual penetration was silly, unnecessary, and rotten with disease. . . . [Serlo] had not allowed another human being to touch him in a sexual way since his grandfather's death" (546).

Phobic of the squalid brown masses that press against his privilege, Serlo is obsessed with purity. Careful that "his sex organ touched only sterile, prewarmed stainless steel cylinders" in which he captures his sperm for preservation, he protects both his person and his bloodline from the pollution he so monomaniacally fears (547). Beaufrey, who procures for himself "rough trade" because of their physical perfection, acknowledges that "one of life's little mysteries" is that "aristocratic bloodlines seemed genetically incompatible with beauty" (537). But unlike Beaufrey, Serlo "had never cared for beauty" because it was not "as lasting as one's lineage, which not even death could diminish" (543).

The metaphorical parallels are clearly drawn: Serlo's psychoses caricature Euro-America's conviction of its own genetic and cultural superiority and its corresponding fear of the corruptions of miscegeny. In much the same way, his gynephobia mirrors in miniature the disdain for women that Silko perceives behind aggressive, hierarchical, and repressive male dominion. Serlo associates purity with white male aristocrats; filth with women and people of color. Cherishing the purity of his bloodline above all else, he can scarcely dismiss his own mother, but he separates the portraits of her family members from those of his father. Sharing his friend's disgust for women and their stench of fecundity, Beaufrey insists that "breeding was for animals" (536). But Serlo — while remaining uncontaminated himself — concedes (at least intellectually) the "God-given duty" of his regal line occasionally to infuse "superior aristocratic blood into the peasant stock" through the passionless rape of young Indian women (541). Procreation was of course a necessity as well as an obligation, but he had learned from his forward-looking grandfather to trust "that reproduction needn't involve the repulsive touch and stink of sex with a woman" (547). Until such time as his private institutions for eugenics research could invent an artificial uterus and identify a means through which both parents could be male, he would follow his grandfather's example and freeze his priceless semen in antiseptic vials.

Serlo as metaphor reveals the loveless phallocentrism that Silko sees as implicit in Euro-American male insolence. His alienation from and disrespect for women parallels his attitudes toward the earth itself — a charge frequently leveled against white men as a whole, both within and without Silko's novel. Imagining himself superior to the seedy miracles of generation, Serlo dreams of escaping them, literally rising above the earth in hermetically sealed Alternative Earth modules where "the select few would continue as they always had, gliding in luxury and ease . . . [on] glass islands where they looked down on earth . . . still sipping cocktails" (542).

Serlo mirrors the justifiable anxieties of the tyrants he represents as well. Until such time as a clean break from the filthy oppressed and their contaminated planet became viable, his central obligations, as he sees it, are to protect the purity of his blood and the sovereign rights that it conferred. Although Beaufrey didn't believe the browns and blacks of the earth had enough "energy or ambition to overrun it," Serlo was persuaded that "those of the *sangre pura* must stop playing games and take action" before the brown breeders "inherit the earth like the cockroaches" (549, 556, 561). To this end, he and a loosely organized confederation of powerful like-minded white men had developed an international "secret agenda" involving a number of highly confidential strategies to exterminate the rabble. Plans already effected included encouraging the political, social, and religious turmoil that would incite "yellows, browns, and blacks" to "slaughter one another" (546); circumventing revolution by numbing young ghetto blacks and Hispanics with cocaine; and introducing AIDS into "targeted groups" so that "the filthy would die. The clean would live" (548). But if revolution came in spite of his efforts to forestall it, he was prepared: his vast estate was a white man's fortress, stockpiled with enough food, water, alcohol, and armaments to repel or withstand any siege.

The figurative cannibalistic qualities of Beaufrey and Serlo are clear. Beaufrey preys upon young homosexual men, fattening his psychoses upon their living and dead bodies; he eats off the mutilated genitals of the victims of his lucrative torture pornography videos. Serlo, gorged with his sense of genetic superiority, never questions that the fat of the land, sucked from the bodies and blood of the hungry, is his to consume or discard. But the metaphor that connects cannibal queers with the egomaniacal greed of Western ideologies becomes startlingly literal in the character of Trigg, who actually sits at a table upon which is spread a living man, and who eats this man alive.

Silko adds even more complexity to the metaphor of loveless, priapically fixated, spiritually impotent Euro-America by creating this character as only half a man. Utterly self-involved and bloated with self-importance, Trigg is in fact paralyzed from the waist down, confined to a wheelchair, literally out of touch with the earth, and furiously denying the finality of his debility. If only he has money enough and science enough, he believes, he will be able to buy wholeness. "Trigg was obsessed with standing up," writes Silko. "More than anything Trigg himself wanted to be erect" (662). Powerless to rise, he shifts the obsession to his penis, which he proudly and frequently kneads into prolonged erections. But even his penis, timeless symbol of regeneration, is barren of seed, and remains "hard and dead as a dildo" (659).

Paralysis, of course, is an apt metaphor for men who are incapable of feeling. The tragedy of contemporary Euro-American men, Silko seems to claim, is that they know they are only half men and must strive mightily to conceal so shameful a truth with hollow bravado and sham masculinity. Trigg, crippled and chronically insecure, has, as the character Max Blue observes, an "absolute" need to prove himself (379). Predictably, he determines to do so in the way his crippled and insecure society most respects: by amassing enormous wealth through the racist strongman strategies of cannibalistic capitalism. In the beginning, he fattens on Tucson real estate, buying up the depressed properties of the poor for resale to rich East Coast investors. The displaced people were nothing but shit to Trigg, but a worry nonetheless because "Mexicans and blacks could drift up from the bottom of the cesspool — and it only took a few of those brown floaters to stink up and ruin an entire neighborhood

Trigg was 'rehabilitating'" (387). He opens his first blood plasma centers because the clinics "busted neighborhoods and drove property prices down without moving in blacks or Mexicans," thereby providing him with delectable new material morsels to feed his avarice (379). But almost from the beginning "Trigg wanted to use the plasma donor centers to obtain donor organs and other valuable tissue" because "he had not been able to forget the price quotes for fresh whole blood, human corneas, and cadaver skin" (387, 389). Yet no accumulation of man-parts can begin to make him a man.

Once again Silko virtually dismisses the sexual aspects of homosexuality to sustain development of her increasingly complex figure. That Trigg's homosexual acts are to be interpreted metaphorically seems emphasized by his equation of sex with his cannibalistic objectives. Probably heterosexual by temperament, Trigg uses sex with either gender to manipulate, master, and devour the object of his appetites. He pumps Leah Blue for information, influence, and ego. He habitually thinks of people as pieces of consumable meat. His projected sex mall — "an entire shopping mall [devoted] only to sex" (664) — is a meat market in an almost literal sense. Among its "tasteful" shops wherein one could find live sex demonstrations and collections of human sex organs pickled in jars, would be vendors selling "the finest food and liquors" (664). He calls his female sex partners "piggies," but he sees even himself as a piece of meat: "Trigg had only ever had one thing on his mind," Silko writes, "and that was the meat dangling between his legs" (383). His associate Peaches calls him Trigg the Pig; and Max Blue, another character who lives off the dead bodies of men he has stalked and killed, scornfully nicknames him "Steak-in-a-Basket."

Trigg as metaphor illuminates Silko's assertions of this culture's limitless capacity for unconscionable exploitation. While Trigg was still a college boy planning his plasma donor centers that would buy blood from the veins of the unemployed and homeless, he had written in his diary, "I could do the world a favor each week and connect a few of the stinking ones up in the back room and drain them dry. They will not be missed" (386). Contemptuous of anyone with less money than he has, and chronically, voraciously hungry for more money for himself, he does just that — and worse. Expanding his plasma centers into an organ and tissue repository, he drains the blood of those who will not be missed, then butchers the cadavers and sells the body parts on the European black market. The figurative cannibalism that drives him is made at least idiomatically literal: he eats his victims alive. To distract an unsuspecting victim from his design, "Trigg gave him a blow job while his blood filled the pint bags; the victim relaxed . . . with his eyes closed, unaware he was being murdered. . . . [Trigg] doubted any of them could hope for a better death" (444).

Beaufrey, Serlo, and Trigg each illuminate a different facet of Silko's complex metaphor for a savage society of "Vampire Capitalists." Feeding off the pain and destruction of others, Beaufrey represents the supreme selfishness that renders ethics, morality, and compassion into absurdities. Creating disorder — breaking whatever tenuous connections he sees — becomes the last remaining amusement for a man to whom nothing is forbidden. Serlo's character reveals the unspeakable arrogance behind racism, misogyny, and disrespect for the earth, and the absolute isolation and sterility that necessarily result from such arrogance. Trigg embodies the crippling effect of unchecked greed, where all things and all people become mere commodities to be wrested from the weak and unwary, where poor men can be bought for small change to be eaten alive by the rich.

Trigg's ending in the final pages of the novel serves as capstone to this elaborate exemplum. Robbed and murdered, his corpse is packed in his own freezer with some of those prime cuts of human meat by which he had thought to become rich and whole. His hoarded wealth, it is implied, will ultimately empower the Army of Homeless, led by the very man Trigg had hired to lure in his unwitting "donors." Beaufrey and Serlo, along with most of their ilk, escape the novel unscathed by their own atrocities. Trigg's end, however, figures the frequently repeated thesis of the entire oeuvre: maybe not yet, but a culture of vicious, impotent half-men must eventually be cut down.

Beaufrey, Serlo, and Trigg are perhaps the three characters who most fully develop the metaphor of cannibal queers. But negative portrayals of male homosexuality infuse every thread of the novel's interwoven subplots. Ferro, the son that Lecha abandoned and Zeta grudgingly reared, scorns the sullen and subservient Paulie for the "smooth, blond thighs" of Jamey, the most "gorgeous" man that dark and dumpy Ferro has ever had (454). The police forces of Tucson and Mexico — collectively, a major character in the novel — are rife with brutal and exploitative homosexuality, and many more men are "faggots who got hot when they wore a pig's uniform" because of the ruthless power it emblematized (456).

Tycoons and high government officials in the novel typically engage in homosexual encounters as well. The "worldly-wise" membership of the prestigious Owls's Club share a predilection for "the rose-bud rumps of all the brown street boys" of Tucson (461); the exclusive Thursday Club, whose members also entertain "pretty Mexican boys" at their posh clubhouse, is known around town as "the old fags sleeping society" (644); members of El Grupo Gun Club swap stories of penis size, sexual exploitation, and titillating theories of sexual violence. This proliferation in the novel of elite clubs of rich and powerful white men that despise and exclude women and butt-fuck poor young men of color is clearly meant to figure the greedy, racist, sexist arrogance that Silko believes characterizes white men in power.

The metaphor works — but the reader cannot escape the irony. Silko is denouncing oppression from the point of view of an oppressed group, the indigenous peoples of the Americas. Yet she is doing so by exploiting the stereotypes by which another group is oppressed — by the same oppressor. White heterosexual males have in the twentieth century systematically tyrannized and persecuted homosexuals with as much mindless vigor as they have tyrannized Native Americans — or any other so-called minority. And needless to say, both the stereotypes and the oppression of gays persist.

Unfortunately, Silko's metaphor works precisely *because* it taps into the very stereotypes that have led to the continuing oppression and denigration of gay males in America. And while Silko may reject any obligation to dispel such stereotypes — she has other legitimate causes to espouse — it might fairly be suggested that she had, in this most moralistic of novels, at least some moral obligation not to promulgate them. Just as racist bigotry has been — and continues to be — validated by so-called scientific proofs, so have hateful prejudices against male homosexuals. Silko's appropriation of vicious stereotypes based on the Euro-American "science" that she attacks as specious and self-serving seems disquietingly incongruous, at best.

Kenneth Lewis, who traces the formulation and development of psychoanalytic attitudes toward male homosexuality from Freud onward, succinctly identifies and reveals the sources of most of this society's popularly received prejudices that continue to marginalize gay men. *Almanac's* characters, unfortunately, echo them. Behind a smoke screen of science, white heterosexual men have branded the male homosexual as either a psychotic or a psychopath. In *The Overt Homosexual* Charles W. Socarides wrote that "[h]omosexuality . . . is filled with aggression, destruction, and self-deceit. It is a masquerade of life . . . [involving] only destruction, mutual defeat, [and] exploitation of the partner" (qtd. in Lewis, 203). Abram Kardiner, noting the "predatory activity" of homosexuals among their other character flaws, concluded after extensive study that they "do not make good citizens in any society" (qtd. in Lewis, 189). Beaufrey and Trigg — among other characters in *Almanac of the Dead* — seem almost patterned upon such spurious representations.

Silko's exploitation of weird-science stereotyping goes further. Edmund Bergler, considered the preeminent American researcher on male homosexuality in the 1950s and 1960s, wrote prolifically, pontifically, and pugnaciously on the subject. He frequently asserts in his books and essays that the male homosexual is conspiratorial, bitter, shifty, and malicious. In his book *One Thousand Homosexuals,* he repeats for emphasis a statement he had previously made in *Homosexuality: Disease or Way of Life?* reminding the reader that he has more clinical experience with such types than anyone else in the world:

> Though I have no bias, if I were asked what kind of person the homosexual is, I would say, Homosexuals are essentially disagreeable people, regardless of their pleasant or unpleasant outward manner. . . . [T]heir unconscious conflicts sap so much of their inner energy that the shell is a mixture of superciliousness, fake aggression, and whimpering. Like all psychotic masochists, they are . . . merciless when in power, unscrupulous about trampling on a weaker person. The only language their unconscious understands is brute force. (197–98)

In the same book, he notes that a homosexual is likely to be "the coldly detached type" who "is an icicle personified — distant, cold, unmoved, frequently so taciturn that he is classed with the 'he gives me the creeps' variety" (200). Beaufrey, Trigg, and Serlo all fit Bergler's profile with unsettling accuracy.

Throughout the seventies, according to Lewis, "most analysts, both orthodox and revisionists, continued to express the traditional themes of the disordered, unhappy, and vicious homosexual," where "a small elite with money, power and prestige prey on their helpless fellows" (216). The theories may be dated among psychoanalysts in the 1990s, but they persist within our culture. In an essay published in 1989, apparently for high school students, Edward Levine quotes physiologists and psychoanalysts "whose findings unequivocally show" that homosexuality "is a psychopathological symptom." Gay men are deranged, evil people who, "by their own accounts, endlessly engage in furtive, promiscuous, and impersonal sex with utter strangers in public men's rooms, parks, bathhouses, and elsewhere" (60–62).

Such outrageous preconceptions, born of supposedly legitimate research and circulated by supposedly learned people, seem to be the molds from which the characters of Beaufrey, Serlo, and Trigg are turned. Typical of homosexuals, we have been asked to believe, they are cold, conspiratorial, brutal, exploitative, aggressive sexual predators who are dangerously crazy and give decent people the creeps.

What is the reader to do with a metaphor at once so effective and so invidious? Bergler's final published essay, "The 'Aristocracy' among Homosexuals: Lovers of 'Trade'," again specifically recalls Beaufrey and his boy toys. Bergler identifies the "half homosexual" male prostitute as "trade"; "the tough-acting, swaggering roughneck" as "rough trade" (1). Beaufrey pursues them both. He is fascinated with the bisexual David, who had formerly worked as a "live-in stud" for "rich old queers in Bel-Air" (59). And he adored "rough trade," the ruggedly handsome "street punks" who "looked blank" if they heard the term *blue blood*" (537). Pursuers of "trade," Bergler claims, are seeking retribution against their overbearing mothers, turning the tables to become at last the all-powerful aggressors toward their weaker objects. Those with an appetite for "trade," says Bergler, consider themselves the "aristocracy" among homosexuals. Beaufrey might have been one of Bergler's case studies.

Silko's characters' stereotypical unwholesome relationships with their mothers seem also to play off of outdated psychoanalytic theories about the elusive or abusive mother. Beaufrey loathes his mother, whom he felt had abandoned him even before he was born. Conceived during an incautious menopausal fling in Paris, Beaufrey learns from his mother that she had tried unsuccessfully to abort him. Serlo's mother divorced his father, then abandoned the child to his pedophilic grandfather. Serlo is nevertheless persuaded that mothers in general are smothering, parasitic "vampires" who will inevitably destroy "even the most perfect genetic specimen" (541–42). Trigg, emotionally abandoned, alternately hates his mother and longs to amass enough money to buy her affection and approval. Ferro, abandoned at birth, cannot abide even the sight of his mother, Lecha. The very first page of the novel makes clear that "Ferro hates Lecha above all others."

Traditional psychoanalytic theorists of the 1950s, 1960s, and 1970s, typically male and culturally gynephobic, would of course find these characters textbook examples: it is because of the absent and/or castrating mother, they claimed, that homosexual men become narcissistic, emotionally stunted, and incapable of love. Crushed by the "giantess of the nursery," boys take "frantic flight" into homosexuality (Bergler, "'Aristocracy,'" 2). The "demonified mother," as Socarides terms her, is the fundamental cause of the psychopathic pattern known as homosexuality. In claiming that the homosexual's splintered ego "attempts to love narcissistic objects and also to vent the rage and sadism aroused by the mother" (qtd. in Lewis, 203), he might be speaking directly about any number of homosexual characters in the novel. Or — more frighteningly — Silko might appear to be lending credence to the vicious myths that have served for decades to justify the oppression of gay men in America.

Silko repeatedly illustrates white men's fear of women's reproductive and maternal power, and their reactionary glorification of the penis. Beaufrey's and Serlo's disgust with the idea of heterosexual contact is one manifestation; armaments dealer Greenlee's lewd ridicule of women is another. Just before Zeta kills him, Greenlee thinks she is laughing at his racist, sexist, phallocentric joke. But "Zeta had laughed out loud because everything essential to the world the white man saw was there in one dirty joke; she laughed again because Freud had accused *women* of penis envy" (704).

Kenneth Lewis identifies this same phallocentric gynephobia as an element in the formulation of psychoanalytic theory about gays. This culture's "centrality of the penis" and fear of castration "served to establish women as defective men." Male homosexuals, who were excluded from participating in the formulation of theories on homosexuality, "were seen as deeply flawed and defective because they shared certain psychic characteristics with women" (237). The stereotype of gays as psychically damaged by the mother reveals the terror and insecurity at the heart of white male culture.

In Silko's defense, however, it must be noted that virtually all the characters in *Almanac*, not just the homosexual men, hate their mothers. Even maternity, it seems, is incapable of engendering love. But women are not the villains of the piece; they are among the victims. All have been blighted by the vicious misogyny of their culture. Some, such as Leah Blue, survive by adopting the male values of self-serving aggression, corruption, and manipulation. Leah, obsessed with pleasing her tycoon father, is utterly indifferent to her sons and only mildly interested in the news that her husband has been killed. Childless Alegría, accepting the natural inferiority of her gender, marries a rich man who disgusts her and joylessly sleeps with abusive and loveless boyfriends. Twin sisters Zeta and Lecha, marked by childhood disdain for both their parents and sexual abuse by an uncle, are likewise incapable of love. Zeta has one repulsive sexual encounter to get a job promotion, then chooses celibacy; Lecha abandons her child immediately after his birth and amuses herself with strings of meaningless affairs with nameless men. Seese, the best mother in the novel, spends her baby's entire short life in the protective fog of alcohol, marijuana, and cocaine. As with the male characters, no one loves anyone; sex is sterile and self-involved. The gruesome slaughter of Monty, the only child in the novel, is scarcely more than a narrative aside.

Love between the genders, based as this culture has traditionally dictated on inequity and contempt, cannot grow. But despite the numberless homosexual men in the novel, there are no homosexual women. Preconceptions of lesbians would not serve the purposes of the metaphor. Lesbian writer Cherry Smyth, among others, points out that notions of gender polarization have influenced stereotypes of homosexuals as well as straights. "Lesbian sex was posited as loving and monogamous," she writes, "in false opposition to gay male sex, which was deemed abusive, exploitative and promiscuous" (36). Her statement recalls Michel Foucault's contention that sexuality is a social construct, the categories of which, once defined, serve to legitimize and sustain power structures. Native American lesbian critic, novelist, and poet Paula Gunn Allen would be slow to agree that the oppositions, however they were derived, are false. It is among women, she repeatedly urges in both her critical and literary works, that the best hope is to be found for redemption from our habits of destruction. In her well-known essay "The Feminine Landscape of Leslie Marmon Silko's *Ceremony*," she outlines the process of feminization/maternalization that delivers Tayo from madness and allows him to "bridge the distance between his isolated consciousness and the universe of being" (12).

If Allen is correct in identifying Silko's belief in the redemptive power of the feminine — and there is nothing in Silko's work to suggest that Allen is not correct — then the absence of lesbian love in *Almanac* makes perfect sense in terms of the metaphor. The thesis that the tyranny of white male values is bringing the Americas to the brink of destruction would be undermined by the existence of loving women, unbruised by the daily contusions of brutal oppression. But to create lesbian lovers incapable of love would undermine the tenacious foundation of hope that undergirds this precariously linked jumble of stories connected only by violence. For hope resides in even the nightmarish wasteland of *Almanac of the Dead:* the ancient book from which the novel is titled itself offers promise that there is a transcendent story that orders the chaos and harmonizes the cacophony; the appearance of the great stone snake precedes an imminent regeneration.

To evade stereotypes altogether and develop a lesbian relationship — or for that matter, a gay male relationship — with sympathetic appreciation for its depth and complexity would be to write another novel altogether. *Almanac of the Dead* is not about love: it is about the death of love; about the love of death. Grossly distorted, wildly exceptional characterizations drawn broad, shallow, and tawdry are among Silko's techniques for portraying the terrifyingly imaginable outcome of our cultural course.

Using the metaphor of cannibal queers, Silko challenges what she identifies as a Euro-male pattern of selfishness, greed, brutality, phallocentrism, racism, misogyny, and arrogance. The reign of the blood-crazed male Death-Eye Dog has spun virtue upside down: that which is horrendous, fearful, and deadly is valued; that which is cooperative, nurturing, and fecund is despised. Cannibalistic homosexuals such as Beaufrey, Serlo, and Trigg serve as emblems of the destructive self-absorption that characterizes for Silko contemporary culture in the Americas. All are sterile, ingrown men capable of neither engendering nor nourishing life. Grotesque predators, rather, who try to nourish their own brutish and deformed lives by sucking to a bloodless husk anyone too weak to resist them. Ruthless men who contrive to ensure that everyone is too weak to resist them. Readers will probably recoil from the shocking metaphor of cannibal queers. But it is appropriate to Silko's apocalyptic landscape, to her all-embracing vision of modern decadence and oppression.

WORKS CITED

Allen, Paula Gunn. "The Feminine Landscape of Leslie Marmon Silko's *Ceremony.*" *American Indian Quarterly* 5 (1979): 7–12.

Bergler, Edmund. "The 'Aristocracy' among Homosexuals: Lovers of 'Trade'." *Bulletin of the Philadelphia Association for Psychoanalysis* 12 (1962): 1–9.

———. *Homosexuality: Disease or Way of Life?* 1956. 2d edition. New York: Collier, 1962.

———. *One Thousand Homosexuals: Conspiracy of Silence or Curing and Deglamorizing Homosexuals?* Paterson, NJ: Pageant, 1959.

Bérubé, Allen. *Coming Out Under Fire: The History of Gay Men and Women in World War Two.* New York: Free Press, 1990.

Foucault, Michel. *The History of Sexuality.* 3 vols. Trans. Robert Hurley. New York: Pantheon, 1978–86.

Levine, Edward M. "Homosexuality Is Unnatural." *Sexual Values: Opposing Viewpoints.* Ed. Lisa Orr. San Diego: Greenhaven Press, 1989. 59–64.

Lewis, Kenneth. *The Psychoanalytic Theory of Male Homosexuality.* New York: Simon and Schuster, 1988.

Silko, Leslie Marmon. *Almanac of the Dead.* New York: Simon and Schuster, 1991.

Smyth, Cherry. *Lesbians Talk Queer Notions.* London: Scarlet Press, 1992.

Socarides, Charles W. *The Overt Homosexual.* New York: Grune and Stratton, 1968.

THE TIMELINESS OF *ALMANAC OF THE DEAD*, OR A POSTMODERN REWRITING OF RADICAL FICTION

Caren Irr

A mong the early reviews of *Almanac of the Dead*, Sven Birkerts's essay in the *New Republic* is notable for its venom. Situating Leslie Marmon Silko's novel in a tradition of suspiciously radical fiction, Birkerts asserts:

> That the oppressed of the world should break their chains and retake what's theirs is not an unappealing idea (for some), but it is so contrary to what we know both of the structures of power and the psychology of the oppressed that the imagination simply balks. . . . [H]er premise of revolutionary insurrection is tethered to airy nothing. It is, frankly, naive to the point of silliness. The appeal to prophecy cannot make up the common-sense deficit. While it is true that a great deal of fiction is an enactment of wish-fulfillment scenarios, it is also true that little of it is of the first order.[1]

The premises here are clear: literature "of the first order" offers a teleological repetition of "what we know." More particularly, it involves a depiction of the "psychology of the oppressed" that is "tethered" to a "common-sense" understanding of the subject in "the world." This subject does not change dramatically, because time as "we" know it is an orderly, consistent, sensible, and nonprophetic repetition of an initial totality. To the extent that

Silko's novel violates these premises, it is in Birkerts' view "airy," "naive," silly — simply wishful thinking.

In both its terms and its implications, this review recalls debates from earlier in the twentieth century about the potential of politically committed fiction. Malcolm Cowley, for instance (another writer associated with the *New Republic,* although in a period when that association meant something else), criticized the proletarian fictions of the 1930s in similar terms:

> [M]ost of the [proletarian novels] have essentially the same plot. A young man comes down from the hills to work in a cotton mill (or a veneer factory or a Harlan County mine). Like all his fellow workers except one, he is innocent of ideas about labor unionism or the class struggle. The exception is always an older man, tough but humorous, who keeps quoting passages from *The Communist Manifesto.* Always the workers are heartlessly oppressed, always they go out on strike, always they form a union with the older man as leader, and always the strike is broken by force of arms.[2]

Insisting on an opposition between the plot of "wish-fulfillment scenarios" and a social reality in which strikes, rebellions, and revolutions are apparently impossible, Cowley like Birkerts ultimately asserts a metaphysics of time. Underlying his hostility to the sentimentalism of proletarian fiction is the theory that change does not happen, since history is the repetition of self-identical defeats. Time is the grid on which these repetitions are made equivalent. Any suggestion otherwise — any prophecy or assertion of an alternative futurity, any quoting for instance from *The Communist Manifesto* — violates the initial premise of temporal consistency and must be disallowed.

Clearly, in such a climate — a climate where the "real" of realist fiction is taken to be a necessary repetition — any fiction involved in the project of figuring radical politics will also be engaged in figuring different, nonidentical temporalities. For this reason, it is not surprising to find Silko asserting in an interview in the *Women's Review of Books* that while writing *Almanac of the Dead* she began researching "post-Einsteinian" theories of time.[3] In so far as Silko is writing a radical fiction, then, she is also confronting and rewriting the Birkerts/Cowley metaphysics of time. Thus, in the themes, structure, and poetics of *Almanac,* we find the simultaneous deployment of multiple versions of temporality. The Birkerts/Cowley model of consistent repetition of an original encounter with power is shown to be part and parcel of the Columbian discovery narrative against which Silko's 1991 narrative is most obviously written; by drawing on a range of Native American cosmologies, Silko supplements and overcomes linear European time lines. Furthermore, the scandalous temporality of the radical fictions that Cowley described is also rewritten; one of the important counternarratives that Silko offers in *Almanac* is a revisionist account of the significance of Marxist revolutionary temporality. Setting this apocalypticism against a reactionary hybrid formed from similar materials, she indicates the multiplicity of temporal registers operative within cultural and political conflict.

Of course, Silko cannot dispose of a temporal metaphysics simply by wishing it away, any more than any other metaphysical totality at the basis of writing can be discarded by fiat. Ultimately, her multiple temporalities settle into an active, circulating, spatialized figure of a possible near future, and this figure is labeled as being in the "Indian style" — clearly investing it in this narrative with a positive vector of authority. Not being a specialist in Native American culture or writing, I will not be concerned here with tracing out the ethnographic sources for this figure, but rather with demonstrating how Silko's use of multiple temporal resources situates her as a postmodern radical novelist. It seems to me that with its ambitious scope and technical bravura, *Almanac of the Dead* does much to fulfill the wish articulated at the conclusion to Fredric Jameson's famous essay "Postmodernism, or the Cultural Logic of Late Capitalism":

> [T]he new political art (if it is possible at all) will have to hold to the truth of postmodernism, that is to say, to its fundamental object — the world space of multinational capital — at the same time at which it achieves a breakthrough to some as yet unimaginable new mode of representing this last, in which we may again begin to grasp our positioning as individual and collective subjects and regain a capacity to act and struggle which is at present neutralized by our spatial as well as our social confusion.[4]

Calling for a new form of political art that will map and thereby alter "our spatial as well as our social confusion," Jameson sets an agenda for postmodern radical fiction. To the extent that Silko takes up this project, we can read *Almanac of the Dead* as an effort to display spatial confusion as the effect of conflicting versions of temporality. In this novel, where the Columbian metaphysics of one-way discovery breaks down, we find a variety of other space-time formations serving as placeholders for an emergent, potentially revolutionary pre- and postmodern near future.

These postmodern concerns appear in Silko's novel as early as the title page. As the title indicates, the book is very much about the dead; it is set in the desert, an environment where "the dead did not rot or dissolve" — a place where people are simply "passing time" while they wait for death (64). In this context, the dead are both bodies that have outlived their social significance and ghosts of those who died before their agendas were complete. Like the 500-pound phantoms who pile onto a cart in one of the traditional stories retold in the novel, these dead souls rest among the living dead until the desert becomes a stockpile of history. Since things do not rot or dissolve in the desert, a vast postmodern array of dated materials accumulates there. Silko's desert is a ghostly postmodern assemblage of dead styles.

The form that binds these styles together is, of course, the almanac. As defined in the novel, an almanac is "a book of tables containing a calendar of months and days" that "predicts or foretells the auspicious days, the ecclesiastical and other anniversaries" and includes "short glyphic passages [that] give the luck of the day"; it derives, in English and Spanish, from the Arabic word "almanakh" (136). Thus, the almanac is simultaneously a record of events (e.g., anniversaries) and a prediction; it occupies a transitive ground between past and future, as well as between English and Spanish, and official and folk religion. This definition holds both for Silko's novel as a whole and for the jumbled assembly of fragments that several of the characters translate throughout the novel. Both are commemorative and prophetic; both cross linguistic and national borders between the U.S. and Mexico; both correlate religious and ecological events. But particularly remarkable among this almanac-within-the-almanac's "short glyphic passages" is one that states the paradox of time: "The image of a memory exists in the present moment" (575). Like the almanac, we are reminded, a memory calls on the past but is retained in an image available in the present. In form and in content, then, the almanac stresses the interpenetration of past and present, promising a renewal that will lessen the weight of dead fellow travelers.

Before reaching these major thematic statements, however, Silko explores the complexity of time in the first chapter. The novel begins on a celebratory anniversary, the sixtieth birthday of the Mexican-born twins Lecha and Zeta. Meditating on aging, the more sober Zeta reflects that "the old ones did not believe the passage of years caused old age. They had not believed in the passage of time at all. It wasn't the years that aged a person but the miles and miles that had been traveled in this world" (19–20). In this and many similar passages, Silko contrasts traditional Native American beliefs about the spatial nature of time with the linear concept of time implicit in white people's gradualist mode of aging. The "miles and miles" traveled are set against a "season by season" progress toward the grave (19).

This initial contrast is complemented at the end of the chapter by the meditations of the twins' gardener, a man from the Laguna Pueblo:

Sterling had been carefully following advice printed recently in a number of magazines concerning depression and the best ways of combating it. He had purposely been living in the present moment as much as he could. One article had pointed out that whatever has happened to you had already happened and can't be changed. Spilled milk. But Sterling knows he's one of those old-fashioned people who has trouble forgetting the past no matter how bad remembering might be for chronic depression. (24)

Here, the "present moment" is not the spatial concept of the "old ones" but a cliché popular with the mass media, and Sterling's "trouble forgetting the past" is not a gradualist linearity but something "old-fashioned." While Zeta contrasts the static with the linear in favor of the static, Sterling does the opposite. While her meditations on native aging interrupt "the passage of time," his personal narrative insistently intrudes on a medicalized, sterilized present. At this early point in the novel, then, at least four theories of time have been presented, and their relative valuation is no doubt one of the "unanswered questions" from which the chapter takes its name.

Of the several time schemes that organize *Almanac of the Dead,* the one most fully considered derives from Navajo myth cycles. The central idea of the traditional concept of time appears just before the prominent definition of the almanac quoted earlier: "Sacred time is always in the Present" (136). In other words, sacred time recognizes no firm divisions between past, present and future; it is a realm of possibility, structured by recurrence, parallels, and patterns within the absolutes of time and space. Time, in this view, is something endlessly available, something spatial; it is something through which one can travel forward and back like a god.

This concept of the everlasting nature of the sacred present does not mean, however, that persons following traditional beliefs recognize no historical differences. In the opening of part 2, the young mestizo Menardo recalls his traditional grandfather's explanation of the relationship between sacred and historical time: "The only true gods were all the days in the Long Count, and no single epoch or time of a world was vast enough or deep enough to call itself God alone. All the ancestors had understood nothing stayed fixed in the universe" (257–58). A concept of epochs is at work here. An epoch seems to be a subdivision of time in general and to carry some sacred significance. A particular epoch will be inhabited by gods, although it is subordinate to the "Long Count," the larger, longer structure that constitutes holiness. One clearly needs to recognize the coexistence of epochs in order to reach "the only true gods."

Menardo's grandfather and Zeta and Lecha's grandmother Yoeme agree that the name of the present epoch is the "Death-Eye Dog." This epoch is characterized by unusual cruelty and viciousness; it has lasted for five hundred years and reigned around the world (252). Clearly, the arrival of Europeans in the Western Hemisphere triggered the new epoch, creating a distinction between "before" and "'now' and tomorrow," as Zeta's friend Calabazas reflects (222). However, while European narratives of this event generally attribute all historical agency to Europeans, in *Almanac of the Dead* as in her previous novel *Ceremony*, Silko does the opposite; she frames the arrival of the Europeans and the epoch of the Death-Eye Dog with developments in native culture. The conquistadors and explorers only made headway into the Americas because "the tribes in Mexico had been drifting toward political disaster for hundreds of years before the Europeans had ever arrived," Calabazas reflects (220). The Europeans exploited preexisting conflicts in indigenous culture, but they did not impose a new order on Native Americans purely of their own volition. This historical thesis is of utmost importance to the novel, since it casts the present as a phase in the unfolding story of native life. It dissolves assumptions of the permanence of ethnic European rule in the Americas and underwrites prophecies of the end of the Death-Eye Dog epoch. Within the recurring patterns of prophecy, it is possible to predict that "the day would come when once more the people would have to flee to the mountains" (233). In the sacred present, the epoch of the Death-Eye Dog represents only a partial incarnation of conflicts between gods; since no one era can complete the full incarnation, this linear, single-actor era can eventually end.

This prophecy of endings is most fully preserved in the almanac-within-the-almanac. As grandmother Yoeme tells Zeta and Lecha, the Almanac "was the 'book' of all the days of their people. These days and years were all alive, and all these days would return again" (247). The Almanac tells the story of living time and recurrence. Thus, it is appropriate that Yoeme put the majority of the Almanac into Lecha's safekeeping, since Lecha herself has psychic power. She can "see the past and tell the future" (46). She "made up the ending to the . . . story" (144). From her vantage point, time is an endless structure through which she is free to travel.

In addition to outlining this theory of time as recurring spatiality in the narrator's commentary, Silko has organized the novel according to the temporal structure of Navajo ceremonial tales. In Navajo cosmology, five worlds overlap one another.[5] The movements of life began in the first world and the symbol associated with this world is fire. In *Almanac of the Dead,* the first part (titled "The United States of America") is primarily devoted to describing the history of the characters; notably, it includes passages on Lecha's experiences in Alaska among the Athabascans, a people who share ethnic origins with the Navajo. It is in Alaska that Lecha meets Rose, a woman haunted by the fire that consumed her siblings. It is also in Alaska that Lecha witnesses the power of an old woman who causes planes to crash and burn in the tundra. Also, in the first part, Sterling visits the Congress Hotel, the site of a fire that led to the capture of his hero John Dillinger. In most of the plot lines dealing with Native Americans, fire is an important recurring image in the first part of the novel.

The second world of Navajo cosmology is associated with air, the third with water, and the fourth with earth and matter, and all these pairings are replicated in *Almanac of the Dead*. In part 2, the house that the beautiful architect Alegría designs for Menardo features the light-filled air of the jungle, and the reflections of this light are central to the plot. In effect, the reflections kill Menardo's wife when she tumbles down the highly polished stairs. In part 3, the defining feature of Venice, the exclusive housing development planned by Mafia wife and real estate tycoon Leah Blue, is water, and the similarly liquid-based plasma center run by her lover Trigg links several plot lines together. Finally, in part 4, land emerges as the central theme. It is the land that the thousands marching with Angelita (aka La Escapía) and the twin brothers want; it is an alternative earth that the purebred Colombian aristocrat Serlo plans; and it is his pony's "rapture of the plain" that finally kills the young photographer David.

In Navajo tales, these four worlds provide the symbolic and cosmological substructure for a fifth world, a world that is home to the Holy People; in this world, the emphasis is on action, since the activities of the Holy People mirror those of real people. The doubleness of this mythic present is described in the novel in part 5, "The Fifth World." In this part, much of the novel's action takes place: many daring escapes are attempted and brewing conflicts are activated. Grandmother Yoeme's great prison break is described; Calabazas's wife and lover aid escaping refugees; a murder with complicated consequences occurs at a Yaqui Easter dance; and Alegría makes an eventful border-crossing. However, despite all this activity, nothing is resolved in this world. Instead, Silko concludes with part six, "One World, Many Tribes," which has a single subsection entitled "Prophecy." From the historical present of the fifth part, Silko returns the narrative to the realm of myth and prophecy. In short, the overall organization of the novel follows traditional Navajo cosmology by ordering temporal events in a five-part spatial structure that culminates in a return to the sacred present.

The effect of this structure, I argue, is to provide a layer of traditional storytelling within the novel. In Walter Benjamin's famous distinction, a story is an irreducible narrative orated by a traveler who makes the far-off world collectively memorable for a local community of listeners, while a novel is a printed communication that takes place in linear time and is produced by, for, and about individuals in a capitalist, rather than artisanal, society.[6] Most of these elements of "story" appear in *Almanac of the Dead*. Although the Navajo cosmology will not be familiar to every reader, it is certainly significant for those who already know the story, that is, to those who have integrated it into their collective memory. In the novel, the cosmology has been reduced to its most essential symbols, and the traveling Europeans are integrated into native history. The story translates white adventurers into its own terms, a practice that strengthens and reaffirms the coherence of the local community in the face of invasion.

The only element of storytelling downplayed in *Almanac of the Dead* is orality, perhaps because for Silko, as for Benjamin, the transmission of stories is endangered — or perhaps because, like Derrida, Silko is interested in taking apart a European metaphysics based on the supposedly primary nature of speaking over writing. As Yoeme's story about the travels of the Almanac reminds us, the carriers of the book fragmented, chewed, boiled, and ate its pages during the struggle to save it. They memorized the contents of the book so it could be retold, and traces of that oral history are retained in the fragmentary nature of the Almanac. But, the Almanac is also insistently graphic; Lecha annotates and translates it, and Seese even enters it onto a computer. Orality here is a survival strategy recalled by means of writing; it is no longer the primary vehicle of story. Even the novel's primary oral storyteller, grandmother Yoeme, shrinks down to a bright-eyed skeletal creature enclosed in a crib, as if a metonym for the infantilization of spoken stories, their reduction to children's entertainment. Interestingly, though, while this loss of storytelling provokes nostalgia in Benjamin, for Silko the fragmentation of stories inspires the double consciousness of time called for in the Fifth World. In *Almanac of the Dead,* the mythic time of stories is made available to the reader through the filter of the progressive time scheme of the novel.

According to the source of Benjamin's definition of the novel, Georg Lukàcs's *Theory of the Novel,* the harmonious wholeness of the ancient world can only appear in story form once it has disappeared from the social world. Then, when even that re-creation disappears, the ground has been laid for the novel. Novels, for Lukàcs, expresses the double loss of one's home in nature and society; by describing the hero's search for home, a novel gives form to the potentially formless series of events called history, and its hero embodies the communal destiny of a community on the verge of dissipation. The novel expresses a "transcendental homelessness" in the course of its re-creation of the individual's quest for home.[7] For Lukàcs and Benjamin, the novel is the historical successor to the story, and its appearance marks a culture's entry into linear time.

Appropriately, then, *Almanac of the Dead* begins with several unique events — that is, events that introduce change and a sense of irreversible sequence. The loss of Seese's child is one such occurrence, and Sterling's conflict with the Tribal Council is another. In the first chapter, Silko emphasizes the dislocation these events have caused. They serve in the novel the same function that the arrival of Columbus serves for Native Americans or the crucifixion serves for Christians; they provide fixed points from which all other events are measured. Of course, both events are also losses. Sterling loses his place in the Laguna community, and Seese loses her place in the complex psychological game that included her lover David, his friend Eric, and the manipulative Beaufrey. She also loses the promise of a future family community with her son. The result is that both Seese and Sterling find themselves homeless at the start of the novel.

In this homeless state, a certain amount of generative action begins. Sterling's story in particular provides a second organizational pattern for the novel. His story line moves in a Lukàcsian development from the "Exile" of the second chapter to the "Home" of the final chapter. He begins with a deep sense of loss and alienation and ends with a feeling of renewal and possibility. His search is not complete in the sense that he has found an adequate solution to all the problems that have beset him, but at the end of the novel he is on the verge of restoring himself to his community. He has opened himself up to the message of the great stone snake that his elders were so eager to protect, and he is ready to settle old grievances. To the extent that Sterling represents a communal destiny, then, he signals a paradox faced by many traditional people caught between two versions of time. In his story, the passage of linear time leads to a return to mythic time. Hence his interest in crime magazines: if crime is an expression of social dislocation, then crime stories make that alienation sensible. They provide a narrative framework for alienation. "True crime" of the type that interests Sterling even goes a step further, since it places the criminal alienation in the double frame of narrative and history. These elements all congeal when Sterling and Seese visit famous crime scenes around Tucson. By returning to the scenes of crimes, Sterling narrativizes his present environment — one in which he does not feel at home. He comforts himself by recalling the barbarism at the root of local history: "The old Tucson mansions along Main Street were the best proof that murderers of innocent Apache women and children had prospered," he reflects. "In only one generation government embezzlers, bootleggers, pimps, and murderers had become Tucson's 'fine old families'" (80). His novelistic feeling of homelessness gives way to storytelling about his own and others' exiles.

Seese's story line, by contrast, does not provide an entry into historical narrative. It does not even run the course of the entire novel. Her character only figures prominently in part 1, and her conflict is resolved by the end of part 4. Her loss has made her homeless, but unlike Sterling she has no home to which she can return. She begins with the knowledge that her baby has been kidnapped, and she seeks out Lecha in hopes of recovering the child. However, as the novel progresses and we learn that Lecha's psychic powers only allow her to locate the dead, it becomes clear that even Seese's success would be a failure; accomplishing her goal and acquiring Lecha's help would only confirm her loss. It would only make her certain of her baby's death and prevent her return home. In the novel, it is unclear whether Seese herself achieves this certainty, but the reader definitely does. We know that the baby is dead. So, what Seese's story line shows us is that fulfilling one's quest is not always a happy task; it does not always produce a homecoming, since the home to which one wishes to return may have been destroyed in the meantime. Instead, it is the search itself that allows hope and encourages action. It is the very linearity of time—the inability to see the future—that generates the novel's hope for a generic reconciliation of wanderer and home.

Of course, both Seese and Sterling's searches take place in time, not space. Neither travels extensively; each searches his or her memory for the causes of exile. This emphasis on memory introduces a temporal complexity typical of the genre of the novel; this complexity is described by narratologists as the difference between the *fabula* (the order of events in a story) and *sujet* (the order of the presentation of events).[8] This difference is evident if we number the events in Sterling's *fabula* from one to ten, in which one stands for the earliest event (the theft of the "little grandparents") and ten for the most recent event (Sterling's return to the Laguna reservation); the order in which these events appear in the novel is roughly as follows: 9–8–1–3–2–6–5–4–7–10. Silko does not arrange the events in chronological order, nor does she use the present as a frame within which one experiences a linear rehearsal of the past (a 9–1–2–3–4–5–6–7–8–10 progression). Instead, she draws attention to the workings of linear time by jumbling the episodes that Sterling recalls. This way, the reader must untangle the series of cause and effect involved in Sterling's banishment from the reservation. The complex arrangement of the *sujet* makes recognition of the linearity of the *fabula* an achievement, not a given. The linearity of the novel genre is actively constructed, not assumed, in *Almanac of the Dead*.

This complex, denaturalized linear time becomes thematically important for Silko at the moment of death. Death is the horizon of an individual's time line, and several of Silko's plot lines suggest that transformations occur at this horizon. Of course, confronting death is a crucial part of a warrior mentality and as such underlies the march of Angelita's army north to the border to take back their land. The marchers face death and confront versions of time that would deny their history. Similarly, Calabazas's helper and cousin Mosca the Fly is fascinated with the motorcycle accident that damaged his friend Root. He sees the accident as a life-altering "journey to the boundaries of the land of the dead"; certainly the accident led Root to align himself with the side of his family that can accommodate a paraplegic with speech defects (199). Conversely, Menardo's attempt to avoid death with the help of a bulletproof vest is part and parcel of his denial of his native heritage. In this novel, attempting to cheat death means hiding from the past, while boldly approaching death enables a kind of transformative access to the grander vistas of history.

In *Almanac of the Dead*, this theme has a Heideggerian ring. In *The Concept of Time,* an outline for the monumental *Being and Time,* Heidegger compares time as measured by clocks and calendars with time as experienced by a particular consciousness. Like Silko, Heidegger seeks a concept of time that will make history a meaningful category. He argues that a strictly linear Newtonian concept of time will not do this, because it bases time on natural phenomena and makes it irreversible and homogenous. Since memory introduces certain types of reversibility and heterogeneity into our experience, Heidegger concludes that the most important problem is the nature of a particular being's experience of time — one's *Dasein* or Being-in-time. Among the most definitive features of the *Dasein* is the orientation toward death. For Heidegger, the Being that exists in time, that actually *is* time, meets the past most fully at the moment of death. Approaching death, one experiences a multivalent, reversible, and heterogeneous time.[9] For Heidegger, as in this line of Silko's novel, death brings one to the limits of linearity. Death is a transformative climax, to which a bold approach will prove historically significant.

Silko's novel, then, is not suggesting that European linear temporality is simply wrong or that it does not describe a range of phenomena. Rather, she illustrates that such a form of temporality is in the process of being challenged from within its own traditions. The grounds of a temporality marking the space of life as the linear progress from birth to death are questioned by a reformulation of the subject as a consciousness openly approaching and even inhabiting the land of the dead from within the sphere of life. Against this decomposing Eurocentric subject, then, Silko's novel positions a reconceptualized native time — a temporality rescued from the archaicism of the eternal return to which most European traditions assign the other. Understood as an endless spatialized temporal zone, this sacred native time encompasses Eurocentric linearity and expands beyond it.

From these two theories of time — a mythic, spatial time associated with storytelling and Native American culture, and a linear clock time associated with the novel and European culture — two hybrid narratives emerge in *Almanac of the Dead*. On the one hand, the concept of an absolute time moving forward in mobile space is tied to the concept of utopian transformation, or a new epoch, through the revolutionary discourse of Marxism espoused by the rebel Indian leader Angelita and sporadically by Clinton, the African American veteran subcommander of the Army of the Homeless. On the other hand, the sequence is also reversed; a counternarrative linking Beaufrey, Serlo, and the corrupt Judge Arne joins a mythic golden era to a narrative of relentless social decay.

The revolutionary narrative that moves from conflict to order is clearly of the most interest to Silko, since a great many passages are devoted to explaining the intricacies of its combination of historical inevitability and Native American time. The most articulate spokesperson for this combination is of course Angelita, aka La Escapía or the Meathook. Most of the action she pursues takes place offstage, and her role in the novel is primarily to provide an opening for theoretical discussion. "The history of the Americas," she announces, "made revolution against European domination inevitable," and this far she sounds like a Marxist. Continuing, though, she qualifies this strain with the reflection that "Marx had also been a European, and he and those following after him had understood the possibilities of communal consciousness only imperfectly" (290–91). These are the poles between which her discourse swings.

Now, although a tradition of radical American fiction discussing communism and socialism stretches from Jack London and Upton Sinclair to Dos Passos, Norman Mailer, and E. L. Doctorow, these authors usually do not invoke the name "Marx" as frequently as Silko does. Especially during the Cold War, the M-word introduced a dissonance; it was thought to leave a haze of ideology in fictional works and its use severely limited their audience. Perhaps for this reason, Silko makes a special effort to account for Angelita's fascination with Marx: "For hundreds of years," Angelita declares, "white men had been telling the people of the Americas to forget the past; but now the white man Marx came along and he was telling people to remember. The old-time people had believed the same thing: they must reckon with the past because within it lay seeds of the present and future. They must reckon with the past because within it lay the present moment and also the future moment" (311). In other words, the source of Angelita's interest in Marxism is Marx's concept of time. The emphasis in Marx's writings on memory makes his thinking consonant with the "old-time" order. The tense is important in this passage, too: "now the white man Marx came along," she says. For Angelita,

Marx inhabits the present (the sacred present?) while "those following after him" do not. For Angelita, Marx is part of the present because he stresses the paradoxes of memory, and his followers are part of the past because they chose to forget the past. Understanding and valuing history is "the true meaning of Marx" for Angelita (314). Marx is relevant for her so far as his theories correspond to the "old-time" Native American worldview.

This revolutionary narrative, however, is not presented only from the point of view of the revolutionists. In counterpoint to Angelita's theorizing, we find the anxious dreaming of insurance executive Menardo. His business is to insure the wealthy against, among other things, revolution, and Silko wittily demonstrates that the ultimate white man's enterprise, insurance, actually depends on a kind of prophecy. Insurance is a bet against the future, and like Angelita, Menardo has been predicting "the dawn of a new age" to his clients; he saw that "the high noon was approaching" (301). These predictions draw on both his political acuity and his childhood attention to grandfather's stories. His native heritage encourages him to respond to cues the others in his circle have not yet perceived: "*Changes were all around*. . . . The old man had always put the phrase at the beginning of the story about Prince Seven Macaws. . . . Changes were everywhere. Aircraft and helicopters supplied by the United States government were on patrol for groups of illegal refugees, who anyone could see were leftist strike units" (494, emphasis in original). Because he combines political and prophetic modes of reasoning, Menardo can see through the disguises of revolutionary groups, despite his own allegiances.

Similarly, the ideas articulated by the leaders of Tucson's Army of the Homeless parallel Angelita's, although like Menardo these men are officially anti-Communist. "Timing was crucial," the homeless men agree because "there are others who are also waiting for the right moment" (410). The veterans also depend on the thesis of historical inevitability: "it was only a matter of time before all captive people on the earth would rise up," adds Clinton (413). Like Angelita, Clinton complements his confidence in the inevitability of revolution with a revived interest in tribal ways. He reinvents worship of the West African god Ogoun, researches slave revolts, and plans radio broadcasts on much the same themes as Angelita's public speeches. His narrative also combines political analysis with prophecy: "The powers who controlled the United States," he asserts, "didn't want the people to know their history. If the people knew their history, they would realize they must rise up" (431).

These parallels — between the Army of the Homeless and Angelita's People's Army, and between Menardo's predictions and the army leaders' conspiracy theory — ultimately support the theory of time that each leader articulates. When the various characters reach the conclusion that revolution is necessary and inevitable, the simultaneity of their decisions affirms their assertion that "there are others who are also waiting for the right moment" (410). Simultaneity places them all in a common "now"; they all inhabit "the right moment" together. At the same time, the very idea of simultaneity, of things occurring in different spaces but at the same time, suggests that one big time connects these different places; it suggests that there is a trans-spatial time, something like "the tidal wave of history" that Angelita is confident will "sweep us along" (518). In short, these parallels and simultaneities make it possible to imagine a hybrid temporality composed of an inevitable history leading up to a transformative, mythic, and widely extensive "now."

However, despite this emphasis on simultaneity, Silko also presents the prospect of another result. The narratives concerning Leah Blue, Judge Arne, Beaufrey, and Serlo set against the revolutionary strain a story of cultural decay and fragmentation. Their Eurocentric temporality charts an irreversible move away from the coherence of an elite, aristocratic order. Thus, their ideologues stress preservation, especially breeding, as a conservative resistance to history. The South American aristocrat Serlo, in particular, is obsessed with sangre pura, or blue blood, and devotes himself to scientific schemes involving alternative earth modules and artificial insemination. This obsession with breeding leads him to maintain a fastidious virginity, substituting discussions of genealogy for sexual intercourse. Similarly, Judge Arne considers himself "an epicurean" with "a cocks man's taste for strange fruits," including the anuses of his own strain of basset hounds (645). Dog breeding is one of the pursuits the Judge has taken up as befitting his role in the Tucson gentry. Like the best blue bloods, he scorns intercourse with persons daring to assume equality with him and so ensures the decline of his stock. For Judge Arne and Serlo, the intergenerational security of genetics substitutes for historical inevitability; their myth of personal superiority relies on a scientifically suspect notion of genetic permanence as does their scant hope for future renewal of their breed.

While the characters most obviously associated with the declining aristocracy move in queer circles, Silko's point seems not to be the creation of "evil, gay characters" but rather the exploration of cruelty and sexuality generally.[10] Even at their worst, the decadent queer characters do not approach the viciousness of the snuff films produced by Menardo's friend the Mexican police chief. After the vehemently heterosexual torture of prostitutes and prisoners, at the conclusion of part 2 the chief orders the hijacking of his Argentinean cameraman and insists his testicles be slit open on film (346). What these scenes have in common with Judge Arne's and Serlo's stories is first of all the denial of sexual interest. The chief pretends to himself that he produces these films so he can "educate the people about the consequences of political extremism" (342). Similarly, for Serlo, "homosexuality involved others" not himself (546), and the Judge "did not consider himself homosexual" (645). In all three cases, it is suggested that there is a link between repression and arousal, between denying one's history and torturing those who remind you of it, and this link occurs in both hetero- and homosexual contexts.

The second important element that these aristocratic plot lines share is a concern with the paradoxes of photography. Judge Arne photographs himself penetrating his dogs; Serlo's plot revolves around David, a young artist who photographs his lover's suicide; and the sexual tension of the police chief's films results in part from the voyeuristic introduction of the video screen. Throughout *Almanac of the Dead,* this kind of photography is associated with brutality, because it is silent, nonnarrative, and instantaneous. In this novel, at least, photography offers the horrific fantasy of an irresponsible present disassociated from the past.

In other texts, however, Silko's use (as opposed to description) of photography often works toward different ends. For instance, *Sacred Water* juxtaposes photographic images of clouds, stones, water lilies, snakes — elemental images of desert life that resonate with the autoethnographic prose poem on facing pages. Similarly, in *Storyteller* Silko includes photographs that serve at once as sites for meditation and as extensions and reflections of themes developed in the text.[11] When placed in contact with narrative, in other words, photos evoke a rich historicism; it is the isolated image, the image that crowds out narrative, that Silko associates with brutality.

At least, this is what is suggested by the descriptions of David's photography. Not only do his photos represent the heartlessness of a photographer disinterested enough to spend the first hours after his lover's death in a photo shoot; they also abort Seese's memory: "after Eric died, Seese had been unable to remember anything except disjointed arrivals and departures in international airports" (53). As a result of her trauma, Seese's memory has become a series of photographs without captions. Fragmented and resistant to narrative, photographs of this type are the ideal form of representation for a culture that actively represses its history.

This last point is underlined in the story of the Blues; for Max, the Mafia assassin, "every time [playing golf] was the first time, a fresh start, the moment before the best possible shot off a driver ever possible" (374). Similarly, his wife Leah dreams of building a city from scratch with no clutter of history and no consideration given to future environmental consequences. This obsession with fresh starts and the denial of history is a major component of Euro-American culture for Silko. "In the Americas," as Angelita puts it, "the white man never referred to the past. . . . The white man didn't seem to understand that he had no future here because he had no past, no spirits of ancestors here" (313). Euro-American culture is at root fragmented, history-less, and barrenly photographic, she suggests.

In addition to fragmenting the past, though, photographs can also make "the white man" vulnerable. Roy/Rambo, the Vietnam veteran who dislikes the movie hero whose nickname he has adopted, realizes that he can deceive the doctors in the veteran's hospital by pretending that "the past was history and no longer mattered" (390). In actuality, though, he understands very well that "a man needed some kind of story to explain himself, to explain why he was here and how he had got here"; he does not mind when drifters far too young to have fought in Vietnam claim veteran status because "the only good they would realize from that war were the stories" (397). These stories and the image provided by the Rambo movie bring the Army of the Homeless together to struggle against the ignorance and disinterest of those who do not care to recognize the past.

The white man's dependence on photography also opens room for a certain form of resistance on the part of the Yaqui. Calabazas relates the story of how the image of a dark-faced Apache with penetrating eyes mysteriously appeared in photographs instead of the four men mistakenly called Geronimo by the *americanos* (224–29). Because the *americanos* were so eager to have their newspapers announce that they had captured Geronimo, they accepted the elderly Old Pancakes as a captive, and this media-dependence, coupled with the mysterious spirit-photographs, enabled the true Geronimos to escape to the mountains in the South. With this story, Silko demonstrates the inadequacy of photographs as a replacement for historical memory while also illustrating the utility of photography for historical counternarratives. The Euro-Americans' repression of historical narrative becomes, in a clever twist, an episode in the longer-lasting story of the Yaqui.

This reappropriation of the image into a narrative history of the image suggests a fifth time strategy in the novel. In "Language and Literature from a Pueblo Indian Perspective," an essay describing the role of the storyteller, Silko explains this fifth technique. Pueblo stories, she asserts, do not follow a linear path from A to B to C; they more closely resemble spider's webs with many "little threads radiating from a center, criss-crossing one another."[12] Each word in this web has a story, and so, when a storyteller uses a word to tell a story, she often needs to go back and tell the story of that word and so on. Thus, whatever the language, each story is the beginning of many stories within the story. Absolute time and space give way to associational links and a social history of language.

For instance, the keyword "bedroom" triggers a story within a story in Sterling's plot line. Entering Lecha's bedroom reminds Sterling of his encounters with a prostitute who specialized in "the deluxe," and the rest of the chapter is a set piece that explains Sterling's associations with that word. The chapter jumps back and forth across chronological time, tangling together memories of work on the railroad, a childhood in boarding school, adult trips to Barstow, and the wishes of his aging aunts (83–86). Each of these elements is then explored further in later chapters so that the story of Sterling unloading a chair for Lecha leads to detours through most of Sterling's life, a story that leads in turn to the history of his people. From the words "bedroom" and "deluxe" a sense of the origins of a whole culture emerges.

This spider-web construction also works at the level of the novel as a whole. To the extent that *Almanac of the Dead* is a novel about social relations in Tucson, its family histories trace strands of a web. The mention of a particular person requires explanation of that person's origin and, as a result, most of the novel is prologue—background on the persons assembled and their migrations. These histories are strung together so that each influences the others, so that Sterling's story of banishment parallels Seese's loss of her child, which reminds us of Zeta and Lecha's childhood, which recalls the origins of Calabazas's smuggling, and so on. Each story's explanation of its origins is linked laterally to the others and all strands join together at Tucson's center.

Perhaps the best example of this kind of linking, though, is the story of the twin brothers El Feo and Tacho. Since they are brothers, their plot lines are connected by their earliest origins, and we are prepared for certain criss-crossings. The People's Army with which El Feo is involved then finds links to Tacho's employer Menardo, and the two brothers become the most distant links in a long chain of lovers connecting El Feo to Angelita to Bartholomeo to Alegría to Menardo, who tells all to Tacho. The twin brothers' connection provides a frame for the entire Mexican portion of the plot. Then, in a further twist, the twin brothers in Mexico are paralleled by the twin sisters in Tucson, the frame for the U.S. plot. When we learn that the twin sisters moved from Sonora to Tucson as the brothers eventually will, the twins are themselves twinned. Further parallels and links become necessary to anchor these two major strands.

In addition to this web weaving, the twin motif has at least two other functions in the novel. The twin brothers are important monster-slaying heroes in Navajo myth, so on the one hand they recall the mythic origins of stories.[13] On the other hand, twins also play an important role in scientific theories that reconceptualize the linearity of time. While Isaac Newton and other Enlightenment thinkers imagined the universe as a clock and time as a homogenous and continuous progression into the future, Einstein's theory of relativity challenged the concept of universal simultaneity. The so-called twins paradox is a famous illustration of Einstein's thesis: if one twin stays on earth, the argument goes, while the other travels in space at something near the speed of light, the two will age differently. Because their motions differ, their relationship to time (and each other) changes. One admirably clear summary restates the central premise of the theory of relativity by saying that "there is no unique absolute time, but instead each individual has his own personal measure of time that depends on where he is and how he is moving."[14] Time and space become mutually determined or relative to one another. It is this Einsteinian view that Calabazas expresses when he reflects that "he did not think time was absolute or universal; rather each location, each place, was a living organism with time running inside it like blood, time that was unique to that place alone" (629). The web narrative, in other words, invokes a relativistic theory of time.

As is well known, however, in the early twentieth century, Einsteinian relativism provoked a widespread intellectual crisis; it seemed to many observers to abandon any concept of order or universal structure within which the space-time units of separated twins might interrelate. One particularly notable response to Einstein was French philosopher Henri Bergson's rejection of the concept of multiple times and defense of the experiential nature of "duration."[15] Bergson asserted the primacy of psychological time over physical science, and his concept appealed to many modernist novelists. For writers who, like Joyce, were attempting to escape the nightmare of history, the world of myth beckoned, and the "stream" of consciousness flowed not so much from past to present to future as laterally across different layers of awareness, integrating them all into an extensive, enduring present.[16] Faulkner's experiments with perspective, Proust's research into memory, and Woolf's polyphonic narratives might all be considered Bergsonian as well.

However, as we might expect, Silko's interest in history pushes many of these modernist devices further. Because she sees history not only as a time line of events (like the uprisings of Native and African Americans recovered through research by Angelita and Clinton) but also as an imminence, as a revolution on the verge of happening simultaneously throughout the hemisphere, Silko represents the larger structure in which relativistic elements cohere as a convergence. The figure for this convergence is the Holistic Healers Convention with which *Almanac of the Dead* concludes. Almost all of the novel's plot lines come together when the healers convene in Tucson. Lecha, Zeta, and Calabazas meet Angelita, the Athabascan prophet Rose, homeless prophet Clinton, and others. Together they absorb the speech given by the Barefoot Hopi, an organizer of prisoner resistance movements: "The Barefoot Hopi's entire philosophy was to wait; a day would come as had not been seen in five thousand years. On this day, *a conjunction would occur;* everywhere at once, spontaneously, the prisoners, the slaves and the dispossessed would rise up" (617, emphasis added). The Barefoot Hopi expresses confidence in a future "conjunction," which is figured by the microcosmic "convention," which in turn is figured by the meeting in room 1212 of the leaders of various movements. When all these leaders meet, each traveling at an individual rate of motion, a spiral of time forms. Coming from all over North and South America to participate in a convention that takes place in the narrative present and the realm of plausible events, Lecha, Zeta, Angelita, and the others unleash forces expected to trigger greater conjunctions that will take place in the unnarrated but foreseeable future. The leaders project an inevitable transformation arising from the plausible present. Thus, by the close of her novel, Silko has set the map printed on its end papers into motion. The arrows tracing various characters' paths to Tucson become vectors, and the whole system begins to revolve like a galaxy with spiraling arms.

I have chosen to conclude with the figure of the spiral because Silko signals us midway through the novel that such a motion constitutes an "Indian style" of narration. When Root, the handicapped mestizo motorcyclist goes to visit Calabazas one day, he "sees that Calabazas is drawing himself into his oratory posture":

> Calabazas calls it "Indian style" when he talks and talks before he turns at the last moment, to the point he wants Root to get. For a long time it drove Root crazy, and he wanted to yell at the old man to just tell him what it was, what was bothering him or what had gone wrong. But over the years Root had learned that there were certain messages in the route Calabazas took when he talked. (215)

As this passage suggests, the message of Silko's long meandering novel is to be learned in the time it takes to tell. The bulk of the novel is given over to prologue interweaving various times — mythic, linear, revolutionary, aristocratic, and relativistic — and all these converge "at the last moment" to suggest how a transition to a qualitatively different future might occur. The narrative circles and spirals telling "what had gone wrong" until Silko is ready to shift into the future tense. At this point, Root is a figure for the sympathetic reader: the mangled mestizo heir to a fortune tainted by duplicity and violence, he

242 : Caren Irr

learns to listen with care. He adapts his sense of timing and becomes a skilled interpreter of content and form; he learns that the storyteller must take his or her own time.

That said, I conclude that if radical novels in the tradition of the 1930s often stumbled on the question of how to combine a sense of historical inevitability with realistic social description, Silko's spiraling convergence provides an important alternative. The novel describes a highly fragmented postmodern social world in which, following the decomposition of the metaphysics of Euro-centric temporality, many people have only partial, photographic access to their history, and these isolated strands of history entangle themselves until they are finally set into motion in a collapsing universe. This notion recalls Stephen Hawking's speculations about such a universe; Hawking proposes that when the arrows of time switch directions broken dishes may cohere and we might remember the future.[17] At the conclusion to Silko's novel, it is possible for a moment to imagine time reversing itself in this fashion. The binational twinning of movements across Mexico and the United States draws far-flung elements into a temporal convergence and, with these fragments bonded, it is possible once again to recall the future predicted by old prophecies. An ancient sense of the future returns. The pre- and postmodern fuse, and a timely new form of radical novel emerges.

NOTES

1. Sven Birkerts, "Apocalypse Now," *New Republic* (4 November 1991): 41.
2. Malcolm Cowley, *The Dream of Golden Mountains* (New York: Penguin, 1964) 250–51.
3. Silko mentions her research into post-Einsteinian theories in an interview with Linda Niemann, "Narratives of Survival," *Women's Review of Books* 9 (July 1992): 10.
4. Fredric Jameson, "The Cultural Logic of Late Capitalism," *Postmodernism, or the Cultural Logic of Late Capitalism* (Durham: Duke University Press, 1991) 54.
5. Gerald Hausman, *The Gift of the Gila Monster: Navajo Ceremonial Tales* (New York: Simon and Schuster, 1993); Trudy Griffin-Pierce, *Earth Is My Mother, Sky Is My Father: Space, Time, and Astronomy in Navajo Sandpainting* (Albuquerque: University of New Mexico Press, 1992).
6. Walter Benjamin, "The Storyteller: Reflections on the Works of Nikolai Leskov," *Illuminations* (New York: Schocken, 1969) 83–111.
7. Georg Lukàcs, *The Theory of the Novel* (1920; Cambridge: MIT Press, 1971).
8. Julio C. M. Pinto summarizes the *sujet/fabula* distinction in *The Reading of Time* (New York: Mouton de Gruyter, 1989).
9. Martin Heidegger, *The Concept of Time*, trans. William McNeill (1924; Cambridge, MA: Blackwell, 1992).

10. Linda Niemann objects to Silko's portrayal of gay characters in "New World Disorder," *Women's Review of Books* 9 (March 1992): 1–4.
11. Leslie Marmon Silko, *Sacred Water: Narratives and Pictures* (Tucson: Flood Plain Press, 1993).
12. Leslie Marmon Silko, "Language and Literature from a Pueblo Indian Perspective," *English Literature: Opening Up the Canon,* ed. Leslie Fiedler (Baltimore: Johns Hopkins University Press, 1981) 54–72.
13. Hausman attributes a prominent role to hero twins in *The Gift of the Gila Monster.*
14. Stephen Hawking, *A Brief History of Time* (New York: Bantam, 1988) 33.
15. Henri Bergson, *Duration and Simultaneity, with Reference to Einstein's Theory,* trans. Leon Jacobson; intro. Herbert Dingle (1922; New York: Bobbs-Merrill, 1965).
16. The classic study of time and modernism is A. A. Mendilow, *Time and the Novel* (1952; New York: Humanities Press, 1972). But see also Wesley A. Kort, *Modern Fiction and Human Time: A Study in Narrative and Belief* (Tampa: University of South Florida Press, 1985), and Ricardo Quinones, *Mapping Literary Modernism* (Princeton: Princeton University Press, 1985).
17. Hawking, 145.

WORKS CITED

Benjamin, Walter. "The Storyteller: Reflections on the Works of Nikolai Leskov." *Illuminations*. New York: Schocken, 1969. 83–111.

Bergson, Henri. *Duration and Simultaneity, with Reference to Einstein's Theory.* Trans. Leon Jacobson. Intro. Herbert Dingle. 1922. New York: Bobbs-Merrill, 1965.

Birkerts, Sven. "Apocalypse Now." Rev. of *Almanac of the Dead,* by Leslie Marmon Silko. *New Republic* 4 November 1991: 41.

Griffin-Pierce, Trudy. *Earth Is My Mother, Sky Is My Father: Space, Time, and Astronomy in Navajo Sandpainting*. Albuquerque: University of New Mexico Press, 1992.

Hausman, Gerald. *The Gift of the Gila Monster: Navajo Ceremonial Tales.* New York: Simon and Schuster, 1993.

Hawking, Stephen. *A Brief History of Time*. New York: Bantam, 1988.

Heidegger, Martin. *The Concept of Time.* Trans. William McNeill. 1924. Cambridge, MA: Blackwell, 1992.

Jameson, Fredric. *Postmodernism, or The Cultural Logic of Late Capitalism.* Durham: Duke University Press, 1991.

Kort, Wesley A. *Modern Fiction and Human Time: A Study in Narrative and Belief.* Tampa: University of South Florida Press, 1985.

Lukàcs, Georg. *The Theory of the Novel.* Cambridge: MIT Press, 1971.

Mendilow, A. A. *Time and the Novel.* 1952. New York: Humanities Press, 1972.

Niemann, Linda. "Narratives of Survival." *Women's Review of Books* 9 (July 1992): 10.

———. "New World Disorder." *Women's Review of Books* 9 (March 1992): 1–4.

Pinto, Julio C. M. *The Reading of Time.* New York: Mouton de Gruyter, 1989.

Quinones, Ricardo. *Mapping Literary Modernism.* Princeton: Princeton University Press, 1985.

Silko, Leslie Marmon. *Almanac of the Dead*. New York: Simon and Schuster, 1991.
———. "Language and Literature from a Pueblo Indian Perspective." *English Litera-ture: Opening Up the Canon*. Ed. Leslie Fiedler. Baltimore: Johns Hopkins, 1981. 54–72.
———. *Sacred Water: Narratives and Pictures*. Tucson: Flood Plain Press, 1993.
Tax, Meredith. "Return of the Native Americans: Leslie Marmon Silko's Vision Quest." *Voice Literary Supplement* (November 1991): 16–17.

OLD AND NEW NOTEBOOKS

Almanac of the Dead *as Revolutionary Entertainment*

Daria Donnelly

> The stories of the people or their "history" had always been sacred, the source of their entire existence. If the people had not retold the stories, or if the stories had somehow been lost, then the people were lost; the ancestors' spirits were summoned by the stories. This man Marx had understood that the stories or "histories" are sacred; that within "history" reside relentless forces, powerful spirits, vengeful, relentlessly seeking justice.
>
> No matter what you or anyone else did, Marx said, history would catch up with you; it was inevitable, it was relentless. The turning, the changing, were inevitable.
> SILKO, Almanac of the Dead

Leslie Marmon Silko's monumental 1991 novel, *Almanac of the Dead*, baffled reviewers. Its difference from *Ceremony* (1977) and *Storyteller* (1981) struck hard and was judged harshly; the scope of the book seemed unmanageable, the subject matter grim, the tone incendiary. Its most enthusiastic reader, Linda Niemann, was alone in hailing *Almanac* as a great and comic novel, and she was sufficiently disturbed by other judgments to interview Silko and get her to explicitly state her intentions and distance herself from the revolutionary violence depicted in the work.[1] That such a repudiation was necessary is ample testimony to the raw nerve Silko touched in her epic portrait of contemporary America, and to the bewildering of fiction and reality she had achieved. It is that latter phenomenon, in particular, that has made the novel so hard to classify and place in relation to the rest of her writing.

Almanac of the Dead, both as it departs from and extends Silko's earlier work, can be best understood in the context of two shifts, one cultural and the other personal. The first is a paradigm shift in the social sciences, particularly history, which reconceives history as the struggle for domination between competing stories. Our understanding of events and ourselves is the result of contest, and that predominant understanding, in turn, can be overthrown by alternative and competing stories, themselves always colored by the established way of interpreting events, when such stories begin to aggregate.[2] This view of history is very much in evidence throughout the book, and Silko draws on it to represent zestfully the processes by which individual explanations of reality become collective action, that is, how homeless veterans, eco-terrorists, psychics, Marxists, bikers, drug addicts, poets, peasants, and mystics end up at a New Age conference in Tucson planning to overthrow the United States of America.

The second shift reflected in *Almanac of the Dead* is in the author herself toward being a more flamboyant and prophetic Laguna storyteller. This shift is most obvious in the sheer length, scope, and digressiveness of the novel. *Almanac of the Dead* is immense: 763 pages, 72 important characters, 12 locations, 500 years of history.[3] In *Storyteller,* a Laguna woman thanks Silko for writing a poem that her grandchildren had read in a library book, and adds, "We all enjoyed it so much, but I was telling the children the way my grandpa used to tell it is longer." Silko responds: "Yes, that's the trouble with writing. . . . You can't go on and on the way we do when we tell stories around here. People who aren't used to it get tired."[4] Silko is clearly no longer worried whether or not readers will resist her Laguna expansiveness.

A more radical aspect of this shift is Silko's embrace of the prophetic mode with all its weird and disruptive energy. In her earlier fiction, Silko integrated Pueblo myths, symbols, and chant into narrative structures that are more or less in the American realist or magical realist tradition. With *Almanac* Silko has put aside her role as a healing writer of tricultural heritage (European, Laguna Indian, and Mexican) in favor of describing contemporary America in light of the pan-Indian prophecy that European culture in the Americas will eventually disappear.[5] The novel's central argument is that this ancient prophecy is visible in everything happening today.

Silko's fidelity to an already written history, steadily advancing to its necessary ending, directly contradicts her presentation of history as an unending struggle for narrative domination. On the face of it, her combination of a supernatural analysis of reality with a Gramscian-inflected Marxist one is idiosyncratic. But it may be that Silko is mounting a two-pronged attack against business and thinking as usual: eroding hegemony through attention to the stories of people who are oppressed and marginal, and unsettling predominant consciousness by placing it within a much larger cosmic narrative, one quite foreign to the dominant culture. In this essay, I explore the tension and cooperation between the two distinct views of history found in the novel and some of the consequences of their combination for the narrative structure of *Almanac of the Dead.*

The title *Almanac of the Dead* refers to a pre-Columbian manuscript circulating within the novel that is said to predict both the arrival of Cortés to the day and the eventual disappearance of all things European from the continent (570).[6] Silko conceived of the almanac/*Almanac* as a fictional companion to the three actual Mayan codices or almanacs that survived the post-Conquest destruction of Mayan written culture.[7] These three surviving almanacs are literally entombed in libraries, and are named for the cities that possess them: Paris, Madrid, and Dresden.[8] Silko's fourth almanac, by contrast, has been circulating among native peoples from the 16th century to the present day, preserved and commented upon by many generations of the dead.

While the extant codices have strong prophetic and apocalyptic dimensions, the explicit prophecy of European invasion and decline derives from other sources: among them, the Toltec stories of Quetzalcoatl's return, which inspired Montezuma to surrender to Cortés as his incarnation, and the Aztec story of Aztlán, which Silko explicitly points to as predicting a resurgence of indigenous peoples. Most importantly, Silko's codex draws on the post-Conquest *Books of Chilam Balam,* which are named for the Mayan priest of the immediate pre-Conquest period who became famous for having predicted the Spanish invasion. These latter manuscripts are written in Mayan, in European script, and are counterparts of the three pre-Columbian hieroglyphic codices.

As a whole, *Almanac of the Dead* confirms the prediction of indigenous resurgence and repossession of the Americas by telling a twofold story: the collapse of white and Hispanic society into sexual perversion and economic parasitism, and the convergence of a variety of Indian, black, and mestizo revolutionary forces (both armed and nonviolent) on present-day Tucson. The novel is designedly prophetic: contemporary local and global phenomena as diverse as the Gulf War, Sendero Luminoso, New Age Spirituality, the Internet, and the 1979 discovery of a giant stone snake at the Jackpile Uranium Mine on Laguna Pueblo land, all stand as heralds of impending social change.[9] Part of the pleasure of reading the book is the realization of how unlikely and persuasive Silko's argument for a pattern is.

In a recent essay, Silko herself is delighted and amused that *Almanac of the Dead* seems to have predicted the unanticipated 1994 emergence of Mayan Zapatistas in Chiapas.[10] The novel is partly set in Chiapas, and revolutionary unrest there marks the onset of indigenous resurgence and retaking of the Americas. When the book was published in 1991, despite the extreme inequality of land distribution and the brutality of land bosses in Chiapas (all well described by Silko), there were no indications that organized resistance would erupt there. A further foreshadowing, unnoticed by Silko, is the likeness between the peaceful mass march northward of indigenous peoples under the twin brothers that occurs in the last section of the novel and three unprecedented indigenous mass marches in Chiapas that occurred after the book's publication: most especially the northward moving 1992 "Ant March" (Xi Nich) from Palenque to Mexico City in which indigenous peoples asserted their rights to land and self-government.[11] The prophetic tenor of *Almanac* and its handling of contemporary events breeches the boundary between the world of the book and the world in which the reader lives so successfully that the novel becomes a credible means by which to interpret ongoing global events.

That *Almanac of the Dead* invites a reader's testimony to the further unfolding of its predictions, perfectly mirrors the extended commentary that the almanac provokes within the novel. The fourth codex, referred to as the "Ancient Notebooks," has horse-gut margins that are filled with the scribbles of past keepers, the stains of their food, wine, blood, and other body fluids, the "vulgar humor" of Yoeme, a mestiza revolutionary who is the almanac's most recent custodian (570). These ancient notebooks are one instance of notebook-keeping found in the novel. Many of the principal characters author notebooks. These homemade books vary widely and include "Thank You Herbert Aptheker!" composed by Clinton, a homeless African American veteran, detailing Indian/black cooperation in liberation struggles since 1526; a cryptic set of notes by a Demerol-addicted Indian psychic named Lecha, encompassing the murders she has supernaturally "witnessed"; and a notebook kept by Mayan revolutionary Angelita (aka the Meat Hook) ironically titled, "Friends of the Indians," which catalogs historical outrages against indigenous peoples.

The new notebooks, as well as the surviving codex and its marginalia, make clear the importance of unauthorized, marginal storytellers to Silko's vision of history. They also underline a central and unresolved tension between the comically digressive character of the novel and the urgency with which it records a history of Western brutality and degeneracy. For example, at the people's trial of a Cuban comrade, the Meat Hook attempts to whip the crowd into a fury by reading excerpts from "Friends of the Indians." Angelita's lists and dates touch off stories in the crowd: "Voices buzzed with enthusiasm and she realized that for a moment the crowd had forgotten the Cuban on trial as people began to recall stories of the old days, not just stories of armed rebellions and uprisings, but stories of colonials sunk into deepest depravity—Europeans who went mad while their Indian slaves looked on" (531).

Angelita is dismayed that the crowd's revolutionary energy has degenerated into a cacophony of storytelling. In this moment, Silko's own novelistic attention to contemporary depravity is disciplined by being placed in a larger history of such depravity, and disciplined in another sense by the Meat Hook's evident horror at the prurient tastes of her people. But if Silko's Pueblo enthusiasm for the proliferation of stories is upbraided by her character, Silko undermines Angelita's simple equation of telling history and fomenting revolution. For Silko, telling does not unambiguously serve social ends; stories can be playful, cryptic, and diffuse precisely because historical change does not finally depend on *how* storytellers tell but that they do. The way we live in and understand America (the way we think about land and history and justice) will not be superseded by one recitation of contrary facts nor by the reinterpretation of material life by an alternative ideology, but rather will be unseated by the improvisations of the weak and powerless, stories that can be statistical or mythical, prurient or prudish, pointed or digressive.

It is Silko's narrative commitment to the inclusion of everyone's testimony, a commitment originating in both her political and spiritual beliefs, that critics have so strongly misunderstood. Because of her attention to marginality and partiality, Silko has been hailed as a postmodernist. She has strenuously resisted the label because she believes that postmodernism severs the connection between language and community, history and cosmology.[12] Other readers have imagined that Silko is writing from a dominantly political point of view. Larry McMurtry's jacket cover praise for *Almanac,* for example, overstates the importance of Silko's materialist analysis: "If Karl Marx had chosen to make *Das Kapital* a novel set in the Americas, he might of come out with a book something like this." Certainly, Silko is indebted to Marx, but she eschews dialectical resolution and materialist determinism with the same vigor that she rejects the postmodern abandonment of cosmology. Where a point of view and a clear trajectory of narrative could be found, it was commented upon (that is, celebrated or decried) by *Almanac*'s reviewers. In a mostly thoughtful review, Sven Birkerts, simply announced that he preferred "the straight on, if somewhat heightened depiction of Western society in its declining phase" to the visionary language of the ancient notebooks.[13]

All these judgments either ignore or misapprehend the almanac, which is not meant to be a site of social commentary, but rather of proliferating storytelling. Silko writes almanac entries that are not only deliberately opaque such as in, "This shall be the end of its prophecy: there is a great war. A parching windstorm" (578), but also rather comical, "Eight is the day called the Dog. Bloody pus pours from the ears of the dog. Persons born on the day of the dog will be habitual fornicators and will be obsessed by dirty thoughts" (573).[14] Rather than try to interpret such entries, the stewards of the almanac — literate and illiterate — add to them. Peasants, children, drunks, mad men and women have made their mark upon the notebooks: the smudges and spills are testimony to the unrecorded commentary of those who could neither read nor write, and the barely legible scrawls of the literate represent the now scarcely accessible record of those who could.

One appended almanac commentary, however, is both legible and extensively discussed in the novel as the archetypal story of those now dead custodians, the story they themselves might have told in their time. This is Yoeme's autobiographical "Day of Deliverance," replete with its own marginalia. In the main body of this story, Yoeme narrates her miraculous escape from certain death when the 1918 influenza wiped out the whole town in which she was imprisoned and condemned to be hung for sedition. Yoeme's granddaughter, Lecha, who is the present holder of the almanac, is amused by her grandmother's seeming deafness to the immense number of lives lost in the great influenza: "That old woman! Years after her death, Lecha still could not top her. . . . Had old Yoeme known or cared that 20 to 40 million perished around the world while she had been saved? Probably not. Lecha could hear the old woman's voice even now. . . . How fitting that Yoeme had required the single worst natural disaster in world history to save her" (580, 581).

Yet "Day of Deliverance" is not simply a comic story illuminating the solipsism of an old revolutionary; it is also a parable about the difference between history as teleological reportage and history as political theater of the deadly earnest absurd. Angelita's notebook recitation of the devastating demographics of the Native American Holocaust reveals the brutal outcome against which men and women like Yoeme pit stories of dazzlingly capricious and triumphant survival:

1500 — 72 million people lived in North, Central, and South America.
1600 — 10 million people live in North, Central, and South America.
1500 — 25 million people live in Mexico.
1600 — 1 million people live in Mexico. (530)

These are the numbers we know, or that we can get, as Angelita does, out of history books. But what the novel keeps giving us are against-all-odds survival stories such as Yoeme's own escape from execution or the bone-chilling story she tells of the four tiny children who originally carried the ancient notebooks to safety across a landscape desolated by the alien invaders, a landscape populated only by a starving murderous old woman, who miraculously cannibalizes only one child, and eats only one page of the horse-gut almanac.

Yoeme's marginal notes to her own tale of deliverance reflect not only Silko's belief that all such stories are vital to the unfolding of the prophesied resurgence of indigenous peoples but also her quite arresting view that the power of such stories does not depend entirely upon their circulation.

Yoeme had believed power resides within certain stories; this power ensures the story to be retold, and with each retelling a slight but permanent shift took place. Yoeme's story of deliverance changed forever the odds against all captives; each time a revolutionist escaped death in one century, two revolutionists escaped certain death in the following century even if they had never heard such an escape story. Where such miraculous escape stories are greatly prized and rapidly circulated, miraculous escapes from death gradually increase. (581)

The final line of this passage perfectly embodies Silko's ongoing interest in the processes by which marginal stories gain value and thus the strength to overthrow the hegemonic narrative and dominant power. But the lines preceding that final thought, about the power residing within stories, regardless of whether they are cherished or find an audience, proceed from her Laguna spirituality. In an interview, Silko affirms Yoeme's position and identifies with older Laguna people's resistance to oral historians coming to record their stories. She says, "If it's important, if it has relevance, it will stay regardless of whether it's on videotape, taped or written down."[15]

That Laguna confidence in the flexibility and supernatural durability of oral narrative and paramount belief in the inherent power of stories are manifested throughout *Almanac of the Dead*. They are most present in Silko's striking lack of concern for the vulnerability of the ancient notebooks and lack of anxiety about the fragmentary nature of the unfolding story. Everything that is lost is meant to be lost: the children had to sacrifice one page of the ancient notebooks in order to preserve themselves and the notebooks (253). This view, of course, is in productive conflict with the one expressed by Angelita, which serves as the epigraph for this paper: "If the people had not retold the stories, or if the stories had somehow been lost, then the people were lost."

When Angelita talks about the proximity of story and history in Marx, the word history is set off by quotations: "This man Marx had understood that the stories or 'histories' are sacred; that within 'history' reside relentless forces, powerful spirits, vengeful, relentlessly seeking justice" (315–16). In the first clause, the quotation marks around "histories" confer the dignity of the term on the variety of means — anecdotal, oral, mythological — by which oppressed and marginated peoples testify. In the second clause, "history" is set within those marks in order to unsettle its status as the whole truth, showing that within the predominant story called history are other stories that will emerge and be known.

There is ample tension in *Almanac of the Dead* about how those stories on the ground can be organized into a movement for justice and a realignment of power. Clinton and Angelita spend time gathering history in order to educate and arouse people. Because "ignorance of the people's history had been the white man's best weapon" (742), Clinton keeps and uses a notebook of facts about black resistance and rebellion drawn from the work of Herbert Aptheker, a radical historian and pioneer in writing history from outside the predominant consciousness. Like Clinton, Angelita is a voracious reader of history and a mad footnoter, filling her notebook with "tiny marks and numbers only she could decipher, for page numbers and titles and authors of books," so that when the Cubans wanted to argue or the 'elder sisters' tried to give her trouble" (314), she could fight back. Angelita feels besieged, because her historical experience as a Mayan is denigrated by fellow Marxists. For her, documenting and recounting events is the principal means of waging the struggle against all those who are oppressing her people, even those with whom she shares ideology. But in Silko's view, Clinton and Angelita's catalogs of events, so carefully crafted from long research, are simply one kind of contribution, no more central to shifting power than is Yoeme's story, or Lecha's woozy notebook meandering, or a marginal stain of wine, or the novel itself.

There will be readers for whom this equivalence will be too mystical and too narratively diverting. Angelita regards those who resist the dominant culture from a spiritual or mythological standpoint as powerful and convenient allies, though their patience and willingness to digress offend her bookish Marxism. But for Silko, a political analysis emerges out of a Pueblo worldview that is committed to making an account of all time and space, and that is heterogeneous and absorptive. As she has said, "Pueblo cultures seek to include rather than to exclude. The Pueblo impulse is to accept and incorporate what works."[16] Pueblo narrative tends to be self-delighted and expansive. In Silko's work, correspondence and repetition are not only pleasurable for their own sake but also necessary since all phenomena are part of the larger prophecy, which she says the Laguna elders believe is "a spiritual process" that "has already begun to happen."[17]

At times, Angelita functions as Silko's superego, drawing attention to the energy and purposiveness that might be lost in the novel's sprawl. (In a similar way, Beaufrey, the most horrific character in the novel, seems to both embody and chasten the uniquely intense rage, unconscious I think, with which Silko limns homosexuals as the most powerful exemplars of European depravity. Beaufrey thinks like an artist and designs events like one, and I think he is meant to trouble her sleep over the annihilating rage that might dwell within an apocalyptic writer).[18] But Silko trusts the improvisations of the powerless far more than any organized political ideology. As readers who know that Angelita has put her Cuban lover on trial for his sexual as much as his social betrayal, we understand that it is precisely when the people are telling stories that they demonstrate a greater sense of justice than their organizers, momentarily forgetting to convict the doomed man.

Because justice is most realized in the act of storytelling, Silko resists narrative resolution, preferring to linger over the formation of revolutionary consciousness. That is why the novel is best described as a revolutionary entertainment. It pleasures the reader by revealing a pattern in the fragments collected by marginal people and implicit in seemingly unconnected events. This comical and wending assemblage is set side by side a narrative so brutal that the reader yearns for an apocalyptic resolution: bestiality, infanticide, torture, disemboweling, and genocide mark not only past European behavior but present-day white and Hispanic degeneracy as well. Above all, this is a novel in which readers are pressed by hyperbole to consider everyday injustices they have not even recognized, things as simple and devastating as where the water in Tucson comes from, how real estate developers pattern the landscape, whom we consider beyond the pale of society.

The prophetic mode, the apocalyptic rage, the brute facts reported in *Almanac of the Dead* mark it as a real departure for Silko. But despite the general amazement that the author of *Ceremony* also wrote *Almanac*, the central concerns of these two novels are the same. Just as *Ceremony* tells the story of the successful reintegration of Tayo into the Laguna community after his traumatic military service fighting the Japanese in World War II, *Almanac of the Dead* ends with the Indianization and return of Sterling to the Laguna community from which he has been exiled. It is the means of reintegration that are so different: Tayo goes through a series of healing rituals and ceremonies. Sterling, in something akin to aversion therapy, learns to loathe the true crime stories he had once passionately read and develops a strong desire for the stories of his elders, to which he formerly had paid so little attention.

Sterling returns to Laguna, fleeing ground zero of the apocalypse in Tucson, where he served as caretaker for the Yaqui twin sisters, Lecha and Zeta, who run drugs and buy arms for various revolutionary groups. Sterling befriends a fellow employee on their isolated estate named Seese, a recovering addict whose infant has been slaughtered for a dissection film by Beaufrey, the lover of her child's father. Sterling is horrified and depleted by the crimes he witnesses at the estate and by the brutality so evident in Seese's story. While the old crime magazines, which recount tales from Dillinger to the present day, once seemed a harmless diversion, Sterling realizes the need for the more brutal comedies of his own people, stories like "Day of Deliverance." He might be the ideal reader for *Almanac of the Dead,* which Silko has likened to "an ogre Kachina to scare bad kids. It's like, read this and be horrified, and then don't let it be this scenario — let it [the fulfillment of the prophecy] be the other scenario, where through just birth-rate and immigration the tide is changing. You can't stop it."[19]

If Silko has changed since *Ceremony,* she has become more interested in the power of *stories* to create and account for reality. The variety of testimony and telling found in the novel accords with Silko's claim that Pueblo storytelling does not erect generic boundaries: "we make no distinctions between the stories — whether they are history, whether they are fact, whether they are gossip — these distinctions are not useful."[20] *Almanac* is both more intensely Laguna in its prophetic and capacious style, and less idealizing of Laguna in its representation. In *Ceremony* Silko used Pueblo myths and rituals to summon Tayo into a community that she imagined as flawed but populated by wise persons and healers. In *Almanac of the Dead* the Laguna community that exiled Sterling is bereft of strong leaders and is characterized by petty grudges and unjust judgments. There are no wise Laguna elders protecting him as there are for Tayo in *Ceremony.* Sterling returns not because he is summoned nor because someone cares about him, but rather because he needs the old stories; he needs help making sense of everything he has seen and heard in Tucson. The stories at Laguna are stronger than the people who, in fragmented and partial ways, narrate and remember them.

This shift toward Pueblo storytelling as the most essential and enduring guarantor of community and a just future accords with a writerly resistance to closure: how can a single author close down or discipline the variety of voices that are adding up to a story. In *Almanac of the Dead* Silko throws off the resolutions of *Ceremony.* She does not resolve the action: the Laguna, for example, ignore Sterling when he returns. She does not resolve the fate of any of her characters; in contrast to the cosmic justice that governs the end of *Ceremony,* the bad characters in *Almanac* do not self-destruct. She does not resolve the timing of the repossession of the Americas.

As a variety of forces and persons converge on Tucson, the novel closes with a sense of both imminent change and infinite delay. Even though the principal revolutionaries gather in a hotel room at the International Holistic Healers Convention, no final strategy is developed. Instead, narrative strands — some comic, some apocalyptic — come together at the convention: eco-warriors with AIDS are shown in a filmed suicide bombing of the Glen Canyon Dam; Wilson Weasel Tail chants poetry; the Barefoot Hopi dramatically announces the imminent end of white culture to an enthusiastic white audience. Lecha is bemused and entertained by how much money Indians are taking in for worthless rocks sold as healing talismans.

As the twin brothers Wacah and El Feo, who are counterparts of the heroic twins of Pueblo cosmology, slowly lead a magnificent unstoppable spiritual procession of brown people into North America, there in Tucson, the wild comedy and heteroglossia of the novel continue. In some sense, Angelita is right: the pleasure of storytelling does moderate revolutionary sentiment. This is because the outcome does not depend upon actions coordinated by a central committee or political program or single author: change is inevitable, charted and promoted by multiple and fragmentary stories told or inscribed in private notebooks, all of which converge upon the prophecies recorded in the ancient notebooks.

NOTES

1. Linda Niemann, "Narratives of Survival," *Women's Review of Books* 9 (July 1992): 10. See also Niemann's enthusiastic March 1992 review in *Women's Review of Books*. Another favorable review, which misses the comedy, is Melissa Hearn, *Prairie Schooner* 67 (summer 1993): 149–51. For typical reviews see John Skow, *Time* 9 Dec. 1991: 86; Malcolm Jones, *Newsweek* 18 Nov. 1991: 84; Elizabeth Tallent, *New York Times Book Review* 22 Dec. 1991: 6; *Library Journal* 15 Oct. 1991: 124; *Choice* Sept. 1992: 119; *Publishers Weekly* 6 Sept. 1991: 94. Sven Birkerts provides a nuanced and intelligent review in *New Republic* 4 Nov. 1991: 39–41.
2. I am indebted to Betsy Aron, a sociologist studying Local 26 (the hotel workers union), for her illuminating conversation on this paradigm shift.
3. In a 1986 interview with Kim Barnes, "A Leslie Marmon Silko Interview," *Journal of Ethnic Studies* 13 (winter 1986), Silko is thinking that 1,600 pages is the right length. In the essay "Notes on Almanac of the Dead" from *Yellow Woman and a Beauty of the Spirit: Essays on Native American Life Today* (New York: Simon and Schuster, 1996) 142, Silko recalls not daring to tell anyone that, having written one thousand manuscript pages, she felt the novel was only about halfway completed.
4. Leslie Marmon Silko, *Storyteller* (New York: Arcade, 1981) 110.
5. Silko is part Laguna Pueblo, part white, and part Mexican. She has said quite famously of herself: "I am of mixed-breed ancestry, but what I know is Laguna. This place I am from is everything I am as a writer and human being." Per Seyersted, *Leslie Marmon Silko* (Boise, ID: Boise State UP, 1980) 15.
6. In her essay "The Fourth World" *Artforum* 27 (summer 1989): 124, Silko emphasizes that European customs, not peoples, are predicted to disappear.
7. Silko has recently published an essay on the writing of *Almanac,* which includes information about the almanacs and the destruction of Mayan libraries. See "Notes

on Almanac of the Dead," *Yellow Woman and a Beauty of the Spirit,* 135–45. Information on the almanacs can be found in Sylvanus Morley and George Brainerd, *The Ancient Maya* (Stanford: Stanford UP, 1983) 513–20, and Norman Hammond, *Ancient Maya Civilization* (New Brunswick, NJ: Rutgers UP, 1982) 34–35, 293–96. Translations of the codices can be found in Yurii Knorozov, *Maya Hieroglyphic Codices,* trans. Sophie D. Coe (Albany: Institute for Mesoamerican Studies, State U of NY at Albany, 1982). In her 1986 interview with Barnes, Silko counts the Mexican Codex (not frequently cited with the others because exposure has congealed it into an unreadable block) and calls her almanac a fictional fifth codex; in her most recent work, she omits the Mexican Codex and calls hers the fourth almanac. See Kim Barnes, "A Leslie Marmon Silko Interview" *Journal of Ethnic Studies* 13 (winter 1986): 103–5, and Leslie Marmon Silko, *Yellow Woman and a Beauty of the Spirit,* 158.

I have not been able to confirm her assertion (made in "Notes on *Almanac of the Dead,*" 137) that the extant codices predict the Spanish invasion. But for information about the *Books of Chilam Balam* as well as Aztec counterparts to Mayan prophecy see Anthony Aveni, *Skywatchers of Ancient Mexico* (Austin: U of Texas P, 1980), a book Silko has said was influential in her conception of her novel; for translations and explications of three of the four central books of the Chilam Balam tradition (Chumayel, Mani, Tizimin, Kava), see E. Craine and R. Reindorp, *The Codex Perez and the Books of Chilam Balam of Mani* (Norman: U of Oklahoma P, 1979); Munro S. Edmonson, *The Ancient Future of the Itza: The Books of Chilam Balam of Tizimin* (Austin: U of Texas P, 1982). Munro S. Edmundson, *Heaven Born Merida and Its Destiny: The Book of Chilam Balam of Chumayel* (Austin: U of Texas P, 1986).

8. For a wonderful contrast between Silko's vision of a freely circulating manuscript and the actual state of the Mayan codices because of the wanton destruction of Mayan libraries, see the facsimile edition of the Paris Codex, which describes its disposition: "Today the precious original of the Codex Paris . . . is sealed in a wooden casket, immovable, with a portfolio frame in which a glass panel allows one to see two pages of the manuscript. As the Keeper of Manuscripts of the Bibliothèque Nationale could not take the risk of opening the casket because of the danger of irreparable damage to the priceless original (which is very fragile indeed), the present facsimile had to be based on the old color facsimile of 1887 *Codex Peresianus* (Graz, Austria: Akademische Druck-u. Verlagsanstalt, 1968) 23.

9. On the stone snake that figures prominently in the novel, see Leslie Marmon Silko, "The Fourth World," *Artforum* 27 (summer 1989): 124–27.

10. In that recent essay, Silko, with equal measures of arch and deadpan expression, inserts her book into the list of Mayan Codices and notes that the almanac that "those two old Yaqui women in my novel *Almanac of the Dead* possess . . . correctly predicted the Zapatista uprising. Their old almanac even purports to explain the unfortunate assassination of Señor Colosio in Tijuana [ruling party PRI candidate for president killed 23 March 1994]." Leslie Marmon Silko, "Books: Notes on Mixtec and Maya Screenfolds, Picture Books of Preconquest Mexico," *Yellow Woman and a Beauty of the Spirit,* 158.

11. Thanks are due here to Alessandro Portelli, editor of *Ácoma,* for making the con-

nection between her Chiapas and the 1994 uprising, and to Jonathan Fox, a political scientist who studies popular movements in Mexico, for drawing my attention to these marches, the other two being the 500th Anniversary of Conquest March and the march to support Bishop Samuel Ruiz (1993 in San Cristóbal with 15,000 indigenous people, the largest march in the history of Chiapas).

12. For perceptive readers of Silko in relation to postmodernism, see Gerald Vizenor, ed., *Narrative Chance: Postmodern Discourse on Native American Indian Literatures* (Albuquerque: U of New Mexico P, 1989) xii–xiii, and Arnold Krupat, "The Dialogic of Silko's *Storyteller*," in Vizenor, 55–68. Silko has resisted the label of postmodernist (and used it as a pejorative) since she identifies postmodernism with language freed from responsibility to community. On her argument with postmodernism see Susan Pérez Castillo, "Postmodernism, Native American Literature, and the Real: The Silko-Erdrich Controversy" *Massachusetts Review* 32 (summer 1991): 285–94.

13. Sven Birkerts, *New Republic* 4 Nov. 1991: 40.

14. Silko appears to be alluding to and burlesquing the Mayan use of portents on the day of birth to predict, usually pessimistically, the future occupation of a child. See Yurii Knorozov, *Maya Hieroglyphic Codices,* trans. Sophie D. Coe (Albany: Institute for Mesoamerican Studies, State U of NY at Albany, 1982) 25. *The Book of Chilam Balam of Mani* offers numerous examples of such physiological and characterological predictions, to our ears comic in their absolutism: "Men born on the days ruled by this sign are small, always sad, very fond of women, and noted for using great quantities of small chilies with their meals." Eugene Craine and Reginald Reindorp, *The Codex Pérez and The Book of Chilam Balam of Mani* (Norman: U of Oklahoma P, 1979), 19–20.

15. Kim Barnes, "A Leslie Marmon Silko Interview," 88.

16. Leslie Marmon Silko, "Videomakers and Basketmakers," *Aperture* 119 (summer 1990): 73.

17. Leslie Marmon Silko, "The Fourth World," 124

18. Silko's representation of homosexuals constitutes Neimann's only qualm about the novel, but when she interviewed Silko she did not ask her about it. Perhaps Silko's expressed view in that interview that indigenous resurgence is being realized partly through birth rates among non-Europeans accounts for why in her imagined version, homosexuals seem particularly decadent. But that seems contrary to the status homosexuals have generally enjoyed in Indian cultures. I don't know how to sort it out, but brutality seems much more intensely drawn in her gay characters, including Lecha's son, Ferro.

19. Niemann, 10. Silko is quite serious about signs of the prophesied indigenous resurgence. See her recent reflections on the border patrol's violent and ineffectual attempt to stop illegal immigration, "The Border Patrol State," *Nation* 259 (17 Oct. 1994): 412–16; reprinted in "Yellow Woman and a Beauty of the Spirit," 115–23, and her reflections on the stone snake at Jackpile in *Artforum* 27 (summer 1989): 124–28.

20. Leslie Marmon Silko, "Language and Literature from a Pueblo Indian Perspective," *English Literature: Opening Up the Canon,* ed. Leslie Fiedler and Houston Baker (Baltimore: Johns Hopkins UP: 1981) 60.

WORKS CITED

Aveni, Anthony. *Skywatchers of Ancient Mexico.* Austin: U of Texas P, 1980.

Barnes, Kim. "A Leslie Marmon Silko Interview." *Journal of Ethnic Studies* 13 (winter 1986): 83–105.

Birkerts, Sven. "Apocalypse Now." Review of *Almanac of the Dead* by Leslie Marmon Silko. *New Republic* 4 Nov. 1991: 39–41.

Bruchac, Joseph. *Survival This Way: Interviews with American Indians Poets.* Tucson: Sun Tracks and the U of Arizona P, 1987.

Castillo, Susan Pérez. "Postmodernism, Native American Literature, and the Real: The Silko-Erdrich Controversy." *Massachusetts Review* 32 (summer 1991): 285–94.

Codex Peresianus. Graz, Austria: Akademische Druck-u. Verlagsanstalt, 1968.

Craine, E., and R. Reindorp. *The Codex Perez and the Books of Chilam Balam of Mani.* Norman: U of Oklahoma P, 1979.

Edmonson, Munro S. *The Ancient Future of the Itza: The Books of Chilam Balam of Tizimin.* Austin: U of Texas P, 1982.

———. *Heaven Born Merida and Its Destiny: The Book of Chilam Balam of Chumayel.* Austin: U of Texas P, 1986.

Hammond, Norman. *Ancient Maya Civilization.* New Brunswick, NJ: Rutgers UP, 1982.

Hearn, Melissa. Rev. of *Almanac of the Dead* by Leslie Marmon Silko. *Prairie Schooner* 67 (summer 1993): 149–51.

Jones, Malcolm. Rev. of *Almanac of the Dead* by Leslie Marmon Silko. *Newsweek* 18 Nov. 1991: 84.

Knorozov, Yurii. *Maya Hieroglyphic Codices.* Trans. Sophie D. Coe. Albany: Institute for Mesoamerican Studies, State U of NY at Albany, 1982.

Morley, Sylvanus, and George Brainerd. *The Ancient Maya.* Stanford: Stanford UP: 1983.

Niemann, Linda. "Narratives of Survival: Linda Niemann Interviews Leslie Marmon Silko." *Women's Review of Books* 9 (July 1992): 10.

———. "New World Disorder." Rev. of *Almanac of the Dead* by Leslie Marmon Silko. *Women's Review of Books* 9 (March 1992): 1, 3–4.

Seyersted, Per. *Leslie Marmon Silko.* Boise, ID: Boise State UP, 1980.

Silko, Leslie Marmon. *Almanac of the Dead.* New York: Simon and Schuster, 1991.

———. "The Border Patrol State." *Nation* 17 Oct. 1994: 412–16.

———. "The Fourth World." *Artforum* 27 (summer 1989): 124–27.

———. "Language and Literature from a Pueblo Indian Perspective." *English Literature: Opening Up the Canon.* Ed. Leslie Fiedler and Houston Baker. Baltimore: Johns Hopkins UP, 1981. 54–72.

———. Rev. of *Almanac of the Dead* by Leslie Marmon Silko. *Choice* Sept. 1992: 119.

———. Rev. of *Almanac of the Dead* by Leslie Marmon Silko. *Library Journal* 15 Oct. 1991: 124.

———. Rev. of *Almanac of the Dead* by Leslie Marmon Silko. *Publishers Weekly* 6 Sept. 1991: 94.

———. *Storyteller.* New York: Arcade, 1981.

———. "Videomakers and Basketmakers." *Aperture* 119 (summer 1990): 72–73.

————. *Yellow Woman and a Beauty of the Spirit: Essays on Native American Life Today.* New York: Simon and Schuster, 1996.

Skow, John. "People of the Monkey Wrench." Rev. of *Almanac of the Dead,* by Leslie Marmon Silko. *Time* 9 Dec. 1991: 86.

Tallent, Elizabeth. "Storytelling with a Vengeance." Rev. of *Almanac of the Dead* by Leslie Marmon Silko. *New York Times Book Review* 22 Dec. 1991: 6.

Vizenor, Gerald, ed. *Narrative Chance: Postmodern Discourse on Native American Indian Literatures.* Albuquerque: U of New Mexico P, 1989.

MAPPING THE PROPHETIC LANDSCAPE IN *ALMANAC OF THE DEAD*

Janet M. Powers

In *Almanac of the Dead*, Leslie Marmon Silko presents a text delineating a complex universe, with geographical, historical, moral, and spiritual dimensions so carefully worked out that it lends itself to linear mapping. Although the similarity at first may seem far-fetched, Silko's prophetic narrative bears striking parallels to Dante's great allegory, the *Commedia*. Indeed, the visionary aspect of her work is not unlike Dante's warning to a world gone wrong, emanating from a personal sense of loss, both of place in society and place in the moral order.

Silko's intensely disturbing novel is intended to shock her readers into full awareness of environmental and moral degradation. It is no coincidence that the only character intact and growing at the end of *Almanac of the Dead* is Sterling, a Laguna Indian who has been banished from his pueblo, yet eventually returns to a quiet life at his family sheep camp. Sterling understands the meaning of the great stone snake that had appeared at Laguna: "The snake didn't care if people were believers or not; the work of the spirits and prophecies went on regardless. . . . Burned and radioactive with all humans dead, the earth would still be sacred. Man was too insignificant to desecrate her" (762).

As a Native American of the late twentieth century, Silko does not present a synchronic Christian cosmology but rather a diachronic one beginning with the arrival of Europeans in the New World at the end of the fifteenth century. Silko, in *Almanac of the Dead,* offers a "Five Hundred Year Map" with historical and prophetic elements embedded in a linear geographical map of the southwestern United States and northern Mexico. Encompassing five hundred years of contact between Native Americans and Europeans, the map celebrates indigenous American uprisings, as listed in the "lost texts," as well as contemporary attempts to speed the disappearance of all things European. With Tucson, Arizona, at the center, representing evil and corruption, the map has moral and spiritual dimensions as well.

Silko's map also records the movements of people, including Sterling, who travels from Laguna to Tucson and back again, and an organized crime family that relocates from Cherry Hill, New Jersey, to Tucson. Twin Brothers, inspired by their spirit macaws, walk north with thousands of indigenous people to reclaim their homeland. Seese, a young mother, comes to Lecha, a visionary, for help in finding her missing child, and the Barefoot Hopi, Wilson Weaseltail, proselytizes about saving the earth. All converge on Tucson, which, like Dante's Firenze, is viewed as the blighted center of the earthly universe. The journeys recorded on Silko's map are multiple, unlike Dante's singular quest, but they are similarly allegorical, forcing readers to confront the evil in a world born of dual colonization, first by the Spanish and later by the Anglos.[1] Like Dante, Silko asks whether that world has any moral reason to continue and constantly reiterates the message of the Mayan almanac: that Native American prophecies have foretold both the arrival and disappearance of the white man. Her complex web of stories leaves no doubt that Eurocentric civilization has begun its downhill slide.

Tracking the movements of her characters from such far-flung places as Alaska, San Diego, and Tuxtla Gutierrez to Tucson, Silko constructs a linear map consisting of a series of signs moving in the dimension of time, both past and forward from the present. In addition, it is a geographical record of contemporary migrations paralleling the migrations that brought the Pueblo people from Sipap to the eighteen pueblos in New Mexico and the Hopi mesas in Arizona. In the visionary tradition so dear to Dante, the journey is a long, hard pilgrimage toward a defined goal, representing the intuitive soul of the traveler moving toward the divine. Yet Silko inverts this tradition as her characters move toward Tucson, "home to an assortment of speculators, confidence men, embezzlers, lawyers, judges, police and other criminals, as well as addicts and pushers, since the 1880s and the Apache Wars" (15, map). Yet at the same time the visionary tradition is upheld, for the vast majority of those moving toward Tucson are the hundreds of thousands inspired by the spirit macaws and their own intuitive links with the sacred.

As a chart of prophetic time, Silko's map is imperfect, for it does not coincide with or even designate the six parts of the novel, intentionally resembling the fragments of the ancient Maya codices, and entitled "The United States of America," "Mexico," "Africa," "The Americas," The Fifth World," and "One World, Many Tribes."[2] With each of these parts further conceived in geographical terms, such as "The Border," "The North," "Rivers," "Mountains," as well as various cities, the novel might better have been mapped by a mandala, a cosmograph, or Navajo sandpainting of the sort described in *Ceremony*. Indeed, the quasi-geographical, single-dimensional map of the white people, based on precise calculation of longitudes and latitudes by chronometer and triangulation, is quite inadequate to contain the powerful prophecies put forward in the novel. Yet the map legends, which refer to the Indian Connection, Tucson's history, and Prophecy, form another sort of triangulation: that of victims, destroyers, and ultimate justice.

Silko's diagram, constructed perhaps originally for her own use in managing a vast cast of characters, includes a list of dramatis personae conveniently located in their respective centers of operation. The map, which points to San Diego in the west and New Jersey in the east, Alaska in the north, and Tuxtla Gutierrez, Mexico City, Cartagena, and Buenos Aires in the south, represents the world of the Americas, and thus the world encompassed by the novel. Silko's map legends also refer to encoding of the future in arcane symbols (The Giant Stone Snake) and old narratives (the almanac), thus balancing the historical with the prophetic. To the extent that Silko diagrams the spiritual message of her narrative, she encourages the reader to penetrate an implicit allegory. Because the story is essentially a web of quests, not only for a lost baby and lost texts but also for the lost will to rebel, it is both like and unlike Dante's dream vision, which is the allegorical narrative of a single soul in search of justice and spiritual identity.

Using Dante's descriptive details, two of his translators, John Ciardi and Dorothy Sayers, have mapped the three areas of the afterlife as envisioned by the poet in the *Commedia*. Hell is a concentric pit with multiple levels; Purgatory, a mountain with a path spiraling upward; and Heaven, a series of spheres revolving each inside the other. Each of the characters inhabiting these worlds, moreover, has a historical role in the struggles between Blacks/Whites, Guelphs/Ghibellenes, the Papacy/French government. Dante's poem came about because, as a member of the White Guelph political faction in Florence, he was banished from the city on trumped-up charges of graft and corruption. One of six supreme magistrates, he was on the verge of a brilliant career. Yet as an opponent of Boniface VIII, he suffered nineteen years of exile under penalty of being burned alive if he returned to his beloved city. The centrality of these events for Dante, and also the sense of injustice with which he struggled, are evident in the fact that he deliberately sets his poem in the past in order to establish a prophetic mode.

264 : Janet M. Powers

Knowing full well the events that will transpire, he seeds the "Inferno" and "Purgatorio" with enigmatic predictions, couched as riddles, of events leading up to the day of his defeat and casting out by the Black Guelphs. Silko achieves a similar effect by the device of the almanac, which has already predicted, to the day, the appearance of Cortés. Although the ancient Mayan almanacs had warned the people hundreds of years before the Europeans arrived about "the appearance, conflict with and disappearance of things European," the Aztecs had ignored the prophecies. Yet Silko identifies both as Destroyers, fellow worshippers of blood and destruction; "Montezuma and Cortés had been meant for each other" (570). Unlike the *Commedia,* Silko's novel is set forward in time, into an undatable future when the Mexican economy has collapsed, fleeing government officials have stripped the National Treasury, and electrical power lines and water mains to the city center have been dynamited. In the United States at the same time, Tucson has lost population as Arizona banks fail and blue-chip industries flee. Combined with earlier accurate almanac prophecies, the events of the novel seem to corroborate the message that the dispossessed will one day have land and the tribes of the Americas retake the continents.

Both the mappings of Dante's journey through a Christian cosmos and Silko's map suggest symbolic schema that have emerged over the centuries to represent experiences of the visionary consciousness. In mystic traditions known to the West, by virtue of the nature of the spirit world, "descriptions of spiritual experience must always be symbolic, elusive, oblique: always suggest, but never tell the truth . . . , the greater the suggestive quality of the symbol used, the more answering emotion it evokes in those to whom it is addressed, the more truth it will convey" (Underhill, 126). Silko, in her unrelieved chronicling of Destroyers at work, belies this quality of suggestiveness, working instead in a matter-of-fact mode typical of tribal storytellers. One problem in comparing Silko's work with Dante's is that the stone snake and the remaining fragments of the Mayan codices lack the color and richness of the symbolic structures Dante was able to create. Silko, by contrast, also devotes far less of her story to these positive elements than to the web of destruction woven by the white man. Yet her way of dealing with these all-important narrative elements is quintessentially Native American. As she explains in *Yellow Woman and a Beauty of the Spirit,* "as with the web, the structure emerges as it is made, and you must simply listen and trust, as the Pueblo people do, that meaning will be made" (49). Only from a Western literary perspective, then, can we ask whether the symbolism of the Almanac and the stone serpent are sufficient to carry the spiritual message that Silko intends to convey.

As Underhill, speaking from that perspective, insists, "a good symbolism will be more than mere diagram or mere allegory: it will use to the utmost the resources of beauty and passion, will bring with it hints of mystery and wonder, bewitch with dreamy periods the mind to which it is addressed. Its appeal will not be to the clever brain, but to the desirous heart, the intuitive sense of man" (126). That Silko achieved such mystery, wonder, and bewitchment with her earlier novel, *Ceremony*, goes unquestioned. And for that reason, many of her readers are confused by *Almanac of the Dead*. As an anonymous resident at Laguna stated, "The novel contains truths, but the ugliness of that book is not necessary."[3] Such responses, however, cause one to reconsider the entire narrative as disruptive, both within the sphere of contemporary Western literature and within the writer's personal corpus. Further, readers are compelled to acknowledge the technique of rupture, used by Renaissance allegorists within a particular text, to force audiences to move from lower to higher levels of understanding (Murren, 146).

The disruptive qualities of Dante's "Inferno" must have had a similar effect on his fourteenth-century audience. It is the vileness of the Inferno that impresses upon the sinner the need to change his ways. Dante's tripartite afterlife is astonishing on all its allegorical levels, and so completely structured as to assure the reader that received truths have become expressible only through divine inspiration. The autobiographical level is a necessary key to the political and historical complexity of the *Commedia*. On the literal level, Dante's spiritual journey is exceedingly detailed and realistic, although the poet's journey must be understood in all of its dimensions: in terms of political and moral concerns (human-centered in time); church doctrine and practice (god-centered in time); anagogical or spiritual concerns (god-centered out of time). Although structured quite differently from the *Commedia*, Silko's novel may also be read on each of these four allegorical levels.

It may be useful to begin with the autobiographical level, which in Silko's narrative is provided by Sterling, who has had difficulties with the tribe and is persona non grata at Laguna. Sterling's error was inadvertent. Appointed to keep a Hollywood film crew under control, he failed to prevent them from filming the giant stone snake and is regarded as having betrayed his people's trust in him.[4] Nothing was stolen or removed, nor did the film crew understand what they had photographed, yet the Caciques and War Captains had viewed the event as sacrilege.[5] Sterling's preoccupation with tribal law parallels Dante's focus on government, both having faced painful expulsion at the hands of local authorities whose governance must be considered no more just than that of larger political structures, the United States or Mexican governments, or in Dante's case, the Holy Roman Empire.

Literal details are significant in Silko's text, just as they are in Dante's *Com-*

media, for they can be read variously from the Anglo perspective or the native perspective. The landscape of the southwestern United States and northern Mexico, with Tucson at the center, might be seen as empty and barren by whites, who require vast amounts of water and greenery to feel at home there. An extreme example of this "European vision" is the canal development of Venice, Arizona, launched by Leah Blue, with the help of a judge who is persuaded to override environmental legislation. Yet the vast skies and rockscapes of Arizona and Mexico are spiritually alive and "full" to the indigenous peoples who have lived there for far longer than the last five centuries. Mosca, for instance, watches the steam rise off the Santa Cruz River "on mornings when cold mountain air settled over Tucson. He understood how the steam was the moisture of the river rising, so that you had a river running in the sky, in all directions of the winds — but also that these were the souls of the dead rising out of the purgatory where they had been imprisoned hundreds and thousands of years waiting to be released so they could return and help their beloved descendants" (603).

Not all the inhabitants of this landscape, however, are so sensitive to its spiritual elements. A complex web of malign characters — Mafiosi, drug addicts, computer pirates, smugglers, homosexuals, human organ and arms traders, corrupt politicians and police — offer a contemporary parallel to the inhabitants of Dante's concentric ledges in the Inferno. Regarding political and moral concerns (human-centered in time), Silko seems intent on showing her readers, as Dante did, that the Eurocentric society, and those who imitate them, are lost in a wilderness of destruction. In their frantic pursuit of capital, spiritual connections with each other and with the earth have been abandoned. Both the map and the text locate and name all the characters but one, placing them in self-contained geographical worlds.[6] The depravity of their lives renders the entire novel an inferno of corruption, with no redemptive vision save those of the almanac prophecies and the enigmatic stone snake.

The Mafia family, Max and Leah Blue and their two sons, emigrate from Cherry Hill, New Jersey, to Tucson, Arizona, where they gain control of real estate, video games, racing, and drugs, and also carry out murders for hire. In multiple locations (San Diego, Cartagena, Buenos Aires), Beaufrey commits horrendous acts: he cannibalizes Seese's baby and manipulates his homosexual lovers, encouraging Eric to commit suicide and David to exhibit photographs of the dead man in an art gallery. A corrupt trio — the Arizona senator, the Tucson judge, and the police chief — who make deals and protect Mafia criminals and arms traders, has its counterpart south of the border in General J, the Mexico City police chief, and his brother, who films police torture interrogations for sale to Argentine pornographic film companies. Both sets of officials are concerned about the Indians flooding their borders from further south. Unaware of the prophecies, they too fear a time when "the world that the whites brought with them would be swept away in a gust of wind" (235).

The Native Americans in the novel at first appear to be problematical figures in that those who are full-blooded are also engaged in destructive acts, while many mestizos are only partially aware of their spiritual connections and consequently linked with violence in both worlds. For instance, an arms trader, Menardo, in full flight from his Indian ancestry, is shaken by powerful dreams, but remains dependent on his Indian chauffeur to interpret them. Yet Silko's earth-oriented logic makes sense of all of the destruction. Rose, an Eskimo who accesses great spiritual power, uses it to down the airplanes of petroleum exploration companies in Alaska. These acts, in defense of the earth, parallel others: the blowing up of a dam by eco-warriors and Awa Gee's computer plan to undermine energy sources all over the United States simultaneously. Root and Mosca work for Calabazas, who indiscriminately smuggles people, drugs, and arms; he knows the desert and pays no attention to borders, which for him and his ancestors are not real. Angelita la Escapía plots with a Cuban, Bartolomeo, to train Chiapas indigenes as a People's Army, then wearies of the Marxist's failure to appreciate the spiritual impetus of the people and kills him. These are not actions of Destroyers, but rather the overturning of conventional moral categories. Destruction and lawlessness are condoned, even celebrated, if one is protecting the earth and indigenous peoples against those who seek only economic gain.

Perhaps because the church seems powerless to address the destructive aspects of contemporary life, Silko deals with church affairs (god-centeredness in time) only briefly. As in Dante's Italy, church officials are painted as corrupt, in particular the monsignor, who drives donated Cadillacs and sleeps with Calabazas's wife. According to old Yoeme, "the Catholic Church had been finished, a dead thing even before the Spanish ships had arrived in the Americas" (717). Fixation on the crucifixion of Jesus, as well as the torturing of heretics and Jews, is linked with the human sacrifices of the Aztecs as the work of Destroyers, "who feed off the energy released by destruction" (336). The Europeans had been human sacrificers too: "'Mother Church' was a cannibal monster. Since the Europeans had no other gods or beliefs left, they had to continue the church rituals and worship; but they knew the truth" (718). Yet the indigenous tribes who migrated north had refused to feed the spirits blood anymore.[7]

Silko's allegations emerge quite logically from the premise that "a church that tortures and kills is a church that can no longer heal; thus the Europeans had arrived in the New World in precarious spiritual health" (718). In their confrontation with the people of the Americas, the colonialists sensed that their

Christianity was inadequate in the face of the powerful spirit beings that inhabited the new land. Although the general public is viewed as hostile toward people with abilities to "see" or "foretell," Lecha, the mestizo psychic, is visited by affluent, educated white people who come to her with a deep sense of something lost: "The white man had violated the Mother Earth, and he had been stricken with the sensation of a gaping emptiness between his throat and his heart" (121). The International Holistic Healers convention comes closest to a spiritual gathering, for it represents a fusion of peoples exploring various modes of psychological and physical healing with Native American prophets and eco-warriors bent on saving the earth. Yet even that gathering verges on parody as people of all ages and origins mill about urgently, spending money in desperate attempts to heal their loss.

The anagogical meaning of Silko's novel (god- or spirit-centered out of time) is presumably what justifies the enormous tapestry of moral depravity that she weaves. Indeed, Silko writes in the manner of a Medieval allegorist, offering us a system of characters and images that will enable the reader to perceive the vision that haunts the visionary. Explicit throughout *Almanac of the Dead* is the bankrupt quality of Anglo life. Seese, although she exhibits maternal attachment to her missing son, is hopelessly addicted to alcohol and cocaine. Trigg makes his fortune dealing in human organs and is not particular about how they are acquired. Numerous male characters seek escape in illicit sex with sleazy women, twisted homosexual lovers, and dogs. A Korean computer genius, Awa Gee, gets high on computers and numbers. The house that Alegría designs for Menardo and Iliana is a virtual temple to greed. Thus, absurdities in the literal narrative function as stairways leading to other levels (Murren, 145–55). Many of Silko's readers, however, refuse to accept the revelation that she offers, perhaps because it is not hidden by a veil of allegory but appears overtly as the accumulated terrible deeds of our civilization. These, implies Silko, must be confronted before they can be transcended. To understand their identity as Destroyers, Anglos must travel through the hell of utter degradation that Silko has constructed, retch at the accumulated horror, and vomit out the values of a wealth-centered Eurocentric culture.

Meanwhile, native peoples who have been induced to sell their souls to the white man, watch and wait, take heart from the slimmest of prophecies, and rouse themselves to action. The many lessons of Native American history woven through the first part of the novel should be common knowledge to everyone in the United States but are not. Instead, they are the horror stories told and retold by the victims: children sent thousands of miles from home to Indian schools that robbed them of their language, culture, and tribal ties; black Indians, a strong race born of escaped African slaves and indigenous Americans;

Geronimo, captured and executed because of a bad-faith promise. The most fundamental point, however, is the illegality of governments: "There was not, and there never had been, a legal government by Europeans anywhere in the Americas. Not by any definition, not even by the Europeans' own definitions and laws. Because no legal government could be established on stolen land. Because stolen land had never had clear title" (133).

In Silko's novel, Native American history is meant to be read spiritually. The Apache in the execution photographs is not the man the U.S. Army has been chasing, and other photographs taken of Geronimo at different times show very different images. These phenomena cannot be explained. Nor can logical sense be made of the great stone snake, which on the map is labeled "ancient spirit messenger," to mark its sudden enigmatic appearance near the open-pit uranium mine, opened in the 1940s, at Laguna Pueblo. The actual mine, operated by the U.S. government, using monetary incentives to override the objections of the tribe, is today a recovering scar on the earth. With very little equipment, tribal members have been working to reclaim the land, a slow process. Stories about these errors of greed and desecration of the earth are now part of the tribal legacy. Wisely, Silko does not attempt to assign precise meaning to the stone image, which she first discovered in 1979 while making a film at Laguna.[8] At the end of the novel, although the snake says nothing, its position tells all: "the snake was looking south, in the direction from which the twin brothers and the people would come" (763).

Without elaborating, or even pressing home the point, Silko's symbol reveals the suppressed power of the plumed serpent. Dante also uses the image of a feathered reptile to represent the corruption of the church, beginning with the Donation of Constantine. Unlike its negative role in Christianity, however, the Native American snake is a positive figure, incorporating modes of goodness, fertility, movement, and survival, barely comprehended by non-native peoples. Union of bird and reptile, Quetzalcoatl is identified both as an ancient deity and legendary ruler of the Toltec. As the god of civilization, the feathered serpent represented the forces of good and light; as a ruler, he is credited with the discovery of maize, the arts, and science. Recent fossil discoveries in South America suggest that in fact feathered dinosaurs existed there, perhaps within the memory of the earliest native people. The earth itself was thought of by the Olmecs as a coiled serpent; Meso-Americans worshipped Coatlicue, a snake goddess, creatrix and mother of celestial deities. Silko has written elsewhere of her impulse to paint a mural featuring a rattlesnake 30 feet long on a wall in her neighborhood: "The snake in my mural is a messenger. He emerges out of a rainstorm and is surrounded by flowers, birds, and other words in Spanish as if they had blossomed out of the flowers and plants that grew around the giant snake. The words, in Spanish, say 'The people are hungry. The people are cold. The rich have stolen the land. The rich have stolen freedom. The people demand justice. Otherwise, Revolution'" (*Yellow Woman,* 144).

In the novel, other feathered creatures, the macaws that advise the Mayan brothers, are not subject to any mode of deductive or inductive analysis. Rather, the blue-and-yellow birds appear mysteriously, cry of big changes coming, and dictate what must be done as people begin moving from the south. The opal in Tacho's spirit bundle foretells the burning of Mexico City; at other times the bundle bleeds mysteriously. Prophecy in Silko's novel is often left undefined. Meaning is apparent, but its precise nature cannot be known, an aspect of native storytelling often frustrating to readers from the dominant culture. Silko herself, in *Yellow Woman and a Beauty of the Spirit,* comments that "a great deal of the story is believed to be within the listener; the storyteller's role is to draw the story out of the listeners" (50). Thus the almanac, preserved at great cost by the children who carry it on the flight north, is incomplete, inchoate, and altogether disappointing to an Anglo mind, schooled in historical record-keeping of another kind. As it is with all native stories, the children who carry the old narratives do not fully understand what has been entrusted to them, only that these fragments are important and must be passed on. Yet these bits of horse-gut, bearing the outline of a giant plumed serpent, possess living power to bring all the tribal people of the Americas together to retake the land. The plumed serpent is thus a powerful spiritual symbol, the key to the lost will to rebel.

Transcendence is similarly what Silko has in mind when she presents the character of Yoeme, grandmother to Lecha and Zeta. One of the old people who understood the significance of the Almanac as well as the language of snakes, Yoeme is among the last whose beings have not been corrupted by Western education or white lifeways. Herself miraculously delivered from death, she passes on significant knowledge: "'You may as well die fighting the white man,' Yoeme had told them when they were girls. 'Because the rain clouds will disappear first; and with them the plants and animals. When the spirits are angry or hurt, they turn their backs on all of us'" (580). Yet as Yoeme also points out, although the white man hates to hear anything about spirits, which are beyond his control, "against the spirits the white man was impotent. . . . Spirits were immune to the white man's threats and to his bribes of money and food. The white man only knew one way to control himself or others and that was with brute force" (580).

It is difficult to deny what old Yoeme teaches. These truths, however painful for Silko's readers, are the core of the allegory. Just as Dante does, she shows us human beings dealing with each other, with minorities, and with the earth—torturing, butchering, shooting, raping, excavating—until we can stand it no longer and cry out, "Stop!" That is precisely Silko's strategy, what earlier mystics called the *via negativa*. If we are truly horrified, we will take steps toward change. *Almanac of the Dead* is not escape fiction. We may not enjoy reading about violence, but that's because it's redundant; our newspapers and TV screens are full of it. Yet Silko's mission in this novel is to present the horror in such a way that it cannot be shunted aside. The uncanny coincidence of historical events that occurred after the novel's publication — the failure of the Mexican economy and the Oklahoma city bombing — with events described in *Almanac of the Dead* drives home Silko's point.

Sven Birkerts, in his review of Silko's *Almanac of the Dead,* remarks, "that the oppressed of the world should break their chains and retake what's theirs is not an unappealing idea (for some), but it is so contrary to what we know both of the structures of power and the psychology of the oppressed that the imagination simply balks. . . . Her premise of revolutionary insurrection is tethered to airy nothing" (41). By this observation, Mr. Birkerts admits himself to be one of those who does not take the spirit world seriously, who does not believe that white culture is destroying itself, that the Destroyers in both of Silko's novels are quite real, that in fact we are they. Silko has staked her life, her tribal loyalties, and her commitment to the earth on getting this message across to an increasingly violent world. As in the dream vision of Dante, similarly intended to put an erring society back on track, the writer reveals her truth to those who are perceptive enough to accept it.

The narrative world that reveals this truth can be mapped in linear fashion, but the vision attained from it transcends that diagram and urges the reader to an immense new spiritual understanding of the Destroyers and the Earth. Yet readers must resist the Eurocentric tendency to label certain actions as good or evil. Silko tells us stories, both traditional myths and modern ones, inviting us to acknowledge the Pueblo vision of the way things are: "In this universe, there is no absolute good or absolute bad; there are only balances and harmonies that ebb and flow" (*Yellow Woman,* 64). Yet the writer leaves no doubt as to which movement is which.

NOTES

1. Native Americans of the Southwest (who refer to themselves as "Indians") use the term "Anglo" to describe white English-speaking settlers who brought with them the English legal system and notions of land ownership, which came into conflict with a more casual system of land tenure under the Spaniards. In common usage today, "Anglo" refers to anyone who is not Hispanic, Native American, or mestizo.

2. In *Yellow Woman and a Beauty of the Spirit,* Silko explains, "By the end of 1981, I

was working on sections that I hoped would fit together much as the old Maya almanacs had fit together.... By 1982, I was writing the novel in sections, much as a movie is filmed for later editing; the sections also resembled the fragments that remained of the ancient Maya codices" (140).

3. Personal conversation, Laguna Pueblo, January 1993.

4. Such a filming did take place at Laguna. The *kiva* was used, and to the minds of some, desecrated, as a setting for a horror film. However, the Laguna Tribal Council maintains the right to declare its *kiva* sacred or not sacred, and therefore "closed" or "open," depending on the occasions for which it is used.

5. These are tribal officers. At Laguna they change yearly, giving individual tribal members, in various combinations with others, frequent opportunities to participate in decision making. As of January 1993, the Laguna Tribal Council was discussing the involvement of women as participants in tribal decision making.

6. For some unknown reason, Root, the disabled victim of a motorcycle accident, is missing from the map. As best I can determine, he belongs with Mosca, Calabazas, Liria, and Sarita, Native American residents of Tucson who are working against, and in spite of, the white world to bring about change.

7. This category presumably includes the Pueblos and Hopis, and perhaps all the Anasazi peoples, who according to the white man's archaeological record, appeared in the Four Corners area of the Southwest in the ninth century A.D.

8. She writes about the stone snake and its role as catalyst for *The Almanac of the Dead* in her recent book of essays, *Yellow Woman and a Beauty of the Spirit*, 138, 144.

WORKS CITED

Alighieri, Dante. *The Inferno.* Trans. John Ciardi. New York: Mentor, 1954.

——. *The Paradiso.* Trans. Dorothy Sayers. New York: Penguin, 1963.

——. *The Purgatorio.* Trans. John Ciardi. New York: Mentor, 1954.

Birkerts, Sven. Rev. of *Almanac of the Dead. New Republic* 4 Nov. 1991: 39–41.

Murren, Michael. *The Veil of Allegory.* Chicago: U of Chicago P, 1969.

Silko, Leslie Marmon. *Almanac of the Dead.* New York: Penguin Books, 1992.

——. *Ceremony.* New York: Penguin Books, 1978.

——. *Yellow Woman and a Beauty of the Spirit: Essays on Native American Life Today.* New York: Simon and Schuster, 1996.

Underhill, Evelyn. *Mysticism.* 1910. New York: New American Library, 1955.

LESLIE MARMON SILKO AND HER WORK

A Bibliographical Essay

Connie Capers Thorson

For the reader interested in further criticism of Leslie Marmon Silko, many sources explore the intricacies of her work. These writings employ a wide variety of critical approaches to appraise Silko's poetry, prose, and fiction. Though this analysis of critical materials on Silko does not attempt to be exhaustive, it discusses a number of essays, chapters from books, and reviews of particular importance, offering both objective and subjective analysis of them. Full bibliographic citations appear at the end of the essay for those articles discussed and for other items of interest by Silko and about her and her work.

A full biography of Silko has yet to be written, but a number of shorter biographical pieces shed light on her childhood and youth, influences on her, her education, and some of her attitudes. Interviews with her spanning nearly twenty years offer a kind of autobiographical perspective on her maturing both as a person and as an artist; they present her attitudes on and thoughts about a number of issues. Some important reviews that include biographical and autobiographical material are discussed below.

The Western Writers series monograph on Leslie Marmon Silko by Per Seyersted provides a lucid, though rather brief, biography of Silko, but its publication date of 1980 indicates, of course, that many years are not covered. A critical biography of Silko would be beneficial for interested readers who must now go to a variety of sources to learn about her life since 1980. In his brief monograph, Seyersted spends several pages recounting the history of Laguna Pueblo in New Mexico where Silko grew up. The information seems relevant because it is, after all, Laguna and its people that are responsible for what Silko is and will be.

In Kenneth Rosen's 1974 anthology in which "The Man to Send Rain Clouds" was reprinted, Silko says, "what I know is Laguna. This place I am from is everything I am as a writer and human being" (176). The women of Laguna — Silko's mother, grandmother, aunts, and others — were all influential in her life. The stories these women told were to become the basis for many of Silko's writings and were to imbue them with a historical and cultural perspective that has pervaded all her work.

Seyersted reinforces his biographical narrative by analyzing a few of Silko's more important stories — "Yellow Woman," "A Geronimo Story," "Lullaby," for example — but he considers *Ceremony* the consummate expression of what her formative years had been preparing her for. Seyersted expands on his convictions about the importance of place and of storytelling for Silko with his analysis of *Storyteller,* a collection of stories and poetry with pictures and drawings.

Many of the interviews with Silko are extremely useful for those wanting to understand her life and what in that life makes her such an important modern writer. She is not reticent to talk about influences on her, about her imagination, about her opinions, and about her work. The interview with Kim Barnes in the *Journal of Ethnic Studies* in 1986 is rewarding because it is long enough to allow Silko to give some thorough and satisfying responses to questions. Silko embarks on what could be her autobiography as an artist in this interview. The idea of an artistic autobiography is continued by a revealing interview published by Donna Perry in *Backtalk: Women Writers Speak Out* (1993). To a question about the strong women in her life, Silko responds, "I was really fortunate because I was surrounded by generations of women. I never thought women weren't as strong as men, as able as men or as valid as men. I was pretty old before I started running into mainstream culture's attitudes about women" (319).

Four other interviews that reward the reader are "A Conversation with Leslie Marmon Silko" by Larry Evers and Denny Carr; "Two Interviews with Leslie Marmon Silko" by Per Seyersted; and "Leslie Marmon Silko" by Laura Coltelli. Evers and Carr's interview is an edited version of a conversation they recorded in 1976 and published in *Sun Tracks* the same year. Silko's answers tell a story about herself, especially about how and why she writes, about her stories, her poetry, and her first novel. Seyersted, Silko's early biographer, focuses a lot of attention in his two interviews on storytelling and memory and their influences on her writing. Silko tells Seyersted what she told a group of high school students at Laguna: "Our [the people of the pueblos] greatest natural resource is stories and storytelling. We have an endless, continuing, ongoing supply of stories" (21). Silko also answers questions about some politically sensitive issues such as the American Indian Movement. Coltelli's interview was conducted in 1985 but not published until 1990. In it Silko talks about some facets of *Almanac of the Dead,* published in 1991, though many answers focus on the more philosophical issues of time, the creative process, and storytelling.

A few reviews advance the understanding of Silko's work by providing analysis of and insight into the piece reviewed. Because of the dearth of scholarly analysis of *Almanac of the Dead* until the present book of essays, three of these seem particularly worth mentioning. One is Joy Harjo's "The World is Round: Some Notes on Leslie Silko's *Almanac of the Dead.*" In this review Harjo praises her friend and former colleague for being an innovator, for "chang[ing] the shape and concept of the American novel" (207). She comments on Silko's use of time, calling it the novel's "main character" (209). Harjo ends her review by voicing concern over the possibility of Silko's being consumed by her creative passion.

Another useful review of *Almanac of the Dead* is "Seeing Our Way Clear" by T. C. Marshall. He sees significance in Silko's "put[ting] contemporary life in the fresh light of larger and older discourses" and reinforces this opinion by saying, "Silko's greatest successes in this book are in bringing forward ignored facts and forces, in telling untold histories" (5). Marshall's review elaborates on these ideas.

The third is actually a review and a critical essay at the same time. While the other two reviews are fairly positive, Sven Birkerts finds much to criticize in this novel he calls "a megalith, a two-hander" (347). The review essay, "Leslie Marmon Silko," appears in his 1992 book *American Energies: Essays on Fiction.* Birkerts asserts, "Silko has ventured nothing less than a paper apocalypse, a vivid enactment of the long-prophesied collapse of white European domination and the simultaneous resurgence of the Native American peoples of much of the continent" (347). It is the vastness of Silko's canvas and the ideas that are outside the boundaries of what he sees as acceptable material for a novel that causes Birkerts finally to censure Silko's creation.

The three reviews mentioned here are important because they go beyond the kind of brief review that may be useful for the book trade or to call Silko's work to the attention of readers. These longer reviews advanced understanding of her work (from both positive and negative perspectives) while readers waited for full-blown studies of *Almanac of the Dead*. Such essays have finally made their way into the scholarly literature with the publication of the current volume and a couple of earlier essays listed in the bibliography.

Comment on the intertwining subjects of biography, autobiography, interviews, and reviews would not be complete without mention of the articles on Silko in several significant reference sources. The most useful of these appears in volume 74 of *Contemporary Literary Criticism* (1993). This long article includes, in addition to a brief biographical sketch, a wide variety of excerpts from criticism and reviews (including several of *Almanac*) and a selective bibliography. An excellent biographical essay, especially for readers coming to Silko for the first time, is that by Elaine A. Jahner in Andrew Wiget's *Dictionary of Native American Literature*. It is the reader's loss that Jahner, an intelligent and insightful commentator on Silko, does not include any reference to *Almanac of the Dead* (1991), though the essay was not published until 1994 and the novel is cited in the brief bibliography.

William M. Clements is the author of a good systematic overview of Silko's work, including *Almanac,* appearing in volume 143 of the *Dictionary of Literary Biography* (1994). This essay is updated by Clements and Kenneth M. Roemer in volume 175 of the *Dictionary of Literary Biography* (1997). A brief, but helpful, entry on Silko appears in volume 45 of the New Revision series of *Contemporary Authors* (1995). These three entries include brief bibliographies.

Many essays using many approaches and espousing many agendas have been written about Silko's novel *Ceremony* since its publication in 1977. Among the earliest essays were those published in a special issue of *American Indian Quarterly* edited by Kathleen M. Sands in 1979. Six of these essays were originally presented at the Rocky Mountain Modern Language Association meeting in 1978 (2). The published essays focus on three topics: "the relationship of the protagonist to nature and the land"; "the way in which ritual provides a means of healing for Tayo"; and the method whereby "the novel is simultaneously an ancient ritual and a contemporary ceremony" (3).

The essays are followed by an edited transcription of the discussion following the presentation of the papers and a response to the seminar discussion by Larry Evers. Evers, after warning the audience of the dangers of believing the ethnologists and what they recorded, carefully explains, "if he [the American Indian writer] is to survive as an American Indian and as a writer, he must not only get his community but all of us to go along with his story. This symposium offers eloquent testimony to Leslie Silko's ability to do just that" (75). By studying these eight essays on *Ceremony,* the reader will begin to develop an understanding of and a sensitivity to the world of the novel and Silko's world.

In *Other Destinies; Understanding the American Indian Novel,* Louis Owens extends the boundaries of our understanding of *Ceremony* in "'The Very Essence of Our Lives': Leslie Silko's Webs of Identity." His discussion of Silko's role as the teller of the story of Tayo's healing illuminates his certainty that *Ceremony* "challenges readers with a new epistemological orientation while altering previously established understandings of the relationship between reader and text" (171). Silko as storyteller is not an informant, according to Owens. Instead, "Silko creates an accretive and a chronological experience for the reader, placing us in the center of the ceremonial cycles like the patient in a Navajo sand painting" (172). While Owens asserts that Silko's novel does not belong within the Euro-American tradition, he nonetheless devotes the majority of the essay to a traditionally Euro-American theoretical analysis.

One group of essays focuses on gender issues for discussing *Ceremony.* As with any focus in which theory may be allowed to overpower art and reason, the feminist focus on Silko's work must be approached with care. Kristin Herzog's essay "Thinking Woman and Feeling Many: Gender in Silko's *Ceremony*" is appealing because it is less doctrinaire than many. Herzog asserts that while feminist criticism has gone beyond the stereotype of the weak woman, "male figures who are sensitive instead of ruthless, gentle instead of heroic, community-conscious instead of individualistic" have rarely been noticed (25). Herzog continues, "Silko's stylistic devices of blending mythical and rational, circular and linear elements correspond to the balance of male and female traits in her characters, and they challenge the reader to question Western ways of portraying gender" (27).

Edith Swan's essay "Laguna Prototypes of Manhood in *Ceremony*" is useful if the reader can get past her theoretical jargon. She catalogs with great care the "key prototypes of manhood which frame and influence [Tayo's] behavior" (40). In the course of these catalogs she explains meticulously the relationships Tayo has with male family members, his maturation as a warrior and hunter, and finally his relationship to Yellow Woman as he strives toward a harmonious reunification with the land.

Robert M. Nelson, in *Place and Vision: The Function of Landscape in Native American Fiction,* devotes the first chapter to *Ceremony.* Nelson concentrates on an analysis of the various encounters Tayo has with places and people on his ceremonial journey as he seeks to heal himself and bring relief to his beleaguered pueblo. As Nelson argues, "Part of the appeal of Tayo's story to the kiva elders is that it establishes the Pueblo as the geographical (and hence spiritual) center of a visible world, a particular landscape that contains, within itself, the power to heal and make whole and sustain life in the face of those destructive forces (both internal and external to human consciousness) that cohabit the universe" (39).

Another essay that rewards study is Rachel Stein's "Contested Ground: Nature, Narrative, and Native American Identity in Leslie Marmon Silko's *Ceremony* and *Almanac of the Dead*" (1997). Stein emphasizes the importance of stories to native peoples as well as the relationships of the native cultures to the European conquerors. She focuses on the " . . . fatal opposition between the aboriginal stories of partnership and reciprocity with nature and the Euro-American stories of detachment and dominion" (122). She concentrates on *Ceremony,* though *Almanac of the Dead* is given equal billing.

Other essays on *Ceremony* abound. Some explore the various symbols and myths that Silko uses, while others are particularly concerned with narrative technique. Some critics analyze Silko's use of land and place, while others consider her use of various discourse strategies. There are essays that deal with witchery and others that focus on healing. Some help readers read and teach Silko. Many of these essays will reward the reader's attention; some will serve to guide the reader toward an understanding of the novel. A few will illuminate Silko's aims and methods.

Storyteller (1981) does not fit the mold of the conventionally illustrated book of short stories or poems or a novel. It is, rather, a book of stories, some in prose and some in poetry, enhanced and illuminated with photographic illustrations. In order to fully appreciate Silko and her art, the reader should work through to an understanding of this important book. While *Storyteller* is a book that critics seem to approach with some trepidation, perhaps because it is iconoclastic, there are essays that offer significant analysis.

Many of Silko's most important short stories appear in *Storyteller,* but the book as a whole is more significant than any one of its parts. "*Storyteller:* Grandmother Spider's Web" by Linda L. Danielson is a good place to start a study of this seemingly elusive creation. Danielson is puzzled that "mainstream feminist scholarship has paid strikingly little attention to the writing of American Indian women" (325). Seven years after its publication in 1981, Danielson offers a feminist reading of this eclectic book that takes into consideration the place of women in Pueblo culture, a place very different from that of women in Euro-American culture. She begins by pointing the reader to feminist expressions of how women's literature should be examined. She then applies these concepts to Silko: "Silko's *Storyteller* represents . . . a re-vision of the world from her vantage point as a Laguna Indian woman" (327).

Focusing on what she sees as Silko's emphasis on the role of the female in the Keresan culture, Danielson looks carefully at the sequencing of the tales within the book. It is obviously important to Danielson that the reader fully grasp that the structure of the book, while "non-linear," is neither "baffling [nor] haphazard" (332). Concentrating on the spider's web as the controlling metaphor that informs the entire book, Danielson offers an analysis that is sensitive as well as intelligent and well argued. Particularly incisive are her comments on "Yellow Woman" and on Coyote, "[who], like the koshare, both subverts and transcends the rules and the ceremonies" (345), and her treatment of the Coyote section of *Storyteller.*

Another perceptive study of *Storyteller* is Kathleen Mullen Sands's "Indian Women's Personal Narrative: Voices Past and Present," which appeared in *American Women's Autobiography: Fea(s)ts of Memory.* The essay is significant and illuminating because of Sands's very cogent, tightly argued explanation of how American Indian women are viewed by the predominantly white culture, why autobiography is not a form easily employed by them, and what the future holds for autobiographical narrative by American Indian women. Examining several autobiographical writings by American Indian women, Sands looks briefly at *Storyteller,* which she considers "a new kind of autobiographical text. In this work Silko uses fragments of personal narrative to bind together traditional expression of collective cultural memory with her contemporary fictional and poetic versions of those stories central to the identity of Laguna people" (283).

Melody Graulich's publication of *"Yellow Woman"/Leslie Marmon Silko* in 1993 was a significant event in Silko scholarship. This book includes Silko's "Yellow Woman" and original and reprinted essays. Graulich's introduction provides substantial analysis of the various permutations and connotations of the word "story" and of the book *Storyteller,* as well as biographical material, the cultural context for the story, and brief reviews of the essays included (several of which are discussed in this essay). Of particular value is Graulich's close reading of "Yellow Woman." By absorbing Graulich's analysis of "the important elements of any short story: its motifs, settings, plot, character development, themes, point of view, and style" (14), readers will enhance their understanding not only of "Yellow Woman" but also of Silko's art.

Bernard A. Hirsch's essay " 'The Telling Which Continues': Oral Tradition and the Written Word in Leslie Marmon Silko's *Storyteller*" reveals other considerations a reader of *Storyteller* must deal with. Hirsch writes about the pivotal place of the photographs within the book: "they involve the reader more fully in the storytelling process itself" (2). Hirsch talks in specific terms about some of the photographs and what they mean in the context of a certain story or group of stories while also emphasizing the significance of the oral tradition for Silko.

Two essays concentrate on possible autobiographical interpretations or implications of *Storyteller.* There end the similarities; both deserve careful study. The earlier of the two is Arnold Krupat's "Dialogic of Silko's *Storyteller.*" The later is Jennifer Browdy de Hernandez's "Laughing, Crying, Surviving: The Pragmatic Politics of Leslie Marmon Silko's *Storyteller.*" Krupat's approach is usefully Bakhtinian and stresses the dialogic discourse of what he distinguishes as autobiographies by Indians: "In autobiographies by Indians, although there is inevitably an element of biculturalism, there is not the element of composite- ness that precisely marks Indian autobiographies [in which there is interven- tion by an Euro-American editor]" (56). Before offering a Bakhtinian reading of Silko's *Storyteller,* Krupat explains, "To examine Native American auto- biography from a Bakhtinian perspective, then, is not only to consider it as a discursive type — a kind of literature, generically closer to the epic or the novel as Bakhtin understands these Western forms — but as a social model which allows for the projection of a particular image of human community" (58– 59). Browdy de Hernandez develops, after looking at several other critics' descriptions of Native American autobiography, her own theoretical construct for reading *Storyteller:* "[I]t seems to me more appropriate to look at Silko's text as an example of decentered, diffused subjectivity, as a written representa- tion of the open borders between self and other, which is consonant with the Native American understanding of identity. There is no 'central' figure in this text, no one voice or story that is more privileged than the other, the result being a composite, polyphonic autobiographical portrait — an interbiogra- phy" (20).

Those wanting to introduce students to the reading of and reading about American Indian literature will find two additional essays of particular value. One is Helen Jaskoski's "Teaching with *Storyteller* at the Center." The other is Matthias Schubnell's "What Other Story? Mythic Subtexts in Leslie Silko's 'Storyteller.'" In particular, the Jaskoski essay on the book provides a descrip- tion of the effective and successful use of Silko's work in the classroom. Schub- nell's essay suggests a way to approach the short story "Storyteller" with students.

Many essays use some portion of Silko's work as a component of a study focusing on ideas such as nature, postmodernism, the supernatural, bi- or multiculturalism, or ecofeminism. Within such a context Silko's work is often analyzed in comparison to or in conjunction with that of other writers. These essays confirm Silko's place within the expanding corpus of American letters while pointing out firmly that "the real weight and profound revolutionary potential of multicultural challenges to the American literary canon, . . . if that potential is to become tangible and transformative, must be undergirded by our willingness to be changed by them" (Adams, 141).

Two essays that include analyses of Silko's poetry will help the readers who are willing to change their understanding of what demands will be made of them. Kenneth M. Roemer, in "Bear and Elk: The Nature(s) of Contemporary American Indian Poetry," begins with an enumeration that attests to the variety of American Indian poetry. He provides lists of poems written by American Indians and publications where poems by American Indians could be found through the 1970s. He then compares and contrasts Momaday's "Bear" and Silko's "Snow Elk" or "In Cold Storm Light," as it was later known. It is the contrast that interests Roemer the most: "If critics simplistically delineate unifying characteristics of contemporary Indian literature, they will repeat the sins of the fathers by manipulating new stereotypes to suit their concepts of 'ethnic' or 'minority' literature" (189).

Kate Adams also insists that the reader recognize the diversity of what is thought of as American Indian poetry in "Northamerican Silences: History, Identity, and Witness in the Poetry of Gloria Anzaldúa, Cherríe Moraga, and Leslie Marmon Silko." The work of these women "complicates . . . our understanding of poetry's range and purpose by merging poetry with other literary forms . . . and tutors us in what has been lost, in what we will regain, and in what will be required of us if we attend to the voices we have become accustomed to rendering silent" (131). Adams's analysis of works by Anzaldúa, Moraga, and Silko helps to liberate the reader from a stultifying view of tradition.

"A Skin of Lakeweed: An Ecofeminist Approach to Erdrich and Silko" by Lee Schweninger is an essay that bears fruit if the dedicated and diligent reader can stick with it. Some of her discussion of ecofeminism may confuse the reader unfamiliar with the rhetoric of that theoretical approach, but Schweninger ultimately provides a comprehensible definition of "ecofeminism," which she then applies in her analysis of Erdrich's *Tracks* (1988) and Silko's *Ceremony* (1977).

Erdrich and Silko are also paired in Susan Pérez Castillo's "Postmodernism, Native American Literature, and the Real: The Silko-Erdrich Controversy," though the approach is quite different. Focusing on ethnic groups and ethnicity, Pérez Castillo tries to reach an understanding of Silko's attack on Erdrich's *Beet Queen* in terms of postmodernist theory.

Scott P. Sanders, in "Southwestern Gothic: On the Frontier between Landscape and Locale," offers yet another perspective on Silko by considering the gothic in Richard Shelton, Rudolfo Anaya, and Leslie Silko. Sanders contends that "in the Southwest, three cultures — Anglo, Chicano, and Indian — are struggling to realize their desires for a sure sense of cultural identity, or rootedness, in a landscape which, with its gothic presence, resists making of it a locale, a homeland where people, events, and places are integrated" (55). After a brief analysis of D. H. Lawrence's responses to the land, Sanders studies how these modern writers depend on the southwestern landscape and culture in all its gothic proportions. Of *Ceremony,* Sanders says, "Much of the gothic tone in Silko's novel rises from the modern Pueblo Indians' need to understand the realities of their culture in the context of the cultural heritage expressed by the ruins of the Great Pueblo culture. . . . The ruins of the Pueblos' Anasazi ancestors evoke the classically gothic mixture of doom and grandeur" (65). Sanders's argument for the importance of the gothic in Silko is not convincing because Silko's use of the land is positive.

Some of the most recent criticism or analysis of Silko's work appears in dissertations. Often her work is studied in relationship to or in conjunction with the work of other important writers: N. Scott Momaday, Louise Erdrich, James Welch, Toni Morrison, Henry David Thoreau, Robinson Jeffers, Eudora Welty, Frank Waters, and Alice Walker, to name a few. Subjects range from women novelists, feminism, and gender issues, to native religion and ritual, storytelling, and nature. The dissertations are evidence that the works of Silko and other Native American writers have assumed their place in the modern literary canon and are legitimate subjects for serious scholarship and theoretical analysis.

Hertha Dawn Wong, in *Sending My Heart Back across the Years: Tradition and Innovation in Native American Autobiography,* tackles, in chapter 6, "Contemporary Innovations of Oral Traditions: N. Scott Momaday and Leslie Marmon Silko," the complex issues surrounding contemporary autobiographical writing by Native Americans as it is informed by their oral traditions. Wong begins with a lucid and well-argued exposition on the ways in which and why Native American autobiography differs from that of the Euro-American. She then applies her theories in a sound analysis of Momaday's *The Way to Rainy Mountain* and *The Names* and Silko's *Storyteller.*

Wong's analysis of the various elements of Silko's *Storyteller,* though focused on autobiography, ties together and illuminates many of the threads that are central to the whole corpus of Silko's storytelling. As Wong so eloquently says, "Just as important . . . [as Momaday's contribution to Native American autobiography] is Silko's contribution to expanding the Euro-American notion of personal identity, of expressing the performance aspect of personal/ tribal stories, and of insisting on the relationship between self and community, self and land, and self and story" (199). Those studying Silko will find these things present in all her work.

In an interview with Kim Barnes in 1986, Silko said,

> At Laguna, [storytelling is] a way of interacting. It isn't like there's only one storyteller designated. That's not it at all. It's a whole way of being.
>
> When I say "storytelling," I don't just mean sitting down and telling a once-upon-a-time kind of story. I mean a whole way of seeing yourself, the people around you, your life, the place of your life in the bigger context, not just in terms of nature and location, but in terms of what has gone on before, what's happened to other people. (86)

There is an abundance of material written about Silko and her life and art, and much of it is worth careful study. It is, however, Silko's storytelling that will ultimately reward the reader's attention and concentration.

BIBLIOGRAPHY

Connie Capers Thorson

SELECTED PRIMARY SOURCES
Novels

Almanac of the Dead. New York: Simon and Schuster, 1991.
Ceremony. New York: Viking, 1977.

Other Book-length Works

The Delicacy and Strength of Lace: Letters between Leslie Marmon Silko and James Wright. Ed. Anne Wright. St. Paul, MN: Graywolf, 1986.
Laguna Woman: Poems by Leslie Silko. Greenfield Center, NY: Greenfield Review Press, 1974.
Rain. [With Lee Marmon]. American Journals Series 4. NY: Library Fellows of the Whitney Museum of American Art, 1996.
Sacred Water: Narratives and Pictures. Tucson, AZ: Flood Plain Press, 1993.
Storyteller. New York: Viking, 1981. Seaver Books.
Yellow Woman and a Beauty of the Spirit: Essays on Native American Life Today. New York: Simon and Schuster, 1996.

Short Fiction

"Bravura." In *The Man to Send Rain Clouds*. Ed. Kenneth Mark Rosen. NY: Viking, 1974. 149–54.
"Coyote Holds a Full House in His Hand." *Tri-Quarterly* 48 (spring 1980), 166–74. Reprinted in various publications.

"From a Novel Not Yet Titled." [Excerpt from *Ceremony* ms.] *Journal of Ethnic Studies* 3.1 (spring 1975), 72–87.
"Gallup, New Mexico — Indian Capital of the World." [Excerpt from *Ceremony* ms.] *New America: A Review* 2.3 (summer–fall 1976): 30–32.
"A Geronimo Story." In *Come to Power: Eleven Contemporary American Indian Poets.* Ed. Lourie. Trumansburg, NY: Crossing Press, 1974. 81–94. Reprinted in various publications.
"Humaweepi, the Warrior Priest." In *The Man to Send Rain Clouds.* Ed. Rosen. 161–68.
"The Invention of White People." Rpt. from *Ceremony.* In *Shaking the Pumpkin: Traditional Poetry of the Indian North Americas.* Ed. Jerome Rothenberg. Rev ed. New York: Alfred Van Der Marck, 1986. 83–88.
"Laughing and Laughing." In *Come to Power: Eleven Contemporary American Indian Poets.* Ed. Dick Lourie. Trumansburg, NY: Crossing Press, 1974. 99.
"Lullaby." *Chicago Review* 26.1 (summer 1974): 10–17. Reprinted in various publications.
"The Man to Send Rain Clouds." *New Mexico Quarterly* 38.4 (winter–spring 1969): 133–36.
"Reasserting Our Claims." *New Letters* 59.1 (fall 1992): 43.
"Storyteller." *Puerto del Sol* 14.1 (fall 1975): 11–25. Reprinted in various publications.
"Tony's Story." *Thunderbird* (literary magazine of the students of the University of New Mexico) (1969): 2–4. Reprinted in various publications.
"Uncle Tony's Goat." *The Man to Send Rain Clouds.* Ed. Rosen. 93–100.
"Yellow Woman." *The Man to Send Rain Clouds.* Ed. Rosen. 33–45. Reprinted in various publications.

Articles, Essays, and Lectures

"America's Iron Curtain: The Border Patrol State." *Nation* 17 Oct. 1994: 412–15.
"Criminal Justice in American Indian Literature." *Oshkaabewis Native Journal* 1.1 (1990): 31.
"An Essay on Rocks: Photographs and Text by Leslie Marmon Silko." *Aperture* 139 (summer 1995): 60–63.
Foreword. Aaron Yava. *Border Towns of the Navajo Nation.* Alamo, CA: Holmganger Press, 1975, 3–4. (Originally in *Yardbird Reader* 3 (1974): 98–103.)
"The Fourth World (Reality and the Laguna Pueblos)." *Artforum* 27.10 (1989): 124–27.
"Here's an Odd Artifact for the Fairy-Tale Shelf." Review of *The Beet Queen* by Louise Erdrich. *Impact/Albuquerque Journal* 8 Oct. 1986: 10–11. Rpt. *Studies in American Indian Literatures* 10.4 (fall 1986): 177–84.
"Interior and Exterior Landscapes: The Pueblo Migration Stories." *Landscape in America.* Ed. George F. Thompson. Austin: U of Texas P, 1995. 154–69.
"Landscape, History, and the Pueblo Imagination." *Antaeus* 57 (autumn 1986): 83–94. Reprinted in various publications.
"Language and Literature from a Pueblo Indian Perspective." In *English Literature: Opening Up the Canon.* Ed. Leslie Fiedler and Houston A. Baker Jr. Selected Papers from the English Institute. N.S.4. [1979] Baltimore: John Hopkins UP, 1981. 54–72.

"An Old-Time Indian Attack Conducted in Two Parts." *Yardbird Reader* 5 (1976): 77–84. Reprinted in various publications.

Review of *Reservation Blues* by Sherman Alexie. *Nation* 12 June 1995: 856–59.

"Through the Stories We Hear Who We Are." *Amicus Journal* 14.4 (winter 1993): 19.

"Tribal Prophecies (after *Almanac of the Dead*)." *Blue Mesa Review* 4 (spring 1992): 12–13.

"Videomakers and Basketmakers." *Aperture* 119 (summer 1990): 72–73.

Plays

"Lullaby." A one-act play for the American Bicentennial Theater Project, sponsored by the San Francisco City Arts Commission. This adaptation by Silko and Frank Chin of Silko's short story was performed in San Francisco in 1976.

Film Scripts

"Coronado Expedition of 1540." Film Script for Jack Beck and Marlon Brando depicting the Coronado Expedition from a Native American perspective was sent to Hollywood in 1977, adapted by Harry Brown, but apparently not used.

"Estoy-eh-muut and the Kunideeyah" ["Arrowboy and the Destroyers"]. Laguna Pueblo Narrative Adapted for Film by Leslie Marmon Silko and Dennis W. Carr. Draft, November 1978, [1–34]. National Endowment for the Humanities, Media Division, 1981.

Interviews, Readings, and Other Autobiographical and Biographical Materials

Autobiographical Information. Letter to Abraham Chapman. In his *Literature of the American Indians: Views and Interpretations*. New York: New American Library, 1975. 5–6.

Barnes, Kim. Interview. "A Leslie Marmon Silko Interview." *Journal of Ethnic Studies* 13.4 (1986): 83–105. Reprinted in various publications.

"Biographical Information," in her *Laguna Woman*, 34–35.

Coltelli, Laura. Interview. "*Almanac of the Dead*: An Interview with Leslie Marmon Silko." In her *Native American Literatures*. Pisa: SEU, 1989. 65–80.

———. Interview. "Leslie Marmon Silko." In her *Winged Words: American Indian Writers Speak*. Lincoln: U of Nebraska P, 1990. 135–53.

"Contributors' Biographical Notes." In *Voices of the Rainbow: Contemporary Poetry by American Indians*. Ed. Kenneth Mark Rosen. New York: Viking. 174.

"A Conversation with Leslie Silko." Videotape (1975). Produced by Lawrence J. Evers and Dennis W. Carr. Available for viewing at Southwest Folklore Center Archive, University of Arizona.

Evers, Lawrence J., ed. "A Conversation with Frank Waters" (with Silko as one of the participants). *Sun Tracks: An American Indian Literary Magazine* 5 (1979): 61–68.

Evers, Lawrence, and Dennis Carr. "A Conversation with Leslie Marmon Silko." *Sun Tracks* 3.1 (1976): 28–33.

Fisher, Dexter. "Stories and Their Tellers: A Conversation with Leslie Marmon Silko." In *Third Woman: Minority Women Writers of the United States*. Ed. Dexter Fisher. Boston: Houghton Mifflin, 1980. 18–23.

Jahner, Elaine. Interview. "The Novel and Oral Tradition: An Interview with Leslie Marmon Silko." *Book Forum: An International Transdisciplinary Quarterly* 5.3 (1981): 383–88.

Kagge, Stein, ed. Interview. "Det er ensomt a skrive" ["Writing Is a Lonely Activity"]. *Aftenposten* (an Oslo, Norway, newspaper), Sept. 14, 1978: 5.

"The Laguna Regulars and Geronimo." (Silko reading "A Geronimo Story," with a brief introduction.) Phonotape, 1977, made available for sale by *Akwesasne Notes,* Mohawk Nation, Rooseveltown, NY, 13683.

Leslie Marmon Silko at the Albuquerque Public Library, 1989. Videocassette. [Readings from *Storyteller, Almanac of the Dead,* "Prayer to the Pacific."]

"Leslie Silko, Laguna Poet and Novelist." *This Song Remembers: Self-Portraits of Native Americans in the Arts.* Ed. Jane B. Katz. Boston: Houghton Mifflin, 1980. 186–94.

Interview. "Leslie Silko: Storyteller." *Persona: University of Arizona Undergraduate Magazine of Literature and Art.* Ed. James Fitzgerald and John Hudak, 1980. 21–38.

Niemann, Linda. Interview. "Narratives of Survival: Linda Niemann Interviews Leslie Marmon Silko." *Women's Review of Books* 9 (July 1992): 10.

Perry, Donna. Interview. "Leslie Marmon Silko." In her *Backtalk: Women Writers Speak Out.* New Brunswick, NJ: Rutgers UP, 1993. 313–41.

"Running on the Edge of Rainbow: Laguna Stories and Poems. With Leslie Marmon Silko." Videotape in the series *Words and Place: Native Literature from the American Southwest.* Produced by Larry Evers. New York: Clearwater Publishing Company, 1978.

Seyersted, Per. Interview. "Two Interviews with Leslie Marmon Silko." *American Studies in Scandinavia* 13.1 (1981): 17–33.

"They Were the Land's." Review of *Creek Mary's Blood* by Dee Brown. *New York Times Book Review* 25 May 1980: 10, 22.

Poems

"Alaskan Mountain Poem No. 1." In *Voices of the Rainbow: Contemporary Poetry by American Indians.* Ed. Kenneth Mark Rosen. New York: Seaver Books, 1975. 17.

"Deer Dance/For Your Return." *Columbia: A Magazine of Poetry and Prose* 1.2 (autumn 1977): 9. Reprinted in various publications.

"Deer Song." *Journal of Ethnic Studies* 2.2 (summer 1974): 69. Reprinted in various publications.

"Four Mountain Wolves." In Silko, *Laguna Woman.* 19–20. Reprinted in various publications.

"Hawk and Snake" (Chinle, June, 1972). *Chicago Review* 24.4 (spring 1973): 8. Reprinted in various publications.

"Horses at Valley Store." *Chicago Review* 24.4 (spring 1973): 99–100. Reprinted in various publications.

"How to Write a Poem about the Sky." In *The First Skin around Me: Contemporary American Tribal Poetry*. Ed. James L. White. Moorhead, MN: Territorial Press, 1976. 76. Reprinted in various publications.

"A Hunting Story." *A: A Journal of Contemporary Literature* 1.1 (fall 1976): 11–13. Reprinted in various publications.

"Incantation." In *The Indian Rio Grande: Recent Poems from 3 Cultures*. Ed. Gene Frumkin and Stanley Noyes. Cerrillos, NM: San Marcos Press, 1977. 101–2.

"In Cold Storm Light." *Quetzal* 2.3 (summer 1972): 46. Reprinted in various publications.

"Indian Song: Survival." *Chicago Review* 24.4 (spring 1973): 94–96. Reprinted in various publications.

"Love Poem." In Silko, *Laguna Woman*. 16. Reprinted in various publications.

"Mesita Men." In Silko, *Laguna Woman*. 22.

"Poem for Ben Barney." In Silko, *Laguna Woman*. 14–15. Reprinted in various publications.

"Poem for Myself and Mei: Concerning Abortion." *Journal of Ethnic Studies* 2.2 (summer 1974): 66. Reprinted in various publications.

"Prayer to the Pacific." *Chicago Review* 24.4 (spring 1973): 93. Reprinted in various publications.

"Preparations." *Chicago Review* 24.4 (spring 1973): 100. Reprinted in various publications.

"Prophecy of Old Woman Mountain." *Journal of Ethnic Studies* 2.2 (summer 1974): 70.

"Si' Anh Aash." In Silko, *Laguna Woman*. 21.

"Skeleton Fixer's Story." *Sun Tracks: An American Indian Literary Magazine* 4 (1978): 2–3. Reprinted in various publications.

"Slim Man Canyon." In Silko, *Laguna Woman*. 17. Reprinted in various publications.

"Snow Elk." *Quetzal* 2 (summer 1972): 46.

"Story from Bear Country." *A: A Journal of Contemporary Literature* 2.2 (fall 1977): 4–6. Reprinted in various publications.

"Storytelling." *Journal of Ethnic Studies* 2.2 (summer 1974): 72–74. Reprinted in various publications.

"Sun Children." *Quetzal* 2.3 (summer 1972): 47. Reprinted in various publications.

"The Time We Climbed Snake Mountain." *Chicago Review* 24.4 (spring 1973): 99. Reprinted in various publications.

"Toe'osh: A Laguna Coyote Story." In Silko, *Laguna Woman*. 9–11. Reprinted in various publications.

"When Sun Came to Riverwoman." *Greenfield Review* 3.2 (1973): 67–68. Reprinted in various publications.

"Where Mountain Lion Laid Down with Deer." *Northwest Review* 13.2 (February 1973): 34. Reprinted in various publications.

SELECTED SECONDARY SOURCES

Adams, Kate. "Northamerican Silences: History, Identity, and Witness in the Poetry of Gloria Anzaldúa, Cherrie Moraga, and Leslie Marmon Silko." *Listening to Silences:*

New Essays in Feminist Criticism. Ed. Elaine Hedges and Shelley Fisher Fishkin. New York: Oxford UP, 1994. 130–45.

Aithal, S. Krishnamoorthy. "American Ethnic Fiction in the Universal Human Context." *American Studies International* 21.5 (1983): 61–66.

Albers, Patricia C. "Voices from Within: Narrative Writings of American Indian Women." *Humanity and Society* 13.4 (1989) 463–70.

Aldama, Frederick Luis. "Structural Configuration of Magic Realism in the Works of Gabriel Garcia Marquez, Leslie Marmon Silko, Charles Johnson, and Julie Dash." *Journal of Narrative and Life History* 5.2 (1995): 147–60.

Allen, Paula Gunn. "The Feminine Landscape of Leslie Marmon Silko's *Ceremony.*" In her *Studies in American Indian Literature: Critical Essays and Course Designs.* New York: MLA, 1983. 127–33. Rpt. in *Critical Perspectives on Native American Fiction.* Ed. Richard F. Fleck. Washington, DC: Three Continents, 1993. 233–39.

——. "Kochinnenako in Academe: Three Approaches to Interpreting a Keres Indian Tale." *"Yellow Woman"/Leslie Marmon Silko.* Ed. Melody Graulich. New Brunswick, NJ: Rutgers UP, 1993. 83–111.

——. "The Psychological Landscape of *Ceremony.*" *American Indian Quarterly* 5.1 (1979): 7–12.

——. *The Sacred Hoop: Recovering the Feminine in American Indian Traditions.* Boston: Beacon Press, 1986.

——. "Special Problems in Teaching Leslie Marmon Silko's *Ceremony.*" *American Indian Quarterly* 14.4 (1990): 379–86.

——. "A Stranger in My Own Life: Alienation in Native American Prose and Poetry: 2." *Newsletter of the Association for Study of American Indian Literatures* (ASAIL), NS 3.2 (1979): 16–23. Rpt. in *MELUS* 7.2 (1980): 3–19.

Anderson, Laurie. "Colorful Revenge in Silko's *Storyteller.*" *Notes on Contemporary Literature* 15.4 (1985): 11–12.

Antell, Judith A. "Momaday, Welch, and Silko: Expressing the Feminine Principle through Male Alienation." *American Indian Quarterly* 12.3 (1988): 213–20.

Barker, Adele Marie. "Crossings." In *Dialogues/Dialogi: Literary and Cultural Exchanges between (Ex)Soviet and American Women.* Ed. Susan Hardy Aiken, Adele Marie Barker, Maya Koreneva, Ekaterina Sttetsenko. Durham: Duke U Press, 1994. 340–53.

Bataille, Gretchen M. "American Indian Novels." *Rocky Mountain Review of Language and Literature* 47.1–2 (1993): 61–66.

Beidler, Peter G. "Animals and Human Development in the Contemporary American Indian Novel." *Western American Literature* 14.2 (1979): 133–48.

——. "Animals and Theme in *Ceremony.*" *American Indian Quarterly* 5.1 (1979): 13–18.

——, ed. "Silko's Originality in "Yellow Woman." *Studies in American Indian Literatures* 8.2 (1996): 61–84.

Beidler, Peter G., and Lavonne A. Ruoff. "A Discussion of *Winter in the Blood.*" *American Indian Quarterly* 4.2 (1978): 159–68.

Bell, Robert C. "Circular Design in *Ceremony.*" *American Indian Quarterly* 5.1 (1979): 47–62.

Benediktsson, Thomas E. "The Reawakening of the Gods: Realism and the Supernatural in Silko and Hulme." *Critique: Studies in Contemporary Fiction* 33.2 (1992): 121–31.

Bennani, Benjamin, and Catherine Warner Bennani. "No Ceremony for Men in the Sun: Sexuality, Personhood, and Nationhood in Ghassan Kanafani's *Men in the Sun,* and Leslie Marmon Silko's *Ceremony.*" *Critical Perspectives on Native American Fiction.* Ed. Richard F. Fleck. Washington, DC: Three Continents, 1993. 246–55.

Berner, Robert L. "Trying to Be Round: Three American Indian Novels." *World Literature Today: A Literary Quarterly of the University of Oklahoma* 58.3 (1984): 341–44.

Bierhorst, John. "Incorporating the Native Voice: A Look Back from 1990." *On the Translation of Native American Literatures.* Ed. Brian Swann. Washington: Smithsonian Institution Press, 1992. 51–63.

Bird, Gloria. "Towards a Decolonization of the Mind and Text 1: Leslie Marmon Silko's *Ceremony.*" *Wicazo Sa Review* 9.2 (1993): 1–8.

Birkerts, Sven. "Leslie Marmon Silko." *American Energies: Essays on Fiction.* New York: William Morrow, 1992. 347–53.

Blaeser, Kimberly M. "Pagans Rewriting the Bible: Heterodoxy and the Representation of Spirituality in Native American Literature." *Ariel* 25.1 (1994): 12–31.

Blair, Barbara. "Textual Expressions of the Search for Cultural Identity." *American Studies in Scandinavia* 27.1 (1995): 48–63.

Blicksilver, Edith. "Traditionalism vs. Modernity: Leslie Silko on American Indian Women." *Southwest Review* 64.2 (1979): 149–60.

Blumenthal, Susan. "Spotted Cattle and Deer: Spirit Guides and Symbols of Endurance and Healing in *Ceremony.*" *American Indian Quarterly* 14.4 (1990): 367–77.

Boynton, Victoria. "Desire's Revision: Feminist Appropriation of Native American Traditional Sources." *Modern Language Studies* 26.2,3 (1996): 53–71.

Brice, Jennifer. "Earth as Mother, Earth as Other in Novels by Silko and Hogan." *Critique* 39 (winter 1998): 127–38.

Brouillette, Liane. "Using Drama as a Cultural Bridge." *Journal of Experiential Education* 15.3 (1992): 41–45.

Browdy de Hernandez, Jennifer. "Laughing, Crying, Surviving: The Pragmatic Politics of Leslie Marmon Silko's *Storyteller.*" *A-B: Auto-Biography Studies* 9.1 (1994): 18–42.

——. "Writing for Survival: Continuity and Change in Four Contemporary Native American Women's Autobiographies." *Wicazo Sa Review* 10.2 (1994): 40–62.

Brown, Alanna Kathleen. "Pulling Silko's Threads through Time: An Exploration of Storytelling." *American Indian Quarterly* 19.2 (1995): 171–79.

Buller, Galen. "New Interpretations of Native American Literature: A Survival Technique." *American Indian Culture and Research Journal* 4.1 & 2 (1980): 165–77.

Castro, Jan Garden. "Indian Storyteller Wins a Pot of Gold." *Greenfield Review* 9.3 & 4 (1981): 103–5.

Cederstrom, Lorelei. "Myth and Ceremony in Contemporary North American Native Fiction." *Canadian Journal of Native Studies* 2.2 (1982): 285–301.

Chapman, Mary. " 'The Belly of This Story': Storytelling and Symbolic Birth in Native American Fiction." *Studies in American Indian Literatures* 7.2 (1995): 3–16.

Clements, William M. "Folk Historical Sense in Two Native American Authors." *MELUS* 12.1 (1985): 65–78.

——. "Leslie Marmon Silko." *American Novelists since World War II.* Ed. James R. Giles and Wanda H. Giles. Vol. 143 of *Dictionary of Literary Biography.* Detroit: Gale Research, 1994. 193–205.

Clements, William M., and Kenneth M. Roemer. "Leslie Marmon Silko." *Native American Writers of the United States.* Ed. Kenneth M. Roemer. Vol. 175 of *Dictionary of Literary Biography.* Detroit: Gale Research, 1997. 276–90.

Cohen, Robin. "Landscape, Story, and Time as Elements of Reality in Silko's 'Yellow Woman.'" *Weber Studies* 12.3 (1995): 141–47.

Coltelli, Laura. "Leslie Marmon Silko's *Sacred Water.*" *Studies in American Indian Literatures* 8.4 (1996): 21–29.

——. "Re-enacting Myths and Stories: Tradition and Renewal in *Ceremony.*" *Native American Literatures.* SEU-Pisa, Forum 1/1989: 173–83.

——. "Le Sacred Waters di Leslie Marmon Silko." *RSA Journal: Rivista di Studi Nord Americani* 4 (1993): 57–65.

——. "The Search for Origins through Storytelling in Native American Literature: Momaday, Silko, Erdrich." *RSA Journal: Rivista di Studi Nord Americani* 3 (1992): 59–71.

Copeland, Marion W. "*Black Elk Speaks* and Leslie Silko's *Ceremony:* Two Visions of Horses." *Critique: Studies in Contemporary Fiction* 24.3 (1983): 158–72.

Couser, G. Thomas. "Oppression and Repression: Personal and Collective Memory in Paule Marshall's *Praisesong for the Widow* and Leslie Marmon Silko's *Ceremony.*" In *Memory and Cultural Politics: New Approaches to American Ethnic Literatures.* Ed. Amritjit Singh, Joseph T. Skerrett Jr., Robert E. Hogan. Boston: Northeastern UP, 1996. 106–20.

Cousineau, Diane. "Leslie Silko's *Ceremony:* The Spiderweb as Text." *Revue Française d'Etudes Américaines* 15.43 (1990): 19–31.

Cummings, Kate. "Reclaiming the Mother(s) Tongue: *Beloved, Ceremony, Mothers, and Shadows. College English* 52.5 (1990): 552–69.

Danielson, Linda. "*Storyteller:* Grandmother Spider's Web." *Journal of the Southwest* 30.3 (1988): 325–55.

——. "The Storytellers in *Storyteller.*" *Studies in American Indian Literatures* 1.2 (1989): 21–31. Rpt. in *"Yellow Woman"/Leslie Marmon Silko.* Ed. Melody Graulich. New Brunswick, NJ: Rutgers UP, 1993. 201–12.

Dasenbrock, Reed Way. "Forms of Biculturalism in Southwestern Literature: The Work of Rudolfo Anaya and Leslie Marmon Silko." *Genre* 21.3 (1988): 307–19.

Dinome, William. "Laguna Woman: An Annotated Leslie Silko Bibliography." *American Indian Culture and Research Journal* 21.1 (1997): 207–80.

Dunsmore, Roger. "No Boundaries, on Silko's *Ceremony.*" In his *Earth's Mind: Essays in Native Literature.* Albuquerque: U of New Mexico P, 1997. 15–32.

Espey, David B. "Endings in Contemporary Indian Fiction." *Western American Literature* 13.2 (1978): 133–39.

Evasdaughter, Elizabeth N. "Leslie Marmon Silko's *Ceremony:* Healing Ethnic Hatred by Mixed-Breed Laughter." *MELUS* 15.1 (1988): 83–95.

Evers, Larry. "A Response: Going along with the Story." *American Indian Quarterly* 5.1 (1979): 71–75.

Evers, Lawrence J. "The Killing of a New Mexican State Trooper: Ways of Telling a

Historical Event." *Wicazo Sa Review* 1.1 (1985): 17–25. Rpt. in *Critical Essays on American Literature*. Ed. Andrew Wiget. Boston: G. K. Hall, 1985. 246–61.

Farrer, Claire R. "Reprise of Swan's Song and Farrer's Chorus." *American Indian Quarterly* 14.2 (1990): 167–71.

———. "The Sun's in Its Heaven, All's *Not* Right with the World: Rejoinder to Swan." *American Indian Quarterly* 14.2 (1990): 155–59.

Fleck, Richard F. "Sacred Land in the Writings of Momaday, Welch, and Silko." In *Entering the 90s: The North American Experience: Proceedings from the Native American Studies Conference at Lake Superior State University, October 27–28, 1989*. Ed. Thomas E. Schirer. Sault Ste. Marie: Lake Superior UP, 1991. 125–33.

Flores, Toni. "Claiming and Making: Ethnicity, Gender, and the Common Sense in Leslie Marmon Silko's *Ceremony* and Zora Neale Hurston's *Their Eyes Were Watching God*." *Frontiers* 10.3 (1989): 52–58.

Freese, Peter. "Marmon Silko's *Ceremony*: Universality versus Ethnocentrism." *Amerikastudien-American-Studies* 37:4 (1992): 613–45.

Garcia, Reyes. "Senses of Place in *Ceremony*." *MELUS* 10.4 (1983): 37–48.

Gilderhus, Nancy. "The Art of Storytelling in Leslie Silko's *Ceremony*." *English Journal* 83.2 (1994): 70–72.

Graulich, Melody, ed. *"Yellow Woman"/Leslie Marmon Silko*. New Brunswick, NJ: Rutgers UP, 1993.

Gross, Konrad. "Survival or Orality in a Literate Culture: Leslie Silko's Novel *Ceremony*." *Modes of Narrative: Approaches to American, Canadian, and British Fiction*. Ed. Reingard M. Nischik and Barbara Korte. Würzburg: Königshausen and Neumann, 1990. 88–99.

Gunton, Sharon R., and Jean C. Stine. "Leslie Marmon Silko 1948–." Vol. 23. *Contemporary Literary Criticism*. Detroit: Gale Research, 1983. 406–12.

Hailey, David E., Jr. "The Visual Elegance of Ts'its'tsi'nako and the Other Invisible Characters in *Ceremony*." *Wicazo Sa Review* 6.2 (1990): 1–6.

Harjo, Joy. "The World Is Round: Some Notes on Leslie Silko's *Almanac of the Dead*." *Blue Mesa Review* 4 (spring 1992): 207–10.

Harvey, Valerie. "Navajo Sandpainting in *Ceremony*." *Critical Perspectives on Native American Fiction*. Ed. Richard F. Fleck. Washington, DC: Three Continents, 1993. 256–59.

Herzog, Kristin. "Thinking Woman and Feeling Man: Gender in Silko's *Ceremony*." *MELUS* 12.1 (1985): 25–36.

Hiatt, Shannon T. "The Oral Tradition as a Nativization Technique in Three Novels." *Journal of Indian Writing in English* 14.1 (1986): 10–21.

Hirsch, Bernard A. " 'The Telling Which Continues': Oral Tradition and the Written Word in Leslie Marmon Silko's *Storyteller*." *American Indian Quarterly* 12.1 (1988): 1–26. Rpt. in *"Yellow Woman"/Leslie Marmon Silko*. Ed. Melody Graulich. New Brunswick, NJ: Rutgers UP, 1993. 151–83.

Hobbs, Michael. "Living In-Between: Tayo as Radical Reader in Leslie Marmon Silko's *Ceremony*." *Western American Literature* 28.4 (1994): 301–12.

Hoilman, Dennis. "The Ethnic Imagination: A Case History." *Canadian Journal of Native Studies* 5.2 (1985): 167–75.

———. " 'A World Made of Stories': An Interpretation of Leslie Silko's *Ceremony*." *South Dakota Review* 17.3 (1979–80): 54–66.

Holland, Sharon P[atricia]. " 'If You Know I Have a History, You Will Respect Me': A Perspective on Afro–Native American Literature." *Callaloo: A Journal of African American and African Arts and Letters* 17.1 (1994): 334–50.

Hunter, Carol. "American Indian Literature." *MELUS* 8.2 (1981): 82–85.

Jahner, Elaine [A.]. "An Act of Attention: Event Structure in *Ceremony.*" *American Indian Quarterly* 5.1 (1979): 37–46.

———. "Leslie Marmon Silko (1 March 1948–)." *Dictionary of Native American Literature.* Ed. Andrew Wiget. New York and London: Garland, 1994. 499–511.

Jaskoski, Helen. "Teaching with *Storyteller* at the Center." *Studies in American Indian Literatures* 5.1 (1993): 51–61.

———. "Words Like Bones." *CEA Critic* 55.1 (1992): 70–86.

———. *Leslie Marmon Silko: A Study of the Short Fiction.* Twayne's Studies in Short Fiction 71. NY: Twayne, 1998.

Jaskoski, Helen, and G. Lynn Nelson. "Thinking Woman's Children and the Bomb." *Explorations in Ethnic Studies* 13.2 (1990): 1–24.

Jones, Patricia. "The Web of Meaning: Naming the Absent Mother in *Storyteller.*" In *"Yellow Woman"/Leslie Marmon Silko.* Ed. Melody Graulich. New Brunswick, NJ: Rutgers UP, 1993. 213–32.

Katz, Jane B., ed. "Leslie Silko, Laguna Poet and Novelist." In *This Song Remembers: Self-Portraits of Native Americans in the Arts.* Boston: Houghton Mifflin, 1980. 186–94.

King, Katherine Callen. "New Epic for an Old World: Leslie Marmon Silko's *Almanac of the Dead.*" In *Native American Literatures.* Ed. Laura Coltelli. Pisa: SEU, 1994. 31–42.

Krumholz, Linda J. " 'To Understand This World Differently': Reading and Subversion in Leslie Marmon Silko's *Storyteller.*" *Ariel* 25.1 (1994): 89–113.

Krupat, Arnold. "The Dialogic of Silko's *Storyteller.*" In *Narrative Chance: Postmodern Discourse on Native American Indian Literatures.* Ed. Gerald Vizenor. Albuquerque: U of New Mexico P, 1989. 55–68. Rpt. in *"Yellow Woman"/Leslie Marmon Silko.* Ed. Melody Graulich. New Brunswick, NJ: Rutgers UP, 1993. 185–200.

Langen, T[oby] C. S. " 'Estoy-eh-muut' and the Morphologists." *Studies in American Indian Literatures* 1.1 (1989): 1–12.

———. "*Storyteller* as Hopi Basket." *Studies in American Indian Literatures.* 5.1 (1993): 7–24.

Lappas, Catherine. " 'The Way I Heard It Was . . .': Myth, Memory, and Autobiography in *Storyteller* and *The Woman Warrior.*" *CEA Critic* 57.1 (1994): 57–67.

Larson, Charles R. "Survivors of the Relocation." In his *American Indian Fiction.* Albuquerque: U of New Mexico P, 1978. 133–64.

———. "Third World Writing in English." *World Literature Today* 56.1–2 (1982): 64–66.

Lee, Valerie. "Responses of White Students to Ethnic Literature: One Teacher's Experience." *Reader [Houghton, Mich.] Essays in Reader-Oriented Theory, Criticism, and Pedagogy* no. 15 (1986): 24–33.

Lincoln, Kenneth. "Grandmother Storyteller: Leslie Silko." In his *Native American Renaissance.* Berkeley: U of California P, 1983. 222–50.

Lucero, Ambrose. "For the People: Leslie Silko's *Storyteller.*" *Minority Voices: An Interdisciplinary Journal of Literature and the Arts* 5.1–2 (1981): 1–10.

Lynch, Tom. "What Josiah Said: Uncle Josiah's Role in *Ceremony*." *North Dakota Quarterly* 63.2 (1996):138–52.

Manley, Kathleen. "Decreasing the Distance: Contemporary Native American Texts, Hypertext, and the Concept of Audience." *Southern Folklore* 51.2 (1994): 121–35.

———. "Leslie Marmon Silko's Use of Color in *Ceremony*." *Southern Folklore* 46.2 (1989): 133–46.

Maranto, Gina. "Storyteller." *Amicus Journal* 14.4 (1993): 16–18.

Marshall, T. C. "Seeing Our Way Clear." *American Book Review* 14.5 (Dec. 1992–Jan. 1993): 5.

Mathewson, Ruth. "Writers and Writing: Ghost Stories." *New Leader* 60.12 (6 June 1977): 14–15.

McAllister, Mick. "Homeward Bound: Wilderness and Frontier in American Indian Literature." *The Frontier Experience and the American Dream: Essays on American Literature*. Ed. David Mogen, Mark Busby, and Paul Bryant. College Station: Texas A&M UP, 1989. 149–58.

McBride, Mary. "Shelter of Refuge: The Art of Mimeses in Leslie Marmon Silko's 'Lullaby.'" *Wicazo Sa Review* 3.2 (1987): 15–17.

McFarland, Ronald E. "Leslie Silko's Story of Stories." *A: A Journal of Contemporary Literature* 4.2 (1979): 18–23.

Metting, Fred. "Exploring Oral Traditions through the Written Text." *Journal of Reading* 38.4 (1994–95): 282–89.

Mitchell, Carol. "*Ceremony* as Ritual." *American Indian Quarterly* 5.1 (1979): 27–35.

Nelson, Robert M. "The Function of the Landscape of *Ceremony*." In *Place and Vision: The Function of Landscape in Native American Fiction*. American Indian Studies. 1. New York: Peter Lang, 1993. 11–39.

———. "He Said/She Said: Writing Oral Tradition in John Gunn's 'Ko-pot Ka-nat' and Leslie Silko's *Storyteller*." *Studies in American Indian Literatures* 5.1 (1993): 31–50.

———. "Place and Vision: The Function of Landscape in *Ceremony*." *Journal of the Southwest* 30.3 (1988): 281–316.

Niemann, Linda. "New World Disorder." Review of *Almanac of the Dead*. *Women's Review of Books* 9 (March 1992): 1,3–4.

Norden, Christopher. "Ecological Restoration as Post-Colonial Ritual of Community in Three Native American Novels." *Studies in American Indian Literatures* 6.4 (1994): 94–106.

Norwood, Vera. "Writing Animal Presence." In her *Made from This Earth: American Women and Nature*. Chapel Hill: U of North Carolina P, 1993. 172–208.

Oandasan, William. "A Familiar Love Component of Love in *Ceremony*." *Critical Perspectives in Native American Fiction*. Ed. Richard F. Fleck. Washington, DC: Three Continents, 1993. 240–45.

Orr, Lisa. "Theorizing the Earth: Feminist Approaches to Nature and Leslie Marmon Silko's *Ceremony*." *American Indian Culture and Research Journal* 18.2 (1994): 145–57.

Ortiz, Simon J. "Towards a National Indian Literature: Cultural Authenticity in Nationalism." *MELUS* 8.2 (1981): 7–12.

Owens, Louis. "'The Very Essence of Our Lives:' Leslie Silko's Webs of Identity." In his *Other Destinies: Understanding the American Indian Novel*. Norman: U of Oklahoma P, 1992. 167–91.

Pace, Stephanie. "Lungfish, or Acts of Survival in Contemporary Female Writing [in Tillie Olsen's "I Stand Here Ironing," Gloria Naylor's *Women of Brewster Place*, Leslie Marmon Silko's *Ceremony*, and Louise Erdrich's *Love Medicine*]." *Frontiers* 10.1 (1988): 29–33.

Parker, Michael. "Searching for the Center: Tayo's Quest in Leslie Silko's *Ceremony*. *Mount Olive Review* 7 (1993–94): 23–29.

Pasquaretta, Paul. "Sacred Chance: Gambling and the Contemporary Native American Indian Novel." *MELUS* 21.2 (1996): 21–33.

Pérez Castillo, Susan. "The Construction of Gender and Ethnicity in the Texts of Leslie Silko and Louise Erdrich." *Yearbook of English Studies* 24 (1994): 228–36.

———. "A Map for Survival: The Community of Laguna Pueblo in Leslie Marmon Silko's *Ceremony*." *Chiba Review* 12 (1990): 41–51.

———. "Postmodernism, Native American Literature, and the Real: The Silko-Erdrich Controversy." *Massachusetts Review* 32.2 (1991): 285–94.

Purdy, John. "The Transformation: Tayo's Genealogy in *Ceremony*." *Studies in American Indian Literatures* 10.3 (1986): 121–33.

Rabinowitz, Paula. "Naming, Magic, and Documentary: The Subversion of the Narrative in *Song of Solomon*, *Ceremony*, and *China Men*." In *Feminist Re-Visions: What Has Been and Might Be*. Ed. Vivian Patraka and Louise A. Tilly. Ann Arbor: Women's Studies Program, U of Michigan, 1983. 26–42.

Rainwater, Catherine. "The Semiotics of Dwelling in Leslie Marmon Silko's *Ceremony*." *American Journal of Semiotics* 9.2–3 (1992): 219–40.

Ramsey, Jarold. "The Teacher of Modern American Indian Writing as Ethnographer and Critic." *College English* 41.2 (1979): 163–69.

Rand, Naomi. "Surviving What Haunts You: The Art of Invisibility in *Ceremony*, *The Ghost Writer*, and *Beloved*." *MELUS* 20.3 (1995): 21–32.

Riley, Patricia. "The Mixed-Blood Writer as Interpreter and Mythmaker." In *Understanding Others: Cultural and Cross-Cultural Studies and the Teaching of Literature*. Ed. Joseph Trimmer and Tilly Warnock. Urbana: NCTE, 1992. 230–42.

Roberts, Jill. "Between Two 'Darknesses': The Adoptive Condition in *Ceremony* and *Jasmine*." *Modern Language Studies* 25.3 (1995): 77–97.

Roemer, Kenneth M. "Bear and Elk: The Nature(s) of Contemporary American Indian Poetry." In *Studies in American Indian Literature: Critical Essays and Course Designs*. Ed. Paula Gunn Allen. New York: MLA, 1983. 178–91.

Ronnow, Gretchen. "Tayo, Death, and Desire: A Lacanian Reading of *Ceremony*." In *Narrative Chance: Postmodern Discourse on Native American Indian Literatures*. Ed. Gerald Vizenor. Albuquerque: U of New Mexico P, 1989. 69–90.

Rosen, Kenneth Mark. Introduction. *The Man to Send Rain Clouds*. New York: Viking, 1974. ix–xiv.

Ruoff, A. LaVonne [Brown]. "Ritual and Renewal: Keres Traditions in Leslie Silko's 'Yellow Woman.'" In *"Yellow Woman"/Leslie Marmon Silko*. Ed. Melody Graulich. New Brunswick, NJ: Rutgers UP, 1993. 69–81.

———. "Ritual and Renewal: Keres Traditions in the Short Fiction of Leslie Silko." *MELUS* 5.4 (1978): 2–17. Rpt. *American Women Short Story Writers: A Collection of Critical Essays*. Ed. Julie Brown. New York: Garland, 1995. 167–89.

———. "The Survival of Tradition: American Indian Oral and Written Narratives." *Massachusetts Review* 27.2 (1986): 274–93.

Ruppert, James [Jim]. "Dialogism and Mediation in Leslie Silko's *Ceremony.*" *Explicator* 51:2 (1993): 129–34.

———. "No Boundaries, Only Transitions: *Ceremony.*" In his *Mediation in Contemporary Native American Fiction.* Norman: U of Oklahoma P, 1995. 74–91.

———. "The Reader's Lessons in *Ceremony.*" *Arizona Quarterly* 44.1 (1988): 78–85. Rpt. Vol. 74. *Contemporary Literary Criticism.* Ed. Thomas Votteler. Detroit: Gale Research, 1994. 338–41.

———. "Story Telling: The Fiction of Leslie Silko." *Journal of Ethnic Studies* 9.1 (1981): 53–58. Rpt. Vol. 74 *Contemporary Literary Criticism.* Ed. Thomas Votteler. Detroit: Gale Research, 1994. 321–23.

St. Andrews, B. A. "Healing the Witchery: Medicine in Silko's *Ceremony.*" *Arizona Quarterly* 44.1 (1988): 86–94.

St. Clair, Janet. "Death of Love/Love of Death: Leslie Marmon Silko's *Almanac of the Dead.*" *MELUS* 21.2 (1996): 141–56.

———. "Uneasy Ethnocentrism: Recent Works of Allen, Silko, and Hogan." *Studies in American Indian Literatures.* 6.1 (1994): 83–98.

St. John, Edward B. Review of *Almanac of the Dead. Library Journal* 15 Oct. 1991: 124.

Sanders, Scott P. "Southwestern Gothic: Alienation, Integration, and Rebirth in the Works of Richard Shelton, Rudolfo Anaya, and Leslie Silko." *Weber Studies* 4.2 (1987): 36–53.

———. "Southwestern Gothic: On the Frontier between Landscape and Locale." *Frontier Gothic: Terror and Wonder at the Frontier in American Literature.* Ed. David Mogen, Scott P. Sanders, and Joanne B. Karpinski. Rutherford, NJ: Fairleigh Dickinson UP. 55–70.

Sands, Kathleen Mullen. "Indian Women's Personal Narrative: Voices Past and Present." In *American Women's Autobiography: Fea(s)ts of Memory.* Ed. Margo Culley. Madison: U of Wisconsin P, 1992. 268–94.

———. Preface. "A Symposium Issue." A Special Symposium Issue on Leslie M. Silko's *Ceremony.* Guest ed. Kathleen M. Sands. *American Indian Quarterly* 5.1 (1979): 1–5.

Sands, Kathleen M., and A. LaVonne Ruoff. "A Discussion of *Ceremony.*" *American Indian Quarterly* 5.1 (1979): 63–70.

Scarberry, Susan J. "Memory as Medicine: The Power of Recollection in *Ceremony.*" *American Indian Quarterly* 5.1 (1979): 19–26.

Schein, Marie. "Identity in Leslie Marmon Silko's *Ceremony* and N. Scott Momaday's *Ancient Child.*" *Southwestern American Literature* 18.2 (1993): 228–36.

Scholer, Bo. "Mythic Realism in Native American Literature." *American Studies in Scandinavia* 17.2 (1985): 65–73.

Schubnell, Matthias. "Frozen Suns and Angry Bears: An Interpretation of Leslie Silko's *Storyteller.*" *European Review of Native American Studies* 1.2 (1987): 21–25.

———. "What Other Story? Mythic Subtexts in Leslie Silko's 'Storyteller.'" *Nebraska English Journal* 38.2 (special issue 1993): 40–48.

Schweninger, Lee. "A Skin of Lakeweed: An Ecofeminist Approach to Erdrich and Silko." In *Multicultural Literatures through Feminist/Poststructuralist Lenses.* Ed. Barbara Frey Waxman. Knoxville: U of Tennessee, 1993. 37–56.

——. "Writing Nature: Silko and Native Americans as Nature Writers." *MELUS* 18.2 (1993): 47–60.

Sequoya-Magdaleno, Jana. "Telling the Différance: Representations of Identity in the Discourse of Indianness." In *The Ethnic Canon: Histories, Institutions, and Interventions.* Ed. David Palumbo-Liu. Minneapolis: U of Minnesota P, 1995. 88–116.

Seyersted, Per. *Leslie Marmon Silko.* Western Writers Series. 45. Boise: Boise State U, 1980.

Shaddock, Jennifer. "Mixed-Blood Women: The Dynamic of Women's Relations in the Novels of Louise Erdrich and Leslie Silko." In *Feminist Nightmares: Women at Odds: Feminism and the Problem of Sisterhood.* Ed. Susan Ostrov-Weisser and Jennifer Fleischner. New York: New York UP, 1994. 106–21.

Sheldon, Mary F. "Reaching for a Universal Audience: The Artistry of Leslie Marmon Silko and James Welch." In *Entering the 90s: The North American Experience: Proceedings from the Native American Studies Conference at Lake Superior State University, October 27–28, 1989.* Ed. Thomas E. Schirer. Sault Ste. Marie: Lake Superior UP, 1991. 114–24.

Slowik, Mary. "Henry James, Meet Spider Woman: A Study of Narrative Form in Leslie Silko's *Ceremony.*" *North Dakota Quarterly* 57.2 (1989): 104–20.

Smith, Patricia Clark, with Paula Gunn Allen. "Earthy Relations, Carnal Knowledge: Southwestern American Indian Women Writers and Landscape." In *The Desert Is No Lady: Southwestern Landscapes in Women's Writing and Art.* Ed. Vera Norwood and Janice Monk. New Haven: Yale UP, 1987. 174–96. Rpt. in *"Yellow Woman"/ Leslie Marmon Silko.* Ed. Melody Graulich. New Brunswick, NJ: Rutgers UP, 1993. 115–50.

Stanford, Ann Folwell. " 'Human Debris': Border Politics, Body Parts, and the Reclamation of the Americas in Leslie Marmon Silko's *Almanac of the Dead.*" *Literature and Medicine* 16.1 (spring 1997): 23–42

Stein, Rachel. "Contested Ground: Nature, Narrative, and Native American Identity in Leslie Marmon Silko's *Ceremony* and *Almanac of the Dead.*" In her *Shifting the Ground: American Women Writers' Revisions of Nature, Gender, and Race.* Charlottesville: University Press of Virginia, 1997. 114–44.

Stetsenko, Ekaterina. "Retelling the Legends." In *Dialogues/Dialogi: Literary and Cultural Exchanges Between (Ex)Soviet and American Women.* Ed. Susan Hardy Aiken, Adele Marie Barker, Maya Koreneva, Ekaterina Stetsenko. Durham: Duke U P, 1994. 327–39.

Stone, Les. (Biographical sketch of Leslie Marmon Silko.) Vol. 122. *Contemporary Authors.* Ed. Hal May and Susan M. Trosky. Detroit: Gale Research, 1988. 424–25.

Swan, Edith. "Answer to Farrer: All Is Right with the Word as Laguna Notions Speak for Themselves." *American Indian Quarterly* 14.2 (1990): 161–66.

——. "Feminine Perspectives at Laguna Pueblo: Silko's *Ceremony.*" *Tulsa Studies in Women's Literature* 11.2 (1992): 309–27.

——. "Healing via the Sunwise Cycle in Silko's *Ceremony.*" *American Indian Quarterly* 12.4 (1988): 313–28.

——. "Laguna Prototypes of Manhood in *Ceremony.*" *MELUS* 17.1 (1991–92): 39–61.

——. "Laguna Symbolic Geography and Silko's *Ceremony.*" *American Indian Quarterly* 12.3 (1988): 229–49.

Taylor, Paul Beekman. "Repetition as Cure in Native American Story: Silko's *Ceremony* and Momaday's *Ancient Child*." In *Repetition*. Ed. Andreas Fischer. Tubingen: Narr, 1994. 221–42.

Thompson, Joan. "Yellow Woman, Old and New: Oral Tradition and Leslie Marmon Silko's *Storyteller*." *Wicazo Sa Review* 5.2 (1989): 22–25.

Truesdale, C. W. "Tradition and *Ceremony*: Leslie Marmon Silko as an American Novelist." *North Dakota Quarterly* 59.4 (1991): 200–28.

Turner, Frederick. "Voice Out of the Land: Leslie Marmon Silko's *Ceremony*." In his *Spirit of Place: The Making of an American Literary Landscape*. San Francisco: Sierra Club Books, 1989. 323–60.

TuSmith, Bonnie. "Storytelling as Communal Survival: Leslie Marmon Silko's *Ceremony*." In her *All My Relatives: Community in Contemporary Ethnic American Literatures*. Ann Arbor: U of Michigan P, 1993. 119–29.

Van Dyke, Annette. "Curing Ceremonies: The Novels of Leslie Marmon Silko and Paula Gunn Allen. In her *Search for a Woman-Centered Spirituality*. New York: New York UP, 1992. 12–40.

———. "'What Do You Do When You Love Everyone on Every Side of the War?': Teaching the Complexities of American Indian Literature." *MELUS* 16.2 (1989–90): 63–68.

Vangen, Kate Shanley. "The Devil's Domain: Leslie Silko's *Storyteller*." In *Coyote Was Here: Essays on Contemporary Native American Literary and Political Mobilization*. Ed. Bo Scholer. The Dolphin. 9. Aarhus, Denmark: Seklos, Department of English, U of Aarhus, 1984. 116–23.

Velie, Alan R. "Leslie Silko's *Ceremony*: A Laguna Grail Story." In his *Four American Indian Literary Masters: N. Scott Momaday, James Welch, Leslie Marmon Silko, and Gerald Vizenor*. Norman: U of Oklahoma P, 1982. 104–21.

Votteler, Thomas, ed. "Leslie Marmon Silko, 1948–." Vol. 74. *Contemporary Literary Criticism*. Detroit: Gale Research, 1993. 317–53.

Wald, Alan. "The Culture of 'Internal Colonialism': A Marxist Perspective." *MELUS* 8.3 (1981): 18–27.

Wallace, Karen L. "Liminality and Myth in Native American Fiction: *Ceremony* and *The Ancient Child*." *American Indian Culture and Research Journal*. 20.4 (1996): 91–119.

Warner, Nicholas O. "Images of Drinking in 'Woman Singing,' *Ceremony*, and *House Made of Dawn*." *MELUS* 11.4 (1984): 15–30.

Wiget, Andrew O. "Contemporary Native American Literature." *Choice* June 1986: 1507–12.

———. "Identity, Voice, and Authority: Artist-Audience Relations in Native American Literature." *World Literature Today* 66.2 (1992): 258–63.

Wilson, Norma C. "Ceremony: From Alienation to Reciprocity. (Leslie Marmon Silko)" In *Teaching American Ethnic Literatures: Nineteen Essays*. Ed. John R. Maitino and David R. Peck. Albuquerque: U of New Mexico P, 1996. 69–82.

———. "Outlook for Survival." *Denver Quarterly* 14.4 (1980): 22–30.

Winsbro, Bonnie. " Calling Tayo Back, Unraveling Coyote's Skin: Individuation in Leslie Marmon Silko's *Ceremony*." In her *Supernatural Forces: Belief, Difference, and Power in Contemporary Works by Ethnic Women*. Amherst: U of Massachusetts P, 1993. 82–108.

Witalec, Janet, ed. *Native North American Literature*. Detroit: Gale Research, 1994. 575–86.

Wong, Hertha Dawn. "Contemporary Innovations of Oral Traditions: N. Scott Momaday and Leslie Marmon Silko." In her *Sending My Heart Back across the Years: Tradition and Innovation in Native American Autobiography*. New York: Oxford UP, 1992. 153–99.

Note: Per Seyersted, in his bibliography of Silko's work, notes that W. David Laird, former university librarian, University of Arizona, Tucson, began a Silko collection at the university library, and Silko has agreed to deposit her material at the University of Arizona (*Leslie Marmon Silko*, 48).

INDEX

Abbey, Edward, 142
Aboriginal cultures, Western culture and, 192
Adams, Kate, 281
Adventures of J. Arthur Pym (Poe), 38
Aeneas, 35, 36, 59n37
African slave revolt (1790–1804), 200
Albuquerque (Anaya), 36
Alcala, Pedro de, 44
Alegría, 46, 54, 219, 229, 239; fetishism and, 192; house by, 268
Alexander, Hartley Burr, 188
Alice, Aunt, 118n8; story of, 105–6
Allen, Paula Gunn, 39–40, 123, 138, 219; on *Ceremony*, 27; on hermeneutic complexity, 28; on ritual, 68; on storytelling, 116
Almanach de Gotha, 45
Almanac of the Dead, The (Silko), 1–3, 8, 10, 12, 19, 20, 35, 45, 151; body/object in, 198; and *Ceremony* compared, 149, 254, 265; cultural/personal shifts in, 245; disengagement/reconvergence in, 43–44; fetishism in, 191, 194, 201; Geronimo sequences in, 165–66; homosexuality in, 178n10, 207, 208–9, 219; hybrid narratives in, 234; impact of, 135, 159, 248, 253; Navajo myth cycles and, 227; as

novel, 46; review of, 223, 245, 271, 275; secrecy and, 39, 49; Silko on, 255n3, 275; social relations in, 239; storytelling in, 159, 230, 246; structure of, 152, 167, 246–47; studies on, 275–76; tension in, 251–52, 271; Time and, 155
Almanacs, 45–46, 47, 54, 58n25, 185, 263; etymology of, 177n5; generic function of, 51; Mayan, 58n26, 262, 264, 272n2; memory and, 226; novel and, 58n29; symbolism from, 264
Almanakh, 44, 45, 46, 177n5
American Association for the Advancement of Science, 189
American Bureau of Ethnology, 187, 202n6
American Energies: Essays on Fiction (Birkerts), 275
American Indian Movement, 275
American Indian Quarterly, 276
American Women's Autobiography: Fea(s)ts of Memory, 279
A'mooh, Gramdma, 73, 104, 105; model for, 16; storytelling by, 17; racism and, 137
Amphibian populations, 146, 147n5
Anaya, Rudolfo, 3, 26, 33, 36, 281
Ancestor spirits, 39, 199
Ancient Child, The (Momaday), 40, 58n24

LIST OF CONTRIBUTORS

Louise K. Barnett teaches American and Native American literature in the English department of Rutgers University. Her most recent book is *Touched by Fire: The Life, Death, and Mythic Afterlife of George Armstrong Custer* (Henry Holt, 1996).

Daria Donnelly has published essays on Emily Dickinson, as well as reviews and articles on contemporary American poetry and criticism. She received her Ph. D. From Brandeis and has taught at Emmanuel College and Boston University.

Robert F. Gish is director of the ethnic studies department at California Polytechnic State University and the author of *Beyond Bounds: Cross Cultural Essays on Anglo, American Indian, and Chicano Literature* (University of New Mexico Press, 1996) and numerous other books on regionalism and ethnicity.

Caren Irr is assistant professor of English and American studies at the Pennsylvania State University and the author of *The Suburb of Dissent: Cultural Politics in the United States and Canada During the 1930s* (Duke, 1998).

Helen Jaskoski is the author of *Leslie Marmon Silko: A Study of the Short Fiction* (Twayne, 1998) and editor of *Early Native American Writers: New Critical Essays* for Cambridge University Press (1998). She has published widely on multi-ethnic American literature and literature and psychology.

Linda Krumholz is associate professor of English at Denison University; her current work is on ritual and reader relations in the novels of Leslie Marmon Silko, Toni Morrison, and Paule Marshall.

Elizabeth McHenry is an assistant professor at New York University, where she teaches American and African-American literature. She is currently completing a study of the literary societies and the reading practices of black Americans in the nineteenth and early twentieth centuries.

David L. Moore, a senior lecturer in the English department and the American Indian Program at Cornell University, is currently on fellowship at the Cornell Society for the Humanities. A former faculty member at Salish Kootenai College, he has published a number of articles in Native American literary studies.

Elizabeth Hoffman Nelson and Malcolm Nelson teach English at the State University of New York at Fredonia. They are co-editors of the American Indian Studies, Peter Lang Publishing. They are collaborating on a critical study of Mari Sandoz's work on American Indians.

Robert M. Nelson is professor of English at the University of Richmond. He has served as production editor of the journal *SAIL* (1989–97) and is the author of *Place and Vision: The Function of Landscape in Native American Fiction* (Peter Lang, 1993).

Janet Powers has been teaching comparative and minority literature at Gettysburg College since 1963. She spent several weeks at Laguna Pueblo with students on a service learning project in January, 1993.

Ami M. Regier is assistant professor of English at Bethel College in North Newton, Kansas. Her articles include work on the teaching of Native American narrative with Greek drama and on the fragmentation of ancestral voices in Mennonite narrative. She is currently writing about women and object collections in a cross-cultural range of contemporary narratives.

Janet St. Clair is an associate professor of American literature at Regis University in Denver. She has published critical essays on novels by a number of Native American women writers, as well as on works by such authors as Faulkner, West, and Hurston.

Paul Beekman Taylor has been professor of Medieval English Literature at the University of Geneva, Switzerland, for some thirty years. A sabbatical visit at the University of New Mexico a decade ago infused him with an interest in Native American and Chicano culture and he has since published a dozen or so articles in this field to add to his numerous books and articles on earlier literary topics.

Connie Capers Thorson is professor of Library Science and Director of the Pelletier Library at Allegheny College in Meadville, Pennsylvania.

James L. Thorson is professor of English at the University of New Mexico in Albuquerque, where he currently holds the Elizabeth Wertheim Endowed Lectureship in English.

Daniel White has contributed to *Critical Reflections on the Fiction of Ernest J. Gaines,* co-scripted a radio documentary on Edward Abbey, and published poetry in various journals. He teaches at Florence-Darlington Technical College in South Carolina and edits *The New Review.*